T0326923

DEVELOPMENTAL MODERNITY IN KERALA

Narayana Guru, SNDP Yogam
and Social Reform

DEVELOPMENTAL MODERNITY IN KERALA

Narayana Guru, SNDP Yogam and Social Reform

P. CHANDRAMOHAN

 Tulika Books

Published by
Tulika Books
35 A/1 Shahpur Jat, New Delhi 110 049, India
tulikabooks.wordpress.com

First published in India in 2016

© P. Chandramohan 2016

ISBN: 978-93-82381-79-2

Printed at Chaman Offset, Delhi 110 002

To my parents
N. DAMODARAN
&
late P. AMMUKUTTY AMMA

Contents

CONTENTS

List of Tables

Foreword

In the wake of globalization and the 'cultural turn' in social science research, the history of socio-religious movements in nineteenth-century India has received a fair amount of attention. Initially the interest was mainly confined to the history of such movements of reform which had an all-India reach. An important work of this genre is Charles H. Heimsath's *Hindu Social Reform and Indian Nationalism*. Since the building blocks of these all-India movements were drawn from regional historical experiences, the focus of attention slowly shifted to regional movements. Quite a few scholars were drawn towards analysing the importance of these movements and their interconnections with nationalism. These studies have considerably enriched the understanding of the 'national' history of social and religious reform movements, and have helped to correct some of the misconceptions about the character of these movements. Susobhan Sarkar's *Bengal Renaissance and Other Essays*, David Kopf's *Study of Orientalism and Bengal Renaissance* and Kenneth Jones' *Arya Dharma* are pioneering efforts.

In the present volume, Chandramohan has attempted the study of a reform movement of Kerala: Sree Narayana Dharma Paripalana Yogam (SNDP). The Yogam drew inspiration from the ideas of Narayana Guru who believed in Advaita philosophy and maintained a universalist outlook. The relationship between the Guru and the Yogam was very close. He was the President of the Yogam for life and actively participated in all its activities particularly during the early phase of the movement, at least till 1913. Chandramohan provides a lively picture of this interplay with a meticulously detailed account of the ideas of the Guru which provided the principles around which the activities of the Yogam were organized. An umbilical connection existed between the Yogam and the Guru, which was nursed carefully by both. This was because the ideas of the Guru suited the aspirations of the upwardly mobile Ezhava middle class, who were the main benefactors of the movement.

The scheme envisioned by Narayana Guru for the regeneration of Kerala society had three important dimensions: the reformation of social and religious practices, the development of education and industrialization. In all these fields the Guru's outlook was very modern. In both religious and social matters he took a rational stand, and he was opposed to all forms of idol worship even if he was instrumental in the consecration of several temples. He conceived the temple as a social space where everybody could meet and exchange ideas. This is reminiscent of the way in which earlier movements like the Brahmo Samaj and Arya Samaj made use of the 'temple' space. Accordingly the worship pattern also underwent change. The new pattern did away with traditional practices in which the priestly class occupied a dominant place. The elimination of the priestly class from officiating during the performance of rituals had a democratic element, inasmuch as it helped the creation of individuals as free agents.

Although of simple looks and simple living, Narayana Guru had a complex and discerning mind. He also had a holistic view of society and an organic conception of progress. As the author rightly points out, he does not fall into the tradition–modernity paradigm; he was a traditionalist who struggled to disseminate a modern outlook among the masses. The most important message of his life was his attempt to reconcile tradition with modernity. Without such reconciliation, he believed that no progress was possible. Therefore, while pursuing his spiritual endeavours, he advocated education of women, industrialization and abolition of caste as necessary for the regeneration of society.

In order to contextualize the life and work of the Guru and of the movement he had helped to organize, Chandramohan has devoted a long chapter on the economic, social and cultural conditions in nineteenth-century Kerala. This is most appropriate as it helps to understand the society and its problems in which the reformers were called upon to intervene. The society was under the vicious grip of obscurantism and superstitions, which accounted for many irrational social practices. Many believed that an association with the blessings of the Guru would go a long way in finding a solution to deal with these practices. When Dr Palpu met Vivekananda the latter reportedly advised him to look for a spiritual leader for the movement. Palpu found one in Narayana Guru, and with his blessings and under his spiritual leadership, organised an association entitled Sree Narayana Dharma Paripalana Yogam (SNDP).

Chandramohan's work demonstrates that the SNDP was mainly an organization of the emerging middle class, which worked as both its strength and weakness. The aspirations of the middle class led them to focus on education, which was essential for social uplift. Because of caste restrictions Ezhavas were not able to get admission into government schools. The Ezhava leaders undertook a sustained agitation, both in the Sree Mulam Popular Assembly and outside. As a result all government schools for boys were thrown open in 1908 and for girls in 1910. The government order did not become fully operational, as we find that only 180 out of 352 girls' schools were open to the Ezhavas by 1919. However, this was a step with far-reaching implications for social change. The Yogam's involvement and advocacy did result in a remarkable increase in literacy. In 1875 the male literacy of Ezhavas was only 3.2 per cent, which increased to 36 per cent by 1931. A similar increase was reported for English education as well: from only 30 in 1890 to 5,202 in 1931. The Guru accorded equal importance to vernacular and English education, as he was aware of the latter's pragmatic value.

The ideas of the Guru were not limited to spiritual and religious matters. His views were organic, and therefore he believed that change should embrace all aspects of society. He was equally concerned with economic problems as he was with religious matters. Therefore, he advised his followers to invest in industries. At the annual meetings of the Yogam industrial exhibitions were organized. The Yogam floated a company, Malabaar Economic Union, of which the Guru himself was a director. Apart from the contribution of the Yogam, several companies were established in different parts of the state.

Looking back, it is not difficult to discern in the interface between the Guru's ideas and the Yogam's reaction, the onset of modernity in Kerala. However, the disjunction between principles and practice has led to a decline of the movement. Now the movement is largely focused on the interests of the privileged sections of the community and has hence lost all reforming zeal.

The empirical details and the conceptual framework of this book make it essential reading for anyone interested in the history of social movements. I have great pleasure in presenting this book to discerning readers.

K.N. PANIKKAR

Acknowledgments

This is a revised version of my M. Phil. dissertation titled 'Social and Political Protest in Travancore: A Study of the Sree Narayana Dharma Paripalana Yogam (1900–1938)', which I submitted at the Centre for Historical Studies, Jawaharlal Nehru University (JNU), in 1982. Initially when I worked on my dissertation and later when I undertook its revision in order to prepare it for publication – and it has gone through fairly extensive revision on account of my further explorations in this subject over the years – I have been helped immensely by a large number of people. The idea for the topic of my dissertation came from Professor K.N. Panikkar and it instantly caught my imagination for it corresponded with my aptitude for studies in the socio-cultural realm. I would especially like to thank Professor Panikkar to whom I am greatly beholden for this project since its inception to its transformation in its present shape, which would not have been possible without his help as my guide and mentor. I am also deeply indebted to him for writing the Foreword to this book.

I owe special thanks to late Professor Bipan Chandra who has been a great source of inspiration and encouragement for me in my academic pursuits from my student days in JNU. To Dr S. Raju of the School of Social Sciences, Mahatma Gandhi University, Kottayam, I extend my unending gratitude for having read the manuscript of this book thoroughly, and made valuable comments and suggestions on its organization and content. He helped me to bring into sharper focus the themes advanced in the course of this book.

I was fortunate to have easy access to Professor M.G.S. Narayanan, Professor M.P. Sreekumaran Nair and Dr M. Gangadhara Menon for their suggestions and comments.

Several friends were kind enough to read the manuscript at various stages of its preparation and to share their ideas with me in discussions. I am particularly grateful in this respect to Dr Amit Kumar Gupta, Dr Gopalankutty, Dr K.P. Shankar, Dr V.S. Nair, Professor Pulapre Balakrishnan and Shri Amrit Tandon.

A few individuals were generous in granting me access to their collections of newspapers and other rare and valuable papers, and spent hours of their valuable time in discussing my subject of research. The most prominent among them were late Shri Puthuppally Raghavan, late Shri K. Prabhakaran and late Shri P.K. Balakrishnan. A major part of the primary source material used in this book has come from Puthuppally Raghavan and K. Prabhakaran.

In the process of writing this book I availed myself of the facilities of research and study at several libraries, archives and research centres. I take this opportunity to record my gratitude to their staff for their services. These institutions are: the Nehru Memorial Museum and Library (NMML), the Central Secretariat Library and the National Archives of India in New Delhi; the Kerala State Archives (Cellar), the Kerala State Legislative Assembly Library, the Library of the Centre for Development Studies and the Kerala University Library in Thiruvananthapuram; the Asan Memorial Library (Thonakkal) and the Shri Krishna Vilasam Library (Malayinkeezh), both near Thiruvananthapuram; the C.H. Memorial Library and the History Department Library, Calicut University, at Tenhipalam; and the Tamil Nadu State Archives and the Connemara Library in Chennai.

I am grateful to the Indian Council for Historical Research and the Jawaharlal Nehru University for providing me with study grants for field trips in South India.

I would like to thank my former colleagues Ms. Neelam Vats, Ravindran K., Satish Kumar, Narender Rana, Ashok Kumar and V.P. Sharma of NMML for their help and cooperation. I owe special thanks to Ms Savita Rani for the marathon bouts of typing which she rendered cheerfully even under tremendous pressure.

On the home front I am indebted to my wife Jaya for her invaluable advice in matters of style and presentation, and for the enthusiasm and support which she has given me in finalizing this book. I am also thankful to my daughters Neelima and Karthika for offering advice on style, somewhat eccentric but nevertheless useful.

Finally, I would like to thank Tulika Books for their interest and cooperation in seeing the book through its many stages.

P. CHANDRAMOHAN

Abbreviations

AICC	All India Congress Committee
AISPC	All India States' People's Conference
CMS	Church Missionary Society
CRR	Crown Representative Records
CWMG	*Collected Works of Mahatma Gandhi*
KPCC	Kerala Pradesh Congress Committee
LMS	London Missionary Society
MNNR	*Madras Native Newspapers Report*
MPP	Madras Political Proceedings
MRR	Madras Residency Records
NAI	National Archives of India
NMML	Nehru Memorial Museum and Library
NSS	Nair Service Society
PWD	Public Works Department
SNDP	Sree Narayana Dharma Paripalana
TGER	Travancore Government English Records
TGG	*Travancore Government Gazette*

Introduction

Change is, and will always remain, a constant in human society – therefore the centrality of its history. Some changes are represented in historiography while others are consigned to oblivion; some of these changes are structural, whereas some may be brought about or influenced by agents.[1] The historical time that we label as 'modern' has witnessed the role of agents in changing the structures that conditioned their functioning; at the same time, this epoch witnessed those conditions being altered and radically ruptured by the interventions of those agents. This study strives to showcase the attempts made by such agents to achieve alterations/changes in existing structures. It also addresses the question of where some of these attempts culminated. In short, this study attempts to provide answers to the question of how certain 'modernizing' agents, influenced and conditioned by existing as well as emerging structures, tried to change 'traditional' structures. It should be stated at the very outset that here I do not allude to 'tradition' and 'modern' as binary opposites, nor do I seek to counterpose them as referents with watertight boundaries. The best examples of such interaction between structures and agents can be drawn from the social reform movements of India. For elucidation, I have selected one such movement from the historical experience of the state of Kerala: the Sree Narayana Dharma Paripalana Yogam, popularly known as the SNDP Yogam. This is one among several such movements that have taken place in Kerala since the turn of the nineteenth century.

It was during this period too that a panoply of practices in Kerala got divided into the categories of 'traditional' and 'modern'. The reformulations had wide ramifications that influenced existing socio-economic organizations and generated new ideas. They ignited a critical and self-reflective appraisal of prevalent institutions, social relations, manifold inter-relations and belief systems. Almost all communities in Kerala were subjected to these influences, although the time of their occurrence, the degree of emphasis, the vantage points and the intensity of change may have differed from community to community. As a result, several movements of reform/reformulation of the self and the other, of dissent and contestation, surfaced. Among the most important of these movements were the SNDP Yogam, the Nair Service Society (NSS), the Yogakshema Sabha, the Sadhu Paripalana Sangam and the Christian Mahajana Sabha.

Rejecting several existing 'socio-religious' practices as belonging to a decadent society, the agents/reformers persuaded those subjected to them to discard these. The reforms sought to create a social climate for modernization. It could even be said that such selective rejection and assimilation of new values was tantamount to the process of modernization itself. The main 'source of inspiration' for the SNDP Yogam was the spiritual–social icon popularly known as Sree Narayana Guru. The Yogam was one of the most effective articulations of such movements. For those who are not familiar with the movements that swept across southern India, it is enough to state that often this particular movement has been compared to the Yadava movement in north India. I have underscored the phrase 'source of inspiration' above because most of the social reform movements in Kerala have had a strong anchorage in 'charisma', in the Weberian sense,[2] and in spiritual leadership. Chattampi Swamikal, Vakbadanandan, Yohannan, Vaikom Abdul Khader Moulavi and Father Nidhiyirikal Mani Kattanar are a few examples among many. Their iconic powers got wide circulation and acceptance because religion was the dominant ideology; their truth regime was constituted in the texture of religion. The world views of these leaders were not shaped by the prevalent language of their religion and religious institutions alone; they were also sensitive to other religions, secular ideas, modernity, notions of freedom, equity, etc. An increasing number of people in Kerala began to be responsive towards them, perhaps impelled by a desire to reformulate themselves in the present for an alternative future.

There are several features common to the social reform movements of the period which may be characterized as modern. In the language of the reforms, new designations and oppositions were conceived: the 'dominant' was distinguished from the 'subordinate'; 'lower' became opposed to 'higher'; 'elite' was differentiated from 'people' or 'popular'; 'magic, animism and superstition' became the other of 'rational', 'economic' and 'useful', and so on. Such sets of distinctions and oppositions were tenable for those with strong positions to oppose or relegate exceedingly well-posited objects and practices. In reform, many religious practices began to be viewed as 'superstition' and wasteful debilitation.

Transgression of these 'debilitating' factors became the desired goal of the social agents, whose world view was constituted within the process of modernization under colonial conditions. They maintained tremendous optimism in the human capacity to change 'what is at present' and what had been 'inherited from tradition and customary practices'. This optimistic mood persuaded people (aspiring for change and mobility across spaces, social strata, going beyond the limits set by immediate environs, religious beliefs, life-worlds, etc.) to challenge the persistent structures they had to encounter in their local social ambience. It was believed that the effectiveness of the challenge depended on collectivity, and thus they organized collective action in which the agent's role was taken as a critical force.

What were the conceptions that upheld the coherence of collectivity in such movements? As already mentioned, there was an unchallenged optimism in one's capacity to change oneself and others. This optimism engendered ventures for total change/rupture, redefinition of distinctions and oppositions, generation of new desires, and alteration of oneself and others according to one's own determination and will. In the process of the 'reform movements', 'self' and 'other' were conceived to be bound by the frontiers set by the caste system, class relations, religious institutions, political units, social hierarchy, etc. These boundary-conditions were decisive in shaping the prevalent relationships between the self and the other. The relationships did not remain static; they were made to slide slowly towards the future because of the stasis of the existent structures. Possibly this is why there were exuberant efforts to move beyond the restrictions of caste, creed, religion and nationalities. People became more and more mobile across all the boundaries set by caste-based traditional practices, and therefore, gradually as well as sporadically, those who experienced suffering and humiliation desired to move beyond and push the limits of contemporary retentions as much as creativity enabled them. Reformulations of the self took place before reformulating others. In other words, the reformulators/reformers first submitted themselves to the ideological compulsions of the desired reforms and then began reforming others.

Reform involves reformulation of one's own condition of existence, as well as reformulating ways of relating to oneself and of placing oneself in relation to others. The dynamics of these relations create individuals and inculcate in them aspirations to become mobile, socially and economically, along a vertical path. Such mobilities enable them to go beyond structures that are enabling and at the same time forbid mobility itself. Reforms or reformulations become a movement when the processes of reform are perpetuated. A certain internal dynamism is achieved when the structures and agents jointly (with or without mutually compatible intentions) make it a continuous process of reformulating each other. If a 'reform movement' is identical to mobility across contemporary limits, either imposed or chosen, then the question before us would be whether the social reform movement that we are focusing on here was one that brought forth an epoch with distinction. This is the urgent question that cuts across, and links, the different chapters of this book, like the string of a garland with varied beads of differing colours and perhaps various shapes as well.

Let me dwell a while on this question. Did the agents or bearers of the reform in Kerala demand that others break free of their limitations, or did they try to go beyond their own restraints? For instance, when they encountered their 'superiors', did they alter their own parameters or did they demand that the superiors change theirs? Did they simply alter their selfhood or did they want others to change theirs in such a way as to suit the reformulation of their own selfhood? When they, as the bearers of reform, encountered 'their' own potential subjects (not as subjects of a sovereign, or as subjected to some or other kind of operation; not even as subjects of history as Marx perceived – that is, labour), namely the Ezhava majority, did they ask them to become like the reformers, or did they try to go beyond the limits that determined them, or did they combine both? The arguments and descriptions presented here are oriented towards this set of questions.

Sree Narayana Guru and the SNDP Yogam found that the most distressing social issue in Kerala was the prevalence of the caste system, which sought to maintain a system of segregation that was hierarchically ordained on the basis of ritual status. Caste structures distributed people across hierarchies and placed them within a stratified social fabric. The reform movement touched on the superficial as well as deep realms of the human condition in Kerala, in terms of religion, marriage, family relations, education, language, ideological and material hegemony of upper-caste Hindus, life-cycle rituals, inheritance systems, touchability/untouchability at public and private spaces, etc. The influence of the movement in these realms and at nodal points was accompanied by a collapse of the traditional powers of the elites, innova-tions in the field of political economy, the incorporation of a universalistic legal system, re-ordering of the administrative system based on the norms of modern governance, introduction of the western (English) educational system, expansion of the market economy, commercialization of agriculture, arrival of modern industries, transformation of agricultural cultivation into agronomy, the opening of new occupations, popularization of communication through the print media, etc. The unfolding of these changes, at both macro and micro levels, led to the formation of a new intelligentsia and a middle class whose main objective was to obliterate the caste system/structure, deconsecrate the centrality of caste, and determine the contours of a new inter-caste society of individuals and inter-individual relationships.

Being so prominent, the SNDP movement gained attention from men of letters, their words in turn reaching the reading public. The works of Nataraja Guru (*The Word of the Guru*) and V.T. Samuel (*One Caste, One Religion and One God*) in English, and those of P. Parameswaran (*Narayana Guru Navothanathinte Pravachakan*) and M.K. Sanoo (*Narayana Guru*) in Malayalam are worth mentioning in this context, although these are primarily biographical and do not refer to the historical conditions that influenced the movement's ideas and practices. One of the seminal academic studies on the

SNDP Yogam is *Social Change and Social Transformation* by M.S.A. Rao. It compares this movement with the Yadava movement in north India, and traces their respective impact on the social mobility of the Ezhavas and the Yadavas. However, though an erudite study, the general changes and developments that coincided with or foregrounded the SNDP movement are barely recognized in this work. There are some other works, such as *Asan and Social Revolution* and *Vaikom Satyagraha and Gandhi* by T.K. Ravindran, and *Abstention Movement* by K.K. Kusuman, which, though general in nature, do shed some light on the movement. But they remain conceptually inadequate. They concentrate on the caste disabilities of the Ezhavas and advocate a proper appreciation of the ideas of Narayana Guru, but miss out on the movement as such; they do not make use of the abundant information that is available on the movement, its context and its consequences.

It is this academic lacuna that prompted me to take up a re-examination of the SNDP movement. To address the questions and to accomplish my objectives, I made use of diverse sources of information (both primary and secondary), such as the archival records of the Government of India and the Travancore Government; institutional archives like the Nehru Memorial Museum and Library; the private archives of various individuals such as Puthupally Raghavan and K. Prabhakaran; government publications, newspapers, journals, private papers of prominent leaders, autobiographies and biographies, and oral history transcripts.

Using these sources of information and observation, this study attempts to examine the socio-economic changes in Travancore society during the late nineteenth and first half of the twentieth century; the emergence of the Ezhava middle class; the socio-religious ideas of Sree Narayana Guru; the formation of the SNDP Yogam; its class character, and its fight against the social, religious, political and administrative deprivations and debilities of the Ezhavas. Further, some of the consequences and limitations of the movement are also examined, but without being judgmental about them. An attempt is also made to examine the attitude of members of the Yogam to the ideas of the Guru and the changes it underwent over time.

In the first chapter, I provide a general profile of society and societal relations in Travancore during the second half of the nineteenth century. This backdrop is presented here so that the SNDP movement can be contextualized within its general milieu. In the second chapter, an attempt is made to delineate the beginnings of the Ezhavas as a caste, the emergence of an Ezhava middle class and the genesis of the SNDP Yogam as a movement. In the third chapter, I proceed to discuss in detail the socio-religious ideas of Narayana Guru in the context of modernity and tradition. In the fourth, I examine the formation of the Yogam, its class character, expansion and struggle against deprivation in the fields of education and employment in government service, as well as its actions for industrial advancement. The fifth chapter discusses the general trends in the socio-religious reform activities of the Guru in comparison with social reforms that were taking place elsewhere in India. The sixth chapter is a discussion on the activities and achievements of the Guru and the Yogam with respect to their attempts towards obliteration of the continued observance of untouchability. The conditions which prompted the reformers to enter into the political field and the consequent activities of the Yogam are discussed in the seventh chapter. It also brings to light the new alignments forged among Ezhavas, Christians and Muslims in Kerala, in their fight for civil rights. Apart from a selective summary of the important observations made in the previous chapters, in the concluding chapter I attempt a certain re-mapping of the aims, objectives and character of the SNDP Yogam.

Notes and References

[1] According to Pierre Bourdieu, while the historical pattern of social relations is in the form of 'structure', the actual actions and interactions of real people are evidence of their agency (for details, see Pierre Bourdieu, *Outline of a Theory of Practice*, Cambridge University Press, Cambridge, 1977). For Antony Giddens, structures must be conceptualized not only as constraints upon human agency, but also as enablers (see Antony Giddens, *New Rules of Sociological Method: A Positive Critique of Interpretative Sociology*, Hutchinson, London, 1976). Elsewhere, Giddens defines structures as consisting of rules and resources involving human action: the rules constrain the actions, the resources make it possible (Antony Giddens, *The Constitution of Society: Outline of the Theory of Structuration*, Polity Press, Cambridge, 1984).

[2] In the Weberian sense, 'charisma' (the gift of grace) is 'a certain quality of an individual personality by virtue of which he is set apart from ordinary men and treated as endowed with supernatural, super human or at least specifically exceptional powers or qualities' (see Max Weber, *The Theory of Social and Economic Organization*, translated by A.M Henderson and Talcott Parson, Free Press, Glencoe, 1947, p. 358). In Weber's sociology, charismatic authority is one of the three forms of authority, the other two being traditional authority and rational–legal authority. Weber's tripartite classification of legitimate authority has been discussed so frequently that it does not seem necessary to elaborate it here. However, as I have referred to the term charismatic authority, a brief summary is given for easy reference. Max Weber defined charismatic authority as 'resting on devotion to the exceptional sanctity, heroism or exemplary character of an individual person and of the normative patterns or order revealed or ordained by him' (ibid., pp. 341–58). In other words, charismatic authority rests upon an individual's influence on authority over a large number of people as a saviour, a prophet or a hero. However, this authority is based neither upon rational rules nor upon tradition. See Max Rheinstein, ed., *Max Weber on Law in Economy and Society*, Clarion Books, New York, 1967, pp. 336–37. For a particularly compact and cogent explanation of the three-part typology of legitimate authority, see Peter M. Balu and W. Richard Scott, *Formal Organizations: A Comparative Approach*, Chandler, San Francisco, 1962, pp. 30–36.

1

The Structure of Society in Travancore

Late Nineteenth Century and Early Twentieth Century

To begin with, let me briefly outline the highly nuanced contours of the socio-economic life of the people of Travancore during the late nineteenth and early twentieth centuries. This may help readers who are not familiar with the conditions prevalent in Travancore at that time to discern the specificities implicit in the following chapters, and also to contextualize these historically.

The princely state of Travancore, located at the southwestern tip of the South Indian Peninsula, was spread across 7,091 square miles[1] and occupied the seventh place in land area among all the Indian states.[2] It was thickly populated,[3] with a multi-religious composition of people. Out of a total population of 2,952,152 in 1901, Hindus constituted 2,035,615 (69.9 per cent), Christians 687,387 (23.6 per cent), Muslims 190,566 (6.5 per cent) and others[4] 28,584.[5] Thus Hindus were numerically dominant in Travancore state. They were divided into several hierarchically ordained castes based on ritual status, concepts of purity and pollution, and property ownership.[6] I proceed now to pay attention to the pyramidical distribution of the Hindu population in terms of caste.

The Hindus and Caste Hierarchy

The Brahmins, who were divided into two broad categories, viz. Malayali Brahmins known as Namboodiris and non-Malayali Brahmins,[7] were at the apex of the caste hierarchy. Although the former were very few in number, they controlled most of the temple lands and a considerable portion of non-governmental land.[8] They enjoyed preferential treatment in matters of revenue payment and command over the powers of the secular authority. Well-versed in Sanskrit and traditional knowledge but reluctant to succumb to the elements of change taking place in the nineteenth century, they remained conservative as they kept themselves away from modern education.

The other category of Brahmins, generally described as 'foreign' Brahmins – for they had immigrated from Tamil Nadu, Karnataka and Maharashtra – were mostly traders, moneylenders and priests. They were quick in taking advantage of the changing socio-economic scenario in general, and the changes in educational infrastructure in particular. Out of a total of 162 Matriculates in Travancore in the year 1872, 71 belonged to this community; and out of 14 Bachelors of Arts, 10 were non-Malayali Brahmins.[9] They had a significant say as well as proportionate representation in the administrative machinery from the time of the ruler Marthanda Varma (especially since the mid-eighteenth century), and by 1881, they seem to have cornered a major portion of government jobs.[10] Compared to the Namboodiris, these Brahmins were more resilient and willing to make use of opportunities that came their way. They were pragmatic and free from the observed sense of social prestige.[11]

Although ranking ritually below the Namboodiris, they were nonetheless economically as powerful as the Namboodiris, the Kshatriyas and the Samantas. Vaisya was a non-existent category in Kerala. In terms of ritual purity, Ambalavasis, a group of castes engaged mainly in temple services, were placed below the Kshatriyas. The most prominent Ambalavasis are Varriers, Pisharodis, Nambissans, Chakkiyars, Nambiars and Nambidis. They are generally described as *antarala jatis* (intermediate castes) because of their position between the two *varnas*.[12]

The Nair caste occupied the next position in the caste hierarchy. The term Nair, in its widest sense, comprises a large number of sub-castes, ranging from washermen and barbers to landed magnates.[13] The total number of Nair sub-castes would be around 130,[14] of whom substantial sections were engaged in military service.[15] Un-partitionable family property formed the vast expanse of landed estates held by Nair *taravad*s or joint families. As the largest body of landholders, the Nairs exercised control over land through different types of tenure. Despite the fact that some of them had conjugal relations with the Namboodiris, conventionally they were subjects of the latter's social and ideological control. However, the Nairs broke away from the Namboodiris during the course of the nineteenth century.[16] Besides, they took advantage of the new educational opportunities offered by the English and Christian missionaries, and by the end of the nineteenth century, they occupied about 60 per cent of government jobs[17] which required knowledge of English and other functions of governance.

About 60 per cent of the total population of Kerala consisted of the untouchable castes – Ezhavas, Pulayas, Parayas, etc. Of the untouchable castes, the Ezhavas were the most numerous and ritually superior. Their primary occupation was cultivation, extraction of palm-tree products like toddy, and manufacture of coir, fibre and jaggery. A large number of Ezhavas worked as woodcutters, farmers and agricultural labourers,[18] and a few as teachers, Ayurvedic physicians, Sanskrit scholars and astrologers.[19] Several Ezhavas were employed as soldiers by the old rulers of Travancore, along with Nairs.[20]

However, their social disabilities were several: they were prevented from using most public roads and buildings, schools and brahminical temples.

Pulayas, Parayas, Velars and Kuravas were at the bottom of the caste hierarchy in Kerala. *Savarna* Hindus were polluted if a member of any of these castes appeared within 50 or 60 yards. Even Ezhavas and Shanars believed that they would get polluted if a slave-caste person such as a Pulaya or Paraya came within a radius of 5 to 6 yards.[21] After the abolition of slavery in 1843 several steps were taken to erase such notions and norms;[22] and during the last decade of the nineteenth century and in the first decade of the twentieth, the Government of Travancore provided many educational facilities for the social uplift of these 'low' castes. But their importance in the changing social and political processes was neither realized nor recognized, and they continued to remain at the bottom of the social and economic pyramid.

The above description of the caste hierarchy in Kerala brings to relief the discernibly stratified Hindu community based on degrees of purity and pollution. Any kind of solidarity among Hindus in terms of religion was almost absent, and caste distinctions and exclusions remained very prominent.[23] The privileges of the caste Hindus were in sharp contrast to the status of the untouchable castes and of outcastes such as the Nayadis.

The Christians

As the most populous non-Hindu community, the Christians occupied a significant place in the society of Travancore; they were economically well placed and far advanced in gaining English education. Ever since its introduction in Kerala, the Christian faith, though alien in its origin, came to be accepted as an indigenous faith[24] – although with some exceptional situations of conflict among Christians.[25] Despite such instances of difference and disputation, propagation of the faith and its path made steady progress. It is interesting to note that Travancore had a larger Christian population than any other state in India.[26] From the time of the British Resident Colonel Munro, the Christians received special privileges and patronage from the Travancore state. The relation of synergy between the Travancore rulers and the British missionaries in the kingdom was influenced by two factors. First, the Christians who came in early times to Kerala were merchants,[27] and therefore, the rulers of Kerala made use of this enterprising business community to advance the trade of the state.[28] Second, the rulers of Travancore believed that supporting the Christians would please the British authorities, particularly the British Resident.[29]

In 1881 the number of Christians in Travancore was 498,542, and by 1921 it increased to 1,172,934.[30] This rapid growth of the Christian population was due to various factors, like the religious tolerance of the Travancore rulers; the British Resident's interest to safeguard the 'legitimate' interests of missionaries and Christians; the incessant work of the Christian missionaries among the depressed classes; the deplorable socio-economic conditions of the untouchable castes; and, finally, the economic status of Christians as traders and merchants, and, later, as estate owners, landholders, manufacturers and publishers of texts printed in their own printing presses. Due to the influence of all these factors, Christianity witnessed steady growth in Travancore. With greater propagation of the faith, more and more followers came into its fold. For instance, while in 1875 Christians formed only 20 per cent of the population, by 1931 their proportion had risen to 31 per cent[31] – a remarkable expansion that happened within a short time-span of a little more than half a century.

Christians in Travancore were generally divided into three distinct groups: Protestants, Catholics and Syrians. These three divided themselves again into several denominations.[32] Such divisions and sub-divisions among the Christians (which bear resemblance to the caste-based distinctions within the fold of Hindus) indeed weakened their cause in the political arena.[33] But the Christians of Travancore had an acknowledged and respectable status in the caste Hindu-dominated Travancore society[34] as they were economically well-off, English-educated and held high positions in the government.

The enterprise of the Christians brought the hilly tracts of Travancore under commercial cultivation (cash crops), and the trade and commerce of the state were largely handled by them. They were at their best in propagating modern education. Most of the private educational institutions belonged to them. The Syrian Christians of Travancore were one of the communities with the largest holdings of land in the state. As regards education, since the Christians had been associated with the English missionaries, they obtained a larger share of the opportunities that were newly emerging. Their association with the Anglican missionaries and British administrators meant that the new economic forces, the spread of English education and the impact of modern western ideas influenced the Christians of Travancore first. They were the first community in Kerala to produce a forward-looking and profit-seeking middle class. At the beginning of the twentieth century, they owned most of the financial institutions, printing presses and other lucrative businesses in the state, and took advantage of the economic downfall of the Nairs by purchasing their landed assets.[35] But all these material advantages did not help them to get equal treatment in the field of politics and administration. This naturally made the Christians resentful, and therefore they cooperated with other non-Hindus and the non-caste Hindus in their social and political struggles against the caste Hindu hegemony.

The Muslims

The Muslims of Travancore were a small but industrious community, mostly engaged in free labour and petty business, except for a few rich traders who controlled the markets of important towns that lay at the confluence of different trade routes from the hills to the sea ports in the state. Just like the Hindus and Christians, the Muslim community also had its own divisions and sub-divisions.[36] Sunnis constituted about 89 per cent and Shias about 10 per cent of the total Muslim population in Travancore.[37] Although, from the economic point of view, the Muslims were not as poor[38] as the untouchables and some sub-groups of Nairs, socially and educationally they were comparatively less developed. A majority of them were converts from low-caste Hindu communities. They were mostly agricultural labourers, fishermen, daily wage earners, petty traders and shopkeepers. Though the educated elite among them were free from caste rigidities, they were treated as inferior to caste Hindus. Muslims were inadequately represented in public services and in the legislature. The social, political and educational awakening of Travancore society did not affect them till the emergence of the Abstention movement in Travancore, in the 1930s.

Casteism and Caste-based Discrimination

The most important feature of Kerala society during the nineteenth century and the beginning of the twentieth century was the existence of a deep-rooted caste system. Casteism began to be looked upon as an evil that corroded the very foundation of a society in need of a transformation. In no other part of India was casteism more rigidly or more fervently observed than in Kerala. Vivekananda, when he visited Kerala at the turn of the nineteenth century, described the Malabaris as 'lunatic' and their homes as 'Lunatic Asylums'.[39] Gandhi's denunciation was equally emphatic. He said, 'Unfortunately for Hinduism, unfortunately for the state, and unfortunately even for the whole of India, there is not much credit to the state in the matter of untouchability.'[40]

Due to the overwhelmingly entrenched casteism within the social fabric, numerous social debilities affected the lives of the lower castes. The most degrading of these sprang from notions of untouchability, unapproachability and unseeability of the outcastes, which were practised with fanatical rigour by the upper castes.[41] The belief, as mentioned earlier, was that even the proximity of certain castes would pollute the higher castes. Hence, members of the lower castes were not permitted to approach members of the upper castes, and were required to stay within degrees of prescribed distance – which, as applied to each caste, was known as *tiyapad*, *cherumapad*, etc.[42] Observations made in this regard by the travel writer Duarte Barbosa are especially revealing. He wrote: 'When they [the high-caste men] go anywhere they shout to the peasants that they may get out of the way where they have to pass and the peasants do so; and if they did not do it, the Nairs kill them without penalty.'[43] Thurston records a case of a Nair killing a *cheruman* in 1904 for coming within the polluting distance prescribed for him.[44] The distance of pollution was observed even among the lower castes.[45]

The untouchables experienced a large number of other forms of caste discrimination too. They were not supposed to dress neatly, and were not allowed to cover their breasts or use head-bands of any sort. Even Nair women, though they could otherwise cover their breasts with a particular style of cloth, were not permitted to do so in front of temple idols and members of superior castes.[46] Caste restrictions also prohibited them from keeping milch cows, and wearing footwear, ornaments or any but coarse cloth.[47] The untouchables were required to use a particular style of self-degrading language (both verbal and physical) when addressing the high castes. They were not to use the language of caste Hindus, and had to address a caste Hindu man as *thampuran* (lord) and woman as *thampuratti* (lady).[48] They could not refer to themselves as 'I' or 'we' (neither first person singular nor plural) but only in the third person, as *adiyan*. They had to cover their mouth with one hand when speaking to a member of a high caste even as they kept the prescribed distance.[49] They were denied the privilege of owning names such as Raman, Krishnan and Ganesan (names of Hindu gods), commonly used by the upper castes, except in their corrupted forms.[50] They had to stand before a caste Hindu in awe and reverence, adopting a humble posture.[51] Rev. Samuel Mateer has succinctly put it as follows:

> The use of public highways was forbidden to outcastes and anyone daring to pass on within polluting distance of a Nair would be down at once. To secure immediate recognition of such classes they were required to keep themselves uncovered above the waist; shoes, umbrellas, fine cloth and costly ornaments were interdicted to them. The holding of umbrella on public occasions was prohibited to all castes except Brahmins even in rainy season. The proper salutation from a female to persons of rank was to 'uncover' the bosom.[52]

The untouchables were compelled to maintain their inferior status even while observing various religious ceremonies. They were not only denied admittance to the temples of the high castes, but also not allowed to approach even the periphery of these temples. They were permitted to build their own temples, but under no circumstances could they consecrate deities worshipped by the higher castes. Their deities were mostly worshipped with offerings of toddy and the blood of fowls and animals.

Even at the beginning of the twentieth century, the untouchables continued to be practically subjected to a number of prohibitions and coercions. They were not permitted to use roads open to members of the higher castes. They were prevented from entering or approaching courts and public offices, and excluded from government schools and public services. Further details of such forms of discrimination are discussed in later chapters.

At a time when these hardships emanating from casteism were at their worst, the Christian missionaries approached the lower castes with their philanthropic and humanitarian activities. Ecumenical evangelism made this possible. Though it was with the aim of protecting the economic interests of European planters and merchants, and of bringing a maximum number of people to the Christian fold, the work of the missionaries among the untouchables, when viewed from a perspective of developmental modernity, was both constructive and regenerative. Whatever their economic or religious motives, the activities they conducted were indeed a solace to the depressed classes. Conversion took away the stigma of untouchability to some extent; the use of roads and other public conveniences gradually opened up for them. Thus conversion to Christianity offered a measure of escape from their miseries although their status of untouchability lingered on for some more time. There is a strong argument that the incentives for conversion were not religion-based, neither a lack of faith in the Hindu religion nor the prospect of Christian salvation.[53] Redressal of social and economic grievances was the main inducement. For example, the Mala Arayans, by themselves and without any prompting from Christian missionaries, approached a priest requesting to be converted. In due course, during the later period of mass conversion, a number of untouchables got converted to Christianity with or without persuasion and promise of social uplift.[54]

Occupational Distribution

The concept of traditional occupations did not receive much preference in Travancore before the nineteenth century. Among Namboodiris only 147 per 1,000, and among Ezhavas only 124 per 1,000, followed their so-called 'traditional' occupations.[55] This was also true for some of the other castes. Therefore, in the context of Kerala, it would be wrong to maintain the commonly held idea that every caste group had a hereditary or traditional occupation that was incessantly followed by all its members.

Government Service

Government service, the most privileged and preferred occupation in Travancore, was monopolized by the caste Hindus, especially Nairs and non-Malayali Brahmins. The caste-wise distribution of persons holding governmental jobs in the late nineteenth century is presented in Table 1.

The table shows that Nairs and non-Malayali Brahmins predominated in

TABLE 1

Distribution of communities and castes in government service, 1875 and 1881[56]

Community/Caste	1875		1881	
	No. of people employed	% share in total employment	No. of people employed	% share in total employment
Malayali Brahmins	158	1.07	239	1.47
Non-Malayali Brahmins	1999	13.59	2031	12.56
Kshatriyas	105	0.71	149	0.92
Nairs	8649	58.82	10654	66.99
Ambalavasis	268	1.82	407	2.51
Ezhavas	92	0.63	131	0.81
Muslims	384	2.61	268	1.65
Christians	798	5.42	1029	6.36
Others	2250	15.30	1159	7.16
Total	14,703		16,167	

Travancore's public services. Non-Malayali Brahmins, who constituted about 1.2 per cent of the total population, accounted for 13.59 per cent of the total number of government servants in 1875. In other words, about 13.65 per cent of the total population of non-Malayali Brahmins were employed in government service. In the same manner, the Nairs who constituted about 19.1 per cent of the total population accounted for about 58.82 per cent of the total government employment; that is, about 4 per cent of the total Nair population were government servants in 1875.[57] By 1881, the share of non-Malayali Brahmins and Nairs employed in government services relative to their total population increased to 15 and 5 per cent respectively.[58] The representation of Christians, Muslims and Ezhavas in government services, on the other hand, was nominal. According to the 1875 Census, these three communities constituted 20.29 per cent, 6.06 and 16.59 per cent, respectively, of the total population of Travancore.[59] Nevertheless their contribution to government services was only 0.34, 0.55 and 0.05 per cent, respectively.[60] The Christians showed a marginal increase in their representation in government services, however, in due course. In 1881, out of a total of 16,167 government employees, only 200 were women. Of these 200 females in *sirkar* (government) service, 194 were Hindus and 6 were Christians.[61] All these details clearly indicate that the privileged government jobs in Travancore were under the control of caste Hindus, especially Nairs and non-Malayali Brahmins.

Agriculture

Being primarily an agrarian society with about 60 per cent of the adult population dependent on land for their livelihood,[62] agriculture and allied activities accounted for nearly half of the state's total income. In the mid-nineteenth century, land in Travancore fell under two distinct categories: *pandaravaka* land and *jenmom* land.[63] The Government of Travancore owned about 80 per cent of the cultivated land and all of the 'waste land' was *pandaravaka*.[64] The government-owned land or *pandaravaka* itself was divided into two, viz. *pandaravaka pattam* and *pandaravaka otti*. The latter did not have the right of 'power to transfer' (alienate), although it enjoyed the right of permanent occupation. The state was in effect the biggest landlord; and it treated tenants as if they were peasant proprietors, demanding only land revenue from them in the form of tax or rent which was not very high.[65] The remaining 20 per cent of cultivated land was in the possession of a few landlords who enjoyed either absolute right or *jenmom*, or paid a light assessment called *rajabogam*. Generally, these *jenmom* lands were owned by Brahmins, temples belonging to Brahmins, or descendants of *naduvazhis* (local chieftains). The government land also came under the control of caste Hindus, especially Namboodiris and Nairs. Nairs held the major portion of state lands, on tenures like *otti* (mortgage) and cognate tenures which had the features of direct mortgage from the state.[66] While the Namboodiris exercised greater control over land as the bigger landlords, the Nairs enjoyed the privilege of being the largest holders or tenants of state lands.

In 1904, in Travancore, the number of persons who paid more than Rs 100 as annual land rent was only 361, of whom 154 were Nairs and 34 were Namboodiri Brahmins. Table 2 below gives the number of big landlords of various communities and castes who paid Rs 100 or more as land tax per year. The table shows that out of 361 such big landlords, 219 belonged to the upper castes. This shows the predominant hold of *savarna*s over landed properties in Travancore in the early twentieth century.

TABLE 2
Number of persons from different castes and communities
paying Rs 100 or more as annual land tax, 1904[67]

Community/Caste	No. of persons
Nairs	154
Christians	98
Malayali Brahmins	34
Non-Malayali Brahmins	18
Muslims	14
Kshatriyas	10
Ezhavas	8
Europeans	5
Ambalavasis	3
Others	17
Total	361

The position of land distribution in the early second half of the nineteenth century was such that Namboodiri *jenmis* owned *jenmom* land, the *kanam* holders (generally Nairs) paid rent, the *verumpattakar* cultivated in lieu of fixed *pattom* and the *pathivaram* cultivators shared the produce equally with the landlords.[68] The number of non-cultivating landholders, cultivating landholders, non-cultivating tenants, cultivating tenants and agricultural labourers, as recorded in the Census of 1891, is given in Table 3.

In 1901, landlords and tenants comprised about 37.1 per cent of the entire population of Travancore.[69] The category of rent receivers included owners of land and rent-free tenants. Rent receivers were a small minority of 181, while rent payers aggregated to 10,94,992.[70] By 1921, the number of rent receivers increased considerably. Table 4 shows the number of rent receivers by castes and communities.

The Census of 1875 figures show about 19 per cent of Hindus, 21 per cent of Muslims and 23 per cent of Christians under the head of cultivation. As predominantly a farming class, 45 per cent of Nairs were involved in agriculture. Farmers among Ezhavas, Malayali Brahmins and non-Malayali Brahmins were 14 per cent, 9 per cent and 18 per cent, respectively.[71] At the

TABLE 3

Number of cultivating/non-cultivating landholders and
tenants, and agricultural labourers, 1891 Census[72]

Class	No. of persons
Non-cultivating landholders	1697
Cultivating landholders	37
Non-cultivating tenants	48
Cultivating tenants	3610
Agricultural labourers	10,46,071

TABLE 4

Number of rent receivers in different communities and
castes, 1901[73]

Community/Caste	No. of rent receivers
Brahmins	177
Nairs	1281
Ezhavas	245
Depressed Hindus	46
Other Hindus	225
Syrian Christians	343
Other Christians	79
Muslims	106

TABLE 5
Number of agricultural labourers in different communities and castes, 1875[74]

Community/Caste	No. of agricultural labourers
Pulayas	55,041
Ezhavas	40,405
Parayas	16,240
Nairs	12,491
Christians	29,573
Muslims	6,582

lowest end of the agricultural sector were the labourers. They consisted of two classes: farm servants and field labourers. The maximum number of male and female workers were employed in agricultural labour. Table 5 shows the source of labourers from various communities.

In 1875, 17.79 per cent of the total population of Travancore were agricultural labourers. By 1901 this proportion came down considerably, to 5.2 per cent. This decrease, however, was not real but apparent, and was due to their inclusion under the head of tenants and occupants.[75]

Professions

The professional class in Travancore society was mainly engaged with the spheres of religion, education, law, medicine, engineering and the fine arts. In 1875, the total number of persons who were returned as being in government service[76] was 7,589 or 0.66 per cent of the total population.[77] A majority of the learned professions were monopolized by caste Hindus. In 1875, out of 7,589 male professionals, 6,073 were Hindus, 459 Muslims and 1,057 Christians.[78] Hindus in this occupational category as a proportion of their male population were 0.72 per cent, Muslims 0.65 per cent and Christians 0.45 per cent.[79] Among Hindus, Malayali Brahmins were the most numerous engaged in religious activities as this was their monopoly. The number of Nairs engaged in such activities was 1,127 (0.52 per cent), non-Malayali Brahmins 583 (4.04 per cent) and Ezhavas 233 (0.13 per cent). The rigid application of caste rules considerably restricted the opportunities of non-caste Hindus to enter into religious activities. Most of the educational institutions, especially professional colleges like Ayurveda College, Sanskrit College, etc., were closed to the untouchables till the end of the second decade of the twentieth century. The economic backwardness of the untouchables was also not conducive to them receiving professional education. While in 1875, the total number of male professionals was 7,589, that is, 0.66 per cent of the population, in 1881 their number increased to 17,674 or 1.48 per cent of the total population. Table 6 shows the details of learned professionals in Travancore in 1891.

TABLE 6
Number of persons engaged in learned professions, Travancore, 1891[80]

Profession	No. of professionals	As a percentage of total population
1. Religion		
Priests and other top jobs	10,101	
Subsidiary religious work	13,701	54.70
2. Education and Literature	2706	4.78
3. Law	4573	10.51
4. Medicine		
Doctors and other medical practitioners	5582	
Subsidiary medical service	156	13.19
5. Engineering		
Engineers and surveyors	81	
Subsidiary staff	464	1.25
6. Fine Arts	2992	6.87
7. Minor Services	3787	8.70
Total	43,513	100.0

TABLE 7
Growth in number of learned professionals, Travancore, 1911 to 1921[81]

Profession	1911		1921	
	Number employed	% of total population	Number employed	% of total population
Professions and Liberal Arts	97721	2.9	142398	3.6
Law	8543	0.2	1575	3.6
Medicine	10206	0.3	25779	0.9
Instruction	26365	0.8	35779	0.9
Letters, Arts and Science	18896	0.6	24113	0.6

Due to the increased spread of English education and changes in the social set-up, the number of learned professionals in Travancore increased considerably by the beginning of the twentieth century. Table 7 shows the growth in the number of learned professionals in Travancore for the years 1911 and 1921.

Trade and Commerce

For centuries Kerala has had the distinction of being one of the regions of the subcontinent to have long-distance maritime trade contact with many countries. These trading activities was not only of financial advantage to the exporters and producers, but also aided people engaged in various marketing or trading 'nodes' (connection points or redistribution points) which were

TABLE 8
Number of persons engaged in trade and commerce, Travancore, 1891[82]

Commercial community	No. of people	As a percentage of total commercial population
Moneylending and Securities	470	0.31
General merchants	120,792	78.20
Unspecified	31,885	20.77
Middlemen, Brokers, Agents, etc.	334	0.22
Total	153,481	100.00

situated not far between in distance; for example, all the nodes in the chain between the collection centres of hill produces to their transportation to ports on the east coast and west/Coromandel coast. In fact there were many intermediary work centres and workers at these different nodes. Therefore, trade and related activities were important means of earning livelihoods in Kerala.

In 1875, there were about 61,750 (5.38 per cent of the male population) persons engaged in trade and commerce.[83] Of this proportion, the percentage of people who made trade their primary occupation increased to 6.42, 8.3 and 8.5 per cent in 1891, 1911 and 1921,[84] respectively. Among Hindus, the number of traders was 25,407 (3.01 per cent), among Muslims 13,919 (19.78 per cent) and among Christians 22,413 (9.55 per cent).[85] Ezhavas constituted the largest number of traders among the different Hindu castes/communities, namely, 7,311 or 3.88 per cent of the total male population. Nairs who were engaged in trade for their livelihood numbered 2,300, that is, 1.05 per cent of the male population; and non-Malayali Brahmins numbered 1,010 or 6.8 per cent of their male population.[86] In port towns of Kerala like Alleppey and Quilon, Muslims, non-Malayali Brahmins, Chettis and Konkanis were the important traders. At the same time, in the interior villages of northern and central Travancore, the shopkeeping trade was largely controlled by Syrian Christians and Muslims.[87] During the course of the twentieth century, Hindus also seem to have entered into the business of trade. In 1921, the number of Nairs involved in trade increased to 15,449 and that of Ezhavas to 42,438.[88]

The commercial community was generally divided into various sections such as moneylenders, general merchants, middlemen, brokers, etc.

Industry

Industrial development in Travancore was confined to the sectors of agro-processing, textile production, wood products, ceramics and chemical products. According to the 1875 Census, the total number of people engaged in these industries comprised 9.11 per cent of the total male population. By 1881 and 1891, this proportion increased to 10.57 per cent and 10.97 per cent, respectively.

TABLE 9
Number of persons engaged in industries, Travancore, 1901 to 1931[89]

Year	No. of persons	% of total population
1901	519,325	17.5
1911	588,410	17.1
1921	721,837	17.9
1931	771,312	15.1

TABLE 10
Ownership and management of factories by different communities/castes/nationalities, 1911[90]

Community/Caste/Nationality	No. of factories	
	Owned by	Managed by
Europeans and Anglo-Indians	11	61
Indians	27	42
a) Christians	7	18
b) Muslims	4	8
c) Brahmins	5	5
d) Ezhavas	2	2
e) Other Hindus	6	6
f) Chettis	1	1
g) Nairs	2	2

By the end of the nineteenth century, a number of coir and cashewnut factories had started to function. According to the 1911 Census, the total number of factories in Travancore at that time was 108. Of these, 5 were owned by the government, 61 jointly by Europeans and Anglo-Indians, and 42 by Indians.[91] Of the European-owned factories, 50 belonged to companies and 11 to individuals. And the corresponding figures for Indians were 15 and 27 respectively.[92] Table 10 presents the ownership and management patterns of the private factories.

According to the 1901 Census, industrial activities were mainly undertaken by non-Hindus and non-caste Hindus. The largest number of industrial workers among the Hindus belonged to the Ezhava community as they accounted for 45.7 per cent of the actual labour force. Muslims and Christians occupied second and third positions in the order.[93]

Labourers

According to the 1875 Census, 18 per cent of Travancore's population were labourers.[94] Though the agricultural labourers were mainly sourced from the

Pulaya and Paraya castes,[95] 6 per cent, 13 per cent and 21 per cent, respectively, of Nairs, Christians and Ezhavas were also labourers. Generally, the conditions of agricultural labourers were deplorable and miserable. In 1850, the daily wage of a coolie labourer was 1 anna and one meal. By the 1870s the wage went up to 4 annas, but without a meal.[96] The working conditions and salaries of plantation labourers, artisans and factory workers were better than that of agricultural labourers. By the 1880s, the wages of non-agricultural labourers, like those employed on plantations, in the public works department and the coir industry, had risen by 167 per cent, and that of artisans by 140 per cent.[97] Among artisans, the highest daily wage was obtained by goldsmiths, which was 18½ *chakras*. [98]

The above description of occupational distribution in terms of caste, religion and nationality indicates that there was a predominance of upper-caste Hindus in the most sought-after occupations such as government services and professional jobs, as well as in the control of land. Muslims had the lion's share in trade; a substantial section of industrial workers and agricultural labourers were Ezhavas; and Christians, while they were more or less evenly represented in all occupations, could not find entry into government services or into age-old and continuing religious activities. The high-end factories of those times were under the direct control of non-Indians who preferred to employ Christians, but as they were not forthcoming to meet the increasing demand for labour they were obliged to employ others as well.

Socio-Economic Changes and the Emergence of New Classes

From the second half of the nineteenth century, Travancore entered a state of unprecedented agency-forming transitions, though these were at times very slow, sporadic and even belated. Various factors such as land reforms and tenancy abolition, growth of the cash economy due to the development of plantation industries, development of public works departments and small-scale industries, and the introduction of English education were the main catalysts of the major changes and shifts that took place. These transitions in the social and economic spheres in turn paved the way for the emergence of new classes in Travancore. Let us now pay attention to each of those causal factors.

Land Reforms and Changes in Land Control

As has already been mentioned, only a small part of the land was owned by *jenmis* and the rest belonged to the state. In order to motivate tenants to increasingly bring more land under cultivation, and to mitigate the continued wedge between the tenurial rights of private *jenmis* and those of tenants of the state,[99] the Government of Travancore issued the Pattom Proclamation on 2 June 1865.[100] This achievement of the state received great acclaim and came to be known as the Magna Carta of Travancore ryots.

There were some other factors that were also responsible for the introduction of land reforms. Since the *sirkar* could not sell land for non-payment of rent and because tenants were reluctant to take up such land for cultivation, the government experienced great difficulties in collecting its dues. Tenants, on the other hand, viewed such land as having no value beyond the paddy it produced. To avoid a stalemate, Madhava Rao, the Dewan of Travancore, issued the Pattom Proclamation granting full ownership rights to the holders of 2,00,000 acres of *sirkar pattom* land.[101] He estimated that Rs 1.5 crores of land value could thus be created.[102] This proclamation enfranchised the *sirkar pattom* lands, irrespective of the agreement between the state and the tenants, and declared that the 'ryots holding these lands may regard them fully as private, heritable, saleable and otherwise transferable property'.[103] Thus it put an end to state landlordism and created peasant proprietorship, as landed 'assets' became landed 'property' in the strict sense of the term. The proclamation brought about serious modifications in the feudal arrangements of joint families in Travancore by enabling the partition of such families, since the *karanavan* (or head of the joint family household) could no longer insist that the *sirkar pattom* lands were inalienable.[104] This was a severe jolt to the traditional joint family system: land was no more the property of the joint family, but that of individual members of families or other individuals.

The reform measure of 1865 benefited only the cultivators of *pandaravaka* lands, however, and the ownership status of tenants of *jenmom* lands and non-*pandaravaka* lands remained intact. These tenants had no security of tenure, the *jenmis* could penalize them in several ways and their assessed land revenue was higher than that of *sirkar* lands. In order to improve these conditions and to systematize the agricultural property of the state,[105] the government issued another Proclamation in 1867 by which the *sirkar* considerably redefined the power of *jenmis* over their tenants. Then onwards eviction became difficult and the tenants became permanent tenants, although they were required to continue giving rent to the *jenmis* as before.[106]

Some of the still-remaining drawbacks of the 1867 Proclamation were partly resolved through another legislation, the *Jenmi–Kudiyan* Act of 1896. This ensured permanent occupancy rights and fixed rents for the *kanam kudiyans*.[107] However, despite the good intentions of the state, the tenants could not get the benefits they were assured. The *jenmis* were given the right to increase the rent at the time of periodical renewal of *kanapattom*.[108] This too did not give much protection to tenants holding land at will – either under *kanam* tenancy or directly from the *jenmis*. Another problem the tenants faced was the incidence of unequal revenue assessment under different tenurial categories, and at times of different cultivators under the same tenure.[109]

A more fundamental and far-reaching change took place in the tenurial system of Travancore in 1932, with the proclamation of the *Jenmi Kudiyan* (Amendment) Regulation. In regard to the *jenmi–kudiyan* relationship this regulation was a benchmark, for it converted all tenants into proprietors (to be known hereafter as *kudiyan*) who were to remit rent to the respective *jenmi*s. The rent payments had to be made only in cash.[110] Thus the *kudiyan* acquired full ownership of the land including all its output.

The land settlement system in Travancore was the 'ryotwari' system, by which the ryots enjoyed private ownership and as such were individually responsible to the state for payment of rent due from their holdings. The land tax was fixed and levied on the basis of accurate measurement of land, assessment of its agricultural productivity, and determination of the individual farmer's entitlement and fixed revenue[111] to be paid.

The new land ownership rights radically revolutionized agrarian relations as well as the joint family system, which were closely interconnected. The land reforms not only gave rise to peasant proprietorship, but also altered relations between members within joint families. As land became alienable, disgruntled members of the Nair *taravad* began to free themselves from the clutches of the autocratic *karanavan* and demand the partition of property; hence, a number of matrilineal Nair *taravad*s in Travancore had to execute partition.[112] Instances of demands for partition of land and non-compliance (which was quite regular) by the *karanavan* gave an entry point for the modern judiciary into the system of the joint family and of land ownership, as it gained the authority to issue the final verdict on land disputes if any. Thus landlordism in Travancore came to be dislodged from its ties with the joint family system. Hereafter, irrespective of community or caste/religious differences, anyone with liquid cash – earned through trade, commerce or any other lucrative business – could purchase and own land.

Information is available about the different castes that were engaged in selling and buying land during the eighteen months between 1906 and 1908.[113] It reveals that the Nairs were selling land as they were losing their hold over it, and those who did not earlier have much control over land began to own more land by purchasing the properties of the Nairs. The Christians and the Ezhavas took maximum advantage of this. Therefore, land reforms in Travancore actually put an end to Nair dominance, and other communities that had been kept aloof till then now had a better opportunity to become landowners.

These land reforms to a large extent also reduced the control of landlords over tenants. The ryotwari system of land tenure considerably pre-empted over-assessment of land. Increase of agricultural products and growth of exports further reduced the miseries of the ryots. No doubt these measures came as a relief to the sufferings of the peasantry of Travancore, which were a result of long-continued oppression and exploitation during the first half and early second half of the nineteenth century. Further, they resulted in the formation of a new middle class due to the emergence of an economy of small peasant proprietors, and tenants with substantial economic independence and sustained interest in land. It is possible to state that the rules of inter-caste and inter-religious relations were rewritten, and that where such relations lingered on, they were marked by a visible difference.

Growth of a Cash Economy and Plantation Industries

The advent of a cash economy in Travancore took place with the entry of British capital into the plantation industries, the development of small-scale industries, shifts in the cropping pattern from food crops to cash crops, and the commercialization of agriculture. Accentuation of these material practices necessitated a build-up of infrastructure, which was accomplished with the government developing its own department of public works. The development of a public works department in turn created both forward and backward linkages in the economy.

Though the British colonial government did not directly invest in the industrial development of the state, it showed a keen interest in building up infrastructure facilities – a prerequisite for any kind of economic growth. This was primarily effected by modernizing the systems of communication and transportation for better exploitation of the state's resources. Lieutenant-General William, the Resident of Travancore from 1840 to 1860, initiated a scheme for the construction of a network of roads. Madhava Rao, the Dewan of Travancore from 1857 to 1872, also took practical steps in this direction. He organized the public works department in 1860, as a consequence of which both job opportunities[114] and wages increased;[115] this in turn increased consumption demand and subsequently the production of consumables. That is, there was a rise in both supply and demand. In general, there was demand-pushed development of production and infrastructure.

Plantation industries developed in Travancore during the second half of the nineteenth century. Some of the factors which helped this process were state ownership of large tracts of land, improvement of transport facilities, rise in prices of plantation products, increased credit facilities[116] and the availability of cheap labour due to the abolition of slavery. In effect, the abolition of slavery generated a work force for the newly established plantation industries of the British capitalists.[117] Though Malabar was directly under British rule, British planters were more enthusiastic to invest in the princely state of Travancore because it was possible for them to lease large tracts of land on favourable terms directly from the state. In Malabar they would have had to lease or buy land from private landlords at relatively higher prices, and buying from private sellers was more difficult than a direct lease from the state.[118] The British entrepreneurs convinced the Travancore rulers about the economic significance of plantation industries, and '[t]he *sarcar* felt satisfied that the country would largely benefit by the introduction of capital, skill and enterprise of Europeans in utilizing the tracts of land which for the most part would otherwise be untouched for generations.'[119]

The first coffee plantation in central Travancore was established in 1862 by J.D. Munro at Hope Estate, and his example was soon followed by Stevenson, Baber and Rechardson.[120] In 1864, a tea plantation was started in the government gardens in Peerumade.[121] The most important and largest plantation companies of the late nineteenth century were the British Kannan Devan Hill Produce Company, registered in 1878, and the Anglo-American Direct Tea Trading Company, registered in 1897.

The government's assessment rates on these lands were very nominal as compared to the income they yielded from plantation crops. 'Even after the amendment (1944) of an early agreement, the state demand on the plantations of the Kannan Devan Hill Produce was ... about five annas per acre.'[122] The assessment rate for coffee and tea cultivation was fixed at Re 1 per acre, and for rubber and cardamom the rates were Rs 2 and Rs 3 per acre, respectively.[123]

Low rates of assessment, cheap labour and good transportation facilities naturally increased the flow of foreign capital into the plantations. By 1896, 6,000 acres of land in the Kannan Devan Hills were under plantation crops, of which tea, cinchona and coffee occupied 3,315, 1,391 and 1,357 acres, respectively.[124] The flow of capital did indeed open up new opportunities for agricultural and non-agricultural expansion, and increased labour mobility across regions, but this did not necessarily translate into upward mobility within the social hierarchy. In short, the positive externalities, both forward and backward, had a far-reaching impact on the uplands of Travancore.

In addition, as a result of consistent persuasion by the British authorities, the Government of Travancore abolished the state monopoly in commodities like pepper in 1860 and tobacco in 1863. Thus 'the commercial resources of the country received an impetus unknown before'.[125] As a consequence of the abolition of monopoly in the pepper trade, local traders were able to freely buy pepper from inland ryots and sell it to their advantage. For a period of nine years, between 1872 and 1880, the pepper market was stable and the pepper trade averaged Rs 2.81 lakhs.[126] In 1863, the tobacco monopoly was also abolished and petty traders were able to acquire their tobacco cheaply. With the withdrawal of the government from imposing duty on tobacco supply and acting as a middleman,[127] the tobacco trade became more profitable.

Extensive cultivation of tapioca in the plains and reclamation of the backwaters for rice cultivation in the coastal belt[128] gave a positive impetus to the economy. The increased demand for labour, 'both skilled and unskilled, in the British Indian provinces and overseas British territories like Ceylon and

Mauritius'[129] also helped the growth of the cash economy in Travancore. Expansion of the area under cultivation,[130] coupled with the development of industries such as coir manufacturing, cashewnut processing, cotton spinning and weaving, and leather manufacturing, effected rapid economic change in the last quarter of the nineteenth century. Trade and commerce, particularly overseas trade, developed in an unprecedented manner. There was a considerable increase in the demand for coconut products from America and Europe between 1870 and 1890, and export earnings from coconut doubled because of the rise not only in the quantity exported but also of prices.[131]

All these economic changes affected the lives of not just the caste Hindus and non-caste Hindus, but also of the untouchables like the Ezhavas and those newly free due to the abolition of slavery. Therefore, the emergence of a middle class in Travancore, unlike in other parts of South India, where 'the new middle class so far [as] Hindus were concerned was almost wholly a single caste class, the Brahmins, and consisted mainly of the white collar profession',[132] was distinct as the change embraced multi-caste and multi-occupational groups. At least some of the changes we have mapped transgressed caste and class differentiation in varying degrees.

Education and the Emergence of a New Class

Travancore was the second most literate state in India, the first being the neighbouring state of Cochin.[133] The main reasons for the growth of education in Travancore were the activities of Christian missionaries, and the enthusiasm shown by the government to

> defray the entire cost of education of its people in order that there might be no Backwardness in the spread of enlightenment among them, but by diffusion of Education that they might become better subjects and public servants that the reputation of the state might be advanced thereby.[134]

In 1834, the Government of Travancore established English schools in the state, and in order to attract more and more students it not only provided free education, but also gave Rs 2 as scholarship for studying English.[135] In addition, the peasant proprietors and tenants who had gained substantial economic independence acted as a stimulant for educational growth.[136]

By 1870 Travancore had one vernacular school per 1.9 square miles and 792 inhabitants.[137] There were 364,810 literate persons in the state in 1901, of whom 14,869 (0.41 per cent) were literate in English.[138] In 1904–05 the total number of schools was 3,630 and the total number of students was 1,95,999, as against 2,337 schools and 1,93,785 students in 1903–04.[139] These figures point to a rapid growth of schools within a year even as the rise in the number of students was marginal. Higher education also registered tremendous progress. In 1911 there were six colleges in the state, comprising four arts colleges, one training college and one Sanskrit college.[140] In 1903, the Government of Travancore spent 9.56 per cent of its total revenue on education.[141] The level of female education was also far in advance of other states. The province had a total number of 19,59,999 students in 1905, out of which 45,570 (2.3 per cent) were women. They constituted 13.2 per cent of the school-going population of girls between the ages of five and fifteen.[142]

But all these educational facilities were obtainable only by upper-class Hindus and by Christians due to the observance of caste rules and pollution till the end of the nineteenth century. Table 11 shows the details of educational status of various castes and communities. In 1895, for the first time, the Government of Travancore provided grant-in-aid for the establishment of schools for backward communities,[143] as a part of its policy of imparting free primary education to all the people irrespective of caste, creed or race.[144] As a result, by 1905, 5,591 backward class students were enrolled in 221 schools, and in the next year both students and schools increased respectively to 5,907 and 276.[145] In 1911 the restrictions on enrolment of Pulaya and other backward class children to government schools were removed,[146] and by 1928–29 all the special schools for backward classes were converted into the general category.[147]

Even though the expansion of education affected all classes and castes of the society, its spread was not uniform. The educational advancement of Christians and caste Hindus was due to preferential facilities and economic viability. The Christians had the support of the missionaries, who managed 416 (22 per cent) schools out of 1,901 schools in the period 1886–87;[148] and the caste Hindus received very good support from the government.

TABLE 11
Educational status of various communitiues and castes in Travancore, 1875 Census[149]

Community/Caste	No. of educated males	As % of total males	No. of educated females	As % of total females
Brahmins	10,183	50.15	241	1.33
Kshatriyas	645	52.02	116	9.56
Ambalavasis	1315	31.67	65	1.52
Nairs	46,373	21.27	2656	1.19
Ezhavas	5928	3.15	93	0.05
Parayas	192	0.60	–	–
Pulayas	183	0.19	–	–
Muslims	6524	9.27	86	0.12
Christians	29,057	12.42	1593	0.68
Europeans	131	87.33	88	79.28
Eurasians	320	45.97	157	22.85

TABLE 12

Number of backward class pupils under instruction in Travancore, 1905 and 1906[150]

Caste	Year	
	1080 ME (AD 1904–05)	*1081 ME (AD 1905–06)*
Pulayas	2266	2513
Parayas	2251	2464
Velans	457	294
Kuravas	340	276
Kanies	220	194
Vedars	56	166

Table 13 shows the growth of native schools in 1886–87, with their percentage share in the total number of schools marginally increasing from 28 per cent to 29 per cent. This shows that schools sponsored by the natives and the missionaries accounted for nearly 75 per cent of the total number of schools, of which more than 46 per cent were under the control of the missionaries. This may help to substantiate the assumption that it was the missionaries who propagated school education in Travancore. At the same time it remains an issue to be probed further, especially because the shift took place within one year.

Table 14 shows the occupations of the parents or guardians of pupils in Travancore for the years 1897 and 1899. In 1897, pupils whose parents had white collar jobs – like in government service, teaching and law – accounted for 8.3 per cent of the total number of students, and this figure slightly increased to 8.7 per cent in 1899. However, at the college level their percentage steadily increased.[151] Children of landlords and agriculturists accounted for 48.4 per cent of the total number of school students. The percentage of children of traders and merchants enrolled in schools was 8.9 and 9.6 in 1897 and 1899, respectively. These three sections together comprised about 65 per cent of the total student population, while the children of labourers, coolies, artisans, etc., together accounted for 34 per cent of students at different stages of school education. It is also worthy of note here that while children of landlords and agriculturists constituted a little more than 48 per cent of students, children of labourers and coolies, at 23–24 per cent, came next. This shows that there were factors beyond caste and wealth behind sending children to school – an important fact but whose further exposition is outside the scope of this study.

Generally speaking, in the sphere of education, caste Hindus and Christians enjoyed an overwhelming superiority over non-caste Hindus and Muslims. Table 15, which shows the number and percentage of educated males and females in the various communities of Travancore for the years 1891 and 1875, points to this disparity between upper castes and lower castes in the

TABLE 13
Number of schools under government and private administration, 1886 and 1887[152]

Description of schools	No. of schools	
	1886	*1887*
Government	226 (26%)	226 (25%)
Mission	398 (46%)	416 (46%)
Native	247 (28%)	259 (29%)
Total	871	901

TABLE 14
Occupation of parents/guardians of pupils, 1897 and 1899[153]

Occupation of parent/ guardian	*1897*		*1899*	
	No. of pupils under instruction	*% to total*	*No. of pupils under instruction*	*% to total*
Government servants	9,823	6.1	11,619	6.5
Teachers	2,174	1.4	2,349	1.3
Landlords/Agriculturists	78,009	48.4	87,765	48.2
Vakils	1,285	0.8	1,750	0.9
Labourers/Coolies	38,127	23.8	40,178	22.6
Artisans	8,557	5.4	8,891	5.3
Other unspecified	8,133	5.2	9,954	5.6

field of education. Caste Hindus and Christians were far ahead of non-caste Hindus and Muslims. However, at the same time, it is noteworthy that the highest caste groups and the lowest caste groups were relatively less educated as compared to the middle-caste groups and Christians. A probable reason for this is that while the Brahmins followed their conventional education rather than the one imparted in the newly established schools, people of the lower castes had neither the opportunity nor the capacity to enrol their children in these schools.

In the sphere of English education too, the caste Hindus and Christians dominated. According to the 1891 Census, there were 3,421 English literates in Travancore – i.e. 13 out of every 10,000 persons were educated in the English language. Of this number, the Brahmins had the highest share, i.e. 881 English-educated persons. The second and third places were occupied by Nairs and Christians with 614 and 600, respectively. The Ezhavas, Muslims and Parayas together accounted for only 126 English-educated persons.[154]

While the educational facilities were not accessible to the low castes, a few Ezhavas who came from landholding families[155] did have some opportunity to learn English. By the early part of the twentieth century, this community had achieved surprising growth in the field of English education. The number of

TABLE 15

Literate males and females in different communities and castes, 1875 and 1891[156]

Community/ Caste	Literate Males			Literate Females		
	Number in 1891	As a % of total male population in 1891	Proportion in 1875	Number in 1891	As a % of total female population in 1891	Proportion in 1875
Brahmins	11,925	51.72	50.18	1469	7.15	1.33
Kshatriyas	499	32.37	52.02	252	20.13	9.55
Ambalavasis	1097	28.20	31.67	183	5.11	1.52
Nairs	90,542	37.47	21.27	16,673	6.89	1.19
Ezhavas	24,996	12.10	3.15	1089	–	0.05
Parayas	858	2.35	0.60	91	0.25	–
Pulayas	4031	0.39	0.19	630	–	–
Muslims	11,709	1.36	9.27	91,280	1.65	0.12
Christians	56,537	21.29	12.42	8454	3.27	0.68

TABLE 16

Development of English education in various communities and castes, 1911, 1921 and 1931[157]

Community/Caste	Literacy in English		
	1911	1921	1931
Brahmins	3007	4221	8226
Nairs	5446	14169	18606
Christians	10129	24059	27296
Muslims	299	1159	1608
Ezhavas	1441	4529	5202

English-educated Ezhavas in 1891 was only 30,[158] but by 1931 it increased to 5,202 (Table 16).

The material and non-material practices and their patterns as discussed in the above sections show that during the period under focus, several modern institutions and processes were introduced in Travancore, and that their spread was quite significant. The ways in which they influenced different sections of the people, the manner in which they were received and the agents who brought them into the social body, all differed substantially. This shows that as in the traditional social formation, modernization also involved social stratification; but the terms and criteria of the stratification under moderniza-tion were quite different. Some of the norms of traditional stratification were obliterated, some redefined, and others introduced. The factors of change that we have delineated show that there were distinct conditions in which a middle class drawn from various religions and castes could emerge in Travancore. With this general social and historical context in mind, in the chapters that follow, we shall proceed to describe and analyse the social reform movement of the SNDP Yogam.

Notes and References

[1] The area of the state is given differently in different sources. The Census of 1891 has recorded it as 6,730 square miles (see *Census of Travancore, 1891*, Vol. I, Report, p. 217), whereas the Census of 1901 has fixed it at 7,091 square miles (see *Census of India, 1901*, Vol. XXVI, Travancore, Part I, p. 11). The estimate of Lieutenants Ward and Conner was 6,731 square miles. See Ward and Conner, *Memoirs of the Survey of the Travancore and Cochin States*, Sirkar Press, Trivandrum, 1863; reprinted 1868. The Census of 1921 estimated an area of 7624.84 square miles. See *Census of India, 1921*, Vol. XXV, Travancore, Part I, p. 136.

[2] All Travancore Joint Political Congress, *Travancore: The Present Political Problem*, Trivandrum, 1934, p. 1.

[3] According to the Census of 1891, the population of Travancore was 2,557,736 with an average density of 380.5 persons to 1 square mile, as against 356.7 in the previous census and 343.4 in the Census of 1875. See *Census of Travancore, 1891*, Vol. I, Report, p. 21. But both the population and the density of population increased respectively to 29, 52, 152 and 416 in 1901. See *Census of India, 1901*, Vol. XXVI, Travancore, Part I, Report, p. 88.

[4] 'Others' refers to Animists, Buddhists, Jews, Jains, etc.

[5] *Census of India, 1901*, Vol. XXVI, Travancore, Part I, Report, p. 88.

[6] *Census of Travancore, 1891*, Vol. I, Report, pp. 647–48.

[7] According to the Census of 1901, Malayali Brahmins themselves were divided into five main groups, such as the Tampurakkal, Adhyas, etc. See *Census of India*, 1901, Vol. XXVI, Travancore, Part I, Report, pp. 296–97.

[8] By the beginning of the nineteenth century, the Government of Travancore had earmarked 80 per cent of the cultivated land under the name of *pandaravaka* land, and the remaining 20 per cent, known as *brahmaswam* lands, were in the possession of a few landlords, mainly Brahmin individuals and Brahmin temples. See T.C. Verghese, *Agrarian Change and Economic Consequences: Land Tenures in Kerala, 1850–1960*, Calcutta, 1970, p. 44.

[9] Robin Jeffrey, *The Decline of Nayar Dominance: Society and Politics in Travancore, 1847–1908*, Vikas Publishing House, Delhi, 1976, pp. 73, 290.

[10] According to the Census of 1881, of the 8,058 males, 2,024 were in government service. See *Census of Travancore, 1881*, Vol. I, Report, p. 196.

[11] According to the Census of 1881 (ibid.), a number of non-Malayali Brahmins worked as domestic servants, coolies, temple servants, bread makers, etc. While the Namboodiri women spent their time in the gloomy interiors of their residences, about 6 per cent of the female population of non-Malayali Brahmins were said to follow some occupation contributing to the family income. The 1881 Census listed 242 females under instruction, 153 under trade, 42 were bread makers, 60 hostel keepers, 50 were put down under agriculture, 36 were cooks, 24 were domestic servants, 20 were beggars, 7 in *sirkar* service, 2 native physicians and 2 were returned as gentlewomen.

[12] Ambalavasis occupied an intermediate position between the Brahmins and Brahmanical Kshatriyas on the one hand, and Sudras on the other. See *Census of India, 1901*, Vol. XXVI, Travancore, Part I, Report, p. 259.

[13] The Nair may be classified as both higher class and lower classes. See L.A. Ravi Varma, 'Caste in Malabar', *Kerala Society Papers*, Vol. II, Series 9, 1932, p. 188.

[14] *Census of India, 1901*, Vol. XXVI, Travancore, Part I, Report, p. 325. Sardar K.M. Panikkar said that the Nairs were not a caste but a race. See K.M. Panikkar, *A History of Kerala*, Annamalai University, Annamalainagar, 1959, p. 10.

[15] Ravi Varma, 'Caste in Malabar', p. 188.

[16] K.N. Panikkar says, 'The Nair acceptance of the Namboodiri privileges as a social idea was the result of the latter's ideological hegemony and control of land.' See K.N. Panikkar, 'Land Control Ideology and Reform: A Study of Change in Family Organizations and Marriage Systems in Kerala', *The Indian Historical Review*, Vol. IV, No. 1, July 1977, p. 35. According to *Keralolpatti*, 'Only through Namboodiri seed would kings be born.' Therefore, 'the women of the royal and noble houses had no need of *brahmaswam* property. All that they wanted was "Namboodiri seed".' This was necessary to get 'good kings'. See Elamkulam P.N. Kunjan Pillai, *Studies in Kerala History*, N.B.S., Kottayam, 1970, p. 315.

[17] This was despite the fact that Nairs accounted for just 20 per cent of the population. *Census of Travancore, 1875*, Vol. I, Report, p. 225.

[18] According to the Census of 1881, 36,310 males and 26,371 females were general labourers; 27,499 males and 1,237 females were agriculturists; 27,331 males were toddy tappers; 59 males and 2,375 females were distillers of arrack; 637 males worked as toddy contractors; 339 males and 2,073 females were rope makers; and 3,187 males and 434 females were engaged in trade. See *Census of Travancore, 1881*, Vol. I, Part I, Report, p. 219.

[19] Francis Buchanan, *A Journey from Madras through the Countries of Mysore, Canara and Malabar*, 2 vols, Higginbotham, Madras, 1870, p. 421.

[20] The chief example being the Raja of Ambalapuzha. See L.K. Anantha Krishna Iyer, *The Cochin Tribes and Castes*, Vol. I, Higginbotham, Madras, 1909, p. 278; reprinted by Johnson Reprint Corporation, New York, 1969.

[21] Jeffrey, *The Decline of Nayar Dominance*, p. 23.

[22] See *Census of India, 1931*, Vol. XXVIII, Travancore, Part I, Report, p. 433.

[23] 'In Kerala,' says D.R. Mankekar, 'much more than elsewhere in the country – a Hindu is not a Hindu, but a Namboodiri, a Nair, or an Ezhava. He cannot easily visualize the larger concept of Hindu as such or think at that level.' D.R. Mankekar, *The Red Riddle of Kerala*, Manaktalas, Bombay, 1965, p. 46.

[24] Francis Day writes: 'The Princes of Malabar treated their Native Christian subjects well. They were given equal or superior rank with the Nairs and allowed to be governed by those of their own sect, in both temporal and spiritual matters.' Francis Day, *The Lands of the Perumals or Cochin, Its Past and Its Present*, Gantz Brothers, Madras, 1863, p. 217.

[25] Between the sixteenth and nineteenth centuries, quarrels and disputes among the various denominations of Christians, such as Syrians and Latins, Jacobites and Marthomas, Carmelites and Jesuits, and Church Missionary Society and London Missionary Society were very common. The Catholic Christians of Malabar were divided into Syrian and Latin Catholics and Jacobites, and a section of the Jacobites split off to form the Marthomas. For details, see K.J. John, ed., *Christian Heritage of Kerala*, Cochin, 1981, pp. 18–19 and 223. Also see Day, *The Lands of the Perumals*, pp. 211–65, and Lawrence Lopez, *A Social History of Modern Kerala*, Trivandrum, 1988, pp. 151–58.

[26] Nagam Aiya says, 'No Indian State or province contains more Christians than Travancore. Nowhere in the world has a state ruled by a non-Christian monarch with such a large Christian population as Travancore.' Nagam Aiya, *The Travancore State Manual*, Government Press, Trivandrum, 1906, Vol. 1, p. 29.

[27] Thomas Cana or Kanni Thomas first visited Kerala as a merchant and later came back as the representative of the Archbishop of Silensia or Tigris, who then governed the Eastern Church under the Patriarch of Antioch. See *Census of Travancore, 1891*, Vol. I, Report, p. 385.

[28] To fill the vacuum created by the absence of Vaisyas, the traditional trading community of the Hindu *varna* system, the rulers of Kerala might have thought of promoting this enterprising business community by awarding them honours and privileges. During the second Chera empire (AD 800–1102) Christians were the prominent business community in the land. The Tarisapalli copper plate, executed in AD 849 by Ayyan Atikal Tiruvatikal of Venad during the reign of Emperor Sthanu Ravi (844–855), confers several important rights and privileges on the Christians of Quilon. See Kunjan Pillai, *Studies in Kerala History*, pp. 224–26. The

Thazhakkad Church inscription of Rajasimha (AD 1028–43) refers to two Christian merchants, Chattan Vadukkan and Iravi Chattan, who were members of the Manigramam guild, being conferred certain privileges. See ibid., p. 243. The copper plate grant popularly known as Syrian Christian Copper Plate of AD 1225, issued by King Vira Raghava Chakravarti of Perumpadappu Swarupam from his headquarters at Mahodayapuram, made Christians the head of the trade guild called Manigramam. See C.M. Agur, *Church History of Travancore*, S.P.S. Press, Madras, 1903, p. 7; A. Sreedhara Menon, *A Survey of Kerala History*, N.B.S., Kottayam, 1973, p. 42.

29 At the instance of Colonel Munro, the British Resident of Travancore, the Maharaja of Travancore gave financial assistance to the cultural activities of the missionaries. In addition, due to the intervention of the Resident, the Travancore rulers granted several concessions to the Christians. See Regional Record Survey Committee (comp.), *History of Freedom Movement in Kerala*, 1970, Vol. I, p. 65. See also Jeffrey, *The Decline of Nayar Dominance*, pp. 37–69; Francis Houtart and Genevieve Lemercinier, 'Socio-Religious Movements in Kerala: A Reaction to the Capitalist Mode of Production', *Social Scientist*, Vol. VI, No. 11, June 1978, pp. 22–23.

30 *Census of Travancore, 1881*, Vol. I, Report, p. 135; *Census of India, 1921*, Vol. XXV, Travancore, Part I, Report, p. 34.

31 *Census of India, 1931*, Vol. XXVIII, Travancore, Part I, Report, p. 383.

32 In 1901, nineteen sects were recorded and were grouped into thirteen sects such as Anglican, Syrian (Jacobites) Salvationist, Lutheran, Church Mission, London Mission, Baptist, etc. *Census of India, 1901*, Vol. XXVI, Travancore, Part I, Report, pp. 114 and 124.

33 All Travancore Joint Political Congress, *Travancore, the Present Political Problem*, p. 14.

34 Agur, *Church History of Travancore*, p. 7.

35 *Travancore Marumakkathayam Committee Report of 1908*, Appendix 11, p. 93. Also see T.C. Verghese, *Agrarian Change and Economic Consequences*, p. 103.

36 According to the Census of 1901, Muslims in Travancore constituted 6.5 per cent of the population, that is 190,556 persons, and they had returned themselves under 47 sub-divisions such as Sayyid, Sheikh, Tangal, Wais, Jonakan, Mettan, etc. See *Census of India, Travancore, 1901*, Part II, pp. 170–74.

37 *Census of Travancore, 1881*, Report, p. 137.

38 All Travancore Joint Political Congress, *Travancore, the Present Political Problem*, p. 13.

39 *Complete Works of Swami Vivekananda*, Vol. III, pp. 294–95.

40 Mahadev Desai, *The Epic of Travancore*, Navajivan Karyalaya, Allahabad, 1937, p. 4.

41 The fear of pollution and its consequences was ingrained into the ethos of the lower castes. Louise Ouwerkerk, *The Untouchables of India*, Oxford University Press, Bombay, 1945, p. 3.

42 The limit of distance of pollution for a Brahmin from a Paraya was 64 feet. A Nair may approach a Namboodiri Brahmin but not touch him. A Tiyan must not come within twelve paces of a Nair, a Malayan must keep three or four paces farther off, and a Pulayan must keep 96 paces away from a Nair as well as Brahmin. See J.H. Hutton, *Caste in India: Its Nature, Functions and Origins*, Oxford University Press, Bombay, 1963, pp. 179–80.

43 Durate Barbosa, *A Description of the Coast of Africa and Malabar*, London, 1866, p. 129.

44 Edgar Thurston, *Castes and Tribes of Southern India*, 7 vols, Government Press, Madras, 1909, Vol. 2, p. 52; second edition, Johnson Reprint Corporation, New York, 1965.

45 A Panan may approach but not touch a Tiyan, but a Pulayan must not even approach a Panan. Pulayans, for instance, if polluted by the proximity of a Nayadi or Ulladan, were enjoined to take seven baths and shed a few drops of blood from a little finger. See ibid., pp. 79–80; L.S.S. O'Malley, *Indian Caste Customs*, Vikas Publishing House, New Delhi, 1974, pp. 141–42; T.K. Ravindran, 'Consequences of Untouchability in Travancore', *Bulletin of the Institute of Traditional Culture*, Madras University, July–December 1975, p. 41.

46 For getting permission to cover their breasts, the untouchables under the leadership of Christian missionaries had to launch a number of movements in Travancore in the nineteenth century. Therefore, a number of conflicts took place between Nairs and the unapproachables

who had converted to Christianity. Ultimately they got permission to wear blouses but on condition that they were not of the same pattern as those worn by the upper castes. For details, see, Agur, *Church History of Travancore*, pp. 780–82; L. Robert Hardgrave, 'The Breast Cloth Controversy: Caste Consciousness and Social Change in Southern Travancore', *The Indian Economic and Social History Review*, Vol. 5, No. 2, June 1968, p. 177. Also see Jeffrey, *The Decline of Nayar Dominance*, pp. 57–61; and Rev. C. Mead, 'A Report of the Neyoor Mission, July 1829', 30 June 1929 (L.M.S. Manuscript), quoted in Hardgrave 'The Breast Cloth Controversy', p. 178.

[47] G.A. Ballard, Resident to the Chief Secretary to the Madras Government, 9 March 1870, *Madras Residency Records*, Madras Political Proceedings, 13 April 1870, G.O. No. 143, National Archives of India (NAI). Also see Robin Jeffrey, 'Social Origins of a Caste Association, 1875–1906: The Founding of the S.N.D.P. Yogam', *South Asia*, No. 4, 1974, p. 40.

[48] T.K. Velu Pillai, *The Travancore State Manual*, 4 vols, Trivandrum Government Press, 1940, Vol. I, p. 844.

[49] Swami John Dharmatheerthan, *The Prophet of Peace*, Sree Narayana Publishing House, Chempazhanti, Kerala, 1931, p. 23.

[50] Ibid., p. 24.

[51] K. Damodaran, *Kerala Charitram*, Trichur, 1962, Part I, p. 162.

[52] Rev. Samuel Mateer, *Native Life of Travancore*, W.H. Allen, London, 1883, p. 291.

[53] *Sahodharan*, March–May 1920 (Meenam–Medam 1095 ME), Vol. 5, No. 8, pp. 31–32.

[54] For a detailed account of the conversion of untouchables from various castes to Christianity, see *Census of India, 1931*, Travancore, Part I, p. 389. As a result of conversion the Christian population in Travancore substantially increased from 20 per cent in 1875 to 31 per cent in 1931. At the same time the population of Pulayas, one of the untouchable castes in Travancore, fell from 8.18 per cent in 1875 to 4.07 per cent in 1931. Ibid., p. 331.

[55] *Census of Travancore, 1875*, Vol. I, Report, p. 253 and *Census of Travancore, 1891*, Vol. I, Report, p. 578.

[56] *Census of Travancore, 1875*, p. 225 and *Census of Travancore, 1881*, pp. 242–43.

[57] *Census of Travancore, 1875*, pp. 255–56.

[58] *Census of Travancore, 1881*, pp. 242–43.

[59] *Census of Travancore, 1875*, pp. 156–78.

[60] Ibid., p. 256. The Censuses of 1875 and 1881 respectively indicate that there were 92 and 131 Ezhavas in government service. But this record creates confusion when compared with the information given in the *Malayali Memorial* and subsequent census reports. *The Malayali Memorial* claimed that there was no Ezhava drawing a salary of Rs 5 and more. See *Kerala Archives News Letter*, Vol. II, Nos. II and III, March and June 1976, p. 5. The Census of 1901 also maintained the same position. See *Census of India, 1901*, Vol. XXVI, Travancore, Part I, Report, p. 435.

[61] *Census of Travancore, 1881*, Vol. I, Report, pp. 242–43.

[62] *Census of Travancore, 1875*, Vol. I, Report, p. 262.

[63] Velu Pillai, *The Travancore State Manual*, Vol. III, p. 116.

[64] T.C. Verghese, *Agrarian Change and Economic Consequences*, 1970, p. 44.

[65] Ibid., p. 45.

[66] Ibid.

[67] According to the Report sent to Dewan Madhava Rao by Dewan Peshkar on 28 September 1904, File No. 113A, 1904, Travancore Political Department, Travancore, Kerala Secretariat (Cellar), Trivandrum.

[68] *Census of Travancore, 1891*, Vol. I, Part I, Report, p. 567.

[69] *Census of India, 1901*, Vol. XXVI, Travancore, Part I, Report, p. 394.

[70] Ibid., p. 395.

[71] *Census of Travancore, 1875*, Vol. I, Report, pp. 261–62.

[72] *Census of Travancore, 1891*, Vol. I, Part I, Report, pp. 732–34.

[73] *Census of India, 1921*, Vol. XXV, Travancore, Part I, Report, p. 492.

[74] *Census of Travancore, 1875, Part I Report*, p. 266.

[75] *Census of India, 1901*, Vol. XXVI, Travancore, Part I, Report, p. 396.

[76] In some cases those who followed some of the learned professions had been included under the government service. Due to these overlaps some differences may be seen in different tables related to the learned professions and government service.

[77] *Census of Travancore, 1875*, Vol. I, Report, pp. 256–57.

[78] Ibid.

[79] Ibid.

[80] *Census of Travancore, 1891*, Vol. I, Report, pp. 603–17.

[81] *Census of India, 1921*, Vol. XXV, Travancore, Part I, Report, pp. 132–35. Also see Jeffrey (1976b), p. 10.

[82] *Census of Travancore, 1891*, Vol. I, Report, p. 602.

[83] *Census of Travancore, 1875*, Part I, Report, pp. 259–60.

[84] *Census of Travancore, 1891*, Vol. I, Report, p. 559; *Census of India, 1911*, Vol. XXIII, Travancore, Part I, Report, pp. 274, 294–96; and *Census of India, 1921*, Vol. XXV, Travancore, Part I, Report, pp. 127, 132–35 and Part II, pp. 102–03.

[85] *Census of Travancore, 1875*, Vol. I, Report, pp. 259–60

[86] Ibid,

[87] Jeffrey, *The Decline of Nayar Dominance*, p. 32.

[88] *Census of India, 1921*, Vol. XXV, Travancore, Part II, pp. 102–03.

[89] Velu Pillai, *Travancore State Manual*, Vol. III, p. 41.

[90] *Census of India, 1911*, Vol. XXIII, Travancore, Part I, Report, p. 295.

[91] Ibid.

[92] Ibid.

[93] *Census of India, 1901*, Vol. XXVI, Travancore, Part I, Report, p. 435.

[94] *Census of Travancore, 1875*, p. 266.

[95] Nagam Aiya, *The Travancore State Manual*, Vol. III, p. 171. Also see *Census of India, 1911*, Vol. XXIII, Travancore, Part I, p. 313.

[96] Ibid., p. 63.

[97] *Census of Cochin, 1891*, Vol. I, Report, p. 144. See also, Samuel Mateer, *Native Life in Travancore*, pp. 235–36.

[98] One *chakram* was equal to 7 paisa.

[99] T.C. Verghese, *Agrarian Change and Economic Consequences*, p. 64.

[100] *Administration Report of Travancore, 1866–67*, p. 37.

[101] Jeffrey, *The Decline of Nayar Dominance*, pp. 88–89.

[102] Ibid.

[103] Notification of His Highness the Maharaja of Travancore on 21 June 1865, quoted in *Travancore Land Revenue Manual*, Vol. 4, p. 375. Also see Madhava Rao to Newill, dated 19 April 1865, *Travancore Government English Records*, Cover No. 228.

[104] According to this proclamation, 'the sales, mortgages etc. of these lands will hence forward be valid. . . . The land may be sold for arrears of tax in execution of decree of courts and such other legitimate purposes, and may also be accepted as security by the Sircar as well as by private individuals.' Notification of His Highness the Maharaja of Travancore on 2 June 1865, quoted in *Travancore Land Revenue Manual*, Vol. 4, p. 375

[105] In a letter to the British Resident from Madhava Rao, Dewan of Travancore, he very clearly mentioned that 'the *jenmies* were not the improvers of the landed property and that if they were permitted to eject tenants, the agricultural prosperity of the state would be adversely affected, apart from the hardships caused to the tenants'. See T. Madhava Rao's letter to the British Resident dated 9 October 1866, quoted in T.C. Verghese, *Agrarian Change and Economic Consequences*, pp. 66–67.

[106] Ibid.

[107] Ibid., p. 67.

[108] See 'Jenmi–Kudiyan Act of 1896', Appendix 1, reproduced in ibid., p. 220.

[109] Ibid., p. 133.

[110] See 'The Jenmi–Kudiyan (Amendment) Act of 1932', Appendix I, quoted in ibid., pp. 220–22.

[111] S. Ramanathan Aiyar, *A Brief Sketch of Travancore, The Model State of India: Its People and Its Progress under the Maharaja*, Western Star Press, Trivandrum, 1903, pp. 103 and 173.

[112] According to the *Travancore Marumakkathayam Committee Report of 1908*, the agreed partitions rose from 301 in 1896 to 516 in 1906–07. See Appendix II, p. 93.

[113] Ibid.

[114] In 1865–66, nearly 10,000 people appointed in Travancore's public services department were on daily wages. See Jeffrey, *The Decline of Nayar Dominance*, p. 91.

[115] The wages increased from one anna or an anna and a half and one meal for a day's work, to four annas and one meal. *Census of Travancore, 1875*, p. 63.

[116] T.C. Verghese, *Agrarian Change and Economic Consequences*, p. 116.

[117] The abolition of slavery in a full-fledged manner took place in 1865, when the Maharaja of Travancore announced a proclamation on 12 Mithunam 1030 ME (June 1865). See Regional Record Survey Committee, *History of Freedom Movement in Kerala*, Vol. I, pp. 57–59. The plantation industries began to develop only after 1860. See Percival Griffiths, *The History of the Indian Tea Industry*, Wiedenfield and Nicolson, London, 1967, p. 157.

[118] In 1879, the Kannan Devan Company obtained a concession from the Pooniate Raja of Rs 5,000 for 27 square miles in Kannan Devan Hills, along with a promise to pay an annual sum of Rs 3,000. See ibid., p. 158.

[119] Velu Pillai, *Travancore State Manual*, Vol. III, p. 18.

[120] Griffiths, *History of the Indian Tea Industry*, p. 157.

[121] Ibid.

[122] T.C. Verghese, *Agrarian Change and Economic Consequences*, p. 117. See P. Parameswaran Pillai, *Report on the Scheme for the Introduction of Basic Land Tax and Revision of Agricultural Income Tax*, Government Press, Trivandrum, 1946, para 65.

[123] Ibid., para 70.

[124] Griffiths, *History of the Indian Tea Industry*, p. 159.

[125] Nagam Aiya, *The Travancore State Manual*, Vol. III, p. 184.

[126] Jeffrey, *The Decline of Nayar Dominance*, p. 96.

[127] Ibid., pp. 96–97.

[128] P.R. Gopinathan Nair, 'Education and Socio-Economic Change in Kerala, 1793–1947', *Social Scientist*, Vol. IV, No. 8, March 1976, pp. 30–31.

[129] Quoted in ibid., p. 30.

[130] In 1920–21, the net area under various crops was 20,08,960 acres and in 1931 it increased to 22,01,295 acres. See *Census of India, 1931*, Vol. XXVIII, Travancore, Part I, Report, p. 22.

[131] *Travancore Administration Reports*, 1870–71 to 1891–92.

[132] B.M. Bhatia, 'Growth and Composition of Middle Class in South India in Nineteenth Century', *The Indian Economic and Social History Review*, Vol. II, No. 4, October 1965, p. 341.

[133] *Proceedings of the Seventeenth Session of the Sree Mulam Popular Assembly of Travancore*, 1921, p. 11.

[134] The state's direct activities in the field of education began in 1817, when the then ruler, Gouri Parvati Bai, issued a receipt which resolved to defray the entire costs of education. Quoted in *Administration Report of Travancore, 1936–37*, p. 197.

[135] *Kerala Kaumudi*, 23 November 1924, pp. 1 and 4.

[136] Gopinathan Nair, 'Education and Socio-Economic Change in Kerala', p. 29.

[137] Nagam Aiya, *The Travancore State Manual*, Vol. II, p. 459.

[138] *Census of India, 1901*, Vol. XXVI, Travancore, Part I, Report, pp. 201–08.

[139] From the Presidential Address of the Dewan at the second meeting of the Sree Mulam Popular Assembly which was held in Trivandrum on 21 October 1905. See *Proceedings of the Second Meeting of the Sree Mulam Popular Assembly*, 1905, p. 17.

[140] *Census of India, 1911*, Vol. XXIII, Travancore, Part I, Report, p. 85.

[141] *Proceedings of the Second Meeting of the Sree Mulam Popular Assembly*, 1905, p. 17.

[142] Ibid., p. 18.

[143] *Census of India, 1931*, Vol. XXVIII, Travancore, Part I, Report, p. 433.

[144] Nagam Aiya, *The Travancore State Manual*, Vol. II, p. 482.

[145] *Administration Report of Travancore, 1905–1906*, p. 53. Also see *Proceedings of the Second Meeting of the Sree Mulam Popular Assembly*, 1905, p. 7.

[146] Velu Pillai, *The Travancore State Manual*, Vol. III, pp. 735–36.

[147] Ibid., p. 737.

[148] Table 13 shows the number of schools under government and private administration for the year 1886–87. See *Administration Report of Travancore, 1886–87*, p. 251.

[149] *Census of Travancore, 1875*, Report, pp. 245–46.

[150] *Administration Report of Travancore, 1905–06*, p. 54.

[151] Gopinathan Nair, 'Education and Socio-Economic Change in Kerala', p. 36.

[152] *Administration Report of Travancore, 1886–87*, p. 251

[153] *Administration Report of Travancore, 1896–97*, para 667, p. 105; and *Administration Report of Travancore, 1899*, p. 105.

[154] *Census of Travancore, 1891*, Vol. I, Report, pp. 504–05.

[155] Robin Jeffrey, 'The Temple Entry Movement in Travancore 1860–1940', *Social Scientist*, Vol. IV, No. 8, 1976, p. 8.

[156] *Census of Travancore, 1891*, Vol. I, Report, pp. 104–05.

[157] See *Census of India, 1931*, Vol. XXVIII, Travancore, Part I, p. 311.

[158] *Census of Travancore, 1891*, Vol. I, Report, pp. 491–93.

2

Genesis of the Sree Narayana Dharma Paripalana (SNDP) Yogam

In this chapter, I attempt to provide the antecedents that necessitated collective action for social mobility among members belonging to the Ezhava caste. I begin with an account of the conditions which enabled some of the members of this caste to gain social mobility in a restricted manner; this is followed by a description of the situation that obligated them to begin caste-based collective action. The refusal of the state to listen to the voice of this community as well as the disinclination, revealed by a majority of the people belonging to this caste, to listen to the appeals of the leader of the community are equally underscored. I end with an account of the convergence of two different agencies which shared the idea of social mobility of the depressed social groups. The account makes note of the emergence of a middle class (or a middle caste) as an agency within this caste, and the positing of Sree Narayana Guru as their spiritual as well as their secular leader. The central theme is the convergence of the Ezhava middle class and Sree Narayana Guru on the podium of the Sree Narayana Dharma Paripalana (SNDP) Yogam.

The first recorded reference to the term 'Ezhava' can be found in the Tharisappally copper plate inscription belonging to the fifth regnal year of King Sthanu Ravi (AD 848–49) of Kerala.[1] It is opined that till twelfth century AD the term 'Ezhava' indicated not a caste but the name of an occupation,[2] but the Tanjore inscription of Raja Raja Chola (AD 985–1013) refers to it both as a caste and as an occupational group.[3] It may be said that in all probability, the formation of the Ezhavas as a caste took place towards the end of the tenth century.[4]

There is no consensus among scholars regarding the origin of the Ezhava community; the absence of unanimity of opinion among ethnologists and historians stems from the prevalence of two opposing views on the genesis of this community. One view maintains that the Ezhavas migrated from Ceylon (Sri Lanka), and the other regards them as an endogenous community. Those who uphold the migration theory argue that they migrated from Ceylon to Kerala between first and fifth century AD.[5] The etymology of the word *Ezhava* is traced to *Ezham*, a corruption of 'Simhalam', by which Ceylon was referred for several centuries;[6] this served to substantiate the migration theory. Likewise, the etymology of the word *Thiyya*[7] may be traced back to the Sanskrit word *dwipa* (island), and on the basis of this it is argued that the Ezhavas originally came from an island, that is, Ceylon.[8] The word *cova* is said to be a corruption of *sevaka*, which means one who works or serves – a description of the status held by Ezhavas in the country of their adoption.[9] Dr Caldwell observes that it is tolerably certain that the Ezhavas and Thiyyas, who cultivate the coconut-palms of Travancore, are descendants of Shanar colonies from Ceylon.[10] There are traces of this common origin among the Travancore Ezhavas. Dr Palpu, the founder of the SNDP Yogam, is also of the view that the Ezhavas came from Ceylon and that they brought coconut and palmyra trees from there to India.[11] There are several others who maintain the migration theory. C.V. Kunjuraman argues that the word *Chovan* was derived from the Tamil word *chuvaka*, which means a mendicant or a *bhikshu* (Buddhist).[12] According to Palpu (junior):

> Assuming then as well as established that the Ezhavas came from Ceylon, the question is what was their religion when they immigrated into Kerala. That it was Buddhism is clear from the following circumstances. (1) In the early centuries of the Christian era when the community in all probability settled in Kerala, the prevailing religion of Ceylon was Buddhism. (2) In several parts of Travancore 'Chithar' is still worshipped as a domestic deity, who can this 'Chitar' be except for Sidha or Sidhartha, one of the Sanskrit synonyms of Lord Buddha. In Paravur, Quilon, there is still a sacred grave called 'Chithan Kavu' and tank called, 'Chithan Kulam'. (3) In Manu's system of castes there is no mention of either 'Chova' or Thiyya as a caste. This omission is significant as a tendency to confirm the view that the Ezhava community did not form a Hindu caste.[13]

K. Damodaran compares the Ezhavas of Travancore and the Simhalas of Ceylon on the basis of the similarities between them in terms of their nomenclature (Ezham and Ezhavar), *marumakkathayam* law of inheritance, absence of priesthood status, Buddhist connection, and body complexion.[14] He argues that like the Buddhists, the Ezhavas were also free from the influence of priests.[15]

As the migration theory is based on various scattered etymological, literary and traditional assumptions, the arrival of the Ezhavas from Ceylon remains a subject of controversy among scholars. Those who renounce the migration theory are of the opinion that the process of evolution of the Ezhavas as a caste group took place within the Kerala society. Elamkulam Kunjan Pillai states that all the communities of Kerala except the Brahmins are indigenous.[16] In distinction to this argument, E.M.S. Namboodiripad holds the view that all communities in Kerala belong to the same race of Nairs and Namboodiris, and that they became divided as a result of the caste system based on landholdings.[17]

K. Damodaran opines that all castes including the Namboodiris emerged out of changes in the mode of production.[18] To Krishnan, the migration theory is a fictitious creation of the Namboodiri Brahmins.[19] Based on their culture, law of inheritance, style of life, etc., T.K. Madhavan observed that the Nairs and the Ezhavas originally belonged to the same *varna*.[20] According to C.V. Kunjuraman, Ezhavas were the natives of Kerala, and they lived along with the Nairs as a sister-group and were separated from them only later. When a group of Buddhists came to Kerala to save the Buddhists there from Brahmin hegemony, the Nairs supported the Brahmins and the Ezhavas supported the Buddhists. Later, when Buddhism declined, the Ezhavas lost their status to Nairs and became an inferior caste.[21]

Among the modern scholars, P.C. Alexander subscribes to the view that the Ezhavas descended from the Buddhist community in Kerala, which included both immigrants from Ceylon and Malayali converts, and that when Buddhism fell on evil days the Buddhists were relegated to an inferior status.[22] For Murkot Kunhappa, the Ezhavas were Buddhist.

> When the Thiyya reverted to pre-Buddhist religion, he preferred pre-Aryan deities like Shiva and Kali for worship. He was therefore an undesirable and outcaste, slipping down into an untouchable and an unapproachable because even the Namboodiri families who practised Ayurveda system of medicine are considered as belonging to a lower rung of the Brahmins and are known as Musads.[23]

The argument here is that when Buddhism completely disappeared from Kerala due to the revivalism of Hinduism and the increasing influence of the Brahmins,[24] the Buddhists were absorbed into Hinduism as an inferior caste.

The dispute regarding the origin of the Ezhavas and the differing interpretations of their historical associations with Ceylon and Buddhism still remain. What is important for us to recognize is the historical fact that for centuries they have been integral to the society and culture of Kerala as a caste group.

Emergence of a Middle Class within the Ezhava Community

Though this caste was regarded as untouchable in Kerala's social hierarchy, both economically and educationally they were not as poor or as backward as other 'polluting' communities. That is why, among the untouchables of Kerala, only this caste could produce a middle class. This argument can be substantiated by different sets of facts and figures.

Agriculture formed the major occupation of the Ezhava community, but they were also actively engaged in industry and trade.[25] Almost all historical accounts of Kerala describe the Ezhavas as toddy tappers, as those who tended the coconut-palm and as liquor distillers. These economic activities were almost a monopoly of this caste, although in reality only a minority was engaged in these activities.[26] By the end of the nineteenth century, only 38 out of 1,000 Ezhavas (3.8 per cent) followed this so-called traditional occupation.[27] In fact, it was the occupation of the poorest section of the community.[28] It is therefore erroneous to represent the Ezhavas as toddy tappers and liquor distillers; such representation would be tantamount to taking 'a part as the whole' and arguing that the part represents the entire community. The sarcastic comment made by Murkoth Kunhappa is worth invoking: 'There is not enough coconut trees to go round if entire community of over half a crore were to clamber up these palms in search of toddy.'[29]

As agriculturists,[30] the Ezhava community in Travancore possessed a sizeable area of arable land, placing them in the third position, just below Nairs and Christians.[31] In northern Travancore, in 1904, out of 261 big landlords who paid Rs 100 or more as annual land tax, 8 landlords (3.1 per cent) belonged to this community; and in central Travancore, at least four 'great' families of this community rivalled with the local Nair lords.[32] Out of a total of 56,775 persons belonging to the propertied classes in Travancore, 7,393 (13 per cent) came from the Ezhava caste.[33] A majority of the members of this community were sub-tenants and landless labourers, but none of them was homeless.[34] In 1875, the total number of Ezhavas engaged in cultivation of land in Travancore was 26,891 or 14.28 per cent of the total male population.[35] Generally, the Namboodiris as the biggest landlords, and the Nairs as the largest body of landholders or tenants, leased out their *kanam* and *verumpattom* tenurial rights to agriculturists of this caste. Thus most of them were employed either as tenant farmers or as agricultural labourers. According to the 1875 Census, the total number of agricultural labourers among Ezhavas was 40,405.[36] For all these reasons we can safely conclude that the majority of the Ezhava population participated in the agrarian economy of Travancore.

The derogatory tone involved in referring to this caste as 'toddy tappers' can be laid bare by tracing the status of Ezhavas in the sphere of education. Their comparatively better economic conditions helped them to avail greater educational facilities, and they were the best educated section among the untouchables. A number of them were traditional Ayurvedic physicians and astrologers. There were also a number of Sanskrit scholars among them;[37] as they had acquired this language through their contact with Buddhism, it relieved them from the prevailing caste restrictions.[38] The Census of 1875 records that out of 7,589 persons belonging to the learned professions, 233 (0.13 per cent) were Ezhavas.[39] They were engaged in occupations like teaching (*asans*), weaving, coir making, trading, business, and the practice of law, astrology and *ayurveda*.[40] In general, out of every 1,000 Ezhava workers, 214 (21.4 per cent) were weavers, 116 (11.6 per cent) field labourers, 163 (16.3 per cent) cultivators and *jenmies*, 163 (16.3 per cent) labourers, 128 (12.8 per cent) businessmen, 110 (11 per cent) toddy tappers, 20 (0.20 per cent) other workers, and 8 (0.08 per cent) *sirkar* servants.[41] Another account providing the distribution of members of this community across occupations states that a large majority (about 30 per cent) of Ezhava workers were agriculturists and more than 22 per cent were industrialists.[42] Their engagement in diverse occupations, acceptance of English education and employment in revenue-earning activities earned them a better position in the 'secular' distribution of castes. These economic advantages and educational improvement helped them to gain vertical social mobility. Those who actively strove to gain such mobility emerged as a 'middle class' within the community.

Another factor that enabled the social mobility of this emerging Ezhava middle class was its exposure to and association with diverse agents of social change. In this context, their interaction with the Christian missionaries was critical. Though missionary activities had swept across all of Travancore by the beginning of the nineteenth century, under the patronage of Colonel Munro,[43] the caste Hindu-dominated society looked down on missionaries as *mlechha*s and ignored their activities by keeping a distance from them. This attitude of the caste Hindus naturally urged the missionaries to have cordial relations with the Ezhavas, who were not only the upper caste among the untouchables, but also comparatively better educated and economically well placed among the low castes. They too on their part had strong reasons to maintain good relations with the Christian communities. If the first was related to their own caste disabilities, the second was concerned with the humanitarian activities of the Christian missionaries coupled with their close proximity to power through British Resident.

The missionaries' activities for abolishing slavery[44] and for giving lower-caste women the right to cover their breasts[45] naturally attracted the middle class of the Ezhava community. Though these two activities of the missionaries were mainly aimed at protecting the economic interests of British and European capitalists in Travancore, they certainly also had a humanitarian angle. While these activities were aimed at creating a work force for the newly established plantation industries of the foreign capitalists, they also considerably contributed to the alleviation of the pitiable conditions of the depressed classes. The prevailing liberal ideology, and the pressures exerted by the Protestant missionaries in Travancore with their ecumenical evangelism and the Latin Catholics in Cochin gave way to the realization of humanitarian 'effects'.[46] This had a chain of consequences leading to several changes in the existing feudal relations between castes, in order to usher in new contractual relations. In addition, the missionary zeal to eradicate the disabilities of the converted Christians[47] and activities for spreading education among the lower castes were factors that attracted those aspiring for social mobility within the Ezhava community. The abolition of different kinds of bondage and the privileges granted to those among the lower castes who converted to Christianity opened the eyes of the Ezhavas, who then started demanding the same privileges as those extended to the converts.[48] Thus the contact with Christians helped to awaken the social consciousness of the untouchables, especially of the Ezhavas, with regard to their rights.[49] This social awakening was accelerated by accompanying changes in their economic conditions and the accomplishment of English education.

We have already seen that during the second half of the nineteenth century, the British capitalists established plantation industries in Travancore. The abolition of state monopoly in commodities like pepper and tobacco, which constituted the commercial resources of the state, brought forth an unprecedented economic impetus.[50] In the 1860s, the Government of Travancore opened a public works department, with the patronage of the British Resident, to build infrastructure consisting of a network of roads and highways. This was in order to encourage trade, commerce and entrepreneurship, and to protect the interests of the British capitalists who had invested money in both plantation and small-scale industries.[51] Between the years 1866 and 1872, the Public Works Department (PWD) established about 1,000 miles of roadways in Travancore.[52] Better constructed roads naturally increased trade and commerce, and the enhancement in trade led to the growth of a cash economy.[53] The expansion of commercialized agriculture converted thousands of low castes as wage labourers and raised their cash earnings.[54] Apart from these new opportunities, a rise in international demand for labourers, 'both skilled and unskilled in the British Indian Provinces and the overseas of the British territories like Ceylon and Mauritius',[55] also helped them to move beyond national boundaries and gain economic benefits.

The opportunities offered by these enterprises especially helped the Christians and Ezhavas because of their interest and experience in commercial and menial occupations, and their association with the evangelists. Nairs and other upper-caste Hindus neither evinced much interest in industry, trade and commerce, nor did they have any experience in these occupations, and so they had no share in the benefits accruing from these occupations. The Nairs concentrated their attention either on land or on government jobs, as they were already more privileged. At the same time, Ezhava leaders asked their people to give more importance to profitable manual labour and industrial activities rather than government jobs, which paid a salary of only Rs 6 per month.[56] In these emerging economic processes they did not face any opposition or competition from the privileged sections of society.

The development of plantation industries, the growth of the PWD, the introduction of postal and telegraph services, and reclamation of the backwaters for rice cultivation in the coastal belt boosted the demand for labour. In 1865–66, nearly 10,000 Ezhavas and slave-caste coolies were absorbed into daily wage occupations in the PWD alone.[57] Along with the increase in the area under cultivation, agro-processing industries like spinning and weaving of cotton and coir manufacture also developed, and this in turn paved the way for an increase in the wages. The daily wage of unskilled labour rose from half an anna and one meal to four annas and a meal.[58] Skilled workers could earn up to a rupee a day by the 1880s.[59] The wages of non-agricultural labourers in the plantation industries rose by 167 per cent and that of artisans by 140 per cent.[60] These newly opened job opportunities and increased wages basically benefited the lower castes, including women and children.

Meanwhile, there was an unprecedented rise in the international demand for coconut products, mainly from America and Europe. This increased the export earnings from coconut products from Rs 30.33 lakhs in 1873 to Rs 68.59 lakhs in 1891.[61] Though the Ezhavas were not the actual owners of the coconut plantations, as the main exploiters of coconut products they certainly got a significant share of the increased profits. Coir processing also developed into a large-scale industry in Travancore due to higher demand for coir products in America.[62] Thus, 'with an expanding market for coir, Iravas, women as well as men, would at least have found full employment, while the traditional aim of the poor Irava to own or rent a few palm trees had the advantage of increasing not only his status but also his wealth.'[63] Ezhavas constituted a majority of the labour force, and they started seeking new vistas and vocations in the material processes that were opening up.[64] By 1900, a few Ezhavas began to invest in agro-processing industries and own coir factories. 'Good work is being turned out here by private industry', wrote the Travancore Dewan to an Ezhava coir factory near Quilon in 1900, 'and some boys are being trained in the work. . . . This institution speaks well for the industry and spirit of self-help of the Elava [Ezhava] community.'[65] The other lucrative business of the time was the manufacture and sale of toddy and arrack. The prices of toddy and arrack doubled between 1860–81.[66] As the Ezhavas had a monopoly over this trade, the increased prices directly helped them to augment their income. Weaving, another traditional occupation of the Ezhavas,[67] also provided them with increased employment. Gradually, from being employees they transformed themselves to occupy the status of employers by investing their surplus in industries. As a result, by the beginning of the twentieth century itself the emerging Ezhava middle class began to become industrialists. One of the industries they established, which is worth mentioning, was the Travancore Weaving and Trading Company, with a capital investment of Rs 1 lakh.[68]

Impact of Economic Transformation and Land Reforms

The land reforms initiated by Madhava Rao (the Pattom Proclamation) in 1865 conferred ownership rights on the holders of the government *pattom* land, so that from then onwards, the owners could divide, mortgage, sell or alienate the land.[69] The state also gave recognition to the relation between the landlord and the *kanam* tenant. The second proclamation of 1867 granted fixity of tenure. The Ezhava sub-tenants became conscious of their legal protection against eviction. While these proclamations were unfavourable to the Nair community, they were of benefit to both Christians and Ezhavas. Following internal family feuds and quarrels, the Nair landlords partitioned their joint property and the number of absolute owners among them increased from 301 in 1896 to 516 in 1906–07.[70] This resulted in a decline in the area of land under single ownership, and land alienation began to proliferate. The relatively rich sections of Ezhavas who had gained under the process of economic transformation in the second half of the nineteenth century seized this opportunity to accumulate the lands alienated by the Nairs.[71]

English Education as an Avenue of Social Progress

The improved financial position among Ezhavas led to a better standard of living. In keeping pace with the ongoing economic development, their perspective and attitude towards life and regarding their social position with respect to others also changed. An immediate effect was that members of the new elite families took interest in sending their children to schools for an English education. After the modernization of the administration and practical recognition of English as the official language of the state, many communities desired to educate their children in modern schools and colleges with a view to qualify them to enter either the state government service or the British Indian service.

The rulers of Travancore had encouraged education in the state from the beginning of the nineteenth century itself. However, educational facilities could be availed of only by the caste Hindus. Ezhavas and other lower-caste people were not admitted to the schools as they were untouchables; education was considered beyond the pale for them. However, the Ezhavas were able to reap the benefits of English education by being admitted into institutions run by private management, mainly Christian missionaries, who controlled most of the educational institutions. By 1885–87, only about 25 per cent of the schools were under the direct control of the state and at the same time the missionaries and the natives controlled 46 and 29 per cent of schools respectively.[72]

Most of the missionary-run schools were open to all communities. When 50 'highly respectable Ezhava boys were refused admission to the government schools in 1872, Samuel Mateer, a member of the London Missionary Society, opened a school for them near Anjengo'.[73] In the 1870s, in order to mitigate the frustration of the Ezhavas, Christian missionaries opened a number of schools meant for Christian and lower-caste boys.[74] In addition, the government was also pressurized to set up schools for the backward communities.[75] This helped the Ezhavas to a great extent. Literacy among them increased from 3.15 per cent in 1875 to 12.10 per cent in 1891.[76] From the 1880s onwards Ezhava students began to graduate from the Trivandrum College.[77] Thus their improved economic conditions and their association with Christian missionaries helped to produce a number of educated people among the Ezhavas. Though the Government of Travancore did not employ them in their own state, a few of them got employment under the British government, and in the princely states of Mysore and Baroda. A number of educated Ezhavas also entered the professions of teaching, law, medicine and journalism.

Self-Assertion

The emerging middle class within the Ezhava community began to realize the limitations imposed on them by society, and sought ways and means to enable members of their community to overcome them. Moreover, the newly emergent social groups in Travancore – the middle class, the working class and the intelligentsia – started to demand 'modernization'.[78] They began to wage war against all obstacles that lay in the way of their development. They became conscious of their basic rights and started to raise their voices in defence of these rights. They gradually built up a movement against the traditional oppression of the higher castes, and pressed for their rights and privileges, eradication of their disabilities and redressal of their grievances.

Palpu, a champion of the Ezhava middle class, devoted his entire life and a good portion of his earnings to fight against caste-based tyranny. They became more self-assertive and opposed the caste structure which prevented their social mobility. They understood that the government and its machinery favoured and protected the interests of the *savarna* middle class. They resented the various restrictions imposed upon them, like prevention of the use of public roads and exclusion from government schools and public services. They were aware that they had no political rights or power, and that virtually nothing was being done for their development. That was why, at the time of the *Malayali Memorial*, the Ezhava middle class joined together with the Nairs and Christians to become one of the signatories. Palpu was the third signatory of the *Malayali Memorial*,[79] in which the conditions of Ezhavas were stated in the following way:

> There is not a single representative of the Thiyya community holding any Government appointment on Rs 5 or upwards a month in the state, whereas several of their caste men in Malabar have been advanced to some of the highest offices of the uncovenanted civil service open to natives of India.[80]

In response to the *Memorial*, the Dewan of Travancore said that the memorialists had dragged the Ezhavas into their fold and asserted that they were not sufficiently educated to understand their grievances by themselves.[81] According to the Dewan, education was not widespread enough among the Ezhavas for them to be eligible for employment in the administration.[82] In 1891, he said, only two among 3,87,176 Ezhavas possessed a university degree.[83] The government also clearly stated that it did not want to interfere with public opinion,[84] which could result in creating conflict within society and thus adversely affect the progress of the state.[85] Singling out the Ezhavas from among the memorialists, the government stated that any attempt to push for their social growth could only culminate in failure; in this way government portrayed them as 'confirmed social inferiors'.[86]

This reply outraged the Ezhava middle class. Dr Palpu and his associates decided to organize the Ezhava community and to promote their cause. Palpu took the initiative to formulate two memorials. He submitted the first memorial on 12 May 1895 to Sankara Soobiar, Dewan to the Maharaja of Travancore. In this memorandum he pleaded for the removal of discrimination against the Ezhavas in education and employment. When it failed to evoke any response, the second one, a community memorial, generally known as *Ezhava Memorial* and signed by 13,176 Ezhavas, was submitted to the Maharaja of Travancore in September 1896.[87] In this petition they requested the Maharaja to grant them the same privileges as those granted to the Christian converts, and especially asked for the right to enter government schools and colleges, and the freedom to seek employment in government services on the basis of the eligibility of the applicants.[88] In addition, the petition recalled that the Ezhavas were numerically the second largest community in the state, and that their counterparts in Malabar, the Thiyyas, had already acquired the same rights as other castes with regard to government service.[89]

The response of the government to this memorial was utterly disappointing and discouraging. It was expressed by the Dewan in the following words:

> In this country, as a body there are uneducated preferring their own occupations of agriculture, coir making and toddy drawing, not going for such education as would fit them for the public service. There are only two of their class out of a population of 88,175 who have graduated in the university and a very few, indeed, if any who are seeking a high education in the local college. Their special position is such that they can hardly be eligible for public offices where a certain amount of respect is expected to be commanded in a state where Hindus are more conservative and superstitious than their brethren in Malabar.[90]

Following this, several petitions, both by individuals and by groups, were submitted to the Maharaja. But the government rejected all these on the ground that they exclusively represented the self-interest of a particular community.[91]

In spite of this rebuff, Palpu continued his endeavour to work for the uplift of his community. He carried on his fight for social justice through several means, like writing in the press, meetings, letters and negotiations with the authorities. In his efforts to transform a marginalized community, he accepted help from all quarters. He made arrangements to raise the grievances of the community in the British Parliament through G.P. Pillai.[92] The British Parliament directed the Indian government to look into the problem and take appropriate measures.[93] Palpu met Lord Curzon when he visited Mysore, and explained to him the plight of Ezhavas in Travancore. He submitted a memorandum to him as well.[94] By this time he had written a small book in English, entitled *Treatment of Thiyyas in Travancore*, to point out the unjust policy of the government towards Ezhavas.[95] Thus he not only mobilized public opinion, but also captured the attention of the state government, the British Resident, the Viceroy and the British Parliament. Acting upon his request, G.P. Pillai highlighted the problems of the Ezhavas on the platform of the Indian National Congress in 1895.[96]

The Question of Collective Action

All these activities were in vain, however, mainly due to the indifference shown by the Government of Travancore. Palpu and other Ezhava elites realized that petitions and memorandums would not change the attitude of the government, i.e. make them countenance the demands of the Ezhavas for ordinary civic rights, without either forming an organization of their own, or converting themselves into Christians, Muslims or Buddhists. In 1891, when Swami Vivekananda visited Bangalore, Palpu met him and explained to him the plight of his community. In response, Vivekananda suggested that they form an organization for collective action.[97] In 1896 Palpu organized an 'Ezhava Mahasabha' to carry on their agitation for achieving social rights in a more systematic and planned way.[98] He and his friends organized a number of meetings at several places like Mayyanad, Paravoor, etc.[99] But these were only initial steps towards realizing the desired goals. Even though Palpu succeeded in organizing the newly emerged Ezhava middle class, his endeavour thoroughly failed to bring the majority of the illiterate but labouring masses under the Ezhava Mahasabha. Many factors were responsible for this failure.

First, there was no unanimity of action among the Ezhavas in their fight against their common grievances as the interests and backgrounds of the members of this community were quite heterogeneous. The community was divided into numerous sub-castes and some groups maintained superiority over others. On 5 December 1895, when Palpu approached C. Krishnan of Malabar for his help in organizing an Ezhava Sabha at Madras (Malabar), the latter discouraged Palpu's efforts due to internal bickering and a feeling of superiority among the Thiyyas of north Malabar over the Ezhavas of Travancore and Cochin.[100]

This feeling of superiority was also evident among certain sections of the Ezhavas of Travancore. C.V. Kunjuraman says:

> Two sections of people namely the status section and non-status section are seen in all communities. But it is so amongst us [Ezhavas]. Ezhavas of one *Kara, Muri* or *Pathikkaram* belong to a separate sect. A sect of a particular province will not enter into marriage relation with another sect belonging to another province. Travancoreans consider themselves to be superior to Paravoor Ezhavas and vice-versa. . . . Ezhavas of one locality consider the Ezhavas of other locality as inferior to them. The weavers, chalians and toddy tappers are attributed as '*nikrishtas*' than *urallimar*.[101]

Ezhava families of upper class and higher status had no social relations with the rest of their own sub-castes.[102] The social life and culture of upper-class Ezhavas, who formed a tiny minority of the total population of the community, were in many respects different from that of lower-class Ezhavas. In some cases persons belonging to this minority refrained from eating food with persons of the lower classes.[103] In other words, this feeling of superiority and sectarianism within the community often split Ezhavas living in the same region into many social atoms, and stood in the way of a united fight for their common cause.

The second reason which prevented the Ezhava middle class from organizing properly and functioning effectively stemmed from their choice of addressee. The Ezhava elites, instead of carrying their message to the villages to secure a mass base for their agitation, concentrated on passing resolutions at public meetings or on addressing the authorities. Though these methods of social activism created a slight change at the governmental level, they had little effect in changing the attitude of the common people or in taking them into confidence. Their craving and admiration for the English language actually created a divide between ordinary Ezhavas and the community's middle-class leadership. During the early part of the 1890s, the total number of English-educated people among the Ezhavas was only thirty.[104] These middle-class individuals used English as their means of communication, thus alienating themselves from the majority of the deprived members of their community. It is important to bear in mind that the enthusiasm of Ezhava leaders to attain command over the English language not only limited their vision and narrowed their appeal, but also strengthened the barrier between them and the rest of the community. This was why in 1896, during the time of the *Ezhava Memorial*, when Palpu approached non-middle-class Ezhavas to sign the petition, most of them refused to oblige.[105]

The third reason was that the illiterate and ignorant Ezhavas were for the most part agricultural labourers working for caste Hindu landlords, and thus were more obliged to their traditional upper-caste lords than to members of the newly emerging Ezhava middle class. The imbibing of a different consciousness required a vigorous propaganda, fit for easy assimilation by the illiterate labourers. No wonder, in the absence of such propaganda, the Ezhava middle class did not receive support from men of their own caste.[106]

Finally, the Ezhava middle class did not have a well-defined ideology and perspective of how to break away from tradition. Their view of the world was still based on caste, and they perceived only suppression by the upper castes as the obstacle to progress. They failed to gauge the wider and complex implications of social stratification. This tended to fudge their understanding.

Religious Halo and Leadership

When Palpu met Vivekananda at Bangalore in 1891, Vivekananda advised him that no movement in India that did not have a leader with a sacred halo of spirituality around him could move the hearts of the masses.[107] This made Palpu realize two things: first, the necessity for an influential spiritual leader as a guiding force in order to persuade an educationally backward community; second, that any movement, to be successful in India, should have a religious hue.[108] It was this advice from Vivekananda that brought Narayana Guru and Dr Palpu together. At that time Narayana Guru, who was living at Aruvippuram after his famous consecration of Shiva, did not have much popular appeal in Kerala, and his area of work and influence was restricted to Aruvippuram and its suburbs.[109] Nevertheless Palpu found in him a spiritual leader with a halo similar to that advocated by Vivekananda. In the Guru's religious concepts, which are discussed later, Palpu found a natural base for a successful reform movement.

The Ezhava middle class utilized the spiritual and religious qualities of Sree Narayana Guru to gain support from cultivators and landless Ezhava peasants.[110] This led to the formation of an organization that was tactically given the name Sree Narayana Dharma Paripalana (SNDP) Yogam. The first generation of leaders who took active part in the Yogam included Palpu, M. Govindan, N. Kumaran Asan, N. Kumaran, Moolur Padmanabha Panikkar, Alummoottil Chanar, C.V. Kunjuraman, C. Krishnan, T.K. Madhavan and Sahodharan Ayyapan.

As stated earlier, by the end of the nineteenth century, a middle class had emerged within the Ezhava community of Travancore which opposed the caste-based discrimination of the government. They were inspired by the idea of acquiring modern education with the expectation that this would privilege them to overcome the limits of the conventional social hierarchy. They also thought that this was the surest way towards vertical and horizontal social

mobility. Although they were able to make some inroads in the desired direction – due to the impact of commercialization of agriculture, the introduction of western education, new systems of law and public administration,
introduction of land reforms, development of means of communication and
philanthropic activities of the Christian missionaries – their contests and
negotiations with the state in the beginning was more or less sporadic and
centered on individual efforts. The entry of Narayana Guru was a watershed in
the community's move towards gaining rights to education and employment.
The Ezhava middle class realized that their fight could be successful only if
the majority of their community arrayed behind them. To gain the support
of the majority of the community and to convince the government that there
were enough educated members in the community, they first had to persuade
members of their community to gain education and imbibe modern perspectives. In short, they realized that their fellow-men should possess a desire for
altering themselves and progress along a different path towards their future.

Narayana Guru and Social Agency

By the end of the nineteenth century, when Sree Narayana Guru took up his
socio-religious reform activities, the Ezhava community could throw up only
a small number of compliant middle-class followers. It was through this class
that Narayana Guru's ideas found social expression. At the same time, it was
precisely this factor that helped gain acceptance for his words and ideas, and
culminated in 'successes'.

It may be noted here that an Ezhava saint, Velayudha Panickar of Karthikappally, had earlier tried to alter the traditional religious beliefs and social practices of the Ezhavas. In 1854 he established the first Ezhava temple for Shiva
at Etakkad, and in 1861 he started the first Kathakali Yogam for Ezhavas.[111]
He persuaded Ezhavas to adopt the hairstyle of the Nairs, and advised women
to wear the blouse and ornaments used exclusively by caste Hindus.[112] But due
to the absence of a strong middle-class support for his movement, Panickar's
endeavours did not acquire the character of a mass movement.

Similarly, the Travancore Ezhava Sabha, a secular organization founded
by Palpu in 1896, failed to conquer the hearts of ordinary Ezhavas as it did
not have any mechanism to address the religious and spiritual prejudices of
the common people,[113] and appealed only to a small section of the educated,
upper layers of the community.[114] Sree Narayana Guru filled this void as he
could effectively address the majority of the Ezhava population. The coming
together of Narayana Guru and the Ezhava middle class eventually led to
the formation of the SNDP Yogam. In the meanwhile he inculcated in the
minds of both laymen and the middle class, the need for developing a social
consciousness imbued with basic human values.

Narayana Guru stressed the importance of forming an organization which, according to him, was inevitable for bringing about socio-religious changes and at the same time essential for attaining power and progress.[115] That was why, in one of his messages, he exhorted his contemporaries to '[s]trengthen themselves by organization, liberate by education'.[116] His intention was not to start an organization for a particular community or caste but one that would bring all men together.[117] He felt the need for an organization which could admit all those who wished to follow the principle of human equality without any discrimination based on religion or caste. The Guru's appeal, of course, was religious; at the same time it was secular, in the sense that the boundaries set by religion did not affect his reasoning. This became an influential underlying principle for the formation of the SNDP Yogam.[118]

Kumaran Asan wrote: 'When Sree Narayana Guru consecrated a Shivalinga at Aruvippuram in 1063 ME [AD 1888], the seed of the SNDP Yogam was sown.'[119] When the Guru consecrated this first temple, a small Kshetra Yogam, generally known as 'Aruvippuram Kshetra Yogam' and consisting of twenty-four members holding eleven shares,[120] was formed with the objective of performing daily *pooja* and conducting annual festivals in the temple.[121] Since this Kshetra Yogam did not have sufficient strength to fulfil the aims and aspirations of the Guru, it was expanded as the SNDP Yogam.[122] It was Palpu who inspired Narayana Guru to expand the Kshetra Yogam into the SNDP Yogam.[123] Thus the efforts of Narayana Guru and his cooperation with the Ezhava middle class under the leadership of Palpu helped to organize and bring together the scattered and divided Ezhavas of the whole of Kerala into a strong caste-based association. Its objective was to strengthen the collective effort in the fields of education, social reform and political action. In short, the genesis of the SNDP Yogam was, on the one hand, an outcome of the desire of middle-class Ezhavas to overcome the caste disabilities which affected their material progress and social status in society,[124] and on the other, to obtain access to the worship of Hindu gods by the low castes and outcastes – an outcome of the Bhakti movement.[125]

Notes and References

[1] In this inscription, Ayyanadigal Thiruvadi, the tenth ruler of Venad, gifted a *viduperu* (a plot of land) to the Tharisappally (Teresa Church) built by Eso da Tapir at Kurakkeni Kolam. In this area lived four families of Ezhavas in which there were eight toddy tappers and one family of washermen. They were exempted from several taxes. Elamkulam P.N. Kunjan Pillai, *Studies in Kerala History*, N.B.S., Kottayam, 1970, p. 372. See also A. Sreedhara Menon, *A Survey of Kerala History*, N.B.S., Kottayam, 1973, pp. 40–41; first edition 1970.

[2] Elamkulam P.N. Kunjan Pillai, *Kerala Charitra Prasanangal* (Malayalam), N.B.S., Kottayam, 1963, p. 119.

[3] M. Srinivasa Aiyangar, *Tamil Studies or Essays on the History of the Tamil People, Language, Religion and Literature*, Guardian Press, 1914, p. 66.

[4] P.K. Gopalakrishnan, 'Ezhavar', in Kerala History Association, *Kerala Charitram*, Ernakulam, Vol. I, 1973, p. 965.

[5] William Logan, *Malabar*, Government Press, Madras, 1951, Vol. I, p. 143; Edgar Thurston, *Castes and Tribes of Southern India*, 7 vols, Government Press, Madras, 1909 and Johnson Reprint Corporation, New York, 1965), Vol. VII, p. 137; L.K. Ananthakrishna Iyer, *The Cochin Tribes and Castes*, Higginbotham, Madras, 1909 and Johnson Reprint Corporation, New York, 1969, Vol. 1, p. 227; C.A. Innes, *Madras District Gazetteer*, Malabar, Madras, 1908, Vol. I, p. 124, first edition 1904; Nagam Aiya, *The Travancore State Manual*, Government Press, Trivandrum, 1906, Vol. II, pp. 298–99; C. Achutha Menon, *Cochin State Manual*, Ernakulam, 1911, p. 203; Francis Day, *The Lands of the Perumals or Cochin, Its Past and Its Present*, Asian Education Services, New Delhi, 1990, first published by Gantz Brothers, Madras, 1863, p. 319; Jacob Canter Visccher, *Letters from Malabar*, Gantz Brothers, Madras, 1882, pp. 127–28.

[6] K.P. Padmanabha Menon, *History of Kerala*, Government Press, Ernakulam, 1933, Vol. III, p. 424.

[7] The Ezhavas of Kerala are known by different names in different parts of the state: in southern Travancore and a part of central Travancore as Ezhavas; in northern Travancore and a part of central Travancore as Chovans; in south Travancore as Shanars; in Malabar as Thiyyas; and in south Canara as Bilwas. *Census of India, 1901*, Vol. XXVI, Travancore, Part I, Report, p. 278; *Vivekodayam*, February–March 1916 (Kumbam, 1091 ME), pp. 344–51.

[8] Padmanabha Menon, *History of Kerala*, Vol. III, p. 424.

[9] Thurston says, 'Chova is supposed to be a corruption of sevaka or servant caste.' Thurston *Castes and Tribes of Southern India*, Vol. II, p. 392.

[10] Dr Caldwell, 'Essays on the Tinnevelli Shanars', quoted in *Census of India, 1901*, Travancore, Part I, Report, p. 278. Also see B.R. Baden Powell, *The Land Systems of British India*, Oriental Publishers, 1974, Vol. III, p. 157.

[11] See Dr Palpu's presidential address in connection with the industrial exhibition held at Quilon in 1904. *Vivekodayam*, 5 February 1905 (30 Makaram 1080 ME), p. 97; *Private Papers of Dr Palpu*, File No. 19, Nehru Memorial Museum and Library (NMML), New Delhi. Also see his letter to Mahatma Gandhi, 12 April 1925, *Private Papers of Dr Palpu*, File No. 1, NMML.

[12] C.V. Kunjuraman, 'The Thiyyas', *Mitavadi*, March 1916, p. 24.

[13] Presidential address of Dr Palpu (junior) at the Thirteenth Annual Meeting held at Quilon on 11 and 12 May 1916, *Vivekodayam*, Vol. XIII, No. 3, June–July 1916 (Mithunam 1091 ME), p. 51.

[14] K. Damodaran, *Ezhava Charitram*, Trivandrum, 1935–36 (1110 ME), Vol. I, p. 306.

[15] It is generally attributed that the Vattis were priests of the Ezhavas. But Damodaran says that Vattis were not their priests and that they were only *parikarmis* or assistants. Ibid., pp. 321–22.

[16] Elamkulam P.N. Kunjan Pillai, *Kerala Charitra Prasanangal*, Part I, pp. 111–12. The strength of the Thiyya community in south India is more than that of the total population of Ceylon. Elamkulam P.N. Kunjan Pillai, *Kerala Charithrathinte Iruladanja Edukal* (Malayalam), third edition, N.B.S., Kottayam, 1963, p. 196.

[17] E.M.S. Namboodiripad, *The National Question in Kerala*, People's Publishing House, Bombay, 1952, p. 40. But he himself admitted, in *Kerala Yesterday, Today, Tomorrow* (National Book Agency, Calcutta, 1967, p. 25), that a group of people migrated to Kerala.

[18] K. Damodaran, *Kerala Charitram*, p. 157.

[19] N.R. Krishnan, *Ezhavar Annum Innum*, Seena Publications, Engadiyar, Trichur, 1969, p. 73.

[20] T.K. Madhavan, *Dr. Palpu (A Life History of Dr. Palpu)*, Vol. I (fully revised by Pallipattu Kunju Krishnan), Cheppad, Alleppey, 1969, p. 8. Murkothu Kunhappa also held the same view in his article, 'Thiyyarude Charitram Oru Vihaga Veekshanam', *SNDP Platinum Jubilee*

Souvenir, 1978, pp. 65–69. See also Kambil Anandhan, 'Thiyyar', *SNDP Yogam Golden Jubilee Souvenir*, 1953, pp. 97–100.

21. C.V. Kunjuraman, 'The Thiyyas', p. 24.

22. P.C. Alexander, *Buddhism in Kerala*, Annamalai University, Annamalai Nagar, 1949, p. 123. To substantiate Alexander's argument, A. Ayyappan points out that a similar thing happened to Buddhists in Bengal during the time of Hindu revivalism: the Buddhists were absorbed into Hinduism and they were considered to be positioned below caste Hindus. A. Ayyappan, *Social Revolution in a Kerala Village: A Study in Culture*, Asia Publishing House, Bombay, 1965, p. 120.

23. Murkothu Kunhappa, *The Thiyyas of Kerala*, Souvenir, Indian History Congress, Calicut, 1976, p. 48. Dr Palpu (junior) said, 'If then our people/Ezhavas were Buddhist when we settled in this land of Perumals, the religious antipathy of the Hindu caste will explain our exclusion from Hindu temples, when we reverted to the old Hindu faith such as the inequality of the distinction shown when they went to worship in the Hindu temples that self respect must have led them to resent the treatment and to establish temples of their own.' Quoted in N.R. Krishnan, *Ezhavar Annum Innum*, p. 73; *Vivekodayam*, June–July 1916, p. 51.

24. *Private Papers of Dr Palpu*, File No. 1, NMML.

25. See, for details, chapter 1.

26. *Census of India, 1921*, Vol. XXV, Travancore, Part I, Report, p. 125. Also see T.K. Velu Pillai, *The Travancore State Manual*, Vol. III, p. 12.

27. Ibid., Vol. I, p. 47.

28. Thurston, *Castes and Tribes of Southern India*, Vol. II, p. 395.

29. Murkothu Kunhappa, *Murkothu Kumaran* (biography), N.B.S., Kottayam, 1975, p. 27. Also see Murkothu Kunhappa, 'Thiyyas of Kerala', p. 47.

30. Logan, *Malabar*, Vol. I, p. 117.

31. *Vivekodayam*, January–February 1909 (Makaram 1084 ME), p. 5.

32. Dewan Pashkar to the Dewan, 28 September 1904, File No. 113 of 1904, Travancore Political Department, Kerala Secretariat.

33. *Census of Travancore, 1875*, Report, p. 267.

34. Murkothu Kunhappa, 'Thiyyas of Kerala', p. 49.

35. *Census of Travancore, 1875*, Report, p. 261.

36. Ibid.

37. For details, see C.R. Kesavan Vaidhyar, 'Ayurvedavum Ezhava Samudhayavum' and Kilimanoor N. Bhaskaran, 'Samskrita Bashayum Ezhavarum'. These two articles were published in the *SNDP Platinum Jubilee Souvenir*, 1978, pp. 74–80 and 168–88, respectively. Also see Murkothu Kunhappa, 'Thiyyas of Kerala', p. 48.

38. A. Ayyappan, *Social Revolution in Kerala Village*, p. 125; P.K. Gopalakrishnan, 'Ezhavar', in *Kerala Charitram*, Vol. 1, 1973, p. 976; C.R. Kesavan Vaidhyar, 'Ayurvedavum Ezhava Samudhayavum', *SNDP Platinum Jubilee Souvenir*, 1978, pp. 74–80.

39. *Census of Travancore, 1875*, Report, p. 256.

40. *Census of India, 1901*, Vol. XXVI, Travancore, Part I, Report, p. 142.

41. *Vivekodayam*, November–December 1912 (Vrichikam 1088 ME), p. 47.

42. T.K. Velu Pillai, *The Travancore State Manual*, 1940, Vol. III, p. 13.

43. During his time as the Resident of Travancore in 1810–19, Colonel Munro patronized missionary activities and secured the title, 'Father of Christian Mission in Travancore'. During his term as the Resident-cum-Dewan of Travancore, Christians obtained a number of privileges. Munro urged the Maharaja of Travancore to provide financial assistance to the activities of Christian missionaries. See Regional Record Survey Committee, 1970, Vol. I, p. 43. The Christians were exempted from poll tax and *uzhiyam* (obligatory service); ibid. Moreover, Christian women were granted the right to cover their breasts as they did in other countries; ibid. In addition, in 1829, it was again under Colonel Munro that a Royal Proclamation was issued authorizing that conversion was to be respected. See Regional Record Survey Committee, 1970, Vol. I, p. 43.

44. As a result of increased agitation by the missionaries, the Government of Madras intervened.

Cullen, the then Resident of Travancore, asked the Maharaja of Travancore to issue a proc-lamation similar to the Government of India Act V of 1843. Cullen to the Chief Secretary, No. 10, 1854, M.P.P. 3 October 1854, Range 321, Vol. XV, pp. 3053–55, National Archives of India (NAI). Also see Jeffrey, *The Decline of Nayar Dominance*, pp. 44–50. Thus, on 24 June 1864, Uttram Thirunal Maharaja issued a proclamation by which slavery in Travancore was abolished. See Regional Record Survey Committee, *History of Freedom Movement in Kerala*, 1970, Vol. I, pp. 123–24. This declaration not only emancipated all *sirkar* slaves from their bondage, but also withdrew legal recognition from all aspects of slavery. See Jeffrey, *The Decline of Nayar Dominance*, p. 49.

45 Till the end of the 1850s, the untouchables were not permitted to cover their breasts. The missionaries, with the support of the British Resident, encouraged them to break away from local customs. At that time, the government circular of 1814 allowed Shanar women to wear clothes on their bosom like the Nair women. See Nagam Aiyya, *The Travancore State Manual*, Vol. I, p. 525; also Hardgrave, 'The Breast Cloth Controversy', p. 177. When they began to cover their breasts it infuriated the Nairs, and as a consequence of this various conflicts took place between the Nairs and the untouchables who had converted to Chris-tianity. C.M. Agur, *Church History of Travancore*, pp. 780–82 and 826. Nairs began to tear off the blouses of these low-caste Christian women, which led to riots, arson and even murder. See Rev. C. Mead, 'A Report of the Neyoor Mission, July 1829', dated 30 June 1829, manuscript (L.M.S.), in Hardgrave, 'The Breast Cloth Controversy', p. 178. Christian missionaries pressurized the Government of Madras time and again, and ultimately, due to the intervention of the Government of Madras in 1869, a Royal Proclamation decreed that there was no objection to the Shanars – a caste with the same function as Ezhava women – wearing a blouse, on condition that it was not in the same pattern as that worn by the high castes. According to the Royal Proclamation of Travancore State on 26 July 1859: 'We hereby proclaim that there is no objection to Shanar women either putting on jacket, like the Christian Shanar women or the Shanar women of all creeds dressing on coarse cloth and tying themselves round with it as the *Mukkuvattigal* (low-caste fisherwomen) do or to cover their bosom in any manner whatever; but not like women of high castes.' See Rev. Samuel Mateer, *The Land of Charity*, John Snow, London, 1871, p. 305; Nagam Aiya, *The Travancore State Manual* Vol. I, p. 531.

46 Houtart and Lemercinier, 'Socio-Religious Movements in Kerala', p. 4.

47 For details, see R.N. Yesudas, *A People's Revolt in Travancore: A Backward Class Movement for Social Freedom*, Kerala Historical Society, Trivandrum, 1975, p. 61; Regional Record Survey Committee, *History of Freedom Movement in Kerala*, 1970, Vol. 1, pp 57–59; Jef-frey *The Decline of Nayar Dominance*, pp. 59–60; Agur, *Church History of Travancore*, Appendix, p. 1.

48 See *Ezhava Memorial*; *Vivekodayam*, Vol. 2, No. 7, 15 November 1905 (30 Tulam 1081 ME), p. 3; *Mitavadi*, Vol. 5, No. 8, August 1917, pp. 31–32.

49 J. Gurunatham describes the impact of Christian missionaries among the educated Telugu men as follows: 'It was Christianity that for the first time in the history of country brought to a consciousness and degeneration'. *Viresalingam Pantulu*, 1911, p. 28, quoted in V. Ramakrishna Acharyulu, 'Social Reform Movements in Andhra (1848–1919)', Ph.D. thesis, Jawaharlal Nehru University, New Delhi, 1977.

50 Nagam Aiya, *The Travancore State Manual*, Vol. III, p. 18.

51 When the new Resident, Maltby, took charge of the office, Dewan Madhava Rao presented a memorandum outlying 'the works required for the improvement of the state'. The Dewan gave first preference to constructing a good road system for boosting the commerce of the state, and constructed the Trivandrum Nagercoil Road, Kottayam Mundakkayam Road, etc. See Maltby to Madhava Rao, 12 April 1860; Memoranda by F.N. Malt, 4 November 1861 and 22 February 1861; Letter to the Dewan, *Madras Residency Records*, Vol. XII; Jeffrey, *The Decline of Nayar Dominance*, p. 94.

52 *Travancore Administration Report*, 1866–67, p. 88 and *Travancore Administration Report*, 1871–72, p. 113.

[53] For details, see chapter 1.

[54] Jeffrey, *The Decline of Nayar Dominance*, p. 91.

[55] P.R. Gopinathan Nair, 'Education and Socio-Economic Change in Kerala, 1793–1947, *Social Scientist*, Vol. IV, No. 8, March 1976, p. 30.

[56] *Vivekodayam*, June–July 1905 (Midhunam 1080 ME), p. 2.

[57] Jeffrey, *The Decline of Nayar Dominance*, p. 91.

[58] *Census of Travancore, 1875*, Report, p. 266. This recent increment of wage was mainly concerned with the development of the PWD in Travancore. The rate stayed roughly at 4 annas until the 1890s, when a new planting boom forced it up to 5 annas. See *Madras Mail*, 30 January 1897 p. 7.

[59] Mateer, *Native Life of Travancore*, pp. 235–36.

[60] Robin Jeffrey, 'The Social Origins of a Caste Association, 1875–1906: The Founding of the S.N.D.P. Yogam', *South Asia*, No 4, 1974, p. 43.

[61] *Travancore Administration Report*, 1870–71 to 1891–92.

[62] *Travancore Administration Report*, 1882–83, pp. 67–68.

[63] Jeffrey, 'The Social Origins of a Caste Association', p. 44.

[64] Robin Jeffrey, 'Temple Entry Movement in Travancore, 1860–1940', *Social Scientist*, Vol. IV, No. 8, 1976, p. 9.

[65] The Dewan's Tour Inspection Notes, 16 May to 18 January 1904, 97/1904, Travancore Political Department, Kerala Secretariat Cellar.

[66] Mateer, *Native Life of Travancore*, p. 281.

[67] K. Damodaran, *Ezhava Charitram*, Vol. I, p. 333.

[68] *Vivekodayam*, June–August 1906 (Midhunam–Karkadakam 1081 ME), p. 12.

[69] For details, see chapter 1.

[70] *Report of the Travancore Marumakkathayam Committee*, 1908, Appendix II, p. 73.

[71] *Vivekodayam*, January–February 1909 (Makaram 1084 ME), pp. 5–6. For details, also see chapter 1.

[72] *Administration Report of Travancore*, 1062 ME (AD 1886–87), pp. 125 and 251.

[73] Jeffrey, 'The Social Origins of a Caste Association', p. 47.

[74] Ibid.

[75] Nagam Aiya, *The Travancore State Manual*, Vol. II, p. 482; *Proceedings of Sree Mulam Popular Assembly*, 1905, p. 7; *Administration Report of Travancore*, 1900–1901, p. 54.

[76] *Census Report of Travancore, 1875*, Report, pp. 245–46; and *Census of Travancore, 1891*, Vol. I, Report, p. 498.

[77] Rao Bahadur P. Velayudhan, elder brother of Dr Palpu, was the first Ezhava graduate to get a BA degree from Travancore University. See M. Govindan, 'Rao Bahadur P. Velayudhan', *SNDP Yogam Golden Jubilee Souvenir*, 1953, p. 59. Velayudhan was followed by his younger brother Palpu and subsequently a number of Ezhavas graduated from various universities in India.

[78] While the industrial labour was comprised overwhelmingly of Ezhavas, a growing number of them were also becoming middlemen and owners of petty industries. A number of Ezhavas worked in various departments of British India with distinction. The most important of them were Dr Palpu, P. Velayudhan and Shangunni.

[79] P.S. Velayudhan, *SNDP Yoga Charitram*, SNDPYogam, Quilon, 1978, p. 41.

[80] *Malayali Memorial*, reproduced in the *Kerala Archives News Letter*, Vol. II, No. 11, and Vol. III, March and June 1975, p. 5.

[81] N. Kumaran Asan, 'Thiruvithamkurinte Rajyabharana Sambhandhamaya Nila', quoted in P.S. Velayudhan, *SNDP Yoga Charitram*, p. 51.

[82] Endorsement of the *Travancore Memorial*, File No.1899/M 884, English Records, Government Secretariat, Trivandrum, pp. 3–4.

[83] Ibid. See also P.K. Balakrishnan, *Narayana Guru Samahara Grandham (An Anthology)*, National Book Stall, Kottayam, 1969, p. 49; first edition 1954.

[84] Endorsement of the *Travancore Memorial*, File No.1899/M 884, English Records, Government Secretariat, Trivandrum.

[85] Ibid.

[86] Endorsement of the *Travancore Memorial*, File No. 1899/M 894, English Records, Government Secretariat, Trivandrum.

[87] File No. C-1231, English Records, Government Secretariat, Trivandrum; *Madras Mail*, 6 October 1896.

[88] See *Ezhava Memorial*, reproduced in M.J. Koshy, *Genesis of Political Consciousness in Kerala*, Kerala Historical Society, Trivandrum, 1972, pp. 190–200.

[89] Ibid.

[90] Endorsement of the *Malayali Memorial*, File No. 1889/M884, English Records, Government Secretariat, Trivandrum.

[91] Robin Jeffrey, 'A Note on the Malayali Origin of Anti-Brahminism in South India', *The Indian Economic and Social History Review*, Vol. XIV, No. 2, 1977, p. 259.

[92] G.P. *Centenary Souvenir 1964: Selected Writings and Speeches of G.P. Pillai*, Trivandrum, 1964, pp. 117–18; K. Bhanu, 'Doctor P. Palpu, D.P.H.', *SNDP Yogam Golden Jubilee Souvenir*, 1953, p. 28. Rs 1,500 had to be spent for sending G.P. Pillai to London to raise the question in British Parliament regarding the treatment of Ezhavas in Travancore, of which all except Rs 300, contributed by others, came from Dr Palpu's own pocket. See Madhavan K.G. Komalezhathu, 'Doctor Palpu', *SNDP Yogam Platinum Jubilee Souvenir*, 1978, p. 376.

[93] G.P. *Centenary Souvenir 1964: Selected Writings and Speeches of G.P. Pillai*, Trivandrum, 1964, pp. 117–18.

[94] *SNDP Yogam Platinum Jubilee Souvenir*, 1978, p. 376.

[95] Ibid.; M.K. Sanoo, *Narayana Guru Swami* (biography), Vivekodayam Printing and Publishing Co., Irinjalakuda, 1976, p. 166.

[96] Dr Palpu sent G.P. Pillai to raise the question of Ezhavas of Travancore to the Poona session of the Indian National Congress in 1895. See G.P. *Centenary Souvenir 1964: Selected Writings and Speeches of G.P. Pillai*, Trivandrum, 1964, pp. 111–14.

[97] P.K. Balakrishnan, *Narayana Guru*, pp. 109–10.

[98] N. Kumaran, 'SNDP Yogam, Chila Smaranakal', *SNDP Yogam Golden Jubilee Souvenir*, 1953, p. 147.

[99] Ibid.

[100] K.R. Achutan, *C. Krishnan* (biography, Malayalam), N.B.S., Kottayam, 1971, pp. 47–48.

[101] A speech delivered by C.V. Kunjuraman at Muttom, reproduced in *Vivekodayam*, 15 November 1904 (30 Thulam 1080 ME), Vol. I, No. 4, p. 70.

[102] Thurston, *Castes and Tribes of Southern India*, Vol. II, p. 394; C. Kesavan, *Jeevitasamaram* (autobiography), 2 vols, N.B.S., Kottayam, Vol. I, 1968, p. 302; Robin Jeffrey, David Arnold and James Manor, 'Caste Associations in South India: A Comparative Analysis', *The Indian Economic and Social History Review*, Vol. XIII, No. 3, 1976, p. 355; Eric J. Miller, 'Caste and Territory in Malabar', *American Anthropologist*, Vol. LVI, 1954, p. 416; and Murkothu Kunhappa, 'Thiyyas of Kerala', p. 49.

[103] C. Kesavan, *Jeevitasamaram*, Vol. I, p. 302.

[104] *Census of Travancore, 1891*, Vol. I, Report, p. 505.

[105] M.K. Sanoo, *Narayana Guru Swami*, p. 160.

[106] Ibid.

[107] Dr Palpu had great regard and veneration for Swami Vivekananda, an iconic figure who triggered a new spiritual wave in the last decade of the nineteenth century with his groundbreaking ideas on religion and philosophy. He therefore invited the Swami to stay with him when the latter visited Bangalore in 1891. The Swami accepted his invitation and an overjoyed Palpu, then a medical officer of the Mysore Government, forgetting his status, himself drove the rickshaw in which the Swami was seated through the city of Bangalore. It was during this time that Palpu sought Swami's advice on ways to redress the grievances of the Ezhavas of Travancore. The Swami advised him to organize the people who had been subjected to socio-religious slavery and awaken them from slumber. The Swami, 'who discovered the soul of India', also told Palpu that in India no movement could move the heart of the masses which did not have the sacred halo of spirituality. See P.K. Balakrishnan, *Narayana Guru*,

p. 109; T.K. Madhavan, *Doctor Palpu*, pp. 94–95; Velayudhan Panikkaseri, *Doctor Palpu* (biography), Seena Publishers, Engadiyar, Trichur, 1970, pp. 94–95; P. Parameswaran, *Sree Narayana Guru Swamikal: Navothanathinte Pravachakan*, Jayabharath Publishers, Calicut, 1979, pp. 74–76; first edition 1971.

[108] P.K. Balakrishnan, *Narayana Guru*, p. 108; M.K. Sanoo, *Narayana Guru Swami*, p. 170.

[109] Ibid., p. 209.

[110] E.M.S. Namboodiripad, *Kerala Yesterday, Today, Tomorrow*, p. 120.

[111] M.S.A. Rao, *Social Movements and Social Transformation: A Study of Two Backward Classes Movements in India*, Macmillan India, New Delhi, 1979, pp. 45–46.

[112] Ibid.

[113] According to Charles Heimsath, the reasons for the failure of other reform movements in Kerala were due to their lack of religious premises. See Charles H. Heimsath, 'The Function of Hindu Social Reformers – With Special Reference to Kerala', *The Indian Economic and Social History Review*, Vol. XV, No. 1, January–March 1978, p. 27.

[114] Woodcock, *Kerala: A Portrait of Malabar Coast*, Faber and Faber, London, 1967, p. 229.

[115] *Sree Narayana Centenary Souvenir*, 1954, p. 182, quoted in Daniel Thomas, *Sree Narayana Guru*, The Christian Institute for Religion and Society, Bangalore, 1965, p. 35.

[116] Quoted in P.S. Velayudhan, 'Sree Narayana Guru: a peep into his life and work', *SNDP Yogam Platinum Jubilee Sourvenir*, 1978, p. 19.

[117] Swami Dharmanandaji, *Sree Narayana Gurudevan*, N.B.S., Kottayam, 1965, p. 173; *Sree Narayana Centenary Souvenir*, p. 182, quoted in Daniel Thomas, *Sree Narayana Guru*, p. 35.

[118] According to Narayana Guru, 'Our organization should unite all people; religion should allow freedom of all faiths and should lead man to higher goals and values in life. This is the *Sanatana Dharma* of one caste, one religion and one God for man.' Ibid.

[119] Kumaran Asan's first report as Secretary of the SNDP Yogam, *Vivekodayam*, 13 May 1904 (31 Medom 1079 ME), p. 15.

[120] The face value of the share was Rs 100. Some members held half a share while others held one-fourth a share.

[121] After Narayana Guru's consecration at Aruvippuram, he acquired the reputation of a distinguished holy man and became the spiritual leader of the Ezhava community. A number of people used to visit his temple as pilgrims and offer donations. The income of the temple, therefore, increased day by day. A sanctum sanctorum was constructed and it was protected by a '*mandapam*', i.e. a canopy. In 1893, Chinmaya Swarupa Swamikal, a sanyasi from south Travancore, approached Narayana Guru to clear his debt; in lieu of this clearance he offered his encumbered property in Thamarakulam near Suchindram. To look after these properties, Pettayil Parameswaran, a brother of Dr Palpu, was appointed as manager of the temple. When the properties increased, in 1889, a committee of eleven members were selected under the name of 'Aruvippuram Kshetra Yogam' to manage the temple. This *Kshetra Yogam* is attributed as the forerunner of the SNDP Yogam. *Vivekodayam*, 13 May 1904, pp. 15–19. Also see Swami Dharmanandaji, *Sree Narayana Gurudevan*, p. 167.

[122] *Vivekodayam*, 13 May 1904, p. 19.

[123] T.K. Madhavan, *Doctor Palpu*, Vol. I , p. 189.

[124] Ramakrishnan Nair, 'Ruling Class and its Governing Elites of Kerala', *Journal of Kerala Studies*, Vol. I, No. 1, July 1973, pp. 41–42.

[125] Houtart and Lemercinier, 'Socio-Religious Reform Movements', p. 13.

3

Narayana Guru

Beyond Tradition–Modernity Dualism

Concepts like tradition and modernity have been conceived as binary opposites in all contemporary societies. Given such an understanding, it has become customary to classify any practice in terms of the contest between tradition and modernity: for example, traditional knowledge versus modern knowledge; traditional dress versus modern dress; traditional education versus modern education; traditional customs versus modern practices; traditional culinary practices versus modern food habits; static tradition versus dynamic modernity, etc; the list would seem endless. But in the subject under study here, Sree Narayana Guru and the SNDP Yogam, it may be possible to bypass this opposition between modernity and tradition. For instance, one could portray the Guru as traditional in the sense that he followed Advaita Vedanta, but on the other hand it is also possible to say that he was modern for he believed in equality and negated all caste distinctions. Therefore, it is necessary to examine the existence of intertwined strands in his ideas; to see him as a synthesizer of the desirable aspects of both modernity and tradition.

Most academic writings on the socio-religious history of Kerala – by those who were introduced to English education[1] and institutions,[2] and the work of the Christian missionaries[3] – have generally viewed the emergence of 'modern ideas' in terms of a critical attitude towards the past as characterized by 'religious superstition' and 'social obscurantism'. While emphasizing the role of the missionaries, and of western knowledge and ideas, the writers have overlooked the true potential of socio-religious ideas rooted in what has been called 'the Indian intellectual tradition'. Had the changes been solely due to the impact of western thought, our society would have undergone a process of westernization.[4] There were ambivalences, contradictions and indecisiveness in conceiving tradition and modern as binary opposites. If tradition served as a powerful weapon in the efforts to realize modernity, modernity did not involve a complete rejection of the past.

There is a belief that western influences automatically lead to 'progressive' social and political consciousness, and that traditional influences invariably encourage 'conservative' and stationary attitudes. One of the arguments that has gained predominance is that Narayana Guru was a product of the Indian intellectual tradition that was based mainly on the Advaita philosophy of Sankara,[5] and that the sources of the evolution of his intellectual thought were derived from traditional knowledge. Nevertheless, rationalism and religious universalism, two important intellectual and ideological strands of the nineteenth century, were the binding principles of Narayana Guru's socio-religious reform activities. This may help us to question the general belief that a western influence automatically leads to 'progressive' consciousness and that a traditional influence promotes 'conservative' attitudes. Here, my attempt is to both place as well as portray Narayana Guru's ideas as a combined outcome of both tradition and modernity, especially since western education in Kerala had already been mediated through the former.

Although a lot has been written on Narayana Guru,[6] most of the writings are not strictly in tune with an academic approach but are more journalistic in character, and devoid of a critical historical perspective. Some of these writings have also been undertaken with the aim of appropriating the legacy of Narayana Guru in order to legitimize one or the other sectarian interest.[7] To some extent, the fairly extensive literature on Narayana Guru owes its existence to the efforts of Malayalis to orient themselves towards their contemporary social, cultural and religious needs, and in order to legitimize themselves with the help of the 'past', going back to the late nineteenth and early twentieth centuries.

Narayana Guru was born, in all probability, on 20 August 1854, in an Ezhava family called Vayalvarath, at Chempazhanti, a village 6 miles north of Thiruvananthapuram.[8] Though untouchable in social status, the Vayalvarath family was held in high esteem in the locality as it jointly owned and enjoyed equal power, along with the Kannakkara Nair *taravad* (descendants of the illustrious Ettuveetil Pillai),[9] over the administration of the Manakkal temple devoted to the Mother Goddess. The male members of Vayalvarath house were well-known as Ayurvedic physicians, astrologers and Sanskrit scholars.[10] Narayana Guru's father, Madan Asan, was a schoolteacher, and his maternal uncle, Krishnan Vaidhyar, was an Ayurvedic physician.[11] His maternal great grand uncle, Achuthan Kochan Asan, had the distinction of being the first Ezhava to perform reinstallation of the idol at Manakkal temple.[12] Thus Kochan Asan paved the way for his grand-nephew, Narayanan, to perform greater and more creative socio-religious reform activities for uplifting the deprived sections of the society. This shows that Narayana Guru belonged to a family of some cultural and intellectual standing, notwithstanding its low position in the caste hierarchy. In short, he inherited considerable cultural and social capital which made him an 'exception' within the general social hierarchy. Perhaps this qualified him to transcend the binaries mentioned above.

As a result of such an intellectual inheritance and cultural background,

Narayana Guru possessed a mind that combined brilliance and incisiveness in finely balanced proportions. Almost all his biographers have narrated in detail how, as a boy, he often revealed his innate nature by reacting in his own naughty way to affairs related to religious rituals and caste sensibilities.[13] Apparently even at that young age when education and conscious thinking had little impact, two significant aspects of the future Guru's mental make-up, i.e. rationalism and humanism,[14] or humour and scepticism about the present, could be discerned.

Like for any other Hindu child of his time, Nanu's (Nanu is a common nick-name for anyone named Narayanan in Kerala) initiation into the letters of the Malayalam alphabet was performed when he was five years old by Kannankkara Narayana Pillai – an aristocratic Nair, a renowned Sanskrit scholar, an astrologer and, above all, the *adhikari* of the village.[15] After learning the basics of the language from his father and maternal uncle, Narayanan was sent to Kummampilli Raman Pillai in 1877 (1053 ME), at the age of twenty-one, to learn more.[16] Under Raman Pillai's tutelage, Nanu learned *Kavya, Nataka, Vyakarana, Alankara, Vedanta, Upanishads,* medicine and astrology.[17] Little is known about this phase of his life.[18] There are no sources to enlighten us on whether he was associated with any other teacher other than Raman Pillai, or other educational institutions and their curricula that may have shaped his thinking. This paucity of information about his formative influences makes it difficult for us to ascertain his evolution as a spiritual intellectual with a vision for socio-religious transformation of the society.

After his education under Raman Pillai, Nanu returned home, in either 1879 or 1880,[19] and started a school in his village at Chempazhanti in 1881.[20] He thus came to be known as Nanu Asan. In 1884, after the death of his father, he left home in search of 'truth'.[21] He travelled extensively during the years 1884–88 across south India,[22] and came in contact with Chattampi Swamikal and Taikkattu Aiyyavu, who influenced his intellectual contours.[23] It was possibly from Chattampi Swamikal that he acquired a critical attitude towards the scriptures and towards the notion that the Vedas were the sole preserve of Brahmins. It was possibly also from him that he learned that non-Brahmins too had the right to consecrate idols in temples.[24] From Taikkattu Aiyyavu[25] he learnt to practise yoga, which helped him to 'open the inner eye'.[26] In addition, he also became familiar with the Bhakti tradition of Tamil Shaivite saints, especially with one of their popular scriptures, the *Thirukkural.*

Narayana Guru read extensively, including books written in Tamil which were available to 'learned Travancoreans' of those days, such as the *Tolkapiam, Nannul, Ozhuvikodukkam* and *Thevarappathikangal.* He even translated a few of them into Malayalam, such as *Thevarappathikangal* in 1887 and the *Thirukkural* in 1894.[27] He also acquired considerable knowledge of Jain and Buddhist philosophies,[28] though from where or how he acquired this remains an enigma. Thus a long-existing corpus of historical and literary knowledge considerably influenced the intellectual make-up of Narayana Guru.[29]

The experiences he underwent during this intellectual journey contributed to his self-transformation. It was during this period that he became especially sensitive to social problems, particularly those faced by the lower castes. Unique both in appearance and demeanour as compared to the conventional sanyasi or sadhu, Narayana Guru mixed with people of all kinds and from all backgrounds, irrespective of their caste or social status.[30] He lived in the midst of the poor, and saw for himself the grinding poverty and superstitions which added to their misery and brought about their ruin.[31] He witnessed the oppression and injustice they were subjected to. This close contact with the weaker sections of society provided him with a clear understanding of their socio-religious and economic conditions, and a conception of possible remedial measures.

The widespread missionary activities in Travancore at the time he was socially active[32] and touring Malabar (a predominantly Muslim area)[33] might have familiarized him with the dictums of Christianity and Islam. His ideas for the social and economic uplift of the lower castes might or might not have been directly derived from Christianity; nevertheless he was inspired to some extent by the activities of Christian missionaries.[34] It is possible that the missionaries' activities and the subsequent changes in society helped Narayana Guru to introspect about the strengths and weaknesses of traditional culture and its institutions, but it would be far-fetched to assume that the missionaries were mainly responsible for his socio-cultural ideas. It would be more appropriate to propose that the socio-cultural ideas of Narayana Guru were occasioned by the presence of the missionaries but not inspired by them. There seems to be no causal link between the two because they had their own independent trajectories and functions in Travancore despite their coexistence in historical time.

The social practices and religious beliefs prevalent in late nineteenth-century Kerala society were perceived as 'religious superstition' and 'social obscurantism'.[35] The popular notion was that the Hindu religion was an admixture of magical animism and superstition.[36] Polytheism and idolatry made the religion full of ceremonious rituals. The common view was that the Brahmins had established a monopoly over scriptural knowledge through the interpretation of rituals. However, at the same time, we find that several individuals belonging to the Ezhava caste were well versed in some of these, including Advaita philosophy and Kerala mathematics which enabled an astrological understanding of the relationship between the cosmos and living beings. The best example was the Guru himself. While the backward communities were not generally allowed to participate in the institutionalized pattern of worship followed by the *savarna*s, the religious beliefs and practices of the *avarna*s resembled the so-called 'abominable' practices: the worship of totems, guardian deities and demons of destruction replete with detestable rites and abhorrent practices.[37] Worship of the snake, very popular among Malayalis, was such an instance; skin diseases, leprosy and sterility, for example, were believed to be caused by the wrath of the serpents.[38] *Mantravada* or the chanting of spells, offering of fermented drinks, sacrifice of roosters and goats, singing obscene songs about female genitals, copulation and masturbation, and devil dancing were all part of the rituals for the worship of the spirits.[39] Religious beliefs and practices were thus a mixture of magic, sorcery, witchcraft, divination and several other forms of popular religion. The forms differed slightly between the *avarna*s and *savarna*s, but the content was common to both the groupings. Gradually, the rites and practices observed at the time of birth, death, puberty and pregnancy began to be treated as absurd and irrational,[40] if not a wasteful expenditure as Narayana Guru propounded. It was often said that such practices led to the decadence of the society. It is at such sites that we find tradition becoming antithetical to modernity.

The Guru understood the interdependencies and interconnections between religious and social life, and also between religious beliefs and social stigmas – the implications of the prevalent forms of worship for social institutions. He became aware of the material, psychological and spiritual problems that affected the deprived sections of Kerala society. The influence of this social experience in the transformation of Nanu the schoolteacher to Narayana Guru the reformer is entrenched in the non-duality between tradition and modernity.

Religious Reforms and Narayana Guru

If the reformers of Kerala can be distinguished into two broad categories, then in the first category are those who believed that social behaviour can be influenced through re-articulating the existent religious idioms. The second group organized themselves under a non-religious leadership, and gained their ends through constitutional means and secular organizations.[41] However, as elsewhere in India, the reformers who belonged to the first category were more successful in Kerala than the second. This was perhaps due to the fact that religion was the dominant ideology of the time and it was not possible to undertake any social action without reference to it.[42] Though the English-educated people were respected by the masses, they were not accepted as their cultural ideal. This was mainly because of their alienation both from the existent culture and their partial affinity with the emergent cultures.[43]

Having understood the interconnections between religious beliefs and social practices, Narayana Guru started his reform activities by making them resonant with religious idioms in order to legitimize the need to reform oneself and others. Keralites met with religion at every turn in their lives – at birth, puberty, marriage, death, etc. As social life was strongly influenced by religious tenets, Narayana Guru realized that religious idioms were a necessary prerequisite for social reform. This is exemplified in the famous consecration of Shiva and the proclamation that he had consecrated 'Ezhava Shiva'. In such instances, along with several others, we see that Narayana Guru sought to replace the existing abominable religious beliefs and practices with a different form of worship. The establishment of temples and consecration of idols by the Guru was an expression of this alternative path. In contrast to the attitude of most nineteenth-century Indian reformers and intellectuals,[44] except Sree Ramakrishna Paramahamsa, Narayana Guru conceded to idolatry, rituals and the practices of traditional religion for the sake of the masses, who could not live peacefully without such practices and beliefs.[45] He believed that idolatry was necessary for the people in the early stages of their religious understanding, before they can grasp the abstract truth embodied in spiritual philosophy. That is why, although he himself did not believe in idolatry,[46] he sanctioned it as the nucleus around which an alternative form of worship could evolve.[47] The first step in this direction was the consecration of an idol of Shiva at Aruvippuram in 1888.

The words he inscribed on the temple wall eloquently declare his vision of universal brotherhood and the oneness of man: 'In this model place all inhabitants irrespective of caste and religion can dwell freely as brothers.'[48] Narayana Guru wished the temple to symbolize the brotherhood of man and equality of all before God. One of the most striking features of his religious reformism was a universal outlook based on the unity of godhead. By his consecration of Shiva, he unleashed an attack on the sacred order of *varna dharma*. That act symbolized a struggle between the status quo and change, or, better, a rational action for change in attitude related to oneself. It was on the basis of religious universalism that the Guru formulated his doctrine, 'One caste, one religion, and one God for mankind.'[49] To him the claim of superiority of one religion over another stemmed from ignorance. He drew a parallel with the story of the seven blind men who felt the parts of an elephant, each giving his own version as he distinguished the animal.[50] The Guru advised his followers, 'Whatever be one's religion it is enough that man becomes good. . . . Whatever a man does for his own pleasure shall be for the benefit of others.'[51]

The Guru's general interest in comparative religion led to the organizing of a *Sarva Mata Sammelanam* (All Religions Conference) on 3 and 4 May 1924. He declared the objective of the conference as follows: 'To know and to make known, not to argue and win.'[52] When the principles of different religions were discussed on a common platform, their underlying unity would be easier to grasp. The principal motives of the conference were: to search for universal truth in religion, to create an interest in comparative religion, to bring home to the people the essential unity of all religions, and finally, to create an atmosphere for developing the idea of religious universalism. Soon after the conference, the Guru decided to start a 'School of All Religions', which he called 'Mata Mahapathashala', at Sivagiri, which would teach the essence of all religions.[53] In this sense he was not against religiosity as such, but against differential (often hierarchical) treatment of people in the name of the religion/caste they adhered to.

After the Aruvippuram consecration, Narayana Guru proceeded to instal deities in 64 temples in different parts of Kerala. Three distinct phases can be discerned in the establishment of these new places of worship. During the first phase, gods of the Brahmanical pantheon were consecrated in place of 'lower satanic gods of primitive religion'. The Guru forbade the worship of evil spirits and the keeping of images representative of such beliefs in temples and houses of well-to-do Ezhavas.[54] Their place was taken by the newly consecrated temples. He also brought about changes in the method of worship; animal sacrifices and offerings of fermented drinks were replaced by flowers and fruits.[55]

The second phase was marked by the establishment of exceedingly simple and inexpensive temples. Though these temples had idols, pujas and celebrations were dispensed with. They were, in fact, conceived more as community spaces with gardens and libraries, which provided a serene and educative atmosphere.[56]

The third category of temples had no idols or images, like the temple at Karamukku where, in 1920, he installed a lamp in place of an idol and pronounced the benediction, 'Let there be light.'[57] At Murukkupuzha, in 1921, he placed a granite slab with the inscription 'Truth, Duty, Kindness and Peace';[58] and at Kalavancode, in 1927, he installed a mirror which symbolically represented the fact that God is present in the self[59] or the principle, 'know yourself'. In the words of Nataraja Guru, 'A plain mirror and lamp was installed by him at one place, so that idolatry might come into line with self-knowledge, for at least one's own image in a mirror told no distorted lie in any hysterical terms.'[60]

These innovations in Narayana Guru's consecratory practices not only differentiate his concept of temples and temple worship from Brahmanical notions, but also illustrate his precept that ideals are more important than idols. The Guru was quite different in inspiration, character and message from the traditional saints of pre-modern reform movements as well as later, westernized movements. That was his uniqueness. But his active participation in the socio-religious movement in Kerala during the late nineteenth and early twentieth centuries endowed him with a halo that combined the aura of a modern Indian reformer with that of a traditional Hindu sanyasi.[61]

Our understanding of Narayana Guru will depend on how we perceive the character of socio-religious movements in nineteenth-century Travancore. A significant aspect of his religious reform was the freedom it afforded to an individual to be critical about one's own tradition and one's position within the unfolding of modern ideas and practices, without either totally renouncing the former or selectively accepting the latter. Irrespective of whether the consecrations were looked upon as Sanskritization or protest, the fact that they sought to change the popular form and attitude of worship among the lower castes is undeniable. At the same time, the system he created was not a replica of what the upper castes followed. It was an intervention intended to create a new mode, distinct from both the popular and the elitist. Unlike his successors in socio-religious reform, he did not demand homogenization of identity among the lower and the upper castes through temple entry but strived for the creation of a new religious ethos.

The objective of Narayana Guru's religious reform efforts was not to enable the low castes to have access to the Brahmanical gods, as has been argued by Genevieve Lemercinier,[62] but to create a system of worship of their own. That he initially consecrated the idol of Shiva, despite his disapproval of idolatry, was an indication of the influence of both the elite and the popular culture. At the same time he was eager to create a system distinct from both, which explains the changes he made in consecration in the later stages, when he was transforming or reformulating his own selfhood.

The consecration of temples by Narayana Guru cannot be viewed either as an attempt to revive the past or as a rebuttal of it. His consecration of temples not only signified a rational approach to customary practices, but also an effort to embellish faith with rationality. If religion did not keep pace with the demands of the times, it would get fossilized and justifiably relegated. While consecrating idols in the temples, he was least concerned about religious sanctions or about whether such practices had existed in the past. When the upper castes questioned his scriptural authority to undertake consecration, the Guru replied, 'My consecration is of an Ezhava Shiva and not of a Brahmin Shiva.'[63] Hearing this, the people, *savarnas* and *avarnas* alike, were torn between their retained sentiments and emerging commitments.[64]

The important intellectual criteria that marked the consecrations were persuasive reason and convincing rhetoric. Very few were able to match the uncompromising reasoning of Narayana Guru. On one occasion, when the Guru was installing an idol in a temple in Trivandrum, a scholar sarcastically expressed his doubt whether the time was auspicious for such a sacred function. The Guru calmly replied, 'A horoscope is cast after the birth of the child. The birth does not take place according to a pre-determined auspicious time. The consecration is over. Now you can do your calculation.'[65] His only concern at that time was the effect the consecration would have on society. He was concerned about creating social mobility and promoting individual initiative rather than toeing the line of the scriptures. Thus his consecrations broke the rules of customary practices, and resulted in emotional and sentimental ruptures in society; but then, the times were such that reason prevailed over both.

The consecration of idols in temples by Narayana Guru was a move against the cultural hegemony of the Brahmins and represented the first expression of social reform. For Gail Omvedt, 'caste struggle', like 'class struggle', can become revolutionary only when it poses as an alternative, a more advanced social system, rather than being simply a negative protest or a competitive struggle for more economic or social–cultural rights within the framework of exploitation.[66] Narayana Guru's reform activities represented the fulfilment of the renaissance's desire for social transformation along revolutionary lines. In other words, he formulated a theo-ideology of reason in order to tilt social relations such that there were no 'ups' and 'downs' within the texture of sociality. His consecration of idols, inscriptions and mirrors were re-formulating practices that had no precedents, but gained prevalence as far as future freedom and self-fulfilment were concerned. Perhaps that is why he was unique and became an icon in all imaginable fields of social action, as someone who could live a life devoid of referential relations to both tradition and modernity – and as an exemplar being in this world for the future to come. A sleek trunk, from which innumerable branches could sprout to transgress that which is given or taken as granted.

For Narayana Guru it was immaterial whether his consecrations had the sanction of religious institutions, as his reform activities were a struggle against cultures that ought to be relegated.[67] They posed a challenge not only to the Brahmin hegemony, but also to the senseless customs that had survived through ages as though by divine ordinance. A sense of freshness was generated by the Guru's efforts, casting a seminal ray of light on the life of the untouchables and unapproachables of Kerala who had been, for centuries, wallowing in darkness and slavery.

Temples, for Narayana Guru, were but a means to an end. Once the end was achieved, he did not bother about the proliferation of temples. In 1917, he advised his followers, 'Do not encourage construction of temples any longer; if at all any temple is to be constructed it should be a small one. The educational institutions should be the chief temples.'[68] In the religious sphere, his reforms sought to remove priestly monopoly of knowledge, and also to simplify rituals on the basis of the ideals of humanism, economic rationalism and perhaps nationalism as well. The social implication of his religious reforms was to liberate individuals from conformity born out of fear and from uncritical submission to exploitation by the priests. The religious activities of Narayana Guru were an explicit expression of his opposition to all distinctions based on caste and *varna*. According to him, there was no fundamental difference between a 'Brahmin and a Pariah'; both belonged to a single human caste.[69] In 'Jati-Mimamsa', he emphasized this oneness: terms like Brahmin and Pariah are ideas that are churned out and superimposed on the reality of humans, which is essentially and fundamentally the same.[70]

The uniqueness of Narayana Guru was that he lived his own life in such a way that what he preached appeared worthwhile to be followed. In other words, he lived the life he desired others to follow and he mirrored the aspirations of others in the process. He started his journey towards dismantling *varna dharma* by liberating himself from its bondage, not by demanding rights from others but by freeing himself of all dependence on caste practices and stipulations.[71] He was a practising model of 'how to take care of oneself' in changing times. The uplift of communities that were lower in social status to the Ezhavas was considered by the Guru as a part of his life's mission. He admitted people from all castes into the temples consecrated by him. He maintained personal relations with those who belonged to castes lower than his own in the hierarchy. In order to uplift the conditions of the Cherumas and the Pulayas, he not only admitted them as students but also employed them as cooks, ignoring all caste taboos.[72] The Guru saw it as a paradox that while the Ezhavas were fighting against the pollution practised by the upper castes, they were themselves treating the Pulayas and Parayas as untouchables.[73] He reminded the Ezhavas that unless they changed their attitude towards the communities considered inferior to them in the caste hierarchy, they had no right to clamour for justice.[74] With this in view, he encouraged inter-caste marriage and inter-caste dining.[75] This goes to show that 'going beyond' was an integral part of his reform lexicon.

Narayana Guru's outlook was quite different from that of the upper-caste elite thinkers of the Indian renaissance. As Hindu culture and the caste system rested upon Brahmanism, Narayana Guru geared his moves in opposition to the cultural and ideological hegemony of the *savarna*s.

Ideas and Ideals of Social Reform

Narayana Guru was simultaneously a social reformer and an icon par excellence of a charismatic religious spearhead. Religious reform for him was tantamount to social reform, since religious beliefs and social practices were so closely intertwined as to be inseparable. Though the Guru's appeal may appear to be religious, the first major public event in his life, the consecration of Aruvippuram temple, was in fact a social reform activity mediated or articulated through the religious idiom. It has been observed that in many of the reform endeavours in nineteenth-century India, religious sanction was invariably sought as a means for bringing about social change.[76] Narayana Guru too formulated his system of thought with social transformation as a necessary prerequisite for the uplift of the downtrodden. His social reform endeavours were mainly concerned with caste, popular customs, beliefs and rituals, education, freedom of work, temperance and economic improvement. As these reform activities will be discussed in detail in the ensuing chapters, here I only briefly outline the ideas he promulgated.

Universalism

Among the social reformers of modern India, the most virulent and direct opposition to the caste system and its corollary of caste hierarchy based on ritual status came from Narayana Guru.[77] To him caste discrimination was out of place and repugnant not only on moral and ethical grounds, but also because it fostered social division, denied individual freedom and negated the growth of democratic ideas. Caste was anti-humanist and sapped individual initiative; it destroyed the self-esteem and sense of dignity of especially the poor and marginalized people.[78] Therefore, in 1914, the Guru formulated his doctrine of 'One caste, one creed and one God for man.'[79] He also advised the people as follows: 'Don't ask about another's caste, do not speak of your own caste and never think of either of them.'[80] His idea was to create a democratic social institution and to remodel the old socio-religious outlook to suit unfolding social needs.

Though a product of traditional knowledge and culture, Narayana Guru held advanced views on several questions related to caste and religious matters as compared to many of his western-educated contemporaries. His conception of caste and his anti-caste stance were radical, perhaps more so than reform-ers like Vivekananda and Mahatma Gandhi. Vivekananda while criticizing the western theory of society, had declared, 'Competition-cruel, cold and heartless is the law of Europe. Our law is caste – the breathing competition, checking its forces, mitigating its cruelties, soothing the passage of the human soul through this mystery of life.'[81] This reveals that Vivekananda preferred the decadent Indian caste system to class struggle, which he considered as a new and peculiar outcome of the materialistic civilization of the west. He regarded the original *chaturvarna* arrangement to be an ideal concept and, therefore, his criticism of caste did not negate this ideal.

In a conversation between Narayana Guru and Gandhiji during the time of the Vaikom Satyagraha in 1925, the latter asked the Guru whether it was not according to nature to have different castes among men. Gandhi cited the example of the leaves of the same tree not being identical in shape and texture. To this the Guru replied that such differences are only superficial, not essential; the juice of all the leaves of a particular tree will have the same essence.[82] Gandhiji believed that *varna dharma* as a system of division of labour was necessary to reduce the tensions of life because everybody would get an opportunity to work.[83] But the Guru believed that the standard of labour would go down because of the caste system. Everybody must get an opportunity to do labour according to his or her talent and liking. One is not intended to one category of labour because he/she happened to be born and brought up in a particular caste. Caste system destroys poor people.[84]

In religious matters too, Narayana Guru was more irreverent than Gandhiji. Gandhi was very perturbed on hearing of the *en masse* conversion of Ezhavas to Christianity and other religions, and sought the Guru's opinion on whether Hinduism was not sufficient for spiritual salvation. To this the Guru, who was essentially a man of religion like the Mahatma, a Hindu to the depths of his being, replied flippantly: 'There are means of salvation in other religions also.'[85] This shows that his concept of religion had nothing to do with dogma or ritual but was rooted in the Advaita philosophy,[86] which resembles modern secularism. Rejecting caste as a feature of a decadent society, Narayana Guru sought to create a socio-religious climate for reformulations of the self which could transcend existing customs and practices.

Questioning Rituals

Social practices and rituals prevalent in Kerala society, such as *thalikettu-kalyanam, thirandukuli* and *pulikudi*, were considered by Narayana Guru as impediments to timely change. His criticism of these customs was trenchant. He vehemently opposed them as having no social, moral or religious significance. Even so, these life-cycle rituals were celebrated with elaborate preparation and involved huge expenditures which impoverished many families.[87] Therefore, in 1904, the Guru summoned a meeting of Ezhavas at Paravoor to discuss the modalities for abolishing such customs.[88] He devised a new order of marriage rites which was simple, uniform, less expensive and involved more transparency so as to avoid impersonation, a common feature in Ezhava marriages of those days.[89] In a sense he was advocating against wasteful expenditure as a utilitarian. Apart from giving marriage a new symbolic significance, he advocated monogamy in the place of polyandry and polygamy.[90] As he saw that the society was under the influence of ostentation rather than necessity, the Guru sent two messages to the Ezhavas, in 1908 and 1911, in which he criticized the unnecessary expenditure incurred in the celebration of these customs.[91] At pilgrim centres, during the time of festivals, he organized lectures on varied subjects like religion, social customs, education, industry and morality.[92] Thus the purpose of the pilgrimage was modified with new aims to suit the demands of changing socio-economic realities.

Another important constraint in the path towards progress of society in general, and particularly of Ezhavas, was the habit of consuming liquor. Apart from economic impoverishment, its effect on health and the social stigma attached to consumption of liquor, the movement of the Guru could be viewed as an intervention in popular beliefs and practices linked to caste and occupation, based on *varna dharma*. He made a scathing attack against the manufacture, sale and consumption of liquor.[93] Comparing toddy-tapping to plague and leprosy, he said: 'Liquor is poison, it should not be manufactured, should not be given to others, or used by oneself. The tapper's body stinks, his clothes stink, and his house stinks, whatever he touches stinks.'[94] He considered the cutting of hair and shaving of beards as much more respectable jobs, and hence he sarcastically remarked that the knife used for tapping toddy should be split into four sharp knives so that they might be used in a barber shop.[95]

Self-Improvement

The source of all the ills that had beset Kerala society was traced by the Guru to the general ignorance of the people. So, dissemination of knowledge occupied a central point in his agenda of social reform. He said: 'Nowadays any caste can be uplifted by means of education. If we have any plan of improving the condition of the downtrodden masses we must educate our children.'[96] He realized that the spread of education was essential for better social mobility.[97] In 1910, he appealed (in his addresses) to the people to 'get enlightened by education'[98] as education, being a 'modern' affair, did not have any space for the injustices which were rampant in the society.

He understood that those who took advantage of educational opportunities controlled the avenues of improvement in the economic and bureaucratic spheres.[99] Therefore he proposed the spread of knowledge which had been limited to the upper strata of the society. In order to improve the overall conditions of his community, he advocated the education of girls;[100] he 'founded a special association for the education of women and girls and for the general improvement of their hard lot'.[101] As K.N. Panikkar stated: 'The struggle against the monopoly of knowledge has been crucial to the evolution of individualism and emancipation of the human mind from superstitions fostered by oppressive religious systems.'[102]

Narayana Guru's concept of education was quite different from that of contemporary intellectuals, who emphasized the vernacular as the only medium through which knowledge could be disseminated among the masses.[103] The Guru asked the people to give more importance to English education than Sanskrit learning.[104] It should be noted that he privileged English not as the best choice but as the second best option for social mobility – both vertical and horizontal. That is why he did not denigrate Sanskrit,[105] as he was certain about the potential of this language as a storehouse of knowledge.[106] His disciple, Nataraja Guru, wrote: 'To modern society and politics Sanskrit is a dead language, although its exactitude makes it ideal for the survival of the wisdom which still lives within it.'[107]

One of Narayana Guru's basic assumptions was that traditional and lit-erary education was inadequate to meet the needs of the time. He wanted libraries and literary associations to be started in every village for inculcating the reading habit and for getting acquainted with the new literature that was forthcoming. He reminded his followers to organize a library at the premises of every temple.[108] At the instance of the Guru, the SNDP Yogam started an Education Fund in 1905, with the objective of providing both technical and general education to the community.[109] He also encouraged professional and scientific education, and appealed to the rich to extend financial help to stu-dents to go abroad for higher studies.[110] He considered technical education as the most urgent need of the hour, and therefore advocated the establishment of technical and agricultural schools along with English, Malayalam and Sanskrit schools. He even stated that there should be a school and industrial training centre attached to every temple.[111]

In spite of his own affinity towards Vedic knowledge, the Guru recognized education in science as a compelling need of the time. His emphasis on scien-tific and technical education could have been the result of a growing realiza-tion that such education was crucial not only for the progress of the society, but also for developing a critical attitude towards obsolete conventions.[112] He encouraged English education as a means of social progress,[113] for its ability to ensure social status and to gain employment, and also because of its libera-tory potential for getting rid of time-worn Hindu customs.[114] In a speech in 1912 to the Vijnana Vardhini Sabha at Cherai, the Guru repeatedly stressed the importance of women's education and the need for imparting technical training in order to establish industries.[115]

In 1917, he advised his followers to stall the building of temples and to concentrate instead on setting up educational institutions, since schools were the real temples which would enlighten the masses.[116] He established residential schools attached to his temples and *ashram*s. As a result of his endeavours and the cooperation of the SNDP Yogam, Ezhavas in Kerala achieved enviable success in the field of education. While the male literacy rate of Ezhavas in 1875 was only 3.2 per cent, it increased to 36 per cent by 1931.[117]

All these instances demonstrate Narayana Guru's attempts to go beyond both 'tradition' and 'modernity'; and, by implication, his attitudinal differ-ence with respect to the recognition of that distinction itself. Moreover, his efforts reveal his sensitivity to the 'present' as what is desirable rather than what is to be retained. The needs of the present time were more important to him than what existed in the 'bygone days'. It is often said that the Guru's views on education are a replica of the missionary/European perception. But I would argue that the Guru did not look upon education in terms of such parameters; rather, his was a selective choice premised on what has to be or ought to be in the present and in the future.

Narayana Guru's philosophy of education included the following aspects: to correlate education with the day-to-day life of the common people; to do away with elitism in the field of education; to create confidence in human reason and individual liberty; to generate awareness of one's own rights and establish the tenets of civil liberty; to demand and procure a better share in employment; to eradicate superstition; and, finally, to enlighten the people, especially the deprived sections of society, to achieve intellectual emancipation from Brahmanical Hinduism and to facilitate a process of reform so that they did not have to feel that they were inferior. In short, the Guru visualized education as a liberating force.

One may be tempted, in this context, to draw parallels between Guru's perspective on education and Immanuel Kant's answer to the question 'what is Enlightenment?'. However, I would propose that Narayana Guru's approach to education or the attainment of knowledge was that it was a means to liberate lower-caste or marginalized communities from the yoke of upper-caste discriminatory practices. Whereas for Kant, the refinement of human reason was a means of salvation and emancipation from the yoke of ignorance.[118]

Against Wasteful Expenditure

Though Narayana Guru had a clear vision of the need for and the basis of a liberation movement, he did not formulate a coherent economic analysis for the movement he led. This could be because he understood that even though one could be economically and, at times, educationally at a higher position, the caste system could still discriminate against one. The best example in front of him was the case of Dr Palpu himself. Therefore, he paid much more attention to social mobility across the caste hierarchy, and his views on economic aspects evolved spontaneously during the course of his conversations with various people,[119] while addressing gatherings of poor Pulayas and other depressed sections of the society[120] and in the messages he issued to the SNDP Yogam.[121] He linked the economic backwardness of *avarnas* with their socio-religious backwardness based on caste. In Kerala, as elsewhere in India, caste and class were interconnected and inseparable. Those who were at the top of the caste hierarchy also occupied higher positions in the class structure. Narayana Guru therefore focused his attention on breaking the *varna* system by which a person's socio-economic status in society was determined on the basis of his birth, and thus predetermined and immutable, to the extent that personal talent or the interests pursued by a person could not alter this *status quo*. The vocation pursued by a person was predetermined by the *varna* into which he/she was born. The Guru questioned the restrictions imposed by the *varna* system of distributing people by occupational status.

In almost all the historical records, the Ezhavas as a community were stigmatized and defiled. Their traditional profession as toddy tappers and liquor traffickers was responsible for this inferior social status.[122] Narayana Guru advocated that the Ezhavas should give up this 'filthy' profession as well as the consumption of toddy in order to elevate their social status and for economic improvement. As mentioned earlier, he firmly believed that one's ability, interest and qualifications, and not caste, should be the basis on which one's occupation is decided. Further, doing the same work for long years would lead to monotony, causing a decline in the quality of the labour.[123] So, on the one hand he denounced choice of vocation on the basis of *varna*, and on the other, he encouraged industrial development[124] and English education for opening new vistas of more desirable types of employment. He exhorted the depressed classes to take up more lucrative vocations and also advised them to undertake various kinds of industrial training.[125] He encouraged small-scale industries to create job opportunities and started a weaving industry in his own ashram at Varkala.[126] This emphasis on the need to change traditional occupations was the result of a growing realization that the *varna* system was the greatest impediment to the economic progress of the *avarna*s. Advocating violation of *varna dharma* was intended to enlighten and awaken the backward communities against oppression and exploitation.

Though Narayana Guru never talked about colonial exploitation, he objected to the dumping of foreign manufactured goods in India and deplored the drain of wealth from India to Europe. Speaking at the Vijnana Vardhini Sabha, Cherai, in 1912, the Guru said: 'We send out to other countries our produce like copra, coconut husks, etc. and pay heavily to buy the consumer goods they manufacture out of them. We are forced to do this because we do not know the manufacturing process.'[127] He requested rich people to start indigenous industries to make use of locally available raw materials.[128] He also advised, 'If it is difficult for one man to meet all the initial expenses to start a factory, then a group of people should join together.'[129] Apart from the drainage of wealth, another aspect that might have influenced the Guru in this context was his support for *swadeshi*: for promoting indigenous industries and giving preference to Indian products over imported commodities.

Apart from setting up a weaving enterprise at his ashram in Varkala, which imparted training in spinning and weaving,[130] he decided to develop a centre for technical and vocational training on his sprawling campus, of about 150 acres of land that he received as a donation, at Sivagiri.[131] He sought the help of Earnest Kirk,[132] an Englishman and the first European disciple of the Guru, for this task. Kirk prepared a detailed plan for the 'Sivagiri Free Industrial and Agricultural Gurukulam',[133] which visualized imparting job-oriented professional education and training youngsters in cottage industries such as handicrafts, weaving, carpentry, dairy farming, metal works, farming, shorthand, typing and pottery.[134] Narayana Guru himself was one of the directors of the Malabar Economic Union, started in 1914.[135] This shows that as a reformer he did not confine himself to socio-religious aspects of the society alone; he tried his best to change the economic life of the people as well.

With the aim of disseminating new methods and modern technical know-how, under the guidance of the Guru, the SNDP Yogam held industrial exhibitions during its annual meetings – at Quilon in 1905[136] and at Cannanore in 1907 – which undertook comparative evaluation of products.[137] The Guru even used his temples as centres for educating pilgrims. While agreeing to the request of the people to convert Sivagiri into a pilgrim centre, he laid down specific aims and objectives. He told the people that they should not make this pilgrimage simply for merrymaking and wasting money, but use the opportunity to augment their knowledge and improve their day-to-day life by arranging lecture programmes by experts on developmental issues pertaining to agriculture, trade, industry and technology.[138] After imbibing new ideas from the experts, when the pilgrims returned home, they were encouraged to apply the newly acquired knowledge to practical use for their own socio-economic betterment.[139] Thus, the purpose of the pilgrimage was modified with new aims to suit the changing socio-economic conditions.

Unlike many other spiritual personalities, Narayana Guru could combine religious and secular practices with coherence and integrity. To him, the every-day life of the people could not be visualized without both. This was another unique feature of the Guru as the leader of a reform movement. 'Armed with his deep insight into the Advaita philosophy, he worked among the common men to raise them up in their personal social and political life. Thus he became instrumental in accelerating the much needed social change.'[140]

While struggling against the ideological influence of Hinduism based on the *varna* system, the Guru strove to formulate and implement an alternative based on industrial and technological development with the cooperation of the well-to-do sections of the society. The crusade against the *varna* system and the subsequent endeavours for improving the economic conditions of the deprived sections have to be understood, primarily, as an expression of developing communities with integrity. Indeed, Narayana Guru spearheaded such a movement without any schism between 'tradition' and 'modernity' with his spiritual aura.

In general, Narayana Guru's interventions in the secular sphere alongside those in the religious and social realms can be viewed without the aid of either the modernity or tradition paradigm, since he transcended their boundaries with grace and in his inimitable way. What he propagated was a selective amalgamation of both modernity and tradition, without considering the distinction between them. This he did as a corrective to the existing state of affairs and in order to lay a unique path towards the future.

Notes and References

1 *Kerala Mitram* (30 April 1881) wrote: 'the study of English language has conferred great many benefits upon the natives of Malabar, who, having read various English books, have now begun to discover defects and flaws in their own habits and proceedings and evince an inclination to improve and reform'. Quoted in *Madras Native News Paper Report*, May 1881. Also see the speech of N. Kumaran in the Travancore Legislative Council, *Proceedings of Travancore Legislative Council*, Vol. VI, No. 2, October 1925, p. 310, and *Report of the Malabar Tenancy Committee*, Vol. II, p. 316.

2 *Malayala Manorama*, 19 February 1898.

3 Rev. Samuel Mateer, *The Land of Charity*, John Snow, London, 1871, pp. 141–57; Rev. Samuel Mateer, *Native Life of Travancore*, W.H. Allen, London, 1883, pp. 396–413; Robin Jeffrey, *The Decline of Nayar Dominance: Society and Politics in Travancore 1847–1908*, Vikas Publishing House, 1976, p. 265; R.N. Yesudas, *A People's Revolt in Travancore: A Backward Class Movement for Social Freedom*, Kerala Historical Society, Trivandrum, 1977, p. 5; B.N. Nair, 'The Problematic of Kerala Society', *Journal of Kerala Studies*, Vol. IV, Part II, June 1977, p. 213; P.G. Edwin, 'British Impact in Kerala', *Journal of Kerala Studies*, Vol. V, Part II, June 1978, pp. 271–86; Lawrence Lopez, *A Social History of Modern Kerala*, Trivandrum, 1988, pp. 40–104; Dick Kooiman, *Conversion and Social Equality in Kerala: The London Missionary Society in South Travancore in the Nineteenth Century*, Manohar, Delhi, 1989, p. 200.

4 K.N. Panikkar, 'Breaking with the Past, Yet Looking Back to it', *The Telegraph*, 7 June 1985, p. 7; K.N. Panikkar, 'Socio-Religious Reforms', in Bipan Chandra *et al.* (eds), *India's Struggle for Independence, 1857–1947*, Viking, New Delhi, 1988, pp. 82–90.

5 Nataraja Guru, *The Word of the Guru: The Life and Teachings of the Guru Narayana*, Paico Publishing House, Ernakulam, 1968, pp. 241–66; first published in 1952. M.K. Sanoo writes, 'Advaita was Swami's declared character of faith. The influence of Raman Pillai should have been a deciding factor in Swami's progress to Advaita Philosophy.' See M.K. Sanoo, *Narayana Guru Swami* (biography), Vivekodayam Printing and Publishing, Irinjalakuda, 1976, p. 53. Also see P. Chandramohan, 'Popular Culture and Socio-Religious Reform: Narayana Guru and Ezhavas of Travancore', *Studies in History*, Vol. 3, No. 1, 1987, pp. 57–74.

6 Sree Narayana literature can be divided into two broad categories: works of and on Narayana Guru. Works on the Guru can again be divided into various categories, such as biographies, memoirs and reminiscences, studies, essays, expositions/commentaries, poetry/ songs, anthologies and souvenirs. All these together amount to about 250 works, of which 54 are biographies, 45 expositions and commentaries, 40 poetry/songs, 80 essays/studies, 15 anthologies and more than 20 are souvenirs. Besides these, there are hundreds of articles published in newspapers, weeklies and magazines. For a detailed account of Sree Narayana literature, see Vijayan Champadan, 'Sree Narayana Sahityam Malayalathil', *Mathrubhumi Varanthappathippu*, 16 September 1900, p. III.

7 There have been attempts by some sections to appropriate his legacy and to paint him as a champion of revived Hinduism. See P. Parameswaran, *Sree Narayana Guru Swamikal: Navothanathinte Pravachakan*, Jayabharath Publishers, Calicut, 1979; first edition 1971. Some have described him as a crusader of the Dalits in their movement for 'social justice'. See P.K. Gopalakrishnan, 'Sree Narayana Guru: Torch Bearer of Enlightenment for Revolutionary Changes', paper presented at a seminar on 'History of Political Development in Kerala', organized by Department of Political Science under the sponsorship of ICHR and University of Kerala at Trivandrum, 11 and 12 December 1985; M.S.A Rao, *Social Movements and Social Transformation: A Study of Two Backward Classes Movements in India*, Macmillan India, New Delhi, 1979, pp. 37–38. For others, he was a messiah of Ezhava liberation in Kerala. See the First Annual Report of the Secretary of the SNDP Yogam in *Vivekodayam*, 13 May 1904, pp. 15–19; Letter by P. Parameswaran to the Dewan of Travancore, 18 January 1903, *Travancore Government English Records*, Cover No. 8338, Kerala Secretariat Cellar (this document is now in the Kerala State Archives, Thiruvananthapuram). Also see

Stephen Fuchs, *Rebellious Prophets: A Study in Messianic Movements in Indian Religion*, Asia Publishing House, Bombay, 1965, pp. 270–71. According to Swami Dharma Theertha, Narayana Guru was a representative of 'Hindu Nationalism'; see Dharma Theertha, *The Menace of Hindu Imperialism*, Har Bhagwan, Lahore, 1946, pp. 264–76.

8 There is no unanimity of opinion among his biographers regarding his year of birth. For details of these different opinions, see P. Chandramohan, 'Social and Political Protest in Travancore', M.Phil. dissertation, Jawaharlal Nehru University, New Delhi, 1981, p. 91 fn 2.

9 P. Parameswaran, *Sree Narayana Guru Swamikal*, pp. 14–15; Kotookoikal Velayudhan, *Sree Narayana Guru: Jeevithacharitram*, Trivandrum, 1983, pp. 23–24, first edition 1975; M.K. Sanoo, *Narayana Guru Swami*, pp. 15–16; Vijayalayam Jayakumar, *Sree Narayana Guru: A Critical Study*, New Delhi, 1999, p. 44.

10 Kotookoikal Velayudhan, *Sree Narayana Guru*, p. 25.

11 M.K. Sanoo, *Narayana Guru Swami*, p. 44.

12 Kotookoikal Velayudhan, *Sree Narayana Guru*, p. 24; P. Parameswaran, *Sree Narayana Guru Swamikal*, p. 15.

13 N. Kumaran Asan's *Brahmasri Sree Narayana Guruswamiyude Jeevacharithra Samgraham*, the first biography of Narayana Guru, was serialized in *Vivekodayam* in 1915. The first chapter was published in *Vivekodayam*, April–May 1915 (Medam 1090 ME), Vol. XII, No. 1, pp. 416–18. In 1979 these *Vivekodayam* articles were compiled, edited and published in a booklet form as *Brahmasri Sri Narayana Guruvinte Jeevacharitra Samgraham* by the Kumaran Asan Memorial Committee, Thonakkal, and its second edition came out in 1984. See the 1984 edition, p. 88. See also M.K. Sanoo, *Narayana Guru Swami*; P. Parameswaran, *Sree Narayana Guru Swamikal*; K. Damodaran, *Shri Narayana Guru Swami Tripadangalude Jeevacharitram*, Quilon, 1929; Kotookoikal Velayudhan, *Sree Narayana Guru*, 1983; Vijayalayam Jayakumar, *Sree Narayana Guru*, p. 44.

14 M.K. Sanoo, *Narayana Guru Swami*, p. 37.

15 Kotookoikal Velayudhan, *Sree Narayana Guru*, p. 33

16 Kumaran Asan, in *Vivekodayam*, April–May 1915, Vol. XII, No. 1, pp. 417–18; Nataraja Guru, *The Word of the Guru: The Life and Teachings of the Guru Narayana*, Paico Publishing House, Ernakulam, 1968, pp. 256 and 387, first edition 1952.

17 Ibid., p. 256; M.K. Sanoo, *Narayana Guru Swami*, pp. 53–54.

18 Realizing this limitation, one of his biographers, M.K. Sanoo (ibid., pp. 35–36), bemoaned: 'It was unfortunate that even his admirers and disciples among his contemporaries did not take care of this aspect.' Even Kumaran Asan, the first biographer and most favourite disciple of the Guru, has given a sketchy account of his boyhood. See *Vivekodayam*, April–May 1915, Vol. XII, No. 1, pp. 416–18.

19 There is a controversy among his biographers about the period of his education under Kummampilli Raman Pillai. While K. Damodaran says that it was between 1877–79, Murkothu Kumaran thinks that it was between 1877 and 1881. For details, see Kotookoikal Velayudhan, *Sree Narayana Guru*, p. 48. According to M.K. Sanoo (*Narayana Guru Swami*, p. 72), he returned to his village in 1879 due to a serious stomach disorder.

20 M.K. Sanoo, *Narayana Guru Swami*, pp. 73 and 548; Kumaran Asan, *Vivekodayam*, April–May 1915, Vol. XII, No. 1, p. 418; P. Parameswaran, *Sree Narayana Guru Swamikal*, pp. 30–31; and Kotookoikal Velayudhan, *Sree Narayana Guru*, p. 49.

21 M.K. Sanoo, *Narayana Guru Swami*, p. 179; P. Parameswaran, *Sree Narayana Guru Swamikal*, pp. 36–37.

22 Nataraja Guru, *The Word of the Guru*, pp. 256–61; M.K. Sanoo, *Narayana Guru Swami*, pp. 77–94; Kotookoikal Velayudhan, *Sree Narayana Guru*, pp. 49–67; P. Parameswaran, *Sree Narayana Guru Swamikal*, pp. 30–52.

23 P.K. Balakrishnan, *Narayana Guru Samahara Grandham* (An Anthology), National Book Stall, Kottayam, 1969, p. 204, first edition 1954; Nataraja Guru, *The Word of the Guru*, pp. 258–60; M.K. Sanoo, *Narayana Guru Swami*, pp. 89–90.

24 *Shri Chattampi Swami Shatabda Smaraka Grantham*, 1953, pp. 14, 98–99 and 206–11.

[25] Thaikkattu Aiyyavu was a devotee of Lord Subramanian and well known for his knowledge of Vedanta, the Tamil spiritual tradition and the mysteries of yoga. See M.K. Sanoo, *Narayana Guru Swami*, p. 90; V.T. Samuel, *One Caste, One Religion, One God: A Study of Sree Narayana Guru*, Sterling Publishers, New Delhi, 1977, p. 46.

[26] P. Parameswaran, *Sree Narayana Guru Swamikal*, pp. 41–42; M.K. Sanoo, *Narayana Guru Swami*, p. 90.

[27] See T. Bhaskaran (ed.), *Sree Narayana Guruvinte Sampoorna Krithikal*, Mathrubhumi Press, Calicut, 1985, pp. 543–89.

[28] V.T. Samuel, *One Caste, One Religion, One God*, pp. 110–15.

[29] Nataraja Guru, *The Word of the Guru*, pp. 254–61.

[30] Nataraja Guru writes: 'Clean shaven, with no ornamental things about him, the Guru Narayana avoided even any stripes or colors in his clothing. He dressed in two seamless pieces of white cloth (in later years tinged orange at the request of his ochre-robed disciples of the Sanyasin tradition). He would sip clean pure water as if drinking a rich beverage, and extol simple foods like fruits or roots. Often he preferred to sleep on a cloth spread on stone for a couch under the clear starlight, with his own arms alone for a pillow; and likewise he preferred bathing in rivers and walking on foot; and he would eat any kind of food from the devoted hands that offered it in village homes as he moved among the people.' Ibid., p. 248.

[31] Ibid., p. 258.

[32] When Colonel Macaulay was the Resident of Travancore, Christian missionaries received considerable help from the colonial government. The London Missionary Society, the Church Missionary Society and the Danish Mission started their evangelical activities in Travancore at the beginning of the nineteenth century. By the last quarter of the century, the Salvation Army also started working in Travancore. See T.K. Velu Pillai, *The Travancore State Manual*, 4 vols, Government Press, Trivandrum, 1940, Vol. I, p. 727.

[33] For Muslim contacts, see Murkothu Kumaran, *Sree Narayana Guru Swamikalude Jeevacharitram*, second edition, P.K. Brothers, Calicut, 1971, pp. 410–12.

[34] Fuchs, *Rebellious Prophets*, p. 271; Swami John Dharmatheerthan, *The Prophet of Peace*, Sree Narayana Publishing House, Chempazhanti, Kerala, 1931, p. 91. After organizing inter-caste dining with the Pulayas on 27 May 1917, when Sahodharan Ayyappan sought the blessing of Narayana Guru for his endeavour to promote inter-caste marriages and inter-dining, for which he faced strong criticism and opposition, the advice of the Guru was: 'Don't feel dejected by opposition. This would grow into a great movement. Just bear in mind to be as forgiving as Christ.' Quoted in M. Prabha, 'Sahodharan Ayyappan', in M. Govindan (ed.), *Poetry and Renaissance: Kumaran Asan Birth Centenary Volume*, Sameeksha, Madras, p. 230. See also M.K. Sanoo, *Narayana Guru Swami*, p. 260.

[35] Durate Barbosa, *A Description of the Coast of Africa and Malabar in the Beginning of the Sixteenth Century*, translated and edited by Henry E.J. Stanler, London, 1866, p. 129; G.A. Ballard, Resident to the Chief Secretary to the Madras Government, dated 9 March 1870, *Madras Residency Records, Madras Political Proceedings*, 13 April 1870, G.O. No. 143, Natonal Archives of India.

[36] Max Weber, *The Sociology of Religion*, Methuen, London, 1965, p. 25.

[37] For their socio-religious practices, see L. Ananthakrishna Iyer, *The Cochin Tribes and Castes*, 2 vols, Higginbotham, Madras, Vol. I, 1909, p. 310, reprinted by Johnson Reprint Corporation, New York, 1969; Mateer, *Land of Charity*, p. 194; Day, *The Land of Perumals*, p. 320; Thurston, *Castes and Tribes of South India*, Vol. II, pp. 406–09; Nagam Aiya, *The Travancore State Manual*, 3 vols, Government Press, Trivandrum, 1906, Vol. II, p. 55; M.S.A Rao, *Social Movements and Social Transformation*, p. 4; *Census of Travancore, 1875*, Report, p. 162.

[38] M.K. Sanoo, *Narayana Guru Swami*, p. 228.

[39] Ibid., pp. 229–30; *Vivekodayam*, 15 July 1904, Vol. I, No. 2.; P. Chandramohan, 'Social and Political Protest in Travancore', pp. 178–80.

[40] *Vivekodayam*, 15 November 1905, Vol. I, No. 4, pp. 73–74; *Census of India, 1901*, Vol.

XXVI, Travancore, Part I, Report, p. 280; C. Kesavan, *Jeevitasamaram* (autobiography), 2 vols, N.B.S., Kottayam, 1968, Vol. I, pp. 126–28; P.K. Gopalakrishnan, 'Ezhavar', in Kerala History Association, *Kerala Charitam,* Vol. I, 1973, p. 985.

[41] Heimsath, 'The Function of Hindu Social Reformers', pp. 21–22.

[42] According to Charles H. Heimsath (ibid., p. 27), the reason for the failure of other reform movements in Kerala was lack of religious premises. Also see P.K. Balakrishnan, *Narayana Guru*, p. 108; M.K. Sanoo, *Narayana Guru Swami*, pp. 170, 175; and K.N. Panikkar, "Socio-Religious Reforms and the National Awakening', in Bipan Chandra *et al.* (eds), *India's Struggle for Independence, 1857–1947*, Viking, New Delhi, 1988, pp. 82–83.

[43] P. Chandramohan, 'Education and Social Consciousness in the Making of Modern Kerala', in Suresh Jnaneswaran (ed.), *Historiography: Structure and Practice, Festschrift in Honour of Dr T.K. Ravindran*, Thiruvananthapuram, 2010, pp. 176–87; P. Chandramohan, 'Social and Political Protest in Travancore', pp. 90 and 112.

[44] Nineteenth-century intellectuals like Ram Mohan Roy believed that polytheism and idolatry negated the development of individuality, and supernaturalism and the authority of religious leaders induced conformity born out of fear. See Ram Mohan Roy, *Tuhfat-ul-Muhawaddin*, in J.C. Ghose (ed.), *The English Works of Raja Ram Mohan Roy*, 3 vols, Panini Office, Allahabad, 1906, Vol. III, pp. 945–46.

[45] For nineteenth-century Indian attitudes towards idolatry, see K.N. Panikkar, 'Presidential Address', Section III, Indian History Congress, 36th Session, Aligarh, 1975, p. 20.

[46] One day a few people approached Narayana Guru with a request that he consecrate an idol in their newly built temple. Instead of installing an idol, the Guru proposed to hang a lamp in the sanctum sanctorum of the temple. But they insisted that he instal an idol and finally he agreed as he knew that they would not be satisfied with anything less than an '*aradhana moorthi*' (idol of worship). For this conversation between the Guru and the devotees, see P.K. Balakrishnan, *Narayana Guru*, p. 154.

[47] P. Chandramohan, 'Popular Culture and Socio-Religious Reform: Narayana Guru and Ezhavas of Travancore', *Studies in History*, Vol. 3, No. 1, p. 62.

[48] The actual translation of the words which Narayana Guru inscribed in Malayalam on the temple wall is:
'Without differences of caste
Nor enmities of creed,
All live like brothers at heart
Here is this ideal place.'
See Swami Dharmatheerthan, *The Prophet of Peace*, p. 33; Nataraja Guru, *The Word of the Guru*, p. 24.

[49] Narayana Guru, 'Jathinirnayam', stanza no. 2, in Narayana Guru, *Sree Narayana Guru Deva Krithikal*, Sree Narayana Dharma Sangam, Varkala, 1967, p. 154; M.K. Sanoo, *Narayana Guru Swami*, pp. 332–35.

[50] See his poem 'Athmopadesha Shathakam', stanza no. 44, in T. Bhaskaran (ed.), *Sree Narayana Guruvinte Sampoorna Krithikal*, Mathrubhumi Press, Calicut, 1985, p. 366.

[51] Narayana Guru, 'Athmopadesha Shathakam', ibid., p. 115. See also Pazhamballi Achyuthan, *Sree Narayana Guru (Smaranakal)*, Sarada Book Depot, Thonnakal, p. 123.

[52] M.K. Sanoo, *Narayana Guru Swami*, pp. 385–86.

[53] Narayana Prasad Muni, *Narayana Guru's Complete Works*, National Book Trust, New Delhi, 2006, p. xviii.

[54] In 1915 the Guru removed twenty-one deities from the Kottattu Arumukam Pillayar Koil and temples in nearby streets. See *Vivekodayam*, Vol. II, No. 10, January 1915, p. 354; Pazhampalli Achyuthan, 'Guruvinte Karmapadharthy', in *SNDP Yogam Platinum Jubilee Souvenir*, 1978, p. 57; P.K. Gopalakrishnan, 'Samudhaya Parishkarana Prasthanangal', in Kerala History Association, *Kerala Charitram*, Vol. I, p. 1208. Apart from removing evil spirits, Narayana Guru also took the initiative to clear the '*sarpakavu*' (snake park), with the intention of removing superstitions connected with snakes and also to avoid the expenses of *Sarpathullal* – a ceremony for the propitiation of snakes which generally lasted one week. See

M.K. Sanoo, *Narayana Guru Swami*, p. 228 and P.K. Balakrishnan, *Narayana Guru*, p. 155.

[55] P. Chandramohan, 'Social and Political Protest in Travancore', pp. 178–81.

[56] The Sarada Temple at Varkala is the best example of this. See M.K. Sanoo, *Narayana Guru Swami*, p. 121.

[57] P. Parámeswaran, *Sree Narayana Guru Swamikal*, p. 122; Kotookoikal Velayudhan, *Sree Narayan Guru Jeevithacharitram*, p. 319; M.K. Sanoo, *Narayana Guru Swami*, p. 550.

[58] Ibid.; Kotookoikal Velayudhan, *Sree Narayan Guru Jeevithacharitram*, pp. 96 and 319.

[59] Ibid., p. 97; P. Parameswaran Pillai, *Report on the Scheme for the Introduction of Basic Land Tax and Revision of Agricultural Income Tax*, Government Press, Trivandrum, 1946, p. 149; M.K. Sanoo, *Narayana Guru Swami*, p. 550.

[60] Nataraja Guru, *The Word of the Guru*, p. 258.

[61] P. Chandramohan, 'Social and Political Protest in Travancore', p. 172.

[62] Genevieve Lemercinier, *Religion and Ideology in Kerala*, New Delhi, 1984, pp. 248–52.

[63] *Vivekodayam*, Vol. XIV, Nos. 1–2, April–May 1917 (Medam–Edavam 1092 ME), pp. 57–65; Murkothu Kumaran, *Sree Narayana Guru Swamikalude Jeevacharitram*, p. 131; P. Parameswaran, *Sree Narayana Guru Swamikal*, p. 50; M.K. Sanoo, *Narayana Guru Swami*, p. 123.

[64] Even Ezhava leaders like Cherunelli Krishnan Vaidhyar and many others seriously doubted whether the Guru had the authority of scriptural sanction for consecrating an idol in a temple. See P. Parameswaran, *Sree Narayana Guru Swamikal*, pp. 57–58.

[65] P.K. Balakrishnan, 'Religion, Temple and God', in *Narayana Guru*, p. 154; see also M.K. Sanoo, *Narayana Guru Swami*, pp. 532–33.

[66] Gail Omvedt, 'Jotirao Phule and the Idea of Revolution in India', *Economic and Political Weekly*, Vol. 6, No. 37, 11 September 1971, pp. 1969–79.

[67] K.N. Panikkar has explained in detail the two dimensions of the cultural–ideological struggle in colonial India, in his First Damodaran Memorial Lecture, 'Rationalism, Humanism and Secularization', delivered at Trivandrum. This was reproduced in *Social Scientist* (Vol. 18, No. 4, April 1990, pp. 3–32) under the title 'Culture and Consciousness in Modern India: A Historical Perspective'. Also see K.N. Panikkar, 'Culture and Ideology', *Economic and Political Weekly*, Vol. XXII, No. 49, 5 December 1987), pp. 2115–20.

[68] For this message of 1917, see P.K. Balakrishnan, *Narayana Guru*, p. 76; P.K. Gopalakrishnan, *Keralathinte Samskarika Charitram (A Cultural History of Kerala)*, Kerala Basha Institute, Trivandrum, 1974, pp. 529–30.

[69] The Guru wrote, 'Of the human species even a Brahmin is born, as is the Pariah too. Where is difference there in caste as between man and man?' See 'Jati Mimamsa', in Narayana Guru, *Sree Narayana Guru Deva Krithikal*; Nataraja Guru, *The Word of the Guru*, pp. 283 and 287.

[70] See 'Jati Mimamsa', in Narayana Guru, *Sree Narayana Guru Deva Krithikal*.

[71] Swami Dharmatheerthan, *The Prophet of Peace*, p. 99.

[72] Pazhamballi Achyuthan, *Sree Narayana Guru (Smaranakal)*, p. 11; P. Parameswaran, *Sree Narayana Guru Swamikal*, pp. 107–08.

[73] *Vivekodayam*, June–August 1906, p. 5 and Vol. 5, No. 9, December–January 1908–09, p. 5; *Kerala Kaumudi*, 14 June 1923, p. 4. See also P.K. Balakrishnan, 'Kerala Navothanathinu Charithraparamaya Oru Mukavura', *Yoganadham*, Vol. 3, No. 7, October 1977, p. 32, and 'Oru Madhyasthan', in P.K. Balakrishnan, *Narayana Guru*, pp. 150–51.

[74] He told them: 'You must look upon the Pulayas and the like with love. The Ezhavas should behave towards their inferior in such a way that those who deem themselves superior to the Ezhavas should see and learn from it. This is a matter you should pay special attention to.' Quoted in P. Parameswaran, *Sree Narayana Guru Swamikal*, p. 108.

[75] A. Ayyappan, 'Iravas and Culture Change', *Madras Government Bulletin*, 1945, p. 156; *Kerala Kaumudi*, 2 June 1921, p. 2; M.K. Sanoo, *Narayana Guru Swami*, p. 261.

[76] K.N. Panikkar, 'Socio-Religious Reform and the National Awakening', in Bipan Chandra *et al.* (eds), *India's Struggle for Independence*, pp. 82–85.

[77] See the following works of Narayana Guru, 'Jatinirnayam' and 'Jatilakshanam', reproduced in T. Bhaskaran (ed.), *Sree Narayana Guruvinte Sampoorna Krithikal*, pp. 487–97.

[78] *Sree Narayana Guru Centenary Souvenir* (1954), p. 62.

[79] Narayana Guru, 'Jati Nirnayam', in T. Bhaskaran (ed.), *Sree Narayana Guruvinte Sampoorna Krithikal*, p. 488.

[80] Quoted in Swami John Dharmatheerthan, *The Prophet of Peace*, p. 149.

[81] *Complete Works of Swami Vivekananda* (1963), Vol. III, p. 205.

[82] M.K. Sanoo, *Narayana Guru Swami*, p. 441.

[83] See *Young India*, 24 November 1927 and 4 January 1931; *Harijan*, 3 March 1937; Daniel Thomas, *Sree Narayana Guru*, p. 26.

[84] *Sree Narayana Guru Centenary Souvenir* (1954), p. 62.

[85] For details of the conversation, see P.K. Balakrishnan, *Narayana Guru*, pp. 164–65; M.K. Sanoo, *Narayana Guru Swami*, pp. 438–41.

[86] Advaita (non-dualism) is a school of Vedanta philosophy that teaches the oneness of God, soul and universe; its chief exponent was Sankaracharya (AD 788–820). For details, see Bina Gupta, *An Introduction to Indian Philosophy: Perspectives on Reality, Knowledge and Freedom*, Routledge, New York, 2012, pp. 224–63.

[87] Daniel Thomas, *Sree Narayana Guru*, p. 31.

[88] On 16 October 1904 (31 Kanni 1080 ME), a meeting of Ezhavas was held at Paravoor near Quilon under the chairmanship of Narayana Guru, for reforming outdated social customs and practices prevalent among the Ezhava community. See *Vivekodayam*, Vol. I, No. 4, 15 November 1904. See also C. Kesavan, *Jeevithasamaram*, Vol. 1, pp. 134–38.

[89] *Vivekodayam*, Vol. I, No. 4, 15 November 1904; C. Kesavan, *Jeevithasamaram*, Vol. 1, pp. 135–36.

[90] *Vivekodayam*, 10 May 1909 (28 Medam 1084 ME).

[91] Ibid., pp. 1–2; *Vivekodayam*, November–December 1911 (Vrischikam–Dhanu 1086 ME).

[92] Narayana Guru, 'Sivagiri Theerthadanam', in P.K. Balakrishnan (ed.), *Narayana Guru*, pp. 146–49. See also M.K. Sanoo, *Narayana Guru Swami*, pp. 483–88.

[93] Swami John Dharmatheerthan, *The Prophet of Peace*, p. 47; Murkothu Kumaran, *Sree Narayana Guru Swamikalude Jeevacharitram*, p. 470.

[94] Ibid.

[95] Ibid.

[96] Ibid., p. 302.

[97] A speech by Narayana Guru at a meeting of Pulayas at Muttathara in 1920. See *Vivekodayam*, August–September 1920 (Chingam 1096 ME); also P.K. Balakrishan, *Narayana Guru*, p. 152.

[98] Ibid., p. 73; M. Prabha, 'Sahodharan Ayyappan', in M. Govindan (ed.), *Poetry and Renaissance*, p. 228.

[99] See the speech by Narayana Guru in 1912 at Vijnana Vardhini Sabha, Cherayi, reproduced in M.K. Sanoo, *Narayana Guru Swami*, p. 251.

[100] Murkothu Kumaran, *Sree Narayana Guru Swamikalude Jeevacharitram*, p. 302; Daniel Thomas, *Sree Narayana Guru*, p. 36.

[101] Fuchs, *Rebellious Prophets*, p. 272.

[102] K.N. Panikkar (1981), p. 36.

[103] See K.N. Panikkar, 'Social and Cultural Trends in Eighteenth Century India: An Overview', in *Eighteenth Century India (Essays in honour of Prof. A.P. Ibrahim Kunju)*, Trivandrum, 1979, p. 11.

[104] In a reply to a citation of the Vijnana Vardhini Sabha, Cherayi in 1912, the Guru said, 'as presently English is the more popular language, we need to pay more attention to it'. Quoted in M.K. Sanoo, *Narayana Guru Swami*, p. 251.

[105] The Guru even started a Sanskrit school at Aruvippuram, which was later shifted to Trivandrum. See *Vivekodayam*, Vol. I, No. 5, 11 February 1905 (30 Makaram 1080 ME), p. 94.

[106] According to Nataraja Guru, 'Of all the channels through which ancient thought reached

the masses of India, the foundation source was the Sanskrit language. Nataraja Guru, *The Word of the Guru*, p. 44.

[107] Ibid., p. 188.

[108] Daniel Thomas, *Sree Narayana Guru*, pp. 36–37.

[109] *Vivekodayam*, Vol. 3, Nos. 2–3, June–August 1906 (Mithunam–Karkkadakam 1081 ME), p. 9.

[110] Daniel Thomas, *Sree Narayana Guru*, p. 36.

[111] C.P. Sivadasan, 'Sree Narayana Guru', in M. Govindan (ed.), *Poetry and Renaissance*, p. 211.

[112] K.N. Panikkar, 'Presidential Address', p. 8.

[113] Daniel Thomas, *Sree Narayana Guru*, p. 36.

[114] M.S.A. Rao, *Social Movements and Social Transformation*, p. 41.

[115] P.K. Balakrishnan, *Narayana Guru*, pp. 73–74; M.K. Sanoo, *Narayana Guru Swami*, pp. 251–52.

[116] See the message of the Guru in 1917 in ibid., p. 253.

[117] *Census of Travancore*, 1875, Report, p. 246; *Census of India, 1931*, Vol. XXVIII, Travancore, Part I, Report, pp. 310–11. In 1914, the number of Ezhava students in Travancore was 23,893; it increased to 51,114 in 1918, that is, a 114 per cent increase in four years. Also see *Mitavadi*, March 1919, p. 109; P.K. Gopalakrishnan, *Keralathinte Samskarika Charitram*, pp. 509–10.

[118] According to Immanuel Kant, enlightenment is a human being's emergence from his self-incurred minority. Minority is the inability to make use of one's own understanding without direction from another. This minority is self-incurred when its cause lies not in lack of understanding, but in lack of resolution and courage to use it without direction from another. Thus 'dare to be wise' (*sapere aude*) is the motto of enlightenment. See Kant's essay, 'An Answer to the Question', written in 1784 and reproduced in Mary J. Gregor (trans. and ed.), *Immanuel Kant: Practical Philosophy*, Cambridge University Press, 1996.

[119] A conversation that occurred in 1928 (1103 ME) between Narayana Guru and T.K. Kittan, writer at Nagambadam Sivakshetram (Kottayam), reproduced in P.K. Balakrishnan, *Narayana Guru*, pp. 146–49.

[120] His reply to the citation of Vijnana Vardhini Sabha, Cherayi in 1912, reproduced in M.K. Sanoo, *Narayana Guru Swami*, p. 251. See also his Presidential Address at a Pulaya conference held at Muttathara near Trivandrum in September 1920, *Vivekodayam*, August–September 1920 (Chingam 1096 ME); P.K. Balakrishnan, *Narayana Guru*, p. 152.

[121] See the messages of the Guru to the SNDP Yogam in 1905, 1908, 1911, 1917, etc., in back volumes of *Vivekodayam*, *Kerala Kaumudi*, *Deshabhimani* and *Sahodharan*.

[122] A. Ayyappan, *Social Revolution in a Kerala Village*, p. 154.

[123] Narayana Guru believed that 'The standard of labour will go down because of the caste system. Everybody should get an opportunity to do labour according to his or her talent. One is not intended to do only one category of labour because he happens to be born and brought up in a particular caste.' Quoted in *Sree Narayana Guru Centenary Souvenir* (1954), p. 62.

[124] Murkothu Kumaran, *Sree Narayana Guru Swamikalude Jeevacharitram*, p. 303.

[125] Ibid.

[126] C. Kesavan, *Jeevitasamaram*, Vol. 1, pp. 330–31; *Kerala Kaumudi*, 22 June 1922, p. 4.

[127] Quoted in Murkothu Kumaran, *Sree Narayana Guru Swamikalude Jeevacharitram*, p. 303. See also P.K. Balakrishnan, *Narayana Guru*, pp. 73–74; M.K. Sanoo, *Narayana Guru Swami*, pp. 251–52.

[128] C.P. Sivadasan, 'Sree Narayana Guru', in M. Govindan (ed.), *Poetry and Renaissance*, pp. 212–13.

[129] Daniel Thomas, *Sree Narayana Guru*, p. 37; Murkothu Kumaran, *Sree Narayana Guru Swamikalude Jeevacharitram*, p. 303; P.K. Balakrishnan, *Narayana Guru*, pp. 75–76; M.K. Sanoo, *Narayana Guru Swami*, pp. 251–52.

[130] Daniel Thomas (1965), p. 37.

[131] *Kerala Kaumudi Sree Narayana Guru Special: Sivagiri Theerthadanam (Pilgrimage)*, 1994, p. 54.

[132] Earnest Kirk came to India as a member of the Theosophical Society and was later attracted to the work of Narayana Guru. He was the twenty-first member of the Sree Narayana Dharma Sangham. For details, see *Kala Kaumudi*, 1 January 1884, pp. 15 and 40; *Kerala Kaumudi Sree Narayana Guru Special: Sivagiri Theerthadanam (Pilgrimage)*, 1994, p. 54.

[133] Ibid.

[134] Ibid.

[135] *Private Papers of Dr Palpu*, File No. 19, Nehru Memorial Museum and Library, New Delhi.

[136] *Malayala Manorama*, 21 January 1905.

[137] *Vivekodayam*, Vol. 6, Nos. 1–2, April–June 1909 (Medam–Edavam 1084 ME), p. 21.

[138] P.K. Balakrishnan, 'Sivagiri Pilgrimage', in *Narayana Guru*, pp. 147–49.

[139] Ibid.

[140] C.P. Sivadasan, 'Sree Narayana Guru', in M. Govindan (ed.), *Poetry and Renaissance*, p. 209.

4

Influence of the Yogam in Non-Religious Domains

The formation of the SNDP Yogam, as discussed earlier, was the result of a combined attempt by Sree Narayana Guru and the newly emerging middle class among the Ezhava community. In this chapter, the internal organization of the Yogam is examined in detail. Its efforts at social and economic advancement with particular reference to the struggle against relative deprivation in the fields of education and employment in government service, and its activities for industrial advancement are also discussed.

The origin of the Yogam may be traced back to Narayana Guru's consecration at Aruvippuram and his founding of an Ashram there in 1888. In 1899, this Ashram was renamed as the Aruvippuram Temple Association; it consisted of twenty-four members,[1] with Kumaran Asan as the founding secretary. Streamlining of the temple, the *madam* and its properties, performance of daily rituals (puja) and celebration of annual festivals were the administrative reasons behind the formation of this Association.[2] In other words, in the beginning this Association was not primarily a secular body or meant for social action; it was more of a religious organization. It was this Association that later transformed itself into the SNDP Yogam, in January 1903.

Dr Palpu and the educated middle class of the Ezhava community were not satisfied with the limited activities of the Aruvippuram Temple Association. It was not that they were against the daily pujas and the annual festivals of the temple, but they felt this was not adequate to fulfil their objectives. Hence they took the initiative to expand its field of activities and to alter its name in order to encapsulate the newly included intentions.[3] In December 1902 (23 Dhanu 1078 ME), the ten life members[4] of the Association – members rich enough to pay Rs 100 as the membership fee – met at Kamalalayam Bungalow in Trivandrum, presumably at the invitation of Kumaran Asan.[5] At this meeting they unanimously decided to register the Temple Association as a joint stock company under the name of the SNDP Yogam.[6] In January 1903, an application for registration/license was drafted by Pettayil Parameswaran, younger brother of Palpu, and submitted to the government. The government granted the license.[7] What needs to be underscored here is that within a short span of four years the Ashram was converted first into a Yogam and then into a joint stock company. One of the inferences that can be drawn from such a metamorphosis is that there was an overwhelming presence of the newly emerging middle class among the Ezhava community at the helm of affairs and in the undermining of the original intent behind the formation of the Ashram. An inevitable question that surfaces is, how was it possible for an ashram to become a joint stock company?

The Yogam as a Joint Stock Company

The objective of the Yogam was the material and moral advancement of the Ezhavas, Chovans and Thiyyas of Travancore, Cochin and British Malabar,[8] in addition, 'to promote and encourage religious and secular education and to inculcate industrious habits among the members of the community'.[9] Though the Yogam was organized around the Ashram and its proclaimed goal was to propagate the Sanatana philosophy of Sree Narayana Guru, a perusal of its Memorandum of Association, Articles of Association and by-laws show that the Yogam was largely commercial in character rather than an organization meant to spread the philosophy of the Guru, or to take an initiative in the social and religious reform movements of Kerala.[10] The membership fee was prohibitively high, and the rules and regulations regarding collection of membership fees for the purpose of building up the assets of the Yogam were stringent and commercial.[11]

The following examples will substantiate this argument. According to the 1903 Articles of Association of the Yogam, not more than one-fourth of the amount collected every year was to be used for that year's expenses. This indicates that ideas of 'prudence' and 'saving for future investment' were the motive force behind such a conditionality. Further, three-fourths of the amount collected was to be loaned out on interest in order to accumulate capital. In other words, it was to act as a bank lending credit for profit-making. Such a rule is clearly consistent with the commercial intentions of a company or business firm. The money spent on works, mentioned in category number 3 of the Memorandum of Association of the Yogam, was not to exceed the income derived from interest in a year.[12] This again shows that the priority of the Yogam, its long-run political–economic strategy, was to accumulate capital assets, rather than to spend its revenues on social uplift. 'Accumulate and accumulate' became the primary motto of the Yogam. Sections 'C' and 'B' of the Articles of Association stipulate that in case a member fails to remit his annual membership once, he may pay the amount the next time with an interest added of 10 per cent. But if any member discontinued payment for more than a year, he was liable to pay the entire amount in a single instalment.[13]

We can infer the initial character of the Yogam/company from these examples. First, ordinary people did not earn sufficient income to become members as the amount to be paid was exorbitant. Second, even if one was able to raise the initial amount, the rules of payment were not at all member-friendly; this was particularly so when we consider the economic status of the majority of the Ezhava population. The rules and regulations regarding membership mirrored the business ethics of corporate structures.

Organizational Structure of the Yogam

The organizational structure of the Yogam was pyramidically hierarchical, with the president at the apex, and the vice-president, secretary, treasurer, board of directors and council members distributed between the apex and the middle level. The domain of the unions was confined to the taluks. Branch offices operated at the village level. At the very bottom of the structure came the community members, whom the Yogam was supposed to represent.

It was unanimously decided to make Sree Narayana Guru, the spiritual leader of the community, the permanent president of the Yogam which was named after him.[14] This was done so that the Yogam could gain legitimacy from his spiritual aura. It was assumed that the Yogam would function according to the direction and wishes of the Guru. However, though the Guru had all the powers and freedom to function in every sphere of the Yogam, he was neither to mortgage his power nor misuse his privileged position in ways that may turn out to be against the objectives of the Yogam.[15]

The vice-president of the Yogam was an annually elected member.[16] His duty was to assist the president in his supervision of the activities of the Yogam.[17] Next in the hierarchy was the secretary, who was the most important in terms of executive powers. His duties included conducting meetings, maintaining the records of the Yogam and distributing certificates to new members with the permission of the president.[18] On the recommendation of Narayana Guru and Palpu, Kumaran Asan was elected as the first secretary of the Yogam,[19] and he continued in this capacity for twelve years without a break.[20] Then, after a gap of a year,[21] he once again occupied the position for another four years.[22] The treasurer maintained the accounts and looked after the finances of the Yogam.

Apart from these office bearers, there were directors. Anyone holding more than twenty shares became a life director,[23] and thus there was no upper limit on the number of directors.[24] In addition to the life directors, every year, according to the total number of shares, the Yogam elected one director from every hundred shareholders.[25] We can observe in the structure of the organization of the Yogam the criticality of 'shares'. Just like any business firm, it was the number of shares one held that decided the relative power exercised by members in the Yogam.

The board of directors of the Yogam consisted of the president, the vice-president, the secretary and a group of elected directors.[26] This was primarily an implementing body, constituted to carry out decisions taken in public meetings.[27] Below the board of directors there was a Yogam council, which comprised of the president, the secretary and two nominated members from the board of directors; internal administration was managed by this council.

In order to spread the activities of the Yogam among the people, unions were established at the taluk level and branch offices at the village level. The taluk unions were administered by a committee consisting of one elected member from each branch office. The branch offices generally worked under an agent who carried out all correspondence with the upper bodies of the Yogam.[28]

The Yogam celebrated its first anniversary on *Shivaratri*, believed to be the birthday of Lord Shiva, in January 1904 (30 Makaram and 1 Kumbam, 1079 ME).[29] The first annual meeting of the Yogam and the composition of its participants reveal the extent of influence that the rich and educated people had over the Yogam. Mattancheri Govindan Vaidhyar, the first Ezhava law graduate in Travancore, presided over the first day of the meeting;[30] the president of the second day's meeting was Chavarkkattu Kochu Cherukkan Vaidhyar, another rich Ezhava from Travancore.[31] On the first day, Palpu delivered a speech which emphasized the importance of education and industry/entrepreneurship for the development of the Ezhava community.[32] We know from different sources that in Kerala, and particularly in Travancore and Cochin, 'development' was a notion that influenced the dominant ideology, which was first propagated by the state. It seems that although there were other conflicts between the Ezhava middle class and the state, there were no disputes between them regarding the worth of this ideology. Within this ideology, English education and industriousness were taken as the surest means to achieve development and progress. An ideology that valued and was based on education and industry brought them together irrespective of disagreements on several other matters.

From the first annual meeting onwards, as a part of the movement aimed at the emancipation of women, the Yogam organized a women's conference.[33] The first women's conference was presided over by Palpu's mother,[34] and it became a regular feature of the Yogam's annual meetings.[35] It created a platform for the redressal of the grievances of Ezhava women, and the organization worked for their social and educational advancement.[36]

At the very first meeting the Yogam took a decision to publish a journal once in two months and called it *Vivekodayam*, with M. Govindan as editor.[37] This decision was influenced by the expectation that the journal would spread the message of the Yogam among the reading public, who could in turn become the torch-bearers among the uneducated masses. Its name was suggested by none other than Narayana Guru,[38] but Palpu referred to it as the

'Ezhava Gazette'.[39] This re-naming reveals the predominance of a bureaucratic attitude and the enforcing power of the leadership of the Yogam.

After a year of service by the first editor, the secretary of the Yogam, Kumaran Asan, took over the editorship of *Vivekodayam*;[40] in 1908, it was converted into a monthly.[41] *Vivekodayam* was in the forefront of the state's literary activities under the leadership and guidance of Kumaran Asan. Most of Asan's writings were first published in it, as also the works of Sree Narayana Guru, especially *Atmopadesa Satakam*.[42] Members of the Yogam like C.V. Kunjuraman, Moolur Padmanabha Panikkar and Murkoth Kumaran were the other literary figures who made contributions to the journal. Besides the publication of literary works, an important aim of this journal was to bring to light the grievances of the community before the Travancore administration, and to articulate their demand for just rights. In addition, the journal focused attention on the frivolous customs and practices followed by the community, and initiated a critique of these.[43] *Vivekodayam* did a lot for the social reform movement, particularly the campaign against the caste system. The journal had two functions: (i) interpretation of Acts issued by the government to the public; and (ii) exposition of the grievances of the backward communities for the benefit of the authorities.[44] Thus the journal mediated between the government and the public; it carried the message of the government to members of the community and articulated their problems in relation to the government. It worked as a mouthpiece of the Yogam and the Ezhava community in general.

Expansion of the Yogam

In the early stages of the Yogam, its main activities revolved around the leading pioneers, such as Sree Narayana Guru, Palpu and Kumaran Asan. The spiritual attributes of the Guru, the enthusiastic activities and generous financial support of Palpu, and the consistent tours, powerful writings and fiery speeches of Kumaran Asan together contributed substantially in laying a strong foundation for the development of the Yogam into a powerful organization of the Ezhavas or Thiyyas of Kerala. Though the influence of these three to a great extent helped the development of the Yogam, its appeal to the unlettered Ezhava masses remained limited. Besides, it did not succeed in bringing all of the Ezhava middle class to its fold. Though the Yogam attracted the attention of a large section of the Ezhava middle class spread across all over India, its membership was confined to the Travancore middle class.

Despite the fact that the Ezhavas were the largest single community in Kerala, comprising 20 per cent of the total population,[45] the number of Ezhava members of the Yogam was only 90[46] in 1903. We may pose a question at this juncture. Why was it that the Yogam could not attract larger numbers of ordinary Ezhavas during its early days? We can ascribe two reasons for this limited role of the Yogam.

The first and foremost was the high rate of membership fee, which only the well-to-do could afford to pay. At the commencement of the Yogam, the face value of its membership was Rs 100, with quarter, half and one-third shares of Rs 25, Rs 50 and Rs 75, respectively, being optional.[47] In the very next year, the Yogam introduced a new system by which no shareholder could possess less than one share, and the share value of Rs 100 was reduced to Rs 25.[48] This was one of the ways in which it tried to extend the limits of its reach.

The Yogam classified its members in terms of the number of shares they held, and they were given different names on that basis. Those possessing up to three shares were called *sahayikal*, those with four to twenty shares were called *samajikanmar*, and those who had more than twenty shares were *pradhanikal*.[49] This classification of shareholders reveals the internal differentiation that existed within the Yogam. Further, from the names given to each stratum, one can infer that they were hierarchized from within. This internal stratification was typical of the way business firms dealt with their shareholders. It also mirrored the social stratification that existed in the society of those days, although the Yogam claimed to be opposed to such hierarchies. At the beginning, *sahayikal* did not have voting rights;[50] but in 1909 the voting system was changed and each shareholder became entitled to a vote. Yet, the number of votes that one could cast changed according to the number of shares, though the maximum limit was fixed at six.[51] In other words, under no circumstances was any member entitled to cast more than six votes even if he held more than twenty shares.[52] This change, along with the reduction of the face-value of shares, showed a shift in the Yogam's perspectives and policies, and was another instance of the Yogam's attempt at extension.

The *samajikanmar* and *pradhanikal* were entitled to very many rights and privileges; without their consent the Yogam proceedings could not take place. The *pradhanikal* had an additional right, to check all the documents of the Yogam and its affiliated bodies.[53] Once again, we can affirm that such internal organization of the governance of the Yogam tended to confine the controlling authority in a few hands, particularly those who belonged to the upper strata of the middle class. Localization of power was imminent in the organizational pattern of the Yogam. What mattered was the purchasing power of the shares; this in turn privileged those with maximum shares as they were endowed with a greater say in the functioning and decisions of the Yogam.

The reduction of the membership fee from Rs 100 to Rs 25 was welcomed by many; but it was still beyond the reach of the majority of the community who were poorly paid agricultural labourers and landless peasants. To pay Rs 25 was impossible for most of them for they earned only 25 *naya paise* per day as their wage. Though the membership fee could be paid in instalments,[54] even that was beyond their capacity. One had to spend individual earnings of nearly four months in order to get membership of an organization that was deemed to have been constituted for one's own emancipation. Thus, although the proclaimed objective of the Yogam was to reach the poorest of the poor and the marginalized sections, it was they who were most distanced from the Yogam, and relegated to the bottom level as spectators and receivers of the Yogam's mercy.

Those who joined the Yogam during the first two decades of its functioning were either rich landlords or upper middle-class people. In January 1904, when the Yogam met at Trivandrum, of the 60 people who attended, 16 were wealthy Ayurvedic doctors.[55] The Yogam failed to capture the minds of the Ezhava masses, and failed also to convince them that it was a representative body of the Ezhavas. Although the Yogam tried to extend its domain to include a larger number of people from the community, there were shortcomings built into the structure of the Yogam which replicated the hierarchical system of the prevalent society.

Although the share money was prohibitive, many members of the community were 'forced' to join the Yogam. They became members not voluntarily, but because of the incessant pressure and insistent persuasion exerted on them by the organizers.[56] As a result, very often, the poorer members failed to deposit their fees in time and ended up paying a large amount of arrears with interest. Table 17 shows the arrears that accrued to poor members of the Yogam in 1912 and 1913. The table shows that in 1912, while 1,037 members deposited Rs 12,530 for 1,661 shares, the balance to be remitted was Rs 30,010; and in 1913, while 1,201 members deposited Rs 14,987 for 1,201 shares, the balance to be deposited was Rs 32,467. This reveals beyond doubt that the membership fee was beyond the capacity of agricultural labourers and other poor Ezhavas who were workers, who constituted about 75 per cent of the total population of the community.[57]

For the purpose of collection of outstanding dues from its members, the Yogam would approach the court. In 1916, the Yogam took court action against 416 Ezhavas for failing to deposit their instalments, and sealed their houses and held up their properties.[58] The inference that one can draw from such coercive action is that the attempts of the Yogam to bring more and

TABLE 17

Balance of share money to be deposited by members for the years 1912 and 1913[59]

Year	Total no. of members	No. of shares	Amount deposited			Balance to be deposited		
			Rs	Anna	Np.	Rs	Anna	Np.
1912	1037	1661	12,530	4	6	30,010	3	6
1913	1201	1851	14,987	0	8	32,467	7	4

more members into its fold were based on its drawing on the assistance of the juridico-political machinery of the state. The mechanics of extension of the Yogam in such instances were legalistic and coercive.

Resorting to the courts was tantamount to resorting to the state for its intervention in the management of the Yogam, in order to discipline its members. This was a paradoxical situation as the Yogam had been formed, in the first instance, to fight against the discrimination of the state against the Ezhavas as a community and the middle class within it in particular. It was this very middle class that relied on the state's judiciary. In other words, the Yogam had internalized the state which was already hierarchical in its structure and hierarchizing in its deeds. As a consequence of such strict modes of collecting membership fees, resembling the collection of taxes by the state, instead of gaining the cooperation of the Ezhavas in its attempts at extension, about 6,000 people became bitter enemies of the Yogam.[60]

In the beginning of the twentieth century, though the number of educated people among Ezhavas was very few and the number of people who had received English education more or less negligible,[61] the presidential addresses and most of the speeches at the annual meetings of the Yogam were in English.[62] It is obvious from this that the Yogam was more a platform of the educated middle class, for whom mass support remained important only in order to lend legitimacy to their claims and self-proclaimed promises. In short, though the Ezhava middle class led the movement in the name of the whole community, they tried to define its objectives primarily to suit their own (middle-class) self-interest.

The ambivalence between class interest and caste interest was of advantage to the new middle class.[63] This naturally led the poorer sections among the Ezhavas to view the Yogam as an organization of the rich and the educated, and to keep aloof from its activities. Acccording to C.V. Kunjuraman: 'Till the time of 1927, the social activities of the Yogam and society's political, social and religious changes affected the upper class civilized people of the society as the wave of the shallow water and it could not touch the bottom of the society.'[64] Though critical in tone, this statement resonates with the hierarchical notion of sociality that existed at that time.

Although many poor Ezhavas raised their voice against and showed apathy towards the activities of Yogam, not all of them disengaged themselves. Some joined the Yogam and cooperated with its activities due to their respect for Sree Narayana Guru and not because they felt the Yogam was their own organization.[65] This was not necessarily because of their understanding of the Guru's Sanatana philosophy or his social reform activities. They were captivated by his charisma and believed in his superhuman powers, such as healing of incurable diseases with simple methods, controlling evil spirits like Kuttichathan, Brahma Rakshasu, etc., and his ability to make women fertile by giving a banana or a bunch of grapes to couples longing to have children.[66] To exploit the weakness of such people among the poor, the Yogam published articles describing various 'miracles' of Narayana Guru in its magazine, *Vivekodayam*.[67] Apart from this, his disciples exaggerated the Guru's abilities and propagated the idea that the 'Swami' could perform miracles among the people,[68] thus elevating him to an incarnation of God.[69] It was these miracles and his alleged 'superhuman' powers that attracted several poor, illiterate and ignorant Ezhavas to him and to the Yogam. In short, while actions to extend the scope of the Yogam appealed to some sections of Ezhavas because of their devotion to the Guru, other sections of the community were opposed to these activities. This reveals the crack that developed between the Guru and Yogam.

The Yogam's inability to rope in the Ezhavas and Thiyyas of Cochin and Malabar was the second factor which prevented its extension across socio-spatial boundaries. As stated earlier, the activities of the Yogam were mainly confined to the Travancore region and were mostly concerned with the problems of the Ezhavas of Travancore. When a few rich Ezhava leaders of the Yogam met in Trivandrum at the invitation of Kumaran Asan in December 1902, six out of the ten shareholders who attended were from an area within 20 miles of Trivandrum, while the remaining four were from Quilon.[70] This goes to show that not even all of the Travancore community was represented. The Ezhavas of British Malabar and Cochin did not take as much interest in the activities of the Yogam as the Ezhavas of Travancore. Although Karattuparambil S. Krishnan was one of the directors of the Yogam at its first meeting,[71] and Ayyakkutty and Sahodharan Ayyappan were very close to the Yogam, till the time of the conversion of the Ezhava Sabha of Cochin (formed in 1915) into the Cochin SNDP Yogam in 1938 (1113 ME)[72], it did not have any presence in Cochin. This reveals the exclusive nature of the Yogam in the first few decades of its inception.

It was at its third annual meeting, which was held in December 1905 in Quilon, that the Malabar Thiyyas participated in the activities of the Yogam for the first time.[73] Their delayed participation was mainly because they had comparatively fewer grievances. Though the position of the Thiyyas of Malabar, and of the Ezhavas of Cochin and Travancore was the same in the caste structure, there were considerable differences in their socio-political position. The Thiyyas of Malabar received a better deal from the colonial rulers than the Ezhavas of Travancore and Cochin. While the Ezhavas of Travancore were struggling for government jobs which fetched them a salary Rs 5 per month and for permission to send their children to schools, the Thiyyas of Malabar held several important posts in the government.[74]

Another factor which kept the Thiyyas of Malabar away from the Yogam was the influence of the nationalist and communist movements. With the formation of the Malabar District Congress Committee in 1908, the nationalist movement spread all across Malabar. Though the leaders of this movement were caste Hindus, their sympathetic attitude towards *avarna*s and the activities of the Home Rule movement under Annie Besant against untouchability[75] convinced the untouchables that the nationalists were not against social development and emancipation. By the end of the 1930s, the communist movement also began to gain roots in Malabar, and it organized the backward castes as if on class lines. All these factors considerably restricted the Thiyyas of Malabar from becoming members of the Yogam. Though the Yogam emerged as a well-knit organization towards the end of the 1920s, and its membership rose to 63,674 by 1929,[76] it had only 121 members from Malabar.[77] A number of organizations like the Thiyya Mahajana Sabha, Ezhava Maha Sabha and Sree Narayana Samajam were formed in Malabar, and actively functioned for a short duration.[78] Yet the spread of nationalism, influence of communism, and class consciousness rather than caste feelings among the *avarna*s, especially Thiyyas, prevented caste organizations from taking deep root in the Malabar soil.

The restrictive practice in membership allocation to only Ezhavas and Thiyyas or Chovans was the third important reason which restrained the Yogam's attempts at extending the size of its membership.[79] Though the Yogam projected itself as an institution to propagate the Sanatana philosophy of Sree Narayana Guru, till 1920 its membership was strictly prohibited to people of other communities.[80] In May 1920, at the seventeenth annual meeting of the Yogam, it was decided to throw open its membership to all genuine sympathizers irrespective of social, caste and religious differences.[81] But this decision remained on paper till T.K. Madhavan, a prominent Congress leader, was elected as the organizing secretary of the Yogam in 1927.

Members of the Ezhava middle class who had been controlling the Yogam realized that the cooperation and support of non-Ezhava masses were crucial in their crusade against the existing social stratification and discrimination, and in the redressal of their socio-economic and political grievances. This was another step towards the extension of their practice. Besides this, the Yogam in 1922 reduced the membership fee from Rs 25 to Rs 5, to be paid in five instalments of Re 1 per year.[82] In addition to the reduction of the membership fee, the Yogam decided to open more branches and unions at the village and taluk levels,[83] with the aim of establishing direct contact with the masses and to acquire the character of a wider mass movement. However, due to the indifference of the people[84] and lack of enthusiasm on the part of Yogam workers,[85] the decision taken at the eighteenth annual meeting remained on paper till 1926, when T.K. Madhavan took charge as organizing secretary of the Yogam.[86]

As an experienced Congress worker Madhavan had learned very many lessons in organizing the masses. Following the example of the Indian National

Congress, he concentrated on expansion of membership even at local levels of the organization. In a special meeting of the Yogam held in Alleppey on 1 January 1927 (17 Dhanu 1102 ME), Madhavan pointed out the limitations of the Yogam and the necessity for establishing more branches at the taluk and village levels,[87] and this was welcomed. It was this meeting that elected him as the organizing secretary. At that time, though the Ezhavas were still the largest community in Kerala with 20 lakh people,[88] the Yogam had only 1,502 permanent members and 2,311 temporary members.[89] Madhavan did his best to organize Ezhavas at the village and taluk levels. Due to his consistent efforts, the Yogam established 250 branches, 8 unions and 60 cooperatives,[90] and its membership registered a tremendous increase from 3,818 to 50,684 by April 1928.[91] In 1930 (Karkkadakam 1105 ME), the membership figure further rose to 63,674.[92] The unions organized by the Yogam at the taluk level functioned as a link connecting the branches at the village level to the main body of the Yogam. Madhavan was the person who brought the Yogam to the ordinary masses. This solitary effort was a landmark in the history of the Yogam's expansion.

Apart from organizing Ezhavas at the local level, Madhavan sought the cooperation of other communities and tried to open up the membership of the Yogam. His nationalist consciousness persuaded him to take such a step.[93] He adopted the tactics of the Congress in organizing the people to gain mass support, namely its appeal to all Indians, irrespective of caste and creed, to become members. In addition, since the Sanatana philosophy of Sree Narayana Guru did not admit of any caste distinctions, Madhavan might have thought that it was meaningless and contradictory to the ideology of the Guru to follow restrictive practices relating to membership in the Yogam. He approached Narayana Guru himself and requested him to write a letter to the Yogam's secretary, N. Kumaran, asking that its membership be thrown open to all communities and religions.[94]

In response to this request, on 30 January 1927 (17 Makaram 1102 ME), Narayana Guru wrote a letter to the Yogam's secretary. In this letter the Guru wrote:

> Without an organization no community will achieve progress or strength. I have founded the SNDP Yogam twenty-five years ago on this principle. Ezhava does not refer to any caste or religion. Therefore, all can join the Yogam irrespective of caste or religion. May many members join this Yogam.[95]

Following this letter, the fifth clause of the by-laws of the Yogam was amended, and from then onwards all those who believed in the Sree Narayana Dharma were permitted to join the Yogam.[96] As a consequence, the Yogam acquired a number of members from other communities.[97] Madhavan thus effected a discontinuity in the history of the Yogam by extending it to a larger number of people and also by transforming it into an organization of mass participation. For this he followed an entirely different ideology from the ideology hitherto in forming it, as also a distinct technique to make the Yogam approachable to men on the streets.

Regional Organizations and Expansion of the Activities of the Yogam

Even though the Yogam attracted the attention of mainly middle-class Ezhavas and was more or less confined to the Travancore region in its activities, it was nevertheless able to create an awakening among Ezhavas all over Kerala. As a consequence of this awakening, a number of Ezhava Sabhas under different regional names emerged in different parts of Kerala. Soon after the formation of the Yogam, in 1904 (1079 ME), the Ezhavas of Karthikappally and Karunagappalli organized associations after the respective names of their provinces.[98] Other important local associations that sprang up included the Karappuram Ezhava Samajam in Shertalai; the Cochin Ezhava Samajam (1915), which later became the Cochin SNDP Yogam; the Sree Narayana Chandrodaya Samajam at Vaikom; the Sanmarga Pradayini Yogam at Pulinkattu; the Jnanodaya Yogam at Tellicherry; the Vijnanodaya Sabha at Palaghat; the Malabar Thiyya Mahajana Sabha; the Ezhava Mahasabha; and the Sree Narayana Sangam in Malabar. The Sahodhara Movement of K. Ayyappan, which was active in the Cochin area for a long time, introduced a number of constructive social and religious reforms all over Kerala. It gained the attention of many and became yet another notable movement.[99] All these organizations got linked with the programmes and activities initiated by the Guru on the one hand, and the Yogam on the other.[100] We may distinguish between the activities of the Yogam on two grounds: ones initiated by the Guru, and those carried out by Yogam. At the same time, we must acknowledge that although separable, they fall within the same rubric.

So far I have confined my attention to discussing the organizational structure of the Yogam, its development and some of its limitations. Now I proceed to examine some of the social interventions it undertook in different fields, which have only been briefly mentioned or tangentially alluded to earlier. I provide more details on the main activities of the Yogam, in the fields of education, employment opportunities and industry.

The Yogam and Education

The agents who brought modern English education to Travancore included, along with others, foreign Christian missionaries such as the London Missionary Society and the Church Missionary Society. Their missionary activities were favourably funded and assisted by the rulers of the princely states of Travancore and Cochin.[101] Although educational facilities were widespread in Travancore, in the beginning they were restricted to the privileged *savarna* sections of Hindus and Christians. Educated sections of the people mainly belonged to either landholding or bureaucratic families.[102] At the same time, among the untouchable castes, a few Ezhavas got the opportunity to get educated. This was due to three social reasons. First, this community was the first to mingle with the European missionaries and so they were able to get English education from the schools run by the missionaries.[103] Second, among all the untouchable castes and other backward communities, there was a middle class only among the Ezhavas. When the Ezhavas submitted the *Ezhava Memorial* to the Maharaja of Travancore in 1896, their main submission was that the schools should be opened to their children, for education was the only secular means by which they could compete with other communities and get placements in government service.[104] When a grant-in-aid scheme introduced by the Government of Travancore in 1868–69 was liberalized in 1873–74,[105] a number of schools were opened for the education of children belonging to the backward communities, which helped the Ezhavas to gain education. The educational facilities available to Ezhavas steadily increased, and the rate of male literacy among Ezhavas increased from 3.15 per cent in 1875 to 12.1 per cent in 1891; there were 30 Ezhavas who were literate in English in the same year.[106] As the Ezhava intelligentsia realized that those who controlled educational facilities also controlled the economic and bureaucratic posts, it gave education a central place in the evolving social formation.

Narayana Guru, like the other reformers and intellectuals of the nineteenth century, was against the opening of English education to the upper strata of the society alone, but his concept of education was very different from theirs. Nineteenth-century intellectuals like Akshay Kumar Dutt, Vidyasagar, Debendranath Tagore, Bal Shastri Jambekar, Sir Sayyed Ahmed Khan and Veeresalingam laid stress on the vernacular languages as the medium of instruction;[107] Narayana Guru, on the other hand, established Sanskrit schools, but also advised his followers to acquire English education. Speaking at the Vijnana Vardhini Sabha at Cherai in 1912, he said: 'Education leads any community to higher standards and therefore, if we are interested in the welfare of our community, we have to encourage it. . . . This would benefit the society as a whole. . . . The chief language now is English. Therefore, our attention has to turn towards English.'[108] The emphasis on acquiring English education was because he was convinced that only this would enable the deprived sections of society to enter into government services, and thereby reach higher positions on the social ladder. In contrast to reformers elsewhere in India who were his contemporaries, the Guru regarded education as a means to gain vertical social mobility. He once said: 'We have only a small number of people who are well educated and holding good positions in the Government service . . . nowadays any caste can be uplifted by means of education. If we have any plan of improving the conditions of downtrodden masses we must educate our children.'[109]

After the modernization of administration and the practical recognition of English as the official language of the state, all communities wanted to send their children to schools and colleges with a view to qualify them for government service.[110] Till the first decade of the twentieth century it was unimaginable for Ezhava children to attend school alongside caste Hindus. The call of the Guru to the Ezhava community to strengthen themselves 'by organization and liberate by education' was like a weapon to free them from the clutches of casteism and traditionalism. Moreover, the Ezhava middle class considered the closing of educational institutions to them as not only an injustice, but also a denial of their basic human rights. A large number of the community members contributed their quota to the state's revenues, with which the government schools were mainly financed, but they were debarred from attending these schools. This situation of denial and exclusion was resented by the Ezhavas, and persuaded them to fight for their right to attend the schools.[111]

As a first step, the Yogam turned its attention to the problems of securing admission in the public schools. Palpu and members of his family were among the first victims of these discriminatory caste restrictions in Travancore.[112] In 1895, when an Ezhava named Raman applied for admission to Attingal English School, he was denied admission by the Inspector of Schools[113] for two reasons. The first was the location of these schools – either within the premises of temples or Brahmin houses, or on paths leading to them – which was socially inaccessible to the *avarna* community.[114] Secondly, upper-caste Hindus opposed admission of low castes to the schools where their children studied.[115] The government did not wish to ignore the sentiments of these upper-caste Hindus.

For better educational opportunities, representatives of the Yogam continued to raise their cause in the Sree Mulam Popular Assembly. In 1905, N. Kumaran Asan, representing the Yogam, put forth in the Assembly the difficulties that Ezhava pupils faced in gaining admission to the government schools, and requested that all Ezhava children be admitted into all government schools without discrimination.[116] In 1907, at the fourth meeting of the Assembly, M. Govindan presented a memorial signed by 64 representatives on free admission of Ezhavas into government schools.[117] But the admission of Ezhava children to public schools remained a vexed problem till 1908. On 6 June 1908, the Government of Travancore issued a notification (No. 82044) throwing open all *sirkar* boys' schools, both English and vernacular, to Ezhava children, except those located in inaccessible places.[118] These inaccessible institutions were also ordered to shift to unobjectionable places without any delay. In 1908, out of 369 government schools, 326 were opened to the Ezhava community;[119] and by 1913, there were only thirteen schools still inaccessible to the Ezhavas.[120]

The *sirkar* girls' schools, however, still remained closed to the Ezhavas. The justification of the government for this was that admitting Ezhava girls into government schools would probably empty these schools of Brahmin and Nair girls.[121] It was generally thought that girls were naturally more conservative. In 1910, the Yogam's representative in the Assembly made an appeal to the government that Ezhava girls should be admitted into at least those schools where Christian girls had access; Kunju Panikkar was the representative at that time.[122] Due to the sustained perseverance of Ezhava representatives in the Assembly, in 1910, for the first time, thirty-five schools were opened to Ezhava girls.[123] Through the Educational Code of 1911, the government removed all restrictions on the admission of children from backward class communities into government schools.[124] Yet, even as late as 1919, out of 352 girls' schools, only 180 were opened to the Ezhava girls.[125]

The next step taken by the Yogam was an agitation for admission to the Sanskrit College and Ayurvedic College, which were situated in localities inaccessible to Ezhavas.[126] However, they had to wait till 1915 to get admitted into the Ayurvedic College,[127] and till 1918 for the Sanskrit College.[128]

Alongside their fight for admission into government or government-aided schools, the Yogam and rich Ezhavas, along with the Guru, started their own educational institutions for Ezhavas. The desire for social and economic development of the community, the aspiration to enhance competitiveness vis-à-vis the relatively forward communities who had an upper hand in economic and bureaucratic positions, and the dearth of government support induced the Yogam to set up a number of educational institutions. In 1906 (1081 ME), the Yogam started an education fund with the objective of providing both technical and general education to students of the community.[129]

The Guru started a Sanskrit School at Aruvippuram, which was later shifted to Trivandrum.[130] Paravoor V. Kesavan Asan started an Ayurvedic School where not only traditional Ayurvedic education was imparted, but the rudiments of anatomy and physiology were also included in the curriculum.[131] In 1917, under the auspices of the Yogam and with the support of the Education Department, an organization by the name of Akhila Ezhava Vidhyabhyasa Mahasabha (All Ezhava Education Conference) was formed with the aim of providing primary education to Ezhavas in Travancore.[132] The main objectives of this Conference were to persuade the government to open all elementary schools to Ezhava children, and to establish new schools in areas where the Ezhavas did not have schools.[133] A central committee was set up at Trivandrum, and taluk-level sub-committees organized for the educational development of the Ezhavas.[134] In 1922, the Yogam started its first English School at Perinadu in Alleppey.[135] A free Anglo-Sanskrit Boarding School was started at Alwaye; this was the largest institution of its kind and showed better results than even the government schools.[136]

In addition to these privately run schools, the community also built many schools and handed them over to the government.[137] Due to all these activities the number of Ezhava graduates, postgraduates and law graduates – both male and female – increased, and they distinguished themselves in various offices of the British Government and the princely states.[138]

Thus, three decades of consistent perseverance by the Yogam earned the Ezhavas of Travancore enviable success in the field of education and ensured social mobility through it. In 1875, the male literacy rate among Ezhavas was only 3.2 per cent; in 1911 and 1931, this proportion increased respectively to 19 per cent and 36 per cent.[139] The number of English literates also increased in hundreds. The number of Ezhavas educated in English was only 30 in 1890; this increased to 5,202 by 1931.[140] By 1917, the number of Ezhava pupils who attended schools rose to 37,508.[141] Out of 1,441 English-educated Ezhavas in 1911, 82 were women.[142]

Modern education was one of the surest means to distance oneself from tradition, and such distancing was the initial step in the Ezhavas' fight against social injustice. Moreover, those who gained education became active in spreading the message of reform, particularly the need for and benefits of education, thereby becoming agents of social change. Education also enabled these agents to negotiate between the popular aspirations of the people and the government. That is why the Yogam took decisive steps to promote education. The centrality of the fight for education in the activities of the Yogam is thus worth underscoring. One of the reasons why the government had to be relentlessly persuaded to permit the entry of lower-caste people into its educational institutions stemmed from the nexus between education and acquiring in employment government jobs.

Agitation for Acquiring Government Jobs

Of all jobs, a government job was the most privileged and thus it was the most preferred one too. This was so not because it enabled higher monetary benefits but because it rendered higher social status to the employee. It was the most respected position and the surest means to reposition oneself in the social hierarchy. Under the aegis of the Yogam, the educated middle class of the Ezhava community turned its attention to government service, a right denied to them in Travancore's public administration.[143] At the time of the *Malayali Memorial* in 1891, there was not a single member of the Ezhava community holding any government job with a monthly salary of Rs 5 or more.[144] We have seen how the government was negative in its response to the *Memorial* and how even after the concerted efforts of the reformers, it did not change its stance.[145] The government's argument was that there were no qualified candidates from this community. Therefore, it became imperative for middle-class members of the Yogam to see to it that there were at least some people who were qualified to be absorbed into government service. Moreover, the argument of the government was considered to be a mere excuse, because the Census of 1891 showed that although the number of educated persons among Ezhavas was 25,000, not a single member of the community was permitted to be even a peon under the *sirkar*.[146] The experiences of P. Velayudhan and Dr Palpu, who graduated as early as the 1880s and were denied *sirkar* jobs, are noteworthy.[147] An Ezhava graduate who applied for the post of a copyist in Travancore High Court was told that the traditional state policy went against his employment.[148] According to a government order, Ezhavas were not admitted into public service chiefly owing to the objections of high-caste Hindus,[149] presumably Nairs.[150] The government order indicated that it did not want to act against the interest of caste Hindus, especially Nairs, since it feared that it would lead to communal conflicts detrimental to the progress of the state.[151] In short, for one reason or the other, till the beginning of the twentieth century, the Ezhavas were completely excluded from Travancore's public services.

The *Ezhava Memorial* requested the government to grant ordinary civic rights (which were granted to converts to Islam and Christianity) to Ezhavas who remained within the fold of Hinduism.[152] The *Memorial* failed to produce any result, however; as noted earlier, even G.P. Pillai's efforts during the ninth Indian National Social Conference at Poona in 1895, and in the British Parliament, did not culminate in success.[153] The government and *savarna* Hindu officials adopted various means and tactics to keep the Ezhavas out of public services. The pressure from the reformers and Assembly proceedings were such that the government could not say an outright 'no' to the requests for employment; rather, it adopted a strategy of deferment and providing indefinite answers.

A few examples can be invoked. According to a correspondent of the *Madras Mail*:

> One candidate is sympathetically advised not to appear. Another is made to await one big official after another till he gets disgusted and leaves the State. A third is 'over-aged' in spite of all proofs to the contrary. A fourth is told he is of a 'lower caste' but no written endorsement to that would be given, 'traditional state policy' precludes a fifth in one department and he is asked to seek employment in other departments where it may be possible to entertain men of his class.[154]

When K.N. Kesavan applied to the Travancore Police Department after acquiring a diploma from Mysore Police School, he was informed by Bezli, then Head of the Department of Police, that there was no vacancy for the time being and he was advised to seek job opportunities elsewhere.[155] In this way the government service remained the preserve of caste Hindus. For educated Ezhavas who realized their predicament, the only alternative was to leave the state in search of employment elsewhere.

As the educated middle class became increasingly conscious of the exclusion principle adopted by the state and by the upper castes, they were compelled to be more self-assertive, and ready to fight for a better status in the bureaucratic and administrative spheres. They perceived the denial of opportunities to them as a major injustice.[156] They had attained education with the conviction that they would get placements in government service,[157] but, owing to the overwhelming influence of nepotism, the bureaucracy remained the sole preserve of the upper castes.

The position of the Ezhavas was the same in many respects as that of the Thiyyas of Malabar and the Christian converts in Travancore, but they stood apart in the matter of appointments in government service. This simultaneous identification and contrast made the reformers all the more disillusioned. Narayana Panikkar requested the government to extend the privileges enjoyed by the Christian converts to the Ezhavas as well, to which the Dewan replied that the government had nothing to do in this matter.[158] Till 1905 there were very few Ezhavas in government service. However there was a relaxation in 'traditional state policy' from 1908 (1083 ME) in the matter of entertaining Ezhavas in public service.[159] This change was mainly because of the incessant pressure of the Yogam on the government, and the attempts of the Ezhava representatives in the Sree Mulam Popular Assembly.[160] From 1905 onwards, one member of the Ezhava community was nominated to the Sree Mulam Popular Assembly, and members like Kumaran Asan and N. Kumaran succeeded in bringing the grievances of their community, particularly with respect to appointments in public services, directly to the notice of the government.[161]

In 1905, out of a total population of 5 lakh Ezhavas, only twenty-five were appointed in government service and only one of them drew a monthly salary of more than Rs 15.[162] Out of these twenty-five Ezhavas, five were police constables and the rest were primary school teachers drawing salaries of Rs 9 to Rs 15 per month.[163] Though, on paper, all jobs but in the department of revenue and judiciary were open to the Ezhavas, in practice almost all departments were closed to them. Their constant pleas within and outside the legislature finally paid off and they were given a few posts in select departments. Table 18 shows the marginal increase of Ezhavas in government service within a decade (by 1914).

Though a few Ezhavas were appointed in government service, their repre-

TABLE 18
Number of Ezhavas in government service in 1914[164]

Department	Monthly salary						Total no.
	Up to Rs 5	Rs 5–10	Rs 10–25	Rs 25–50	Rs 50–100	Above Rs 100	
Police	–	1	1	2	3	–	7
Excise	–	11	–	1	–	–	12
Forest	1	10	2	–	–	–	13
Public Works	–	–	2	1	–	–	3
Education	–	14	13	–	–	–	27
Registration	–	–	2	–	–	–	2
Medical	–	–	1	–	–	–	1
Judicial	–	6	2	1	–	–	9
Revenue	–	–	1	1	–	–	2
Agriculture	–	2	–	–	–	1	3
Postal	–	2	–	–	–	–	2
Prison	–	2	1	–	–	–	3
Total	1	48	25	6	3	1	84

sentation was nowhere near proportionate to their population and the number of educationally qualified people among them. We have already seen that the justification of the Dewan for appointing such a small number of Ezhavas in the Police Department was that if more Ezhavas were recruited the work would be limited, as they could not freely enter all places such as temples, Brahmin houses and the like.[165] The Revenue Department, the largest department with maximum avenues for employment because it was a part of the Devaswam, was closed to untouchables and non-Hindus.[166] This considerably affected the job opportunities of Ezhavas in government.

Another problem faced by the Ezhavas was that their chances of promotion in government service were very limited. This prompted Kumaran Asan to make a request to the government that instructions be issued to the heads of departments to entertain the applications of qualified Ezhavas and give them legitimate promotions.[167] By that time, resentment among Christians and Muslims too had began to build up against the bias of the government against non-caste Hindus and non-Hindus. On 1 March 1919, K.C. Mamman Mappilla presented a memorandum to the Dewan of Travancore, demanding that the Revenue Department should be separated from the Dewaswam and opened up to non-Hindus and untouchables.[168] The agitators believed that such a separation would provide better job opportunities to the Ezhavas, the Christians and the Muslims, as this Department of the Government of Travancore was the largest with 4,000 jobs. The Ezhavas utilized this opportunity to fight for their rights and privileges by joining together with the

Christians and Muslims. Under Christian leadership, a League for Equal Civic Rights was launched to agitate for the opening of all branches of government service to them, and to put an end to untouchability.[169] After the *Malayali Memorial* this was the first collective movement by disgruntled sections of Christians, Muslims and Ezhavas. The League was primarily an expression of the unsatiated aspirations of the middle classes of these communities. It represented 26 lakh people who were denied civil liberties in their own state.[170] In 1922 out of 4,000 jobs in the Revenue Department, more than 3,800 were held by caste Hindus alone.[171]

On 20 March 1919, the working committee of the Civic Rights League was formed with John Chandy as the president. On 5 April, a mammoth meeting was held at Tirunakkara maidan in Kottayam district under the chairmanship of E.J. John, to discuss the future programme of the League.[172] This meeting questioned the exclusion of Christians and Muslims on the basis of religion, and Ezhavas on the basis of caste, from government jobs. In 1920, on the basis of a decision taken at the Tirunakkara meeting, T.K. Madhavan led a delegation to submit a memorandum to the Travancore Government asking to throw open all government departments to non-Hindus and *avarnas*.[173] But this memorandum had very little consequence.[174] Therefore one more petition was submitted by E.J. John pointing out their grievances, including the exclusion of law-abiding Ezhavas, Christians and Muslims from the Revenue Department and Imperial Service Brigade.[175]

On 20 February 1919, the Dewan had made it clear in a meeting of the Sree Mulam Popular Assembly that the separation of the Revenue Department from the Devaswam was neither desirable nor practicable under the circumstances.[176] Later, as a result of the consistent struggle of the League, the government constituted a committee consisting of Hindus and non-Hindus to report on the feasibility of separating the departments.[177] On the basis of the recommendations of this committee, which was supported by the Madras Governor, Lord Wilington,[178] the Maharaja of Travancore issued a proclamation known as the Devaswam Proclamation on 12 April 1922, bifurcating the Devaswam and the Revenue Department;[179] this enabled non-Hindus and non-caste Hindus to get appointments in the Revenue Department.[180]

Though such slight improvements did take place in the sphere of government employment, they did not seriously alter the predominance of caste Hindus in the Travancore administration.[181] The Civic Rights League became inactive much before achieving its aims and objectives. Therefore the Yogam, under T.K. Madhavan, organized a Public Service Bureau at its annual meeting held in Quilon on 9 May 1926, with the twin aims of collecting and publishing information regarding the representation of each caste and community in government service, and to press for representation of candidates belonging to the Ezhava community in government service.[182] On 4 August 1926, a meeting of the Public Service Bureau was held at L.M.S. Hall, Trivandrum, to request the government to earmark a major proportion of new appointments in various departments like Education, Police, etc., to the Ezhavas, and to appoint at least one Divisional Peshkar, one Hazur Secretary and one District Judge from the Ezhava Community.[183] During the visit of the Simon Commission in 1928, C.V. Kunjuraman, the then general secretary of the Yogam, submitted a memorandum (on 26 May 1928) in which he enumerated the various disabilities suffered by the Ezhavas due to caste Hindu domination.

Gradually, there was an increase in the percentage of Ezhavas in government jobs. By 1931, the community had produced thirty-two gazetted officers.[184] Similarly, out of 503 posts carrying a monthly salary of Rs 150 or more, there were five incumbents who belonged to the Ezhava community. One can observe a radical change in the demands of Ezhavas over three decades since 1895. In the 1890s, their demand was to get privileges and facilities similar to that of untouchables who had been converted to Christianity. In the course of the next thirty years, the demand became 'equal civic rights enjoyed by the Brahmins and Nairs'.[185] Though there were some remarkable achievements, they had not yet got their share in the administration as warranted by the strength of their population. Table 19 shows the monopoly of caste Hindus, especially of Nairs and Tamil Brahmins, and the meagre presence of other communities, in government service in 1932.

The table shows that the Nairs, accounting for about 17 per cent of the total population, held about 52 per cent of the total number of government jobs in the state. Similarly, the Brahmins, comprising 0.83 per cent of the total population, occupied 17.87 per cent of the total number of jobs. All the other communities – together comprising 82 per cent of the population – held less than 36 per cent of the total number of jobs in government services. This was excluding the Military and the Devaswam Department. The Military was constituted entirely of Nairs. The Devaswam was staffed exclusively by caste Hindus of whom the large majority was Nairs.[187]

TABLE 19

Monopoly of caste Hindus and poor status of other communities in government service, 1932[186]

Community/Caste	Population (total 6,092,237)	% of total population	Government jobs (total 20,378)	% of population
Nairs	868,411	17.05	10,585	51.94
Ezhavas	872,174	17.13	787	3.86
Christians	1,605,475	31.51	3,537	17.36
Muslims	353,274	6.94	436	2.14
Brahmins	42,040	0.83	2,622	17.87
Other Hindus	351,863	26.55	2,411	11.83

The history of the struggle for government jobs conducted by the Yogam shows us that it was not as successful as its struggle to get entry into educational institutions run by the government and other institutions. However, there were some limited achievements within a short span of time in gaining government jobs. Although the Yogam did not accomplish its desired objectives, it was able to convince the general public that in matters of employment in government posts, not caste differences but educational qualifications should be the yardstick to decide whether the applicants were accomplished enough.

Another alternative that was open to the Ezhava community for their social uplift was to earn wealth through industrial activities; on this front also the Yogam took initiatives.

Industrial Activities

Alongside the attempts at educational advancement and improvement of opportunities in gaining government service, the Yogam concentrated its attention on economic progress of the Ezhava community by promoting industrial activities. The Ezhavas had no hesitation to take up any work if it was found to be lucrative.[188] According to C.V. Kunjuraman, the motto of the Ezhavas was: 'If you cannot find any job, go and steal something. Do not sit idle. He who lives on other's charity without doing any kind of work is a great gentleman thief.'[189] Even though they struggled hard to get into government service, in general, the Ezhavas preferred more profitable occupations like trade, commerce and industry.[190] Many sections of the community had contempt towards low-paid government jobs, and preferred occupations in cultivation and industry. According to them:

> Those who walk wearing a red cap and khaki uniform on a salary of Rs 6 bid farewell to this world in the end leaving behind some wives and many children in the wilderness. Instead of these petty offices we have to respect forefathers who created a new world by clearing away the forest and by cultivating virgin land. In lieu of aping the pomposity of the government employee, we have to follow the capitalists who sit and write bills in the shop and take the money of the government employees.[191]

The trend among Ezhavas traditionally to be engaged in occupations in various industries was further strengthened by: (i) their realization that it was difficult for them to get government jobs, and (ii) the advice and encouragement Narayana Guru gave them to undertake new ventures. Though the Guru did not put forward an economic programme to improve the conditions of the working-class section of the community, who constituted about 75 per cent of the total Ezhava population,[192] he advised Ezhava pilgrims at Sivagiri to organize presentations and speeches on trade, industry and commerce so that the members of the community could turn their attention to such ventures.[193] He also recommended that the relatively rich members of the community invest in manufacturing industries so that they could provide jobs for the poor. He said:

> If it is difficult for one man to take all the initial expense to run a factory then a group of people should get together. Factories will provide jobs for people. There are so many ways for making progress but our people will not follow them. We must manufacture goods from coconut fibre here ourselves instead of exporting them and then importing the manufactured goods from foreign countries.[194]

He advised people to acquire different kinds of industrial training.[195] He encouraged small-scale industries and heralded such activity by opening a weaving industry in his ashram at Varkala for imparting skills in spinning and weaving.[196] As a consequence of the advice of their spiritual leader, well-to-do Ezhavas invested in a number of industrial units, such as textile mills, cashew factories, etc., in various parts of Kerala.[197]

These ventures set an example of how to go beyond traditional and outdated methods and practices in the industrial sphere by innovating through improved modern methods and technical know-how. With this in mind, two industrial exhibitions were held under the auspices of the Yogam: one at Quilon in 1905 and the other at Cannanore in 1907, as part of the annual meetings of the Yogam. These exhibitions, as mentioned earlier, were held for the purpose of 'comparative evaluation of products'.[198] They resulted in an unprecedented awakening within the Ezhava community.[199] In 1906, due to the attempts of Palpu and some other wealthy Ezhavas, the Travancore Weaving and Trading Company was set up with a capital of Rs 1 lakh.[200] In 1909, with the aim of providing financial aid to Ezhava weavers and traders, a cooperative was established under the name of Weaving and Trading Association, and registered in Travancore under the influence of the Yogam.[201] In 1910–11, C. Krishnan and Chozhy Vaidhyar started Calicut Bank with a capital of Rs 50,000.[202] In 1930, the Ezhavas of Travancore established another bank, The Travancore Ezhava Bank, with an initial capital of Rs 2 lakhs, to improve the economic conditions of the Ezhavas.[203]

In 1914, according to a decision taken by the Yogam in its eleventh annual meeting, a company by the name of Malabar Economic Union was started with a capital of Rs 1 lakh, for encouraging entrepreneurship, and for providing financial help and employment opportunities to Ezhavas.[204] This far-sighted project was inaugurated by Narayana Guru.[205] After his retirement in 1920, Palpu organized an industrial museum in Trivandrum for the development of cottage and small-scale industries.[206]

By 1920, Ezhavas owned a number of industries in Kerala, such as Malabar Produces and Industrials,[207] Malayala Vyavasaya Company, Quilon

Thamarakkulam Ottu company, Malabar Economic Union and Kerala Vyavasaya Company.[208] The Yogam had an intention to bring all Ezhava-owned companies under a united venture under the supervision of N. Kumaran as its managing director.[209] But this did not materialize due to lack of interest of the concerned people.

Though the Yogam did considerable work for the industrial development of the Ezhava community, it did little to organize and improve the conditions of the peasants and agricultural workers who constituted the majority of the community. The Yogam had toyed with the idea of organizing Ezhava labourers under the leadership of K. Ayyappan,[210] but this did not arouse any enthusiasm among the leaders. In the field of industrial development too, although some of the individual initiatives succeeded, the collective action did not lead to impressive outcomes.

The main achievements of the Yogam were in the field of education: that is, in extending educational facilities to aspiring pupils of the community. Further, though in a limited sense, the Yogam was successful in propagating the demand for government employment as a just claim. Its attempts at expansion in the social fabric also made some headway. Such expansion was limited, however, in terms of organized efforts to gain vertical labour mobility. Hence, one question that crops up is, were the articulations of the Yogam, and the resistances and struggles led by it, a reflection of only the interests of the emerging middle class? The foregoing discussion tempts us to give an answer in the affirmative.

Notes and References

[1] For details about the nature of the membership, see chapter 2.

[2] See the first Annual Report of the secretary of the Yogam in *Vivekodayam*, 13 May 1904 (31 Medam 1079 ME), pp. 15–19.

[3] T.K. Madhavan, *Dr. Palpu (A Life History of Dr. Palpu)*, fully revised by Pallipattu Kunju Krishnan, Cheppad, Alleppey, 1969, Vol. I, pp. 170–71; P.K. Balakrishnan, *Narayana Guru Samahara Grandham* (An Anthology), National Book Stall, Kottayam, 1969, p. 111, first edition 1954; *Vivekodayam*, May–July 1915 (Edavam–Mithunam 1090 ME), Vol. II, p. 52.

[4] The ten members were: Mattamcheri Govindan Vaidhyar, Muttathara B. Kochutty Muthalaly, Koyipuzha Kochayyappan Channar, Karattuparambu Peringottukara S. Krishnan Asan, Perinadu Mangalaesseriyil Govindan Channar, Perinadu S. Govindan Asan, Neyyattinkara Kottakkal Kumaran Madan, Thiruvanathapuram Puthanchanda P.M. Madhavan Vaidhyar, Kuttiyappi Asan and Paravoor Kesavan Asan. See P.S. Velayudhan, 'SNDP Yogam Oru Charitravalokhanam', *Yoganatham Antharashtra Sree Narayana Guruvarsha Visheshal Prathi*, SNDP Yogam, Quilon, 1977, p. 7. But Dr Palpu, the patron of the Yogam, could not attend its inaugural meeting. See Robin Jeffrey, 'Social Origins of a Caste Association, 1875–1906: The Founding of the SNDP Yogam', *South Asia*, No. 4, 1974, p. 52.

[5] N. Kumaran, 'SNDP Yogam, Chila Smaranakal', *SNDP Yogam Golden Jubilee Souvenir*, 1953, p. 47. Also see P.S. Velayudhan, 'Sree Narayana Guru: A Peep into His Life and Work', *SNDP Yogam Platinum Jubilee Souvenir*, Quilon, 1978, pp. 94–95; P. Parameswaran, *Sree*

Narayana Guru Swamikal: Navothanathinte Pravachakan, Jayabharath Publishers, Calicut, 1979, pp. 76–77, first edition 1971.

6 Ibid., p. 95.

7 Letter from P. Parameswaran to the Dewan of Travancore, 8 January 1903, *English Records*, Cover No. 8338, Travancore Government, Kerala Secretariat, Trivandrum.

8 *Vivekodayam*, Vol. 1, No. 5, 11 February 1905 (30 Makaram 1080 ME), p. 100; *Vivekodayam*, Vol. IV, Nos. 8–9, November 1907 to January 1908, pp. 13–14, and May–July 1915 (Edavam–Mithunam 1090 ME), p. 53.

9 Letter from Pettayil Parameswaran to the Dewan of Travancore, 8 January 1903, *English Records*, Cover No. 8338, Travancore Government, Kerala Secretariat, Trivandrum.

10 See the amended Articles of Association of the Yogam in 1903, Category 19; *Vivekodayam*, Vol. I, No. I, 13 May 1904 (31 Medam 1079 ME), p. 8.

11 Ibid.

12 Ibid.

13 Section 'B' of the Articles of Association says: 'As agreed upon by the members [of the Association] they may remit the amount of their share in advance. If it is inconvenient they may pay the sum in not more than four equal instalments spread over a period of four years. However, as per the earlier Article of Association, those members who opt to pay an annual interest of 10 per cent continuously for a period of twenty years may also be deemed to have paid up the entire amount.' The Articles of Association of the Yogam was prepared at a meeting held at Kamalalayam Bungalow in Trivandrum on 23 Dhanu 1078 ME (December 1902), Category 4, Section 'B'. See *Vivekodayam*, Vol. I, No. 5, 11 February 1905 (30 Makaram 1080 ME), p. 101.

14 *Vivekodayam*, Vol. II, May–July 1915 (Edavam–Mithunam 1090 ME), p. 53.

15 Ibid., p. 103.

16 The amended Articles of Association of the SNDP Yogam in the fourth annual meeting which was held at Cannanore on 29 and 30 March 1907. See *Vivekodayam*, Vol. IV, Nos. 8 and 9, November–January 1907 (Vrishchikam–Dhanu 1083 ME), p. 14.

17 Ibid.

18 *Vivekodayam*, 13 May 1904 (31 Medam 1079 ME), p. 7.

19 M.K. Sanoo, *Narayana Guru Swami* (biography), Vivekodayam Printing and Publishing Co., Irinjalakuda, p. 168.

20 P.S. Velayudhan, *SNDP Yoga Charitram*, SNDP Yogam, Quilon, 1978 p. 97.

21 On 16 January 1915, Kumaran Asan left the secretaryship and Mr N. Krishnan became the secretary for one year. See *Vivekodayam*, May–July 1915, p. 66.

22 P.S. Velayudhan, *SNDP Yoga Charitram*, p. 97.

23 *Vivekodayam*, November–January 1907, p. 19.

24 Ibid.

25 Ibid.

26 Ibid., p. 14.

27 Ibid.

28 These unions and branch offices actually functioned only after T.K. Madhavan became the secretary of the Yogam. See 'The SNDP Organization Scheme', *Vivekodayam*, January 1929 (Dhanu 1104 ME), pp. 4–13. Before Madhavan, in 1907, the Articles of Association mentioned the branch offices; at that time, a *samajam* which was run by members who had not less than 200 shares came to be known as a branch office. See the by-laws of the SNDP Yogam of 1907 in *Vivekodayam*, November–January 1907–08, p. 19.

29 *Vivekodayam*, 13 May 1904, p. 2; *SNDP Yogam Golden Jubilee Souvenir*, 1953, p. 47.

30 *Vivekodayam*, 13 May 1904, p. 3.

31 N. Kumaran, 'SNDP Yogam, Chila Smaranakal', *SNDP Yogam Golden Jubilee Souvenir*, 1953, p. 48.

32 *Vivekodayam*, 13 May 1904, pp. 13–22.

33 N. Kumaran, 'SNDP Yogam, Chila Smaranakal', p. 48.

34 Ibid.

[35] Ibid.
[36] See back volumes of *Vivekodayam*, 1904–12.
[37] *Vivekodayam*, 13 May 1904, p. 1.
[38] *Vivekodayam*, Vol. 20, December 1928–January 1929 (Dhanu 1104 ME), p. 20. By this time *Vivekodayam* was being edited by K.N. Kunhikrishnan.
[39] Ibid.
[40] *Vivekodayam*, Vol. 2, No. 9, 13 January 1906 (30 Dhanu 1081 ME), p. 14.
[41] The meeting of the SNDP Yogam held in April 1908 decided to publish *Vivekodayam* as a monthly instead of a quarterly. See *Vivekodayam*, Vol. 5, Nos. 1 and 2, April–June 1908 (1083 Medam–Edavam ME), p. 8.
[42] *Vivekodayam*, 13 May 1904, p. 10.
[43] Ibid., p. 1.
[44] *Vivekodayam*, Vol. XII, April–June 1915 (Medam–Edavam 1090 ME), p. 53.
[45] According to the 1909 Census, the Ezhava populations of Malabar, Cochin and Travancore were 660,608, 185,446 and 491,774, respectively. These constituted about 20 per cent of the total population of Kerala. See *Vivekodayam*, October–November 1910 (Thulam 1086 ME), p. 176.
[46] *Vivekodayam*, 13 May 1904, p. 17.
[47] Ibid., p. 5.
[48] This information is from the Article of Association 'A' (1), ibid. However, P.S. Velayudhan says that the amendment for reducing the value of the share from Rs 100 to Rs 25 took place in 1908; see P.S. Velayudhan, 'SNDP Yogam Oru Charitravalokhanam', p. 7.
[49] Ibid.
[50] Ibid., p. 6.
[51] The share and number of votes were as follows:

No. of shares	No. of votes
1	1
4	2
8	3
12	4
16	5
20	6

See *Vivekodayam*, Vol. IV, November–January 1907 (Vrischikam–Dhanu 1083 ME), p. 18.
[52] Ibid.
[53] *Vivekodayam*, 13 May 1904, p. 5.
[54] The members could remit the amount of their share either in instalments or the entire amount at once. Those who remitted the amount in instalments could make annual deposits of Rs 2.50 over a period of ten years. See the by-law amended in the fourth annual meeting of the Yogam, held at Cannanore on 29 and 30 March 1907 (16 and 17 Meenam 1082 ME). Categories 6 and 7 of the by-law were reproduced in *Vivekodayam*, Vol. IV, Nos. 8 and 9, November–January 1907 (Vrischikam–Dhanu 1083 ME), p. 18.
[55] Jeffrey, 'Social Origins of a Caste Association', p. 52.
[56] See the thirteenth Annual Report of the Yogam by M. Krishnan, general secretary, reproduced in *Vivekodayam*, Vol. XIII, April–June 1916 (Medam–Edavam 1091 ME), pp. 12–15.
[57] *Kerala Kaumudi*, 6 May 1920, p. 2.
[58] See the thirteenth Annual Report of the Yogam by M. Krishnan, *Vivekodayam*, Vol. XIII, April–June 1916 (Medam–Edavam 1091 ME), pp. 12–15.
[59] *Vivekodayam*, April–June 1912 (Medam–Edavam 1087 ME), pp. 26 and 312, and Ibid., April–June 1913 (Medam–Edavam 1089 ME), p. 93.
[60] Ibid.
[61] According to the Census of 1901, 10 per cent of Ezhava males were literate. But out of more than 5 lakh Ezhavas in Travancore, only 175 were literate in English. *Census of India, 1901*, Vol. XXVI, Travancore, Part I, Report, p. 214.
[62] See back volumes of *Vivekodayam*, 1904–12.

[63] Francis Houtart and Genevieve Lemercinier, 'Socio-Religious Movements in Kerala: A Reaction to the Capitalist Mode of Production', *Social Scientist*, Vol. VI, No. 11, June 1978, p. 20.

[64] C.V. Kunjuraman, 'The Annual Report of the 27th Session of the SNDP Yogam', *Vivekodayam*, Vol. 20, No. 6, 31 July 1930 (15 Karkadakam 1105 ME), pp. 9–10.

[65] *Kerala Kaumudi*, 7 July 1921, p. 1.

[66] N. Kumaran Asan, 'Brahmasri Sree Narayana Guruswamiyude Jeevacharitra Samgraham', *Vivekodayam*, Vol. 12, Nos. 2–3, May–June 1915 (Edavam–Midhunam 1090 ME), pp. 39–41.

[67] See *Vivekodayam*: Vol. 10, Nos. 1 and 2, April–June 1913 (Medam–Edavam 1088 ME), p. 64; Vol. 12, Nos. 2 and 3, May–June 1915, pp. 39–41; No. 5, 16 September 1907 (31 Chingam 1082 ME), p. 11; Vol. 3, No. 1, April–May 1906 (Medam 1081 ME), p. 4.

[68] See Swami Dharmanandaji, *Sree Narayana Gurudevan*, N.B.S., Kottayam, 1965.

[69] *Vivekodayam*, 16 September 1906, p. 11.

[70] Jeffrey, 'Social Origins of a Caste Association', p. 52.

[71] Gopi, 'Cochin SNDP Yogam', *SNDP Yogam Golden Jubliee Souvenir*, 1953, p. 257.

[72] Ibid., p. 235.

[73] *Vivekodayam*, February–April 1907 (Kumbam–Meenam 1082 ME), p. 13.

[74] In 1869, a Thiyya, Churayyi Kanaran, was the first Malayali to be appointed as the Deputy Collector in Malabar. See C. Aboo, 'Shriman Churayyi Kanaran', *SNDP Yogam Golden Jubilee Souvenir*, 1953, p. 246. P.C. Govindan passed the ICS in 1880 and became the Political Agent of Aden. P. Sankunni was the first Malayali principal of Victoria College, Palghat (1916–22). See Murkothu Kunhappa, 'Thiyyarude Charitram Oru Vihaka Veekshanam', *SNDP Yogam Platinum Jubilee Souvenir*, 1978, p. 72.

[75] *Mitavadi*, Vol. 5, No. 5, May 1917, pp. 1–2.

[76] *Vivekodayam*, Vol. 21, No. 1, August–September 1930 (Chingam 1106 ME), p. 10.

[77] *Vivekodayam*, Vol. 20, No. 6, 30 July 1930 (15 Karkkadakam 1105 ME), p. 5.

[78] Of the above-mentioned three organizations, Sree Narayana Samajam, which was founded in 1925, functioned actively for some time. Within a decade it established forty branches with 1,200 members, and it had a volunteer corps of 1,000 members which maintained a particular uniform. However, by the end of 1930s, it ceased to exist. See V.K. Kumaran, 'Malabar SNDP Yogam', *SNDP Yogam Golden Jubilee Souvenir*, 1953, pp. 235–36.

[79] The Articles of Association and by-laws of the Yogam specified that membership should be given to members of the 'Samudayam', that is, Ezhavas, Thiyyas or Chovans of Travancore, Cochin and Malabar. See *Vivekodayam*, Vol. I, No. 5, 11 February 1905 (30 Makaram 1080 ME), p. 100, and Vol. IV, Nos. 8–9, November 1907–January 1908, pp. 13–14.

[80] *Sahodharan*, May–July 1920 (Edavam–Midhunam 1095 ME), p. 5.

[81] *Kerala Kaumudi*, Vol. 11, No. 13, 27 May 1920.

[82] *Kerala Kaumudi*, 29 May 1924, p. 1; *Vivekodayam*, Vol. 20, July–August 1930 (Karkkadakam 1105 ME), p. 9.

[83] In the eighteenth annual meeting of the Yogam, it was decided to establish branches at the village level and unions at the taluk level. See *Kerala Kaumudi*, 12 May 1921, pp. 21–22.

[84] *Kerala Kaumudi*, 29 May 1924, p. 21.

[85] The editor of *Mitavadi*, C. Krishnan, criticized the activities of the Yogam for being limited to the organizing of annual meetings. See *Vivekodayam*, Vol. 24, No. 1, August–September 1930 (Chingam 1106 ME), p. 9.

[86] K.R. Narayanan, 'Sree T.K. Madhavan: Chila Anusmaranakal', *SNDP Yogam Golden Jubilee Souvenir*, 1953, p. 206.

[87] Ibid.

[88] Presidential address of N. Kumaran Asan at the twentieth annual meeting of the Yogam, *Kerala Kaumudi*, 27 May 1923, p. 1.

[89] Temporary and permanent members were classified on the basis of the membership fee deposited by them. Those who paid the fee of Rs 5 in full were known as permanent members, and those who did not pay the full amount continued as temporary members till the time they did so. See *Vivekodayam*, Vol. 20, No. 6, 30 July 1930, p. 9.

[90] *Vivekodayam*, Vol. 20, July–August 1930, pp. 9–10. K.R. Narayanan, however, notes that by 5 May 1928 (23 Medam 1103 ME), the Yogam had established 255 branches and ten unions. See K.R. Narayanan, 'Sree T.K. Madhavan, Chila Anusmaranakal', *SNDP Yogam Golden Jubilee Souvenir*, 1953, p. 222.

[91] Ibid.

[92] *Vivekodayam*, July–August 1930, pp. 9–10.

[93] P.K. Madhavan, *The Life of T.K. Madhavan* (*T.K. Madhavante Jeevacharitram*), Sarada Book Depot, Trivandrum, 1936, Vol. II, p. 580.

[94] Ibid., pp. 496–98; K.K. Panicker, *Sree Narayana Paramahamsan* (biography), Vidyarambham Press, Alleppey, 1968, p. 347

[95] *Vivekodayam*, March 1978, p. VIII.

[96] *Yoganadham Antharashtra Sree Narayana Guru Varsha Visheshal Prathi*, 1977, p. 5.

[97] Ibid.

[98] *Vivekodayam*, 13 May 1904, p. 23.

[99] See M.K. Sanoo, *Narayana Guru Swami*, p. 260.

[100] M.S.A. Rao, *Social Movements and Social Transformation: A Study of Two Backward Classes Movements in India*, Macmillan India, New Delhi, 1979, p. 53.

[101] Financial and material aid to missionaries and societies for the promotion of English education was more generous from the rulers of these princely states. See C.M. Agur, *Church History of Travancore*, S.P.S. Press, Madras, 1903, p. 21.

[102] *Administration Report, Travancore*, 1899, p. 105. (For details see chapter 1.)

[103] *Private Papers of Dr Palpu*, File No. 12, p. 129, Nehru Memorial Museum and Library, New Delhi. Samuel Mateer of the London Missionary Society opened a school near Anjengo, between Trivandrum and Quilon, for 50 'highly respectable' Ezhava boys who 'were refused admission to the *sircar* schools'. See LMS, *TDC Report*, 1872, p. 18 quoted in Jeffrey, 'Social Origins of a Caste Association', p. 47. Also see M. Govindan, 'Rao Bahadur P. Velayudhan', *SNDP Yogam Golden Jubilee Souvenir*, 1953, p. 59.

[104] *Private Papers of Dr Palpu*, File No. 12, p. 129, Nehru Memorial Museum and Library, New Delhi.

[105] P.R. Gopinathan Nair, 'Education and Socio-Economic Change in Kerala, 1793–1947', *Social Scientist*, Vol. IV, No. 8, March 1976, p. 32.

[106] *Census of Travancore, 1891*, Vol. I, Report, pp. 492 and 505.

[107] Most of them, like Sir Syed Ahmed Khan and Akshay Kumar Dutt, argued that the mother tongue should be made the medium of instruction, and totally opposed English-medium education. See Mohammad Shan (ed.), *Writings and Speeches of Sir Syed Ahmed Khan*, Nachiketa Publications, Bombay, 1972, pp. 231–32; *Tattwabodhini Patrika*, No. 36, Shrawan 1768, pp. 309–11; K.N. Panikkar, 'Presidential Address', Section III, Indian History Congress, 36th Session, Aligarh, 1975, pp. 7–13. Though Syed Ahmed Khan opted for the mother tongue in the beginning, he changed his views later when he was confronted with the problem of translating English works into regional languages; he did not champion the cause of vernacular education consistently. For details, see Sayyid Yusuf Shah, 'Politicization of Education in British India: A Case Study of the Establishment of Aligarh Muslim University (1875–1920)', Ph.D. Thesis, Jawaharlal Nehru University, New Delhi, 1981, pp. 159–70.

[108] Quoted in M.K. Sanoo, *Narayana Guru Swami*, pp. 251–52. When Narayana Guru asked his followers to turn their attention to English education, Akshay Kumar Dutt's response was that English education would create a group of people alienated from their national culture and from their own countrymen. See K.N. Panikkar, 'Presidential Address', p. 12.

[109] Murkothu Kumaran, *Sree Narayana Guru Swamikalude Jeevacharitram*, second edition, P.K. Brothers, Calicut, 1971, pp. 261–62.

[110] *Report of the Unemployment Enquiry Committee of Travancore*, 1928, p. 23.

[111] See the arguments of M. Govindan, representative of the SNDP Yogam, in the fourth session of the Sree Mulam Popular Assembly: *Proceedings of the Sree Mulam Popular Assembly*, 1907, pp. 45–46.

[112] P.T. Palpu, Dr Palpu's father, applied for the government pleadership examination in Travancore. Though his application fee was accepted, he was not allowed to appear for the examination as he belonged to an *avarna* community. Similarly, Dr Palpu secured the second position in the entrance examination for medicine in Travancore, but was refused admission. This compelled him to go to Madras from where he secured his medical degree. See *Private Papers of Dr Palpu*, File No. 12, Nehru Memorial Museum and Library, New Delhi, pp. 126–30.

[113] This letter had been reproduced in *Kerala Kaumudi*, 23 November 1922, p.1.

[114] *Proceedings of the Sree Mulam Popular Assembly*, 1908, pp. 45–46.

[115] Ibid.; P.K.K. Menon, *The History of the Freedom Movement in Kerala*, Vol. II (1885–1938), Regional Record Survey Committee, Government of Kerala, Trivandrum, 1972), p. 456.

[116] *Proceedings of the Sree Mulam Popular Assembly*, 1905, p. 73. Also see the Editorial in *Vivekodayam*, Vol. 2, No. 1, p. 1, 11 February 1905 (30 Medam 1080 ME).

[117] *Proceedings of the Sree Mulam Popular Assembly*, 1907, p. 40.

[118] File No. 355 of 1910, Education Department, Travancore, Kerala Secretariat, Trivandrum.

[119] *Proceedings of the Sree Mulam Popular Assembly*, 1908, p. 73.

[120] Dewan's reply to the question of a member, *Proceedings of the Sree Mulam Popular Assembly*, 1913, p. 137.

[121] *Proceedings of the Sree Mulam Popular Assembly*, 1907, p. 46; File No. 355 of 1910, p. 2, Education Department, Travancore, Kerala Secretariat, Trivandrum.

[122] *Proceedings of the Sree Mulam Popular Assembly*, 1910, pp. 39–40; *Vivekodayam*, Vol. 6, Nos. 8–9, November 1909 to January 1910 (Vrischikam–Dhanu 1085 ME), p. 252.

[123] P.K. Gopalakrishnan, 'Samudhaya Parishkarana Prasthanangal', in Kerala History Association, *Kerala Charitram*, Government Press, Ernakulam, 1973, Vol. I, p. 1218.

[124] T.K. Velu Pillai, *The Travancore State Manual*, 4 vols, Government Press, Trivandrum, 1940, Vol. III, pp. 735 and 756.

[125] *Proceedings of the Sree Mulam Popular Assembly*, 1919, p. 91.

[126] Reply of the Dewan to the demand of an Ezhava member in the Assembly to remove the restrictions on admission of Ezhavas in the Ayurvedic and Sanskrit College: *Proceedings of the Sree Mulam Popular Assembly*, 1907, p. 46.

[127] *Vivekodayam*, Vol. 11, No. 6, September–October 1914 (Kanni 1090 ME), p. 233.

[128] *Proceedings of the Sree Mulam Popular Assembly*, 1918, p. 12.

[129] *Vivekodayam*, Vol. 3, Nos 2 and 3, June–August 1905 (Mithunam–Karkkadakam 1081 ME), p. 9.

[130] *Vivekodayam*, Vol. 1, No. 5, 11 February 1905 (30 Makaram 1080 ME), p. 94.

[131] *Vivekodayam*, Vol. 4, Nos. 4 and 5, July and September 1907 (Karkkadakam 1082 and Chingam 1083 ME), p. 3.

[132] *Mitavadi*, Vol. 5, No. 6, June 1917, p. 7.

[133] *Vivekodayam*, Vol. 13, Nos. 10–11, January–March 1917 (Makaram–Kumbam 1902 ME).

[134] *Mitavadi*, Vol. 5, No. 7, June 1971, p. 5. The president of this central committee was P. Ramaswami Ayyar who was the Deputy Director of Education in Travancore, and N. Kumaran Asan was elected as secretary.

[135] *Kerala Kaumudi*, 24 May 1923, p. 1.

[136] *Private Papers of Dr Palpu*, File No. 6, p. 109, Nehru Memorial Museum and Library, New Delhi.

[137] Ibid., p. 108.

[138] Murkothu Kunhappa, 'Thiyyarude Charitram Oru Vihaga Veekshanam', *SNDP Yogam Platinum Jubilee Souvenir*, 1978, pp. 71–72; *Private Papers of Dr Palpu*, File No. 4, p. 109, Nehru Memorial Museum and Library, New Delhi.

[139] *Census of Travancore, 1875*, Report, p. 246, and *Census of India, 1931*, Vol. XXVIII, Travancore, Part I, Report, pp. 310–11.

[140] See chapter 1.

[141] *Mitavadi*, Vol. 5, No. 6, June 1917.

[142] *Vivekodayam*, Vol. I, No. 8, November–December 1912 (Vrischikam 1088 ME).

[143] The government made it clear in 1891 that the social position of the untouchables 'is such

that they can hardly be eligible for public offices where a certain amount of respect is expected to be commanded in a state where Hindus are more conservative and superstitious than their brethren in Malabar'. See Government Endorsement to the *Malayali Memorial* No. 1899 M 888, *English Records*, Government Secretariat, Trivandrum.

144 *Malayali Memorial*, reproduced in *Kerala Archives News Letter*, Vol. II, Nos. II and III, March and June 1976, p. 5.

145 According to the Dewan, 'There are only two of their class out of a population of 887,175, who have graduated from the university and a very few, indeed, if any, who are seeking a higher education in the local college'. See Endorsement to Travancore Memorial, File No. 1899/M 884, *English Records*, Government Secretariat (Cellar), Trivandrum; *Vivekodayam*, Vol. 3, No. 7, 18 October 1906 (32 Kanni 1082 ME), p. 4.

146 *Kerala Sanchari*, 7 October 1896; *Madras Native News Paper Report*, 1896, p. 273.

147 *Private Papers of Dr Palpu*, File No. 12, pp. 128–30, Nehru Memorial Museum and Library, New Delhi. Also see the reply to P. Velayudhan from J.C. Harrington relating to his application for a job in Travancore, dated 21 July 1888, where he talks about his attempt and failure to get him a job in Travancore and Cochin. Quoted in P.S. Velayudhan, *SNDP Yoga Charitram*, 1978, p. 28. After getting his medical degree from Madras University, when Dr Palpu applied to the Travancore Government for a job, he was informed that not only was there no vacancy in the Medical Department at that time but that there was no chance in the impending future. See *Vivekodayam*, Vol. 4, Nos. 4 and 5, July–September 1907 (Karkkadakam 1082 and Chingam 1083 ME), p. 6.

148 *Kerala Sanchari*, 7 October 1896; *Madras Native News Paper Report*, 1896, p. 273.

149 'Disabilities of Thiyyas of Travancore', *Kerala Sanchari*, 1 January 1896; *Madras Native Newspaper Report*, 1896, p. 11.

150 See P.K. Balakrishnan, *Sree Narayana Guru*, pp. 49–50. But the statement of Nair objection was denied by *Sujanandhini*, an Ezhava journal, which described this as an excuse of orthodox Brahmin Dewans. See *Vivekodayam*, Vol. 2, No. 3, 15 July 1905 (32 Midhunam 1080 ME), p. 1.

151 P.K. Balakrishnan, *Sree Narayana Guru*, pp. 49–50.

152 See full text of *Ezhava Memorial*, in M.J. Koshy, *Genesis of Political Consciousness in Kerala*, Kerala Historical Society, Trivandrum, 1972, Appendix No. IV, pp. 190–200.

153 G.P. Sekhar (ed.), *G.P. Centenary Souvenir: Select Writings and Speeches of G.P. Pillai*, Trivandrum, 1964, pp. 111–16.

154 Quoted in the Memorandum submitted to His Excellency, the last Governor of Madras, by Dr Palpu. See *Private Papers of Dr Palpu*, File no. 6, Nehru Memorial Museum and Library, New Delhi.

155 *Vivekodayam*, Vol. 3, No. 7, 17 November 1906 (32 Thulam 1082 ME), p. 4.

156 *Vivekodayam*, Vol. 2, No. 3, 15 July 1905 (32 Midhunam 1080 ME), p. 3.

157 Ibid.

158 *Vivekodayam*, Vol. 2, No. 7, 15 November 1906 (30 Thulam 1081 ME), p. 3.

159 *Proceedings of the Sree Mulam Popular Assembly*, 1913, p. 160.

160 *Vivekodayam*, Vol. 2, No. 3, 15 July 1905 (32 Midhunam 1080 ME), Editorial, p. 1; 17 November 1906, p. 4; and other back issues.

161 See T.K. Ravindran, *Asan and Social Revolution in Kerala: A Study of His Assembly Speeches*, Kerala Historical Society, Trivandrum, 1972.

162 *Vivekodayam*, Vol. 2, No. 3, 15 July 1905 (32 Midhunam 1080 ME), p. 13.

163 Ibid.

164 *Vivekodayam*, Vol. II, Nos. 1 and 2, April–June 1914 (Medam–Edavam 1089 ME).

165 *Proceeding of the Sree Mulam Popular Assembly*, 1913, p. 163.

166 *Vivekodayam*, Vol. II, Nos. 1 and 2, April–June 1914 (Medam–Edavam 1089 ME).

167 *Proceedings of the Sree Mulam Popular Assembly*, 1914, p. 116.

168 P.K.K. Menon, *History of the Freedom Movement in Kerala*, Vol. II, p. 284.

169 Ibid., p. 283.

170 *Caste and Citizenships in Travancore*, Travancore Civic Rights League, Kottayam, 1919, p. 3.

[171] P.K.K. Menon, *History of the Freedom Movement in Kerala*, Vol. II, p. 289; *Malayala Manorama*, 14 December 1922.

[172] File No. 53, 1919, Political Department, *English Records*, Kerala Secretariat, Trivandrum.

[173] Ibid.; K.R. Narayanan, 'Shri T.K. Madhavan', *SNDP Yogam Golden Jubilee Souvenir*, 1953, p. 103.

[174] File No. 53, 1919, Political Department, *English Records*, Kerala Secretariat, Trivandrum.

[175] Ibid.

[176] *Proceedings of the Sree Mulam Popular Assembly*, 1919.

[177] 'Press communiqué on the Devaswam Proclamation of 1922', in P.K.K. Menon, *History of the Freedom Movement in Kerala*, Vol. II, p. 287.

[178] Ibid., p. 288.

[179] *Devaswam Hand Book*, Section I, File No. 53, 1919, Political Department, *English Records*, Kerala Secretariat, Trivandrum; P.S. Velayudhan, *SNDP Charitram*, p. 198; P.K.K. Menon, *History of the Freedom Movement in Kerala*, Vol. II, p. 283.

[180] K.R. Narayanan, 'Shri T.K. Madhavan', p. 103.

[181] *Malayala Manorama*, 14 December 1922.

[182] P.K. Madhavan, *The Life of T.K. Madhavan*, Vol. II, p. 458.

[183] Ibid., pp. 469–70; *Vivekodayam*, January–March 1932 (Makaram–Kumbam 1107 ME), pp. 18–22.

[184] *Vivekodayam*, Vol. 21, Nos. 1 and 2, September–November 1930 (Kanni–Thulam 1106 ME), p. 17.

[185] Ibid., p. 18; *Kerala Kaumudi*, 16 October 1929, p. 5.

[186] *The Dasan*, 27 August 1932.

[187] All Travancore Joint Political Congress (1934), p. 27.

[188] C.V. Kunjuraman, 'Samuhya Parishkkaranam', *Vivekodayam*, Vol. I, No. 4, 15 November 1904 (30 Thulam 1080 ME), p. 64.

[189] Ibid.

[190] *Vivekodayam*, Vol. 2, No. 3, 15 July 1905 (32 Mithunam 1080 ME), p. 3.

[191] Ibid.

[192] *Kerala Kaumudi*, 6 May 1920, p. 2.

[193] See P.K. Balakrishnan, 'Sivagiri Pilgrimage', in *Narayana Guru*, pp. 146–49, and M.K. Sanoo, *Narayana Guru Swami*, pp. 487–88.

[194] Ibid.; Murkothu Kumaran, *Sree Narayana Guru Swamikalude Jeevacharitram*, p. 303.

[195] Ibid.

[196] C. Kesavan, *Jeevitasamaram*, Vol. I, pp. 330–31.

[197] M.S.A. Rao, *Social Movements and Social Transformation*, p. 109.

[198] *Vivekodayam*, Vol. 6, Nos. 1–2, April–June 1909 (Medam–Edavam 1084 ME), p. 21.

[199] C. Kesavan, *Jeevitasamaram*, Vol. I, pp. 407–11.

[200] *Vivekodayam*, Vol. 3, Nos. 3–4, June–August 1906 (Mithunam–Karkkadakam 1081 ME).

[201] *Vivekodayam*, Vol. 6, Nos. 1–2, April–June 1909 (Medam–Edavam 1084 ME), p. 21.

[202] *Vivekodayam*, January–March 1911 (Makaram–Kumbam 1086 ME), p. 264; K.R. Achuthan, *C. Krishnan* (biography, Malayalam), N.B.S., Kottayam, 1971, pp. 71–76 and 244–75.

[203] *Vivekodayam*, January–February 1930 (Makaram 1105 ME).

[204] *Private Papers of Dr Palpu*, File No. 19, Nehru Memorial Museum and Library, New Delhi; *Vivekodayam*, Vol. II, Nos. 1–2, April–June 1914 (Medam–Edavam 1086 ME), p. 159.

[205] *Private Papers of Dr Palpu*, File No. 19, Nehru Memorial Museum and Library, New Delhi.

[206] *Private Papers of Dr Palpu*, File No. 17, Nehru Memorial Museum and Library, New Delhi.

[207] Although this name sounds strange, this is exactly how it is mentioned in my source: *Kerala Kaumudi*, 6 May 1920, p. 2. Hence it has been retained as such.

[208] Ibid.

[209] Ibid.

[210] Ibid.

5

Religiosity–Sociality Continuum

India witnessed several social and religious reform movements during the nineteenth and twentieth centuries. While there was differentiation among them in terms of content and context, the inseparability of the religious and social spheres in Hindu society led the 'reformers' to combine them as if they were integral parts of the same process.[1] Religious reformers like Raja Ram Mohan Roy, Keshub Chandra Sen, Debendranath Tagore, Sasipada Banerjee, Gopal Hari Deshmukh, Ramakrishna Paramahamsa, Dayananda Saraswati, Swami Vivekananda and Sree Narayana Guru, all combined their social reform activities with religious reforms. Emancipation of women, abolition of caste, questioning of taboos on sea voyage, and eradication of 'outdated' customs and other objectionable practices were some of the socio-religious issues that were addressed by these reformers.[2] Almost all of them gave priority to the resolution of local problems which overlapped self-evident contemporary categories in the social, religious, political and economic spheres. It is important to underscore the fact that their activities were not influenced by a notion of homogeneous sociality.

As already mentioned, in the beginning of the second half of the nineteenth century,[3] Christian missionaries played an enabling role in Travancore, in the contexts of legal abolition of slavery, social equality, introducing English education, achieving permission to wear the breast cloth, etc. These have been widely accepted as remarkable achievements of the missionaries.[4] In addition, the western-educated middle class, especially of the Nair community, expressed their disenchantment with prevailing social practices and customs.[5] There was also the presence of several printed journals and forums (such as debating societies) for spreading new messages about what ought to be relegated and what imbibed.[6] These exemplars clearly reveal the recognition of a compelling need for reforms, which permeated every walk of life and was felt by the educated high-caste people of Travancore even before the advent of Sree Narayana Guru. Needless to say, these waves of recognition were confined to a small section of the educated and upper middle-class sections of the society.

We have already seen that after the consecration of Shiva in 1888, Sree

Narayana Guru earned the reputation of a great and inspiring teacher who strove to create awareness and social consciousness among both the unlettered masses and the educated. His social and religious reform ideas were imbued with the progressive tendencies that had already appeared in Indian society in the nineteenth century.[7] Besides Narayana Guru, western-educated Ezhavas in Kerala who were aware of the potential of social reform movements elsewhere, and for whom advancement of their caste implied adoption of modern social ideals, stood up against irrational and dehumanizing social practices. The middle class of the SNDP Yogam therefore ventured towards social reform of members of the Ezhava community.

The scattered, disparate and individual ideas of the early reformers needed to be mobilized and organized, and systematic efforts were made in this direction by Sree Narayana Guru and the SNDP Yogam. Emancipation of women was a major issue of social reform movements in other parts of India[8] as women were subjected to discriminatory practices like *sati,* the *purdah* system, female infanticide, denial of widow remarriage, non-inheritance of property and lack of sexual freedom. In Kerala, however, a majority of women, except Namboodiris and Muslims, enjoyed relatively better social and economic freedoms under the matrilineal system.[9] The majority of Ezhavas followed the matrilineal system under which womenfolk were self-reliant, and so the Guru and the Yogam chose to target social issues that affected the community at large.[10] The agenda of their social reform activities included teaching members of the Ezhava caste about the need to erase the existing differences within their caste; eradication of outdated and expensive customs and practices, particularly life-cycle rituals; opposing social evils like consumption of liquor and substitution of matriliny by patrilineal law; and abolition of casteism and untouchability.

Achieving Homogeneity within the Ezhava Community

The existence of differentiated sub-castes among Ezhavas hampered the efforts to congregate them within a shared domain; it also hindered the inculcation of ideas of reform among them equally. Since the reforms were addressed to the caste as a whole, homogeneity within the community was critical in gaining the all-round support of different sections of Ezhavas. Therefore, the reformers made efforts to break the barriers of sub-casteism and to unite them within a single fold. Sub-casteism functioned more or less like casteism; untouchability and unapproachability were prevalent in sub-caste relations, similar to their influence on inter-caste relations.[11] For instance, untouchability was practised between Ezhavas and Thiyyas. Further, Ezhavas belonging to the upper class and of higher status had no social relations with the rest of the community.[12] In short, the persistence of untouchability and unapproachability were integral to both intra-caste relations among the Ezhavas, as well as relations between Ezhavas and the *savarna*s. The hierarchical stratification of the Ezhava caste was the severest obstacle in the way of the spread of reform ideas among members of this caste.

The first attempt of the reformers was to bring all Ezhavas and Thiyyas on a united platform, without any discrimination regarding inferior and superior status. They propagated the idea of unity through lectures, the vernacular press, local seminars and discussions. They emphasized the importance of relegating endogenous stratification and the need for unification of the community to redress their grievances. Sree Narayana Guru was a champion of the campaigns against both intra-caste and inter-caste discrimination. He called upon the people to find their way out of the caste system and to become socially united.[13] In a message issued to the All Kerala Conference of the Sahodhara Sangam (Brotherhood Association) of K. Ayyappan, which was held at Alwaye in 1921, he asserted: 'Whatever be the religion, customs, language, etc., of men, since their species is the same there is no harm in inter-marriage and inter-dining.'[14] As an exponent of the Advaita philosophy and a staunch follower of religious universalism, for Narayana Guru, any religion and any caste was as good as the other. In order to create a feeling of oneness among the Ezhavas, the SNDP Yogam decided to adopt a common name for the entire community, in lieu of different names like Ezhavas, Thiyyas, Chovans, etc. Therefore, in 1923, at the twentieth annual meeting of the Yogam, a resolution was passed to use the name Thiyya for all sections of the caste in Kerala, and the government was requested to use only this name and not to invoke the name Ezhava in all government records and documents.[15]

The idea of adopting the name Thiyya came about due to various reasons. First, the sub-caste-based stratification of the community worked against its larger interests, with the various sub-castes objecting to any sort of understanding among the members of the community as a whole.[16] In order to build the community as a united force by dissolving the sub-castes, the leaders of the movement thought of changing the title of the community itself. That is how this idea found expression at the twentieth annual meeting of the Yogam. Secondly, the name 'Ezhava' signified the Ceylonese origin of the community;[17] the reformers, who wanted to identify themselves as indigenous and erase the migration theory from collective memory, preferred the name Thiyya.[18] Finally, for the pro-changers, the name Thiyya was a more attractive and suitable alternative, since the Thiyyas of Malabar occupied important positions in government service,[19] and were comparatively better off than the Ezhavas of Cochin and Travancore.[20]

However, this attempt to adopt the name Thiyya as a comprehensive term for the community did not materialize due to the opposition of a section of the Ezhavas in Travancore.[21] Despite the best efforts of the Yogam, it could not uproot caste feelings among its own members. In the context of the proposed name change, Kumaran Asan, the general secretary of the Yogam, was subjected to humiliation by some members who belonged to a sub-caste that was considered superior to the one to which he belonged. This instance alone is sufficient to indicate how the Yogam was not able to erase intra-caste hierarchy within the community, or to establish an order of harmonious coexistence that derecognized the system of sub-castes.[22] Though the Yogam did not succeed in eradicating sectarian feelings among the Ezhavas, as a result of its activities, the Ezhavas of Travancore were officially recorded as a single caste in the 1931 Census. Before this they had been classified under twenty-two sub-castes, as in the 1891 Census.[23] In the context of social advancement, the Yogam did not recognize differences between sects or classes within the community.[24] However, its efforts at reducing hierarchical stratification and conflicts based on sub-castes did not get the desired results.

Modification of Worship Patterns and Construction of Temples

The reformers initiated activities for ameliorating age-old forms of worship such as animal sacrifice, offerings of toddy and the blood of roosters, and the singing of obscene songs. The religious worship of the Ezhavas was a mixture of traditional Hinduism tinged with animism and other local-specific beliefs.[25] Being non-caste Hindus, they worshipped gods and goddesses of 'lesser status' like Paycoil, Ammancoil, Kuttichhathan, Shodalamadan, Bhoothathan, Mari Amman, Venkaramadan, Bhadrakali, etc.;[26] they were forbidden from worshipping 'higher' gods and goddesses belonging to the Sanskritic Hindu tradition, like Vishnu and Shiva. The deity they worshipped most commonly was Bhadrakali, a demon-goddess described as a mixture of mischief and cruelty. Bloody sacrifices and offerings, and devil dancing were essential elements of the ceremonies of her worshippers. Similarly, Kodungallur Bhagavati was also a very popular deity among them. For pleasing this goddess they would sing obscene songs[27] and conduct fowl sacrifice called *kozhivettu*.

The emerging Ezhava middle class viewed such practices of worship as 'primitive' and termed them 'uncultured practices'. At the first annual meeting of the Yogam, Palpu said: 'Whatever be the prosperity of a society in other walks of life, if it is practised with cruel and dishonest appeal and civility no doubt that it is very wicked and ignorant.'[28] This interpretation of conventional religious/social practices was to a great extent influenced by western education and the discourse of Christian missionaries. In this context, the consecration of a Hindu god by Narayana Guru gains great significance. It may be postulated that the above-mentioned practices being viewed by the reformers as 'primitive' and 'uncultured', as something to be discarded by the community and obliterated from social memory, was due to the influence of orientalist representations,[29] internalized by them through their exposure to English education.

As a substitute for the 'primitive gods' and in imitation of the pantheistic caste Hindus, they began to adopt Hindu deities and the associated worship practices. Sree Narayana Guru not only consecrated the gods of upper-caste Hindus in the Ezhava pantheon, but also removed older 'demonic' deities from Ezhava temples. In 1915, the Guru removed twenty-one such deities – such as Yakshi, Madanpeedam, Bhoothathan, Chodalamadan, Ezhakathi Peedom, Mallan, Karunkali Peedam, Karuppan and Erulan – from the Kottattu Arumukhan Pillayar Koil and other nearby temples.[30] He removed these deities from Ezhava temples as well as exhorted Ezhavas to discard them from their homes.[31] At that time, many well-to-do Ezhava houses had their own private temples where they consecrated deities like Chathan, Chamundi, Kandaran and Madan.[32] Although there was some response from the community to these calls, the older religious beliefs and practices could not be discontinued abruptly or altogether, as they were deep-rooted as well as strongly reproduced in the social memory.

The Yogam distributed a notice among members of the Ezhava community, appealing that they put an end to the worship of 'evil deities' and animal sacrifice. The twelfth annual meeting of the Yogam, held in Trivandrum in May 1915, passed a resolution to discard these forms of worship, and requested the government to issue an order to stop animal sacrifice which was still being practised in some Travancore temples.[33] There were also other individuals and associations that opposed and fought against these practices. Prominent among them were A. Ayyappan and Harippad Madhavan, founders of the Sahodhara Sangam and Sree Narayana Karunavilasini Yogam, respectively. Sahodharan Ayyappan particularly attacked the practice of singing obscene songs at temples and fowl sacrifice in the Kodungallur Temple. Similarly, Harippad Madhavan did his best to stop such practices at the Kolattupuzha Bhagavati temple in Karunagappally.[34]

These activities of Narayana Guru, his followers and others could be understood as primarily an expression of the developing trend of reforms in the religious life of the people. But it is also possible to discern in these attempts a movement towards Hinduization – through the creation of a discontinuity in the worship patterns of the Ezhavas and establishment of a continuity with the worship practices of upper-caste Hindus.

As a consequence of these religious reform activities, Ezhavas gradually began to give up their traditional system of worship and started worshipping deities like Shiva, Subramanyan and Ganapathy; most Ezhavas became worshippers of Shiva.[35] As a community they are more Shaivite than Vaishnavaite, but they did not eschew worship of Vishnu altogether.[36] The popularization of Shiva worship might have been induced by the belief that Shiva was a

God of Dravidian origin, and the lack of interest in Vishnu and Brahma (the other two Gods in the Hindu trinity) might have been due to the belief that they were products of the Aryanization of India. We have already seen that the temples consecrated by Narayana Guru were not simply a replica of the temples of caste Hindus; rather, they posed a challenge to the age-old hegemony of Brahmin tutelage. The priests for these temples were chosen from the community and they were generally known as Ezhavatti.[37]

In short, in the field of religious practice, the reformers advocated deconsecration of the Ezhava community's favoured gods and goddesses, and the worship practices associated with them, and introduced idols of the caste Hindus but minus their priests. As these endeavors were spearheaded by Narayana Guru, his legitimization as a secular saint was not difficult to achieve.

Abolition of Superstitious Customs and Practices

Another important activity of the Yogam was its crusade to liberate the unlettered untouchables from the grip of 'superstitious customs' and obscure social practices. Life-cycle practices such as *talikettu kalyanam*, *tirandukuli*, *pulikudi* and marriage practices were the initial targets. At that time almost all *marumakkathayam* or matrilineal communities in Kerala celebrated the above-mentioned customs with ritualistic pomp. Though the educated Nair middle class had started a campaign against such practices within their community, and heterodox Ezhava youths like C.V. Kunjuraman and others were inspired by them,[38] it had not found an appreciable response among the Ezhava community as a whole. But soon, due to the persistent initiatives of Narayana Guru and the Yogam, and the enthusiastic efforts of C.V. Kunjuraman, this movement gained a new vitality and strength.

On 16 October 1904 (31 Kanni 1080 ME), a historical Ezhava conference was held at Paravoor near Quilon under the chairmanship of the Guru.[39] Its aim was to pave the way for social and economic amelioration of Ezhavas by breaking away from irrational and unscientific social institutions. It was at this conference that Narayana Guru laid down the guidelines for putting an end to socially regressive practices like *talikettu*, *tirandukuli* and *pulikudi*, and introduced a new code of conduct for marriage.[40] Let us now briefly examine these life-cycle rituals which were held up as undesirable by the Guru and the Yogam.

All girls belonging to matrilineal families, before they attained puberty, had to undergo a ritual marriage by tying a *tali* – a small gold ornament in the shape of a pipal leaf that was threaded on a cotton cord and worn round the neck; this could be performed only by a member of her own caste or a higher caste, but never by someone from a lower caste.[41] The ceremony was popularly known as *talikettukalyanam*. It was considered a dishonour to the family if a girl were to attain puberty before undergoing this customary ritual.[42] However, till 1869, tenant-farmers and other lower sections of society, irrespective of caste differences, had to take prior permission of the government to perform this expensive ceremony with its accompanying pomp and show.[43]

The ceremony was generally conducted as follows. All girls below the age of twelve from a *taravad* (joint family) with various *tavazhis* (lineages) would be seated facing south to north in a decorated pandal.[44] Either a single boy or a group of boys,[45] brought in a procession, would tie the *tali* around their necks as in an adult marriage. The boys were escorted to the girls' house on an elephant or horse, or on foot, depending on the status and dignity of the families.[46] The celebration, with complicated rituals and festivities, lasted four days.[47] At the end of the fourth day the bridegroom had to surrender his ceremonial robes and depart after obtaining a fixed fee.[48] In some places there was a custom of tearing up a cloth called the *kachcha* on the fourth day of the ceremony,[49] while in other places the *tali* – signifying the marital status of the girl – was removed shortly after the ceremony.[50] Both these symbolized termination of the marriage. Following this formal divorce after the *tali* ceremony, neither the boy nor the girl had any rights or duties towards each other.[51]

According to the famous jurist T. Muthuswamy Aiyer, 'As a religious ceremony the *kettukalyanam* is intended to give the girl a marriageable status.'[52] The *tali* rite as a 'ritual formality'[53] was primarily a means of declaring a girl's social maturity.[54] Heterodox, educated youths and social reformers looked down upon this ceremony as an empty ritual,[55] and considered it absurd and unnecessary.[56]

Another prevalent custom was *tirandukuli* – a ceremonial bath ceremony performed after a girl attained her first menstruation. This expensive and elaborate ceremony involving revelry and a sumptuous feast also lasted four days, and ended in a procession leading the girl to a pond or river for a bath.[57] This was in the nature of a public declaration that the girl had attained the age of marriage.[58]

The actual marriage, called *pudavakoda* or cloth-giving ceremony, usually took place only after the girl had attained puberty.[59] In different parts of Kerala the marriage of Ezhavas was known by various names, such as 'mangalam', and 'kalyanam'.[60] To conduct a marriage, neither the consent of the boy or the girl was necessary for it was the *karanavan*'s decision that was binding. The proposal for the marriage had to come from the bridegroom's side.[61] During the marriage itself, not even the presence of the bridegroom was necessary; in lieu of the bridegroom, his sister would give the *pudava* or cloth to the bride,[62] and then the bride would be taken to her husband's house for *kudivaippu*.[63] The 'gift of cloth' was made in a room of the house which, owing to the traditional architectural style, used to be dark. Therefore, it was not uncommon for impersonation to take place.[64] Another feature of marriage was the existence of polygamy and polyandry. As Ezhavas practised fraternal polyandry,[65] the women's choice of more than one husband extended to brothers of her husband or members of the same family.[66] Divorce and remarriage were common; widow remarriage was also permitted.[67]

Another traditionally observed ceremony was *pulikudi*, a ritual performed in the seventh month of the first pregnancy of a woman.[68] This ritual involved ceremonial drinking of a juice prepared by mixing seven different ingredients of sour taste.[69] A part of the ceremony was the pouring of oil over the head of the pregnant woman to determine the sex of the child. 'If the oil flows over the left side it predicts the birth of a female and on the right side, a male.'[70] As in the case of other ceremonies, this too was followed by a sumptuous feast provided to all relatives and friends; but unlike the others, this one lasted only for two days.[71]

All these customs and festivities involved huge expenditures. They persisted, however, because such occasions enabled social interaction of otherwise disparate family groupings. Intimate associations and relationships were reinforced through feasts and the offering of gifts. Perhaps, as time evolved, the priorities were inverted; that is, if conventionally the 'social' was prioritized over the 'economic' through such customary expenditures, it was the economic that got prioritized over the social in the modern era of reforms. Therefore, to the reformers, members of their community appeared not to be introspecting about the relevance of such customs in a changing socio-cultural and economic scenario.[72] As the social status of families was dictated by the grandeur of these functions, they were willing to meet the expenditures involved by even going to the extent of selling their properties, although knowing fully well that this could lead to economic deprivation.[73]

Every system has a rationale within the structure in which it comes into being. It becomes outdated and meaningless only when structural changes take place. These extravagant ceremonies, as mentioned above, ceased to exist or be justified amidst the enthusiasm for social reform. Such a change took place in Travancore society as a result of missionary activities, modern education, reform activities, and changed notions of prudence and economy. It is also true that there existed protest and dissent both in the Indian intellectual tradition and in subsequent social developments in the eighteenth century, i.e. prior to the intervention of the British.[74] Therefore, reformers who belonged to both the strands – traditional as well as the modern, educated intellectuals – contributed to the emergence of social reform movements in Travancore. Though they were products of divergent intellectual backgrounds, they shared the belief that several social customs and practices prevalent in nineteenth-century Malayali society were hindering social and economic progress, or the process of 'catching up' with the colonial masters. This united Narayana

Guru, a product of the earlier Indian intellectual tradition, and the modern, educated, middle-class Ezhava reformers, in their fight against religious orthodoxy and social obscurantism. The activities of the Guru and the leaders of the Yogam against *talikettukalyanam, tirandukuli* and *pulikudi*, and their endeavour to reform marriage and other life-cycle ceremonies could be considered as constitutive of as well as constituted in the reform movement.

In opposing these customs and practices, Narayana Guru and the emerging middle class had economic, social and intellectual considerations.[75] Economically, they wanted to put an end to the extravagant expenses incurred by observance of these customs, which impoverished a large number of Ezhavas in Travancore.[76] C.V. Kunjuraman roughly calculated the expenditure for *talikettukalyanam, tirandukuli* and *pulikudi* in Karunagappally taluk in 1904 as amounting to Řs 18,47,100.[77] In opposing *pulikudi*, Kunjuraman was more concerned with the medical repercussions of compelling women to drink a mixture of seven different ingredients of sour taste in an advanced stage of pregnancy.[78] In the first report of the Yogam, the general secretary Kumaran Asan wrote that the main aim of abolishing these customs was to prevent people from wasting money on illusionary pomp and prestige of the family by conducting ceremonies on such a large scale with grand feasts.[79]

In other words, the movement led by Narayana Guru against hollow social customs suited the ideological and economic perspectives of the emerging Ezhava middle class. His call against ignorance, laziness, extravagance and unnecessary expenditures helped to develop virtues like thrift, frugality and hard work. As the reforms advocated the introduction and acceptance of such values characteristic of a bourgeois order, it is no wonder that they appealed to the Yogam, a representative organization of the emerging Ezhava middle class.

Socially, they were keen to bring about a change in norms characteristic of a decadent society.[80] The reformers wanted to protect the dignity of the community by repudiating such customs, as well as to purify the society by erasing obsolete practices. In a letter to Parayil Kochu Raman Vaidhyar, dated 11 September 1906 (26 Chingam 1081 ME), Narayana Guru stressed the need for reform for the welfare of the community. However, he had no objection to retaining useful and essential traditional practices.[81] Thus he sought to create a social climate for modernization without overlooking tradition as a whole.

The reformers' intellectual considerations were aligned to rationalism, an important ideological strand of nineteenth-century thought.[82] Narayana Guru and heterodox Ezhava youths regarded outdated social customs as irrelevant and unacceptable to the swiftly changing socio-economic rationality. The most virulent attack was against *talikettukalyanam*. They opposed people wasting their hard-earned money on a 'mock marriage'[83] which had no social or religious significance, and in which a bridegroom was not essential since a deity or a sword could substitute for him. Besides, the practice which allowed a bridegroom to marry any number of sisters, that too subject to a divorce shortly after the ceremony, could not be considered a marriage. Instead of making marriage a permanent and sacred obligation, it was brought down to the level of a mockery or an initiation ritual.[84] As rationalism was his precept, the Guru adopted a rational approach to evaluate tradition within the contemporary socio-religious norms of social utility, and replaced unreasonable faith with judicious beliefs.[85] The main dictums of the Yogam were freedom, reason and human dignity. In short, while opposing the hegemonic values of a feudal society, they were supporting a new phase in the evolution of bourgeois capitalism. It is clear from their endeavours that avoidance of extravagant expenditure on superstitious, unproductive and retrograde customs was considered to be a step forward in the path of progress.

While the Yogam called upon Ezhavas to spend their money on productive purposes instead of wasting it on ostentation,[86] it did not ask for everything inherited from the past to be banished. For instance, marriage procedures[87] remained a mixture of both the Dravidian and Sanskritic traditions. The high influence of the Vedas led L.A. Krishna Aiyer to say that 'the Ezhava rituals received a Sanskritic orientation'.[88] In the new system of marriage, the Guru introduced or insisted on the following changes:[89]: (i) the marriage should be conducted in an open or public place,[90] which ought to be neat and clean, and in the presence of a priest, relatives and friends; (ii) the presence of the bridegroom was essential during the time of the marriage; (iii) the marriage ceremony was to be performed under the guidance of a priest who could recite hymns and verses either in Malayalam or Sanskrit; (iv) the marriage should be solemnized in front of a sacrificial lamp called the *nilavilakku*, and ceremonial articles like the *ashtamangalyam* and *nirapara*, and should be accompanied by *mangalavadhyam* (playing of auspicious musical instruments); (v) the important rituals of marriage were to be the tying of a *mangalasutram* (in place of a *tali*) by the bridegroom around the bride's neck to signify her marital status,[91] followed by an exchange of garlands of flowers;[92] (vi) finally, the bride and bridegroom had to go around the sacrificial lamp and *ashtamangalyam* three times.[93] With the denouncing of elaborate domestic rituals and weeding out of unnecessary procedures, marriage became more simple and less expensive affair, and attained a new symbolic significance. These newly introduced marriage rituals upheld the values of monogamy as against the earlier practices of polyandry and polygamy.[94] As he was firmly against pomp and show, the Guru also directed that not more than ten persons should be present at the marriage ceremony.[95]

Though the priorities of social reform for the Guru were the economic, political, social and educational development of the Ezhava community as a whole, he did not ignore issues concerning women. He included the grievances of women in his agenda of social work and started educational institutions for their overall development.[96] In a message to the secretary of the Yogam on 10 May 1909, he outlined various issues relating to women. As polygamy and polyandry were still being practised by Ezhavas in some places, he asked the Yogam to take necessary steps to stop these practices.[97] He was convinced that no substantial improvement could be brought about in the condition of women without giving them the right to inherit property. So he appealed to the matrilineal sections of Ezhavas to make necessary provisions for giving a part of the self-acquired property of a man to his wife and children.[98] Resolutions supporting such measures were often passed in the meetings of the Yogam and its local associations, and at women's conferences.

The main speaker at the Paravoor conference was C.V. Kunjuraman, who was already popular among the educated middle class as a rationalist and crusader against the irrational and expensive social customs prevalent among matrilineal families.[99] In his speech, Kunjuraman made a scathing attack against *talikettukalyanam, tirandukuli* and *pulikudi*, and criticized the evils resulting from these norms. He ridiculed *talikettukalyanam* as a practice that may have been meant to educate girls at a tender age in practical knowledge about marital life, but which gave them the idea instead that they could change their husbands as they wished.[100] In other words, he explained that this ceremony prepared girls for polyandric unions.[101] Similarly, the procession leading girls to a tank or river for a bath on reaching puberty, called *tirandukuli,* was mocked as a declaration that 'the ground is ready for sowing seeds'.[102] His criticism of *pulikudi was* equally emphatic. He denounced it as a function to advertise the fact that the pregnancy is legitimate, and that the husband himself is the the biological father of the child.[103] The impact of his speech infuriated the orthodox Chanars of Paravoor, who said: 'A mad dog from Mayyanad came and bit many dogs in Paravoor.'[104]

As the opposition to reform was very strong, the basic strategy that the Guru and the Yogam adopted was to educate people and mobilize opinion against customary ceremonies hitherto considered obligatory. First, they decided to use the *Vivekodayam,* the mouthpiece of the Yogam, to mediate between the reformers and the public. *Vivekodayam* published a large number of articles highlighting the negative aspects of these customs and the need for social reform.[105] Second, the Guru asked the Yogam to organize lecture tours by able and educated speakers in order to enlighten the masses to approach socio-religious issues with a critical and scientific attitude, and also to disseminate new ideas of social reform among the people. In January 1905, the Guru sent a message to the Yogam specifying the topics for these lectures, namely, religion, morality, education and industry.[106] The objective was that these lectures would be conducive to the welfare of the community in general. The selection of the topics and the points he wanted to emphasize in each lecture show the Guru's far-sightedness and maturity of thinking,[107] which, while opposing the hegemonic values of a feudal society, were in tune with values characteristic of a bourgeois order. He reminded his followers of the need for detecting the morbid influences that affected the community and for adopting adequate curative measures, along with efforts to get their rights recognized.[108] He also gave special instructions to the speakers not to speak on subjects they were not sure of, and warned that the tone and style of language they used should neither be provocative to the so-called upper castes nor derogatory to the lower castes.[109] He reminded them to take special care to inculcate interest in the minds of the people for the welfare of the downtrodden.[110] The speakers undertook extensive tours for delivering speeches and distributed pamphlets to educate the general public. *Vivekodayam* regularly published the messages, letters and instructions of the Guru pertaining to reforms in the social, religious, economic, educational and cultural spheres.[111]

But all these social reform activities of Sree Narayana Guru and the Yogam were confined mainly to a certain section of the society, comprising educated youths, teachers, lawyers, Ayurvedic doctors and government officials. In northern and central Travancore, middle-class peasants and petty traders also took part in this movement. The reformers lacked the support of the masses, however, as their ideas and programmes failed to go beyond the middle class. At the same time, as a result of the limited spread of education, extremely restricted social mobility and, above all, the prevalence of old feudal relations, the rich peasants, big traders and even a section of the educated people not only kept away from this movement, but continued to practise the retrograde customs. Many rich and educated Ezhavas, in spite of their respect and reverence for the Guru, were not in a position to eschew their age-old customs as they were deeply influenced by tradition, or living in the clutches of a false consciousness pertaining to the feudal concept of 'family prestige', or for fear of 'social criticism'.[112] On some occasions, people found themselves compelled to celebrate these rituals because of emotional attachment to their dear ones.[113] In many such situations the Guru directly intervened, and wrote personal letters to rich and influential Ezhavas who were indifferent to the reforms.[114]

In his message to the secretary of the SNDP Yogam on 10 May 1909, the Guru evaluated the impact of reforms as follows: 'The ceremonies like *tirandukuli* and *pulikudi* are observed without much festivities and expenditure. However, advice of discarding *talikettu* is, of course, getting accepted, but the message has not created the same impact everywhere uniformly. This practice should be eradicated at the earliest as it is unprincipled and unnecessary.'[115] This shows how minutely and meticulously the Guru observed the development of social reforms. For a holy man like him to consider the material prosperity of the people to be as important as their spiritual well-being was a rare phenomenon.[116]

An interesting instance of the Guru's direct intervention was reported in the January–March 1911 (Makaram–Kumbam 1086 ME) issue of *Vivekodayam*, under the heading, 'An Amusing *Talikettukalyanam*'. On hearing the news of grand preparations for a *talikettukalyanam* at the residence of Valiya Vilakathu Arathan Kumaran at Kurunkulam in Neyyattinkara, the Guru went there just before the appointed day, 18 January 1911 (5 Makaram 1086 ME), and stopped the ritual by explaining politely yet firmly the futility of the ceremony.[117] Everybody present, including the women, accepted his advice. He blessed the girls who had gathered for the *talikettu* with flowers and fruits.[118] Similarly, when M. Govindan, a highly educated and prominent member of the Yogam, decided to celebrate the *talikettukalyanam* of his daughter in 1912, the Guru, who was extremely disappointed, wrote him a letter asking him not to conduct the ceremony.[119] Govindan promptly gave up the idea in obedience to the wishes of the Guru. As people had 'blind faith' in customary practices, they could not completely cut themselves off from tradition; however, they could not turn down the advice of the Guru. Thus he brought about some favourable changes in the attitude of the people.

The need for abolition and removal of such customs continued to remain a matter of concern, and repeated discussions took place in the annual meetings of the Yogam.[120] As mentioned earlier, this is evident from the Guru's letter to Parayil Kochu Raman Vaidhyar where he stressed the need for uniform social customs and practices and eschewing wasteful expenditure, and called for cooperation from all sections. As a result, slowly but steadily, a favourable change was discernable. In the words of Swamy Sathyvridhan: 'Thus according to the activities of Swamy and the SNDP Yogam, *talikettu* and other ceremonies were abandoned, and within a period of 20 years since the beginning of the present century, the Thiyyas had affected a saving of ten crores of rupees from its unnecessary expense.'[121]

To summarise, however slowly the ripples of reform activities may have spread among the people, their direction, and the work and achievements of Narayana Guru and the Yogam, were noteworthy. The Guru's affectionate advice coupled with his charisma and spirituality on the one side, and the persistent work of the Yogam on the other, helped considerably to reduce the influence of customs and rituals that had become a heavy financial burden, and were a hurdle in the way of the desired social progress.

Challenges to Changes in the Law of Inheritance

Another important social reform activity of the Yogam was its effort to change the system of inheritance and succession rights. There was no uniform law of inheritance among the Ezhavas of Travancore. In fact, they followed three distinct types of law of inheritance, viz. *marumakkathayam* or matriliny, *makkathayam* or patriliny, and *misradayam* or a mixed system of both *marumakkathayam* and *makkathayam*. According to *marumakkathayam* – a system of inheritance and descent through the female line – a man's legal heirs were his sister's children. Paternal property was never given to the wife and children.[122] Under the *misradayam* system of inheritance, both children and *anantharavas* (younger male members of the family) inherited equal shares of the assets of the deceased.[123] In Travancore, a majority of the Ezhavas were followers of the matrilineal system. About 60 per cent of Ezhava families followed *marumakkathayam*, whereas 30 per cent of the rest followed *misradayam*. Matriliny was mainly followed by Ezhavas in all taluks of the north of Quilon, patriliny was popular in the extreme south, and *misradayam* mainly in Neyyattinkara.[124]

By the beginning of the twentieth century, the reformers started a movement for changing the laws of inheritance. Various factors like the economic changes in the society,[125] new means of independent income for junior members of the family, the overwhelming influence of the *karanavan* over *anantharavas*, new ideological and cultural perspectives acquired by the educated middle class, emergence of the nuclear family, and, finally, the Nair Regulation of 1912, urged the Ezhavas to demand a change in their laws of inheritance.

In addition to the factors mentioned above, the increase in prices of coconut products like coir, copra, oil, toddy, etc., contributed towards favourable economic circumstances of the Ezhavas. These opportunities provided by British colonialism helped junior members of Ezhava families to acquire independent incomes. But under matriliny the wealth acquired from any source by either the males or the females of a *taravad* was considered as joint property,[126] under the management of the *karanavan*. As manager of the *taravad* property the *karanavan* not only controlled the income, but also used up the surplus money from *taravad* properties for satiating his own needs or that of his spouse and children.[127] Income distribution among family members thus became a problem. Rather than sharing the income of *taravad* properties equally, junior members of the family were only entitled to money required to meet the expenses of their basic needs like food, clothing and oil; childbirth expenses of their wives; and token gifts to their wives at festivals like *Onam* and *Vishu*.[128] The spread of education and increase in social mobility considerably changed their concept of family life. The needs of junior members of the family 'increased due to changes in the social climate and in the nature of the internal market, and they soon perceived the disparity between what was due to them and what was actually received by them'.[129]

Dissatisfaction with the management of the *karanavan* of the joint family created dissension within the *taravad*. Apart from being partial towards his own wife and children, the *karanavan* often failed to treat all members of the *taravad* equally. There was an increasing desire among the well-to-do families of that time to send their children to English schools with the aim of gaining employment in government service. Though the *taravads* were not too badly off financially, they could not afford school fees for all the male members of the joint family. Therefore, the *karanavan* facilitated the education of his direct nephews, while the nephews of other *tavazhis* (lineages) were retained as agriculturists and servants in the *taravad*. The increasing importance of education and the bias of the *karanavan* created dissensions within the *taravad*, and induced young men to break away from the matrilineal system.[130]

Another feature of matriliny was that an adult belonging to a *taravad* did not have the power to dispose of his self-acquired property by will, and if he died intestate, his wife and children were not entitled to any of his property. This discouraged many from engaging in productive and revenue-earning activities, and to the slowing down of economic progress. The existence of the *taravad* and the *karanavan*'s management of property proved to be of no advantage to junior members of the joint family. Fathers had little responsibility for their children, for these children lived under the yoke of the *karanavan*.[131] The existence of such a family situation and the outdated law of inheritance inspired the social reformers to try and change the law. On 10 May 1909, Sree Narayana Guru sent a message to the Yogam in which he appealed: 'Where *marumakkathayam* system is followed in the community, legal provision should be made to give to the wedded wife and children the right to a portion of a man's individual earnings. Otherwise marriage would be meaningless. Necessary steps in this direction should be taken after careful consideration.'[132]

The changes in the attitude of the Ezhava elites and persuasion from Sree Narayana Guru undermined the cohesion and unity of matrilineal joint families. Another factor which induced the Ezhavas to change their law of inheritance was the disproportionately large share that the women could claim of *taravad* property. Under matriliny, inheritance and succession was through the mother, and all the children (sons and daughters) of daughters of the family had rights to matrilineal property, whereas the children of sons, whether male or female, had no such rights.[133]

A further motivation that induced Ezhavas to change their law of inheritance was the desire for unity. The fact that Ezhavas followed three distinct systems of inheritance had considerably reduced the feeling of oneness among them. There were a number of restrictions on marital relations between these different groups. Therefore, they thought that a common law of inheritance would help to unite them[134] and eradicate the sub-caste distinctions in terms of lineage.

The immediate inspiration to change the law of inheritance came from the Nair Regulation of 1088 ME (1912). From the last quarter of the nineteenth century onwards, the Nair elites of Malabar[135] and Travancore started a movement for changing their law of inheritance and claiming legal validity for the practice of *sambandham*. In 1887, the Malayali Sabha, an organization of Travancore Nairs, circulated a draft marriage bill for Nairs. But the Government of Travancore did not take it seriously. In 1896, Thanu Pillai introduced a bill in the Travancore Legislative Council to provide legal recognition for all marriages solemnized by the presentation of cloth or any other such recognized ceremony. But this bill did not undertake to change the system of inheritance, so that when a Nair man died, his nephews in the *taravad* remained the rightful heirs of his personal property.

The Travancore Act of 1899 provided marginal reform by conferring on *marumakkathayi* Nairs the right to bequeath up to one-half of their self-acquired property to their wives and children. The Nairs were not satisfied with this, however, and continued their efforts to achieve their goal. In 1907, in the second annual meeting of the Kerala Nair Samajam, P.G. Govinda Pillai introduced a resolution which advocated three things: (1) giving children a legal claim for maintenance from their father; (2) making a man's self-acquired property heritable only by descendants of that branch of his *taravad* originating from his mother; (3) allotting half of a man's self-acquired property to his wife and children on his death. Another resolution that was passed at the same meeting demanded recognition of the ceremony of *sambandham* as legal marriage. As a result of their consistent demands, P. Rajagopalachari, then Dewan of Travancore, appointed a committee in 1907 to investigate and report on the reforms proposed by the Nair elites regarding marriage, inheritance, partition of *taravad*, etc., within joint families of Nairs.[136] The committee, after thorough investigation, submitted its report in 1908, recommending the recognition of *sambandham* as legal marriage, maintenance of accounts by the *karanavan*, granting to wives and children a half share of the self-acquired property of a man dying intestate, as well as the right of any *tavazhi* of a *taravad* to demand partition.[137] The report, with some modifications, was accepted by the government and the Regulation of 1088 (ME) was passed in 1912. It recognized *sambandham* as legal marriage, and gave wives and children of Nairs who died intestate the right to half of the husbands' self-acquired property. The powers of *karanavans* were limited, simple procedures for divorce were laid down, and sub-caste distinctions among Nairs were theoretically ignored.[138]

The Nair Regulation came as an eye-opener to the Ezhava reformers.[139] Certain provisions of the Nair Regulation were very attractive to the Ezhavas[140] of central Travancore as their own laws of inheritance, and social customs and practices, were very similar to those of the Nairs.[141] The Ezhavas thought that a law like the Nair Regulation, with slight changes,[142] would help them to improve their social and economic condition.[143] As soon as the Nair Regulation was passed, the Ezhava elites began to act; *Vivekodayam* and *Kerala Kaumudi* published several articles and suggestions relating to this issue.[144] Charles H. Heimsath wrote, 'Because many Illavas followed *marumakkathayam law*, reforms strickingly similar to those of Nairs were embraced by the SNDP Yogam. Following closely the Nair reform strategy, Illavas petitioned for communal legislation.'[145]

In 1912, Kumaran Asan published an appeal in *Vivekodayam* inviting the attention of Ezhava leaders and to know the response of the *marumakkathayam tavazhi*s towards the need for an Ezhava Regulation.[146] On 14 February 1913 (3 Kumbam 1088 ME), at the ninth session of the Sree Mulam Popular Assembly, the Ezhava representatives K.M. Krishnan, K.C. Krishnan, P. Kesavan Vaidhyan, R. Padmanabhan and N. Kumaran submitted a memorandum to the Dewan, which asked for a common law of inheritance to protect them from internal quarrels and bickering, and unnecessary litigation due to the absence of a law to regulate inheritance in the Ezhava community.[147] From this year onwards the demand for an Ezhava Regulation became a recurring feature in the Assembly. Ultimately, in March 1916, the Government of Travancore appointed an Ezhava Law Committee consisting of five members, including a president, two officials and two non-official members,[148] to gather evidence and to frame a draft bill for regulating the law of inheritance and marriage among Ezhavas.[149] U. Subba Iyyer, an additional head *sirkar vakil*, was appointed the president of this committee, with M. Govindan, S. Padmanabha Pannikar, N. Kumaran and N. Kumaran Asan as members.[150] In June the same year, two more non-official members were appointed to serve in the committee.[151] With the addition of these two members the committee became representative of all sections of the Ezhava community, following three distinct types of the law of inheritance.[152]

In February 1917, the committee suggested that they should be empowered to enquire into the question of partition of property, and that the draft bill should contain a provision regarding testamentary deposition.[153] The Ezhava members of the Assembly supported this suggestion at the thirteenth session of the Assembly. As a consequence, the government constituted another committee with P.N. Boothalingam Iyer as president, and M. Govindan, N. Kumaran, N. Kumaran Asan, K.M. Krishnan, V. Kochunni Vaidhyan and K.C. Kunjuraman as members.[154] On 1 January 1919, the committee submitted both a report and a draft bill; the committee proposed that the *makkathayam* Ezhavas and Ezhava converts to other religions should be excluded from the purview of the proposed legislation.[155] The important recommendations of the committee were legal recognition of marriage, abolition of polyandry and polygamy, the devolution of self-acquired property to wife and children in case of intestacy, *tavazhi* partition in respect of *taravad* property, individual partition with respect to *makkathayam* property, and the right to dispose of one's self-acquired property by making a will.[156]

The bill was introduced in the Legislative Council in 1920. The *misradayam* group of Ezhavas in Travancore, under P. Parameswaran, Karuva

S. Krishnan Asan, Padmanabhan Vaidhyan and others, opposed the bill vehemently. Parameswaran, especially, was a vociferous opponent of the Ezhava Regulation.[157] Under his leadership, protest meetings were organized in various parts of Travancore. On 25 January 1925, the annual meeting of the *misradaya* section of Ezhavas was held at Trivandrum Jubilee Hall. This meeting opposed the Ezhava Regulation;[158] Parameswaran collected a letter from Sree Narayana Guru opposing the regulation, and the letter was sent to the government to indicate that even the spiritual leader of the community was against it.[159] When Parameswaran published the Guru's letter in order to get Ezhava support for the *misradayam* group, T.K. Madhavan and some of his followers who were in favour of Ezhava Regulation approached Narayana Guru to issue another letter supporting the regulation. Not wishing to disappoint Madhavan, the Guru issued another letter favouring his stand.[160] This created great confusion among the Ezhavas.

The *misradayam* group continued its opposition till the time of the passing of the bill in the Council.[161] Karuva S. Krishnan Asan, the chief representative of this section in the Council, protested the passing of the regulation saying that it was a result of mischievous activity by the modernized section of Ezhavas. He impressed upon the government the fact that the bill would never benefit the *misradayam* section, and submitted that the government was bound to protect them in preserving their ancient law of inheritance.[162] When Krishnan Asan and Padmanabhan Vaidhyar opposed the passing of the Ezhava Regulation in the Assembly, C. Krishnan Vaidhyar, a supporter of the regulation, pointed out that the representation made by the two members should not be taken as a reflection of the opinion of the entire Ezhava community.[163]

In spite of all the opposition, the government was compelled to pay due regard to the sentiments of the majority of the community, and the bill became law on 12 February 1925.[164] The Ezhava Regulation (Regulation III of 1100 [1925]) settled the problems relating to marriage, succession, family management and partition among Ezhavas.[165] It was certainly an achievement due to consistent attempts, for more than one decade, by leaders in the Sree Mulam Popular Assembly. But the dissenting voice splintered the coherence of the community and accentuated existing differences.

The Temperance Movement

Before the social reform activities of Sree Narayana Guru and the formation of the Yogam, the Christian missionaries and social reformers of the nineteenth and twentieth centuries had taken up the issue of temperance as a part of their work. The temperance agitation in India is generally connected with Sanskritization and westernization.[166] The influence and importance of these two processes must not be overlooked.

In India, one of the first reformers to make temperance a crucial issue was Swami Narayana (1771–1830) of Gujarat, who propagated the need for renouncing alcohol.[167] But in the early stages, the temperance movement was confined to just a few individuals who gave expression to their views in their writings and speeches. By the second half of the nineteenth century, due to the activities of Sasipada Banerjee,[168] the Anglo-Indian Temperance Association,[169] the Kayastha Temperance Association,[170] the Indian Social Conference[171] and the Indian National Congress,[172] the earlier individual efforts became well organized and systematic. Therefore, by 1921, when the Yogam took up this issue as part of their social reform activities, 'temperance' was already an important movement for social purity – as the habit of drinking alcohol was believed to be dangerous and immoral – in northern India and also in Madras Presidency.[173]

Even though Sree Narayana Guru and the Yogam were not the originators of the anti-alcohol movement, the movement launched by them against intemperance was very conspicuous and more noticeable than the attempts of other social reformers and organizations promoting temperance. This was because through their anti-alcohol movement they openly declared war not only against the 'traditional occupation' which was the livelihood of a large number of Ezhavas, but also against the most lucrative and monopolistic business of their community.[174] While temperance in general was mostly promoted by reformers who had some economic power or social influence,[175] the movement of the Yogam, in contrast, was led by people who had neither. The abolition of alcohol in Kerala under their spiritual leader Sree Narayana Guru, and educated Ezhavas like T.K. Madhavan and Sahodharan Ayyappan, was considered by the Ezhavas to be a means of self-purification, and of attaining social status and self-respect. It was thought that this would in turn qualify them to enter temples – where they had hitherto been prevented from entering on account of their 'filthy' profession. In Ayyappan's words:

> Sree Narayana Guru and the Ezhava leaders were of the view that adherence to the occupation of manufacturing and selling of liquor was one of the factors which contributed to the low caste status of the Iravas. Iravas of economic status took pride in claiming that it is only the poorer Iravas who were tappers.[176]

Palpu strongly believed that a major reason for the degradation of Ezhavas in the society was that some of them were engaged in the manufacture and sale of intoxicating drinks.[177] Involvement in this profession was certainly one of the reasons why the upper castes considered the Ezhavas as untouchables. According to Kavalappara Muppil Nair, a legislator and leader of the landed aristocracy of Malabar, 'it will want a lot of time and patience for us to mingle with the unwashed Thiya who carries about his person live crabs and a pot of toddy'.[178] Consumption of alcohol had become a taboo attached to members of the community. With the spread of socio-religious activities of the Guru and education among the Ezhavas, social stigma became attached to consumption of liquor. The spread of education infused in the Ezhavas a greater sense of dignity based on the notion of higher professions.[179] Besides self-purification and respectability, other factors largely responsible for this were thrift, public order, rationality, and, above all, the influence of Mahatma Gandhi and Indian nationalism on Ezhavas like T.K. Madhavan and a few others.[180]

We have already noted that the temperance movement in India was generally connected with either Sanskritization or westernization. Narayana Guru's movement in favour of abstention had elements of both: on the one hand, he wanted to improve the individual internally, morally and spiritually; on the other, he wished to propagate an ideology closely associated with the Protestant ethic of the nineteenth century, with values such as respectability, thrift, public order, rationality and puritanism. However, a close examination of his movement for 'temperance' reveals that it can be viewed as an intervention in popular beliefs and practices based on caste and *varnadharma*-based occupations. According to *varnadharma*, the vocation pursued by a person was predetermined by the *varna* into which he was born. An individual had no choice as birth alone determined his occupation. The talents or interests pursued by a person could not alter this status, which was believed and practised in Hindu society as divine order.[181] Ezhavas, in general, were considered as toddy tappers, as persons who tended coconut palms and as manufacturers of liquor in almost all historical accounts of Kerala.[182] As a community they were identified with the toddy and liquor business, their 'traditional' occupation. The social anthropolgist A. Ayyappan has observed, 'Most castes have generic terms of contempt applied to them by their neighbours, e.g., an Irava is contemptuously referred to as a *"kotti"* or "beater".' The reference here is to the process of making toddy, in the course of which the inflorescence of the palm is beaten and pressed.[183] Narayana Guru ascribed the low-caste status of Ezhavas to the filthy profession of trafficking liquor.[184] According to a follower of the Guru, 'Our Guru has said that it is a sin to make and sell liquor. Our caste can rise up only if no one among us is a toddy tapper.'[185] The low-caste status cost the Ezhavas not only a better social position but also denied them opportunities in the bureaucracy and other learned professions. Narayana Guru therefore advocated that the Ezhavas should give up their so-called traditional occupation for their social and economic betterment, as there was no ordained code that Ezhavas should engage in liquor traffic alone.

The actions of the Guru as a social reformer were similar to the liberal tendencies of the modern bourgeoisie. This led him to encourage the development of a modernized version of religion whose futile fuss about *varna* sought to drown the din of class struggle. Abolition of the *varna* system was therefore bound with a basic economic restructuring of Indian society. Narayana Guru attacked the so-called traditional occupation on the one hand, and on the other, encouraged industrial and educational development to open up new vistas of employment.

Sree Narayana Guru thus attacked the consumption of alcohol on social, religious and economic grounds. His conclusion was that the evil effects of drink, such as drunkenness, violence, loss of work and money, and impoverishment of society (both socially and economically), would lead to an increase in crime and also ruin the health of those addicted to it. Economically, it was one of the causes of impoverishment, especially among the poorer sections of society. Narayana Guru, like Sasipada Banerjee,[186] showed a keen interest to reform and discipline poor Parayas, Pulayas and Ezhavas who were agricultural and field labourers. He taught them middle-class virtues of industry, ambition, sobriety and thrift. The motive behind his anti-drinking movement was to ameliorate the conditions of life of poor labourers. Addressing a Pulaya assembly at Muttathara (Trivandrum) in 1916, the Guru said:

> Pulayas lack money and education. These deficiencies should be made up. Education is the chief thing. Once it is had, money, cleanliness etc. would follow. It is wrong to say that you have no wealth. You are yourself wealth. You earn money every day by your work. But you waste it – say on drinks. If you set apart one anna a day for a common fund you can educate your children . . . you should stop the habit of drinking. Hereafter, you should not allow your children to drink. Even elders should try to stop the habit. It is for such purposes that you should gather in assemblies . . . and discuss your problems and do the needful.[187]

No one in the history of the temperance movement attacked alcoholism as vehemently as Narayana Guru.[188] As we have already mentioned, he once flippantly remarked that the knife used for toddy-tapping should be cut into four pieces and used as razors in barber shops.[189] In a message sent by him dated 27 August 1920 he stated: 'Liquor is poison. It should not be manufactured, served or drunk. The toddy tapper's body will stink, his clothes will stink, his house will stink and whatever he touches will stink.'[190] He even compared toddy-tapping with diseases like plague and leprosy.[191] He said: 'As we cut off the diseased limb, so the tappers should be cut off from society. We should have no social relations with them. When they give up tapping we may take them back.'[192] While in other parts of India, the temperance movement appears to have been confined mostly to urban areas,[193] in Kerala this movement became widespread in urban and rural areas alike.

Though the Indian National Congress passed a number of resolutions against intemperance and the *abkari* policy of the government in Kerala from the time of its inception, it did not include anti-drinking as part of its programme. At the time of the first civil disobedience movement, as part of Gandhiji's constructive programme, the Congress started to picket and boycott liquor shops. Narayana Guru had advocated abstinence from drinking much earlier than its inclusion in the Congress's progamme. Therefore, when the Congress started picketing and boycotting liquor shops, it was not something new for Keralites. Nevertheless, the policy of the Congress gave added impetus to the temperance movement. It was at that time also that Mahatma Gandhi and his ideology, coupled with nationalist sentiments, began to spread and gain popularity all over Kerala.

From the very beginning of the anti-alcohol movement, the SNDP Yogam faced many difficulties from the government as well from within its own community. As far as the government was concerned, since excise earnings from *abkari* was one of the main sources of income for the state,[194] this economic motive prevented it from cooperating with the anti-drinking movement. The prohibition movement among Ezhavas was beset with several problems. When the Yogam passed a resolution in its twentieth annual meeting for social boycott of drunkards and tappers, a strong protest was organized by a section of the Ezhavas against this resolution.[195]

However, T.K. Madhavan, C. Krishnan and other Ezhava leaders ignored the opposition and plunged into the temperance movement. Many volunteer organizations like the Sanmargadayini in Paravoor, the Karthikappally Ezhava Samajam and the Ezhava Mahajana Sabha in Kottayam played leading roles in the movement.[196] As a result of these consistent activities of the Yogam and its affiliated local organizations, a number of drunkards, toddy tappers, contractors and liquor businessmen took a pledge of abstinence.[197] The eighteenth annual meeting of the Yogam, held at Karunagappally in June 1921, unanimously passed a resolution moved by T.K. Madhavan calling on Ezhavas to stop toddy-tapping and withdraw from the liquor business. In the twentieth annual meeting of the Yogam another resolution was passed for social boycott of drunkards and those engaged in the liquor industry.[198] This stigmatization, however, hampered the economic progress and moral status of Ezhavas and contributed to a feeling of inferiority among them.[199]

In a meeting organized by the Ezhava Mahajana Sabha of Kottayam in Velur in 1922, presided over by T.K. Madhavan, twenty-two toddy shop agents and a number of toddy tappers took a pledge to abstain from toddy-tapping and the toddy business before a portrait of Sree Narayana Guru.[200] To rehabilitate retrenched labourers from the liquor business, the meeting laid down a scheme for starting an industry by investing capital of Rs 10,000, which would provide jobs for them.[201] Due to the strenuous efforts of T.K. Madhavan and other heterodox youths, a number of mass meetings were organized at Alleppey, Meenthalakkara in Tiruvalla, Ramankara, Karthikappally and other places during 1921–24.[202] These public meetings as well as the vernacular papers, like *Vivekodayam, Deshabhimani* and *Kerala Kaumudi*, discussed the evils of drinking and criticized the indifference of the government in not taking stern measures against intemperance. A meeting held at Karthikappally on 29 September 1922 (13 Kanni 1098 ME) organized a vigilance committee to report violations of the *abkari* regulation by tappers, contractors, shop owners, sellers and excise officials.[203] For the knowledge of this 'vigilance committee', Madhavan published the relevant rules of the *abkari* regulation in *Deshabhimani*.[204] The committee functioned well in Travancore, and the movement became strong and widespread over a large area of Travancore.

The decision to excommunicate tappers and the advice of the Yogam to its community members not to bid for shops at the time of the next auction in 1922 had a strong impact on the people. In 1922, in contrast to the excessive competition seen in previous years when auctions were held for toddy shops, the number of bidders was less than the total number of shops up for auction. In Kottayam, out of a total of 69 shops, only 41 were auctioned; and of these 41 shops, only 30 were auctioned to Ezhavas.[205] As a result, during the period 1922–23, the government incurred a loss of Rs 4 lakhs on *abkari*.[206] A worried Government of Travancore decided to counter the Yogam's temperance movement by starting a school for imparting training in the art of toddy-tapping to non-Ezhava[207]communities, and also sought to brew liquor from cereals without the help of Ezhavas.[208] These attempts failed, however, upon which the government tried to suppress the movement through coercion – and police arrests and imprisonment became common.[209] These arrests and incarceration only strengthened the vigour and vitality of the movement. A number of protest meetings were organized in Trivandrum, Alleppey and Quilon, at which strong voices raised against the coercive measures of the government.[210] These meetings continued the Yogam's crusade by exposing the economic motives of the government in not taking stern measures against intemperance and in trying to suppress the temperance movement. Criticism was also directed against the system of auctioning liquor shops, which served as inducement to promote liquor trafficking.

In the meanwhile, the Yogam approached M.E. Madhava Varrier, the then leader of the Legislative Council, to introduce a resolution on prohibition in the legislature. On 23 November 1922 (8 Vrischikam 1098 ME), Varrier introduced a resolution asking the government to permit use of alcoholic drinks only for medical and industrial purposes, and banning production and import of liquor.[211] An excise committee was appointed by the government to study the problem; on the basis of the recommendation of this committee, the government decided to gradually introduce prohibition.[212] As this was not satisfactory to Madhavan and his colleagues, they revived their movement with greater vigour. Eventually, the government promised that total prohibition on drinking would be effected within a period of forty years.[213] As they had no other alternative, the reformers finally accepted the stand of the government. Thus, through clever use of the anti-alcohol movement which had been started by Narayana Guru as a social reform movement, T.K. Madhavan forced the government to tighten the *abkari* rules and regulations despite the threat of an annual loss of Rs 4 lakhs as income[214] earned through excise.

Although the movement succeeded in creating a stigma about drinking and thus reduce excessive alcohol intake, it failed to meet the aspiration of the Guru to cut off Ezhavas from this occupation and to keep people away from the habit of drinking. This partial failure of the movement was mainly due to three reasons: (i) stiff opposition from the government; (ii) the indifference of a section of the Ezhava leaders; and (iii) because tapping was the sole means of livelihood for a large number of people and the organizers of the movement did not have enough financial capital to provide alternative jobs to those who gave up their age old occupation. Yogam leaders like Palpu and C.V. Kunjuraman, though not opposed to the movement, did not strongly support it. According to Palpu, 'It was the only available means they had of getting back at least a portion of the enormous sums that were being systematically wasted here on the so-called Brahmins in the name of God and religion.'[215] After his retirement in 1919, Palpu started a 'non-alcoholic *madhu* campaign' and tried to develop his community's 'traditional occupation' as an industry.[216]

The indifference of leaders like Palpu and Kunjuraman towards the temperance movement was mainly due to economic reasons. Toddy tapping was the sole means of livelihood for many poor Ezhava families in Kerala, and its sudden stoppage would have rendered many of them jobless. Therefore the more pragmatic-minded among the Ezhava leaders did not agree with the views of the Guru and other nationalist-minded leaders like T.K. Madhavan; they believed that the material conditions were not conducive for the success of the struggle. However, at the same time, many businessmen, tappers and contractors pledged to put a stop to their involvement in the liquor trade, pointing to the fact that narrow economic self-interest did not necessarily prevent acceptance of prohibition. This explains the steep decline in the involvement of Ezhavas in the production and trade of liquor, from 11 per cent in 1912[217] to 8 per cent in 1921.[218]

There were two economic issues that arose in the course of the temperance movement. Abstaining from consumption of liquor reduced the expenditure of consumers, and was seen as encouraging them to work harder and increase personal savings, which was a positive economic factor. The other was that the production of liquor and its sale, if stopped, would reduce the income of those engaged in these activities, which was a negative economic outcome. In short, economic reasons could serve both as justification for refraining from consumption of liquor, and to promote the production and sale of liquor.

This chapter began with an account of the efforts directed at unifying the caste by obliterating the internal heterogeneity of the Ezhavas as a community. Such heterogeneity was detrimental to efforts at uniting the Ezhavas, and in eradicating practices of untouchability and unapproachability among them. Effective relegation of many primitive and superstitious practices could be effected only after unification, as unification alone could sustain a common platform. However, in spite of various efforts, heterogeneity within the community persisted, with only the English-educated, to a large extent, stopping the practice of blind faith. Even the proposal for a common name for the internally stratified community could not gain consensus. The attempts to de-consecrate several gods and goddesses also met with partial success. The laws of inheritance of the community varied from region to region, and there were some attempts to unify these. Once again this move also reached only half-way due to the differential ramifications of alterations in the observed laws of inheritance. The effect of the temperance movement was felt far and wide, especially because it was carried on as part of the nationalist freedom movement. However, an inherent economic logic prevented its full realization.

Notes and References

[1] See K.N. Panikkar, 'Socio-Religious Reforms and the National Awakening', in Bipan Chandra et al., *India's Struggle for Independence, 1857–1947*, Viking, New Delhi, 1988, pp. 82–90; V. Ramakrishna Acharyulu, 'Social Reform Movements in Andhra (1848–1919)', Ph.D. thesis, Jawaharlal Nehru University, New Delhi, 1977, p. 452.

[2] For details, see H. Charles Heimsath, *Indian Nationalism and Hindu Social Reform*, Oxford University Press, Bombay, 1964.

[3] For a critical appraisal of the role of Christian missionaries in social and religious reform movements in Kerala, see P. Chandramohan, 'Colonial Connections of Protestant Missionaries in Travancore', *Indian Historical Review*, Vol. XXVI, July 1999, pp. 60–83.

[4] L. Robert Hardgrave, 'The Breast Cloth Controversy: Caste Consciousness and Social Change in Southern Travancore', *Indian Economic and Social History Review*, Vol. 5, No. 2, June 1968, pp. 171–87; R.N. Yesudas, *A People's Revolt in Travancore: A Backward Class Movement for Social Freedom*, Kerala Historical Society, Trivandrum, 1975; K.K. Kusuman (n.d.), *Slavery in Travancore*, Kerala Historical Society, Trivandrum, pp. 28–73; Robin Jeffrey, *The Decline of Nayar Dominance: Society and Politics in Travancore 1847–1908*, Vikas Publishing House, Delhi, 1976; Dick Kooiman, 'The Gospel of Coffee: Mission, Education and Employment in the 19th Century Travancore', *Economic and Political Weekly*, Vol. XIX, No. 35, 1 September 1984, pp. 1535–43; Dick Kooiman, *Conversion and Social Equality in India*, New Delhi, 1989.

[5] The first movement for the amelioration of social evils in Travancore was started by C. Krishna Pillai and Thanu Pillai, two college-educated Nairs. C.V. Kunjuraman and other heterodox youths followed and adapted their activities for the Ezhava community. See C. Kesavan, *Jeevitasamaram* (autobiography), 2 vols., National Book Stall, Kottayam, Vol. I, 1968, pp. 126–27.

[6] Rama Varma, *Our Industrial Status*, Trivandrum Debating Society, printed at C.M.S Press, Kottayam, 1874; P. Bhaskaranunni, *Pathonpatham Noottantile Keralam*, Kerala Sahitya Akademi, Trichur, 1988; P. Bhaskaranunni, *Keralam Irupathamnootantinte Arambathil*, Kerala Sahitya Akademi, Trichur, 2005.

[7] For details, see K.N. Panikkar, 'Presidential Address', Section III, Indian History Congress, 36th Session, Aligarh, 1975.

[8] See Ram Mohan Roy, *Tuhfat-ul-Muhawaddin*, in J.C. Ghose, ed., *The English Works of Raja Ram Mohan Roy*, 3 vols, Panini Office, Allahabad, 1906, Vol. III, p. 929; Mahadev Govind

Ranade, *The Miscellaneous Writings*, published by Mrs Ramabai Ranade, The Manoranjan Press, Bombay, 1915, pp. 236–37; and Keshub Chandra Sen, 'Promotion of Education in India' and 'The Reconstruction of Native Society', in Prem Sundar Basu, comp., *Life and Works of Brahmanand Keshav*, Navavidhan Publication Committee, Calcutta, second edition, 1940, pp. 45–49 and 286–89. Also see Heimsath, *Indian Nationalism and Hindu Social Reform*, p. 248.

[9] As the nucleus of the family in the matrilineal society, women held a position that was higher than that enjoyed by their counterparts in patrilineal societies of similar culture. Women under matriliny enjoyed a greater degree of equality with men; they could hold property in their own right and enter any profession they chose. The rapid progress made in women's education strengthened their spirit of self-reliance and independence. Moreover, the persons with whom matrilineal women entered into sexual relationships were not those on whom they depended for economic survival. An added advantage of Ezhava women was that they worked in the fields and factories as wage earners, which gave them equal status with men as breadwinners. For the superior status of matrilineal women in Kerala, see K.M. Panikkar, 'Some Aspects of Dravidian Culture', *Journal of the Royal Anthropological Institute*, London, 1919; L.A. Krishna Aiyer, 'Matriliny in Kerala', *Man in India*, Vol. 24, March 1944; L.A. Krishna Aiyer, *Social History of Kerala*, 2 vols, Book Centre Publications, Madras, Vol. II, 1970; D.M. Schneider and Kathleen E. Gough, eds., *Matrilineal Kinship*, University of California Press, Berkeley, 1961; K.N. Panikkar, 'Land Control Ideology and Reform: A Study of Change in Family Organizations and Marriage Systems in Kerala', *Indian Historical Review*, Vol. IV, No. 1, July 1977. To know about the economic independence of women under matriliny, see the memorandum submitted by K.P. Padmanabha Menon, filed in the *Report of the Marumakkathayam Committee*, Travancore, 1908, Kerala State Legislative Library (KSLL), Trivandrum: 'Enclosure B', p. VII. The miserable plight of women was primarily an issue relating to upper-caste patrilineal Hindu communities like the Namboodiris, and Muslims. See Bhavadasan Bhattathiripad, 'Antharjanagaludeyum Kuttikaludeyum Anatha Sthithi', *Mitavadi*, June 1916, pp. 12–15.

[10] H. Charles Heimsath, 'The Functions of Hindu Social Reformers – With Special Reference to Kerala', *Indian Economic and Social History Review*, Vol. XV, No. 1, January–March 1978, pp. 21–39.

[11] *Vivekodayam*, Vol. 1, No. 4, 15 November 1904.

[12] Edgar Thurston, *Castes and Tribes of Southern India*, 7 vols, Government Press, Madras, 1909 and Johnson Reprint Corporation, New York, 1965 (second edition), Vol. II, p. 394; Eric J. Miller, 'Village Structure in North Kerala', *Economic Weekly*, Vol. IV, No. 6, 9 February 1952; C. Kesavan, *Jeevitasamaram*, 1968, Vol. I, p. 302; David Arnold, Robin Jeffrey and James Manor, 'Caste Associations in South India: A Comparative Analysis', *Indian Economic and Social History Review*, Vol. XIII, No. 3, 1976, p. 355.

[13] *Kerala Kaumudi*, 2 June 1921, p. 2.

[14] Ibid.

[15] *Kerala Kaumudi*, 24 May 1923, p. 3. But many of the Ezhavas did not like this change and they protested against it. See *Kerala Kaumudi*, 14 June 1923, p. 1.

[16] K.R. Achutan, *C. Krishnan* (biography, Malayalam), National Book Stall, Kottayam, 1971, p. 48.

[17] Dr Palpu was prominent among them. For details, see Chapter 2.

[18] Ibid.; C.V. Kunjuraman, 'The Thiyyas', in *Mitavadi*, March 1916.

[19] Robin Jeffrey writes, 'The British, unlike Kerala's princes, readily employed Tiyyas, and the Tiyya factotum became a constant companion of some British officials'; see Robin Jeffrey, 'Politics, Women and Well-Being: How Kerala Became "A Model"', Macmillan, London, 1992, p. 50. See also E.K. Krishnan, 'A Brief Account of the Life of the Late Mr Churia Kanaran: Deputy Collector of Malabar', *Malabar Quarterly Review*, Vol. III, No. 3, September 1904, pp. 209–20; *Madras Mail*, 6 January 1916, p. 5.

[20] *Kerala Kaumudi*, 14 June 1923, p. 1. L.A. Krishna Aiyer writes that the Ezhavas of north

Malabar are more affluent and westernized than those in the rest of Kerala. See L.A. Krishna Aiyer, *Social History of Kerala*, Vol. II, p. 67.

21 *Kerala Kaumudi*, 14 June 1923, p. 1.

22 Kumaran Asan and Chevrukattu P.M. Kunchu Sankaran Vaidhyar were very close friends from their boyhood. The marriage of the latter's elder daughter was celebrated with grandeur in 1919. Asan was also invited to the marriage. The bridegroom was a rich college-educated boy from Kaikkara, Kumaran Asan's native place. On the day of the marriage, when Asan arrived at the gate of his friend's house, the latter approached Asan and sadly informed him that if he was present at the marriage ceremony, the bridegroom and his group would leave the place. The reason for this threat was that the bridegroom belonged to an upper-caste section of Ezhavas and so they would not dine with Kumaran Asan, who belonged to a low-caste section. Staying outside the gate, Asan conveyed his blessings to the couple and left the place. See K. Surendran, *Kumaran Asan* (literary biography), National Book Stall, Kottayam, 1971, pp. 233–34.

23 *Census of India, 1941,* Vol. XXV, Travancore, Part I, Report, p. 131.

24 *Vivekodayam*, April–June 1909 (Medam–Edavam 1084 ME), Nos. 1 and 2, p. 22.

25 K.P. Padmanabha Menon, *History of Kerala*, 4 vols, Government Press, Ernakulam, Vol. III, 1933, p. 442.

26 *Census of Travancore, 1875*, p. 162; Thurston, *Castes and Tribes of Southern India*, Vol. II, pp. 406–09; Rev. Samuel Mateer, *Travancore and its People*, John Snow and Co., London, 1871, p. 194; L.K. Ananthakrishna Iyer, *The Cochin Tribes and Castes*, 2 vols, Higginbotham, Madras, 1909, Vol. I, p. 310 (reprint, Johnson Reprint Corporation, New York, 1969).

27 During the time of Kodungallur *Bharani*, pilgrims from all over Kerala visit this temple. On their way, they sing *Bharani pattu* (songs). The peculiarity of these songs is that they centre round themes such as male and female sex organs, copulation and masturbation.

28 *Vivekodayam*, Vol. I, No. 2, 15 July 1904 (32 Mithunam 1079 ME).

29 See Edward Said, *Orientalism*, Random House, New York, 1979. Said is very critical of the Eurocentric prejudice of the west against the cultures and peoples of Asia with special reference to the Middle East. He effectively redefined the term 'orientalism', equating it with a constellation of false assumptions underlying the western attitude towards the Middle East. Also see Edward Said, *Culture and Imperialism*, Vintage Books, 1994.

30 *Vivekodayam*, Vol. II, No. 10, January 1915 (Makaram 1090 ME), p. 354.

31 K. Damodaran, *Shri Narayana Guru Swami Tripadangalude Jeevacharitram*, Quilon, 1929, p. 63; P.K. Gopalakrishnan, 'Samudhaya Parishkarana Prasthanangal', in Kerala History Association, *Kerala Charitram*, Government Press, Ernakulam, 1973, Vol. I, p. 1208.

32 Pazhambally Achuthan, 'Guruvinte Karmapadhathy', in *SNDP Yogam Platinum Jubilee Souvenir*, 1978, p. 57.

33 *Vivekodayam*, Vol. XII, No. 1, April–May 1915 (Medam 1090 ME), p. 21.

34 M.S.A. Rao, *Social Movements and Social Transformation: A Study of Two Backward Classes Movements in India*, Macmillan India, New Delhi, 1979, p. 55.

35 L.K. Ananthakrishna Iyer, *The Cochin Tribes and Castes*, Vol. I, p. 310.

36 K.P. Padmanabha Menon, *History of Kerala*, Vol. I, p. 443.

37 Ezhavatti was a sub-caste of Ezhavas which functioned both as barbers and priests. See *Census of India, 1901*, Vol. XXVI, Travancore, Part I, Report, p. 280. According to A. Ayyappan, Ezhavatti functioned in the capacity of quasi-priests at all important rites connected to birth initiation and death. See A. Ayyappan, 'Iravas and Culture Change', Madras Government Bulletin, 1943, p. 58.

38 C. Kesavan, *Jeevitasamaram*, Vol. I, pp. 138–47.

39 *Vivekodayam*, Vol. I, No. 4, 15 November 1904 (30 Thulam 1080 ME), p. 72; C. Kesavan, *Jeevitasamaram*, Vol. I, pp. 134–35.

40 *Ibid.*, p. 135; *Vivekodayam*, Vol. I, No. 4, 15 November 1904 (30 Thulam 1080 ME), p. 72.

41 For a detailed account of the ceremony, see U. Balakrishnan Nair, 'The Marriage System in Malabar', *Calcutta Review*, Vol. XCIX, 1894, p. 387; Rev. Samuel Mateer, *Native Life of*

Travancore, W.H. Allen, London, 1883, p. 174; Kathleen E. Gough, 'Female Initiation Rites on the Malabar Coast', *Royal Anthropological Institute Journal*, 1955; K.G. Narayanan, *Ezhava–Thiyya Charitra Padanam*, Anaswara Publishers, Kayamkulam, 1984, pp. 88–99; speech of C.V. Kunjuraman at Muttom on 'Samudaya Parishkaranam', *Vivekodayam*, Thulam 1080 ME, reproduced in Puthuppally Raghavan, ed., *C.V. Kunjuramante Thiranjedutha Krithikal*, Prathibha Publications, Quilon, 1971, pp. 295–302; L.A. Krishna Aiyer, *Social History of Kerala*, Vol. II, 1970, pp. 54–55 and 63.

[42] L.A. Krishna Aiyer writes, 'It was considered "religious impurity" for a girl to attain puberty before the *talikettukalyanam* was performed.' See ibid., p. 60; Nagam Aiya, *The Travancore State Manual*, 3 vols, Government Press, Trivandrum, 1906, Vol. II, p. 399; L.K. Ananthakrishna Iyer, *The Cochin Tribes and Castes*, Vol. II, p. 15; P.K. Gopalakrishnan, 'Ezhavar', in Kerala History Association, *Kerala Charitram*, Vol. I, pp. 985 and 1213–15; C. Kesavan, *Jeevitasamaram*, Vol. I, p. 128.

[43] All tenants and other lower sections of society, whether Nairs or Ezhavas, had to pay a fee to the government for procuring the privilege of erecting decorative pandals and singing songs in connection with the *talikettukalyanam*. However, in 1869, Ayilyam Tirunal Maharaja Rama Varma, the ruler of Travancore, issued an order (dated 20 Midhunam 1044 ME), stating that such fees for the purchase of privileges would be discontinued for the welfare of the plebeians. See C. Kesavan, *Jeevitasamaram*, Vol. I, p. 131.

[44] The sitting arrangement from south to north was an indication of the status of the girls. Those having less (economic) status in the family would be seated in the north. See *Vivekodayam*, Vol. 1, No. 4, 15 November 1905 (30 Thulam 1080 ME), pp. 73–74; C. Kesavan, *Jeevitasamaram*, Vol. 1, p. 129; Puthuppally Raghavan, ed., *C.V. Kunjuramante Thiranjedutha Krithikal*, p. 299; M.K. Sanoo, *Narayana Guru Swami* (biography), Vivekodayam Printing and Publishing Co., Irinjalakuda, 1976, p. 211.

[45] M.K. Sanoo, *Narayana Guru Swami*, p. 213. On rare occasions the *tali* rite was performed even without the bridegroom, with a sword or a deity – preferably Vishnu or one of his manifestations – made to represent the bridegroom, and the mother would invest the girl with the *tali* in its presence. See L.K. Ananthakrishna Iyer, *The Cochin Tribes and Castes*, Vol. II, p. 27; Nagam Aiya, *The Travancore State Manual*, Vol. II, p. 357.

[46] *Vivekodayam*, Vol. I, No. 4, 15 November 1905 (Thulam 1080 ME), pp. 73–74.

[47] C. Kesavan, *Jeevitasamaram*, Vol. I, p. 130; M.K. Sanoo, *Narayana Guru Swami*, p. 212.

[48] As a rule the person who tied the *tali* was paid a small sum, generally 25 Travancore *panam* (equal to Rs 3.5), together with expenses incurred by him in connection with the ceremony. See *Census of India, 1901*, Vol. XXVI, Travancore, Part I, Report, p. 280; Samuel Mateer, *Native Life of Travancore*, p. 174; L.K. Ananthakrishna Iyer, *The Cochin Tribes and Castes*, Vol. II, p. 27.

[49] U. Balakrishnan Nair, 'The Marriage System in Malabar', pp. 338–39; *Census of India, 1901*, Vol. XXVI, Travancore, Part I, Report, pp. 231 and 328; *Report of the Marumakkathayam Committee*, Travancore, p. 6.

[50] *Census of India, 1901*, Vol. XX, Cochin, Part I, Report, p. 158; C.A. Innes, *Madras District Gazetteer*, Malabar, Madras, 1904, Vol. I, p. 177; C.J. Fuller, *The Nayars Today*, Cambridge University Press, London, 1976, p. 104.

[51] Samuel Mateer, *Native Life of Travancore*, p.172; *Census of India, 1901*, Vol. XXVI, Travancore, Part I, Report, pp. 411–13. However, in some areas, the girl had to mourn the death of her *tali* husband and also observe death pollution for a day or a week or two, as his death made her impure. See L.K. Ananthakrishna Iyer, *The Cochin Tribes and Castes*, Vol. II, p. 154; also L.A. Krishna Aiyer, *Social History of Kerala*, Vol. II, p. 55. This shows that in some cases the *tali* husband, in spite of the divorce, established a permanent tie by remaining a ritual husband. See Louis Dumont, 'Nair Marriage as Indian Fact', *Affinity as a Value in South India with Comparative Essays on Australia*, University of Chicago Press, Chicago, 1983, p. 116; Gough, 'Female Initiation Rites in the Malabar Coast', p. 50.

[52] Quoted in *Census of India, 1901*, Vol. XXVI, Travancore, Part I, Report, p. 328.

[53] Dumont, 'Nair Marriage as Indian Fact', p. 115.

[54] According to Dumont, the *tali* rite marked the transformation of a girl from the category of child to that of a woman. Ibid., p. 114.

[55] See *Report of the Malabar Marriage Commission*, 1891.

[56] *Vivekodayam*, Vol. 6, Nos. 1–2, April–June 1909 (Medam–Edavam 1084 ME), p. 1.

[57] L.K. Ananthakrishna Iyer, *The Cochin Tribes and Castes*, Vol. II, pp. 29–30. However, Edgar Thurston writes that the ceremonial procession took place on the seventh day of menarche. See Thurston, *Castes and Tribes of Southern India*, Vol. II, p. 416.

[58] M.K. Sanoo, *Narayana Guru Swami*, p. 214.

[59] *Census of India, 1901*, Vol. XXVI, Travancore, Report, p. 280; Nagam Aiya, *The Travancore State Manual*, Vol. II, pp. 399–400.

[60] L.K. Ananthakrishna Iyer, *The Cochin Tribes and Castes*, Vol. I, p. 291.

[61] Ibid., p. 288.

[62] Nagam Aiya, *The Travancore State Manual*, Vol. II, p. 400; C. Kesavan, *Jeevitasamaram*, Vol. I, p. 135.

[63] After the marriage, the bride was taken to the house of the husband and installed as a member of his family. This rite was known as *kudivaippu*. See Thurston, *Castes and Tribes of Southern India*, Vol. II, pp. 413–15.

[64] C. Kesavan, *Jeevitasamaram*, Vol. I, pp. 135–36.

[65] A. Ayyappan, 'Iravas and Culture Change', p. 98.

[66] Nagam Aiya, *The Travancore State Manual*, Vol. II, p. 400. Ananthakrishna Iyer writes, 'The practice of two or more brothers was very common in Central Travancore, northern side of the Cochin and some parts of Malabar'. See L.K. Ananthakrishna Iyer, *The Cochin Tribes and Castes*, Vol. I, 285–301.

[67] Nagam Aiya, *The Travancore State Manual*, Vol. II, p. 400.

[68] Thurston, *Castes and Tribes of Southern India*, Vol. II, p. 416; L.K. Ananthakrishna Iyer, *The Cochin Tribes and Castes*, Vol. II, p. 43; C. Kesavan, *Jeevitasamaram*, pp. 137–38.

[69] M.K. Sanoo, *Narayana Guru Swami*, p. 214.

[70] L.K. Ananthakrishna Iyer, *The Cochin Tribes and Castes*, Vol. II, p. 43.

[71] *Pulikudi* was a two-day ceremony. See Thurston, *Castes and Tribes of Southern India*, Vol. II, p. 43.

[72] Puthuppally Raghavan, ed., *C.V. Kunjuramante Thiranjedutha Krithikal*, pp. 298–302; see also M.K. Sanoo, *Narayana Guru Swami*, p. 216.

[73] Jeffrey, *Decline of Nayar Dominance*, pp. 89 and 105.

[74] K.N. Panikkar, 'Presidential Address', pp. 3–5. Also see K.N. Panikkar, 'Breaking with the Past, Yet Looking Back to It', *The Telegraph*, 7 June 1985, p. 7.

[75] P.K. Balakrishnan, *Narayana Guru Samahara Grandham*, p. 75.

[76] See the speech of C.V. Kunjuraman at Muttathara, in Puthupally Raghavan, ed., *C.V. Kunjuramante Thiranjedutha Krithikal*, pp. 295–302.

[77] Ibid., pp. 300–01. Although it was an exaggerated calculation, it still gives an idea of the huge expenditure in conducting these ceremonies.

[78] Ibid., p. 297.

[79] *Vivekodayam*, Vol. I, No. 2, 15 July 1904 (32 Mithunam 1079 ME), p. 28.

[80] Ibid.

[81] This letter of Narayana Guru, dated 26 Chingam 1081 ME (11 September 1906), to Parayil Kochu Raman Vaidhyan, is reproduced in K. Damodaran, *Shri Narayana Guru Swami Tripadangalude Jeevacharitram*, p. 45; P.S. Velayudhan, *S.N.D.P. Yoga Charitram*, S.N.D.P. Yogam, Quilon, 1978, p. 130; M.K. Sanoo, *Narayana Guru Swami*, p. 221; and P. Parameswaran, *Sree Narayana Guru Swamikal: Navothanathinte Pravachakan*, Jayabharath Publishers, Calicut, 1971, pp. 84–85.

[82] K.N. Panikkar, 'Presidential Address', p. 18.

[83] Samuel Mateer, *Native Life in Travancore*, p. 172. See also *Malabar Marriage Commission Report*, 1891.

[84] A. Ayyappan, 'The Meaning of Tali Rite', *Bulletin of Rama Varma Research Institute*, Vol. IX, July 1941, Trichur, p. 83.

[85] This was applicable to a large number of social reformers of modern India who were con-temporaries of Narayana Guru. See K.N. Panikkar, 'Breaking with the Past, Yet Looking Back to It', p. 7.

[86] *Vivekodayam*, Vol. I, No. 2, 15 July 1904 (32 Mithunam 1079 ME), p. 28.

[87] For procedures, see ibid.

[88] L.A. Krishna Aiyer, *Kerala and Her People*, Education Supplies Depot, Palghat, 1961, p. 90.

[89] *Vivekodayam*, 15 November 1904, p. 72; C. Kesavan, *Jeevitasamaram*, Vol. I, p. 136.

[90] He insisted to conduct marriage in an open place to prevent impersonation, which was very common among Ezhavas. See C. Kesavan, *Jeevitasamaram*, Vol. I, pp. 135–36; C.P. Sivadasan, 'Narayana Guru', in M. Govindan, ed., *Poetry and Renaissance: Kumaran Asan Birth Centenary Volume*, Sameeksha, Madras, 1974, p. 212.

[91] See *Irava Law Commission Report*, para II, in *Regulations and Proclamations of Travancore*, Vol. V, p. 775 (Regulation 111 of 1100). However, the Guru insisted in his message dated 28 Medam 1084 (10 May 1909) that a widow or divorcee, at the time of her re-marriage, should not wear anything in memory of her dead or divorced husband. Therefore, a woman who gets married again should not wear, either during the subsequent marriage or there-after, the *tali* used at the time of the earlier marriage. See *Vivekodayam*, Vol. 6, Nos. 1–2, April–June 1909 (Medam–Edavam 1084 ME), p. 2.

[92] According to Robin Jeffrey, Narayana Guru adopted the practice of garlanding with flowers from Tamil regions where he travelled extensively during his *avaduta* life. Robin Jeffrey, *Politics, Women and Well-Being*, p. 52.

[93] C. Kesavan, *Jeevitasamaram*, Vol. I, p. 136; M.K. Sanoo, *Narayana Guru Swami*, pp. 222–23; and P. Parameswaran, *Sree Narayana Guru Swamikal*, pp. 80–81.

[94] M.S.A. Rao, *Social Movements and Social Transformation*, p. 39.

[95] *Vivekodayam*, Vol. I, No. 4, 15 November 1904 (30 Thulam 1080 ME), p. 72. See M.K. Sanoo, *Narayana Guru Swami*, pp. 222–23.

[96] Stephen Fuchs, *Rebellious Prophets: A Study in Messianic Movements in Indian Religion*, Asia Publishing House, Bombay, 1965, p. 272. Almost all reformers of modern India emphasized the need for female education. Keshub Chandra Sen wrote, 'no country on earth ever made sufficient progress in civilization whose females were sunk in ignorance'. See Prem Sundar Basu, comp., *Life and Works of Brahmananda Keshav*, pp. 286–89.

[97] *Vivekodayam*, Vol. 6, Nos. 1–2, April–June 1909 (Medam–Edavam 1084 ME), p. 2.

[98] Ibid.

[99] C. Kesavan, *Jeevitasamaram*, Vol. I, p. 135; Puthupally Raghavan, ed., *C.V. Kunjuramante Thiranjedutha Krithikal*, pp. 280–300.

[100] Ibid., pp. 299–300; *Vivekodayam*, Vol. I, No. 4, 15 November 1904 (30 Thulam 1080 ME), p. 72.

[101] See also Fuchs, *Rebellious Prophets*, p. 271.

[102] C. Kesavan, *Jeevitasamaram*, Vol. I, p. 134.

[103] Ibid., p. 137.

[104] Ibid., p. 135.

[105] See the back volumes of *Vivekodayam* from 1904 to 1912.

[106] *Vivekodayam*, 12 May 1905 (30 Medam 1080 ME), p. 14.

[107] P. Parameswaran, *Sree Narayana Guru Swamikal*, p. 81.

[108] M.K. Sanoo, *Narayana Guru Swami*, p. 217.

[109] *Vivekodayam*, 12 May 1905, p. 14.

[110] Ibid.

[111] See the back volumes of *Vivekodayam*, 1905, 1908, 1909, 1911 (1080 ME to 1086 ME), etc. See also P.K. Balakrishnan, *Narayana Guru*, pp. 71–76. His messages dated 10 May 1909 (28 Medam 1084 ME) and 31 August 1909 are worth mentioning.

[112] M.K. Sanoo, *Narayana Guru Swami*, p. 224.

[113] C.V. Kunjuraman, a rationalist par excellence who once ridiculed life-cycle social rituals, was compelled to celebrate the *tirandukalyanam* of his only daughter, Vasanthy, to fulfil the last

wishes of his wife who was on her deathbed. See C. Kesavan, *Jeevitasamaram*, Vol. I, p. 134.

[114] The Guru directly stopped the *kettukalyanam* ceremonies in Kunnuvilla House, Trivandrum. See *Vivekodayam*, Vol. 1, No. 3, June–July 1904 (Mithunam 1079 ME), p. 40. He did the same in the house of Cochchammini in Pettah. See *Vivekodayam*, Vol. 1, No. 3, August–September 1904 (Chingam 1080 ME); P.S. Velayudhan, *S.N.D.P. Yoga Charitram*, p. 129.

[115] *Vivekodayam*, Vol. 6, Nos. 1–2, April–June 1909 (Medam–Edavam 1084 ME), p. 1.

[116] C.P. Sivadasan, 'Narayana Guru', in M. Govindan, ed., *Poetry and Renaissance*, p. 209.

[117] In the presence of a large number of invitees the Guru said: '*Talikettukalyanam* is an unnecessary ceremony. It is disgusting, as you do not pay enough attention to my words in spite of my repeated advice. It is for your benefit. I am telling you that these unnecessary ceremonies should be discarded. If you have faith in my words, you must give up this ceremony.' Everybody who had gathered there wholeheartedly accepted his words. See *Vivekodayam*, January–March 1911 (Makaram–Kumbam 1086 ME).

[118] Ibid. Almost all the biographers of Narayana Guru record in detail this incident. Also see M.K. Sanoo, *Narayana Guru Swami*, pp. 224–27; P. Parameswaran, *Sree Narayana Guru Swamikal*, pp. 87–88; P.S. Veluyudhan, *S.N.D.P. Yoga Charitram*, pp. 130–32.

[119] On 8 May 1912 (26 Medam 1087 ME), Swami wrote a letter to the Nellaman Muttathara Thayarvillakathu House criticizing the activities of a person like M. Govindan. *Vivekodayam*, Vol. 6, Nos. 1–2, April–June 1913 (Medam–Edavam 1087 ME), p. 1.

[120] *Vivekodayam*, Vol. XIII, Nos. 1–2, April–June 1916 (Medam–Edavam 1091 ME), p. 14.

[121] M.K. Sanoo, *Narayana Guru Swami*, p. 282.

[122] *Census of India, 1901*, Vol. XXVI, Travancore, Part I, Report, p. 279.

[123] *Proceedings of the Twelfth Session of the Sree Mulam Popular Assembly*, 1916, p. 43.

[124] Ibid.; Thurston, *Castes and Tribes of Southern India*, Vol. II, p. 410.

[125] In Chapter 2, I have discussed the influence of factors like the development of the public works department, penetration of British capital which led to the development of plantation industries, introduction of laws patterned on the western concept of private property in land, the demand for coconut articles from abroad, and the demand for manual labour in Ceylon and Burma, making way for economic changes among the Ezhavas. A number of Ezhavas were appointed in services of the British Indian government, and a number of them were accommodated in plantation industries, the public works department and the forest department in the Government of Travancore.

[126] U. Balakrishnan Nair, 'Marriage System in Malabar', pp. 385–98.

[127] For all practical purposes, the *karanavan* was an 'absolute ruler' and a 'dictator'. He had full control over the distribution of family income. He was not bound to give any account of his stewardship. See *Travancore Legislation Record*, Vol. XVIII, pp. 81–87 and Vol. XIX, p. 87, KSLL. See also Mannath Padmanabhan, *Ente Jeevitha Smaranakal*, Vol. I, Nair Service Society Press, Trivandrum, 1964.

[128] Kathleen E. Gough, 'Nayars and the Definition of Marriage', *Journal of Royal Anthropological Institute*, Vol. LXXXIX, 1959, pp. 23–34.

[129] K.N. Panikkar, 'Land Control Ideology and Reform', p. 40.

[130] O. Chandu Menon, distinguished judge of British Malabar and a member of the Marumakkathayam Committee, in his famous social novel *Indulekha*, has beautifully depicted the resentment of junior members of matrilineal families at not getting equal opportunities for education from the *karanavan*. O. Chandu Menon, *Indulekha*, National Book Stall, Kottayam, 1971 (first published 1889).

[131] See the preface of *Indulekha*, which describes the autocracy of the *karanavan* and the miserable condition of junior members of the family. This description of Nair *taravads* is applicable to all communities which followed the matrilineal law of inheritance. Chandu Menon, *Indulekha*, pp. 31–32. Also see the editorials of *Vivekodayam*, Vol. 9, Nos. 9–10, December 1912 and February 1913 (Dhanu–Makaram 1088 ME).

[132] A message dated 10 May 1909 (28 Medam 1084 ME) sent to the SNDP Yogam by Sree Narayana Guru. *Vivekodayam*, Vol. 6, Nos. 1–2, April–June 1909 (Medam–Edavam 1084 ME), p. 2.

[133] Murkoth Kunhappa, 'The Thiyyas of Kerala', *Souvenir*, Indian History Congress, Calicut, 1976, p. 49.

[134] *Vivekodayam*, December–February 1912–13 (Dhanu–Makaram 1088 ME), p. 311.

[135] In 1879, the Malabar Marriage Association was founded; this Association drafted and presented a bill to the government seeking legal sanction for the Nair marriage. But the government did not consider it seriously. Mr William Logan, Malabar Collector, in his report on the tenancy problem, pressed the need to change the marriage and law of inheritance of the Nairs. Acting on Logan's recommendation, the Madras government constituted a committee of four members to investigate the legal recognition of Nair marriages. The committee unanimously recommended the enactment of a marriage and succession law. In 1890, Sir C. Sankaran Nair, a member of the Madras Legislative Council, introduced a bill to permit Nairs in British India to register their *sambandham*, make it legally binding, and enable Nairs to dispose a part of their self-acquired property to their wives and children. Before sanctioning this bill, the Government of India asked the Madras government to collect more details on this subject. Thus the Malabar Marriage Commission was appointed in 1891 with T. Muthuswamy Aiyer as president. Although the commission published its report by the end of the same year, the government waited till 1896 to pass the Malabar Marriage Bill. According to this Bill, *sambandham* acquired the status of a legal marriage, and entitled a man to make over his self-acquired property to his wife and children if he died intestate. But these rules were applicable only to those who registered their *sambandham* with the government. See Legislative Department Proceedings, Judicial Proceedings, *Malabar Marriage Commission Report*, 1891, and *Madras Native News Paper Reports*. For details, see K.N. Panikkar, 'Land Control, Ideology and Reform', pp. 39–45. The Malabar Marriage Bill inspired the Ezhavas to change their law of inheritance. See *Vivekodayam*, Vol. 2, No. 8, November–December 1905 (Vrischikam 1081 ME), pp. 1–2.

[136] The important suggestions for reform were recognition of *sambandham* as a legal marriage; statutory control over the power of *karanavan*s; and rights to bequeath all of one's self-acquired property, to arrange partition of distantly related branches of *taravad*s, and to claim a share for wives and children from the self-acquired property of a man dying intestate. *Report of the Marumakkathayam Committee*, Travancore, p. 1.

[137] Ibid., pp. 1–70.

[138] Regulation I of 1088 ME, *Regulation and Proclamation of Travancore*, Vol. V, p. 820.

[139] *Vivekodayam*, Vol. IX, Nos. 9–10, December 1912 to February 1913 (Dhanu–Makaram 1088 ME), pp. 296, 311.

[140] C.O. Madhavan, 'Ezhavarum Nayar Regulationum', ibid., pp. 295–96.

[141] 'Editorial', ibid., p. 311.

[142] *Vivekodayam*, November–December 1912 (Vrischikam 1088 ME), p. 258; *Vivekodayam*, Vol. II, Nos. 3 and 4, June–August 1914 (Midhunam–Karkkadakam 1089 ME), p. 130.

[143] *Vivekodayam*, December 1912; *Vivekodayam*, February 1913 (Dhanu–Makaram 1088 ME), p. 311.

[144] *Vivekodayam*, Vol. 9, No. 8, November–December 1912 (Vrischikam 1088 ME), p. 258.

[145] Heimsath, 'The Functions of Hindu Social Reformers – With Special Reference to Kerala', pp. 33–34.

[146] *Vivekodayam*, Vol. 9, No. 8, November–December 1912 (Vrischikam 1088 ME), p. 258.

[147] In this memorandum, there were no arguments for changing their inheritance. The memorandum was nothing but a request. See *Vivekodayam*, Vol. IX, Nos. 11–12, February–April 1912 (Kumbam–Meenam 1088 ME), pp. 350–51.

[148] M. Govindan and S. Padmanabha Panikkar were the official members, and N. Kumaran and N. Kumaran Asan the non-official members. See *Vivekodayam*, Vol. XII, No. 12, March–April 1916 (Meenam 1091 ME), p. 403.

[149] Ibid., pp. 402–03; G.O. No. J-2888, dated 19 March 1916, cited in P.K.K. Menon, *The History of the Freedom Movement in Kerala*, Vol. II: 1885–1938, The Regional Record Survey Committee, Government of Kerala, Trivandrum, 1972, pp. 468–69.

[150] *Vivekodayam*, March–April 1916, pp. 402–03; G.O. No. J.5184, dated 21 June 1916, cited

in P.K.K. Menon, *The History of the Freedom Movement in Kerala*, Vol. II, pp. 468–69.

151 G.O. No. J-5184, dated 21 June 1916, cited in P.K.K. Menon, *The History of the Freedom Movement in Kerala*, Vol. II, pp. 468–69.

152 When this committee was constituted in March 1916, it was represented only by the members those who followed mixed system of inheritance and *marumakkathayam* system. By adding two more non-official members from Kottayam area, the followers of *makkathayam* system also got representation. See P.K.K. Menon, *The History of the Freedom Movement in Kerala*, Vol. II, p. 463.

153 Ibid., p. 169.

154 G.O. No. J-2255, dated 6 March 1918, cited in P.K.K. Menon, *The History of the Freedom Movement in Kerala*, Vol. II, pp. 468–69.

155 See *Report of the Ezhava Law Committee with Draft Bill and Appendices*, Government of Travancore, 1919; also P.K.K. Menon, *The History of the Freedom Movement in Kerala*, Vol. II, p. 468.

156 See the Ezhava Regulation relating to marriage, succession, family management and partition among Ezhavas, reproduced in *Vivekodayam*, Vol. 17, No. 3, October–November 1923 (Thulam 1099 ME), pp. 123–25; *Vivekodayam*, Vol. 17, No. 4, December 1923 (Vrischikam 1099 ME); *Vivekodayam*, Vol. 18, No. 19, February–March 1925 (Kumbam 1100 ME).

157 In order to gain favour for the *misradaya* group from the government, Parameswaran even opposed the bill which was introduced in the Assembly to give freedom to Ezhavas and other backward communities to use public roads. The bill was defeated by one vote, that of Parameswasran. See C. Kesavan, *Jeevitasamaram*, Vol. I, pp. 366–67.

158 *Vivekodayam*, Vol. 18, No. 9, January–February 1925 (Makaram 1100 ME), p. 303.

159 Ibid.; P.K. Madhavan, *The Life of T.K. Madhavan (T.K. Madhavante Jeevacharitram)*, Vol. II, Sarada Book Depot, Trivandrum, 1936, p. 584.

160 Ibid., p. 580.

161 The following reasons were given by Mr Kochunni to consider this bill defective. (1) The system of inheritance therein proposed tended to pave the way for *makkathayam*, which was too radical a change and unsuited to the present condition of the community. (2) The evidence collected by the Ezhava Law Committee was not satisfactory because most of the witnesses who deposed before the committee in support of the principle were ignorant persons who did not know what they were speaking about. (3) The provision that the self-acquired property of an Ezhava dying with issue should devolve on his wife was inequitable, inasmuch as it left out of account old parents, if any, of the deceased; only half the property should go to the wife. (4) The provisions of the Ezhava Regulation did not affect *makkathayam* Ezhavas; that would be destructive of unanimity among the community as a whole, and was not, therefore, a desirable restriction of the scope of the proposed law. (5) Finally he touched upon *tavazhi* partition, which he said was highly desirable, but he suggested two modifications to clause 27 of the bill, viz. (i) that partition should be so effected as to give equal share to all *tavazhis*, irrespective of the number of members in each; and (ii) that partition should give only right of enjoyment and not that of alienation. See *Proceedings of the Sree Mulam Popular Assembly*, 1924, p. 52.

162 *Proceedings of the Sree Mulam Popular Assembly*, 1924, pp. 216–17; T.K. Ravindran, *Asan and Social Revolution in Kerala: A Study of His Assembly Speeches*, Kerala Historical Society, Trivandrum, 1972, p. 92.

163 Ibid.

164 *Vivekodayam*, Vol. 18, No. 10, February–March 1925 (Kumbham 1100 ME), pp. 330–41; *Travancore Gazette*, April 1925.

165 *Vivekodayam*, February–March 1925 (Kumbham 1100 ME), pp. 330–41. According to Raghavayya, the Dewan of Travancore, 'the Ezhava bill which is an important piece of social legislation purports to define and amend the law relating to marriage succession, partition and family management among the Ezhavas . . . I think that this bill as passed by the Council ought to meet the legitimate wishes of all sections of the community.' See Dewan's Address, *Proceedings of the Sree Mulam Popular Assembly*, 1924, p. 21.

[166] Some Indian scholars like M.N. Srinivasan have connected the liquor question with the Sanskrit tradition. See M.N. Srinivasan, *Social Change in Modern India*, University of California Press, Berkeley, 1966, pp. 387–88. But western scholars like Lucy Carnoli have seen close connections between the temperance agitation in India in the late nineteenth century and the temperance agitation in England. See Lucy Carnoli, 'Origin of the Kayastha Temperance Movement', *Indian Economic and Social History Review*, Vol. III, No. 4, December 1974, pp. 432–47.

[167] Heimsath, *Indian Nationalism and Hindu Social Reform*, pp. 34–40.

[168] Sasipada Banerjee, a Bengal social reformer, started a Temperance Society in his native town Baranagar in 1863; this society was later affiliated to the Bengal Temperance Society of Calcutta. Bannerjee's temperance movement highly influenced the working class of Baranagar. See Albion Raja Kumar Banerjee, *An Indian Path Finder: Being the Memoirs of Sevabrata Sasipada Banerjee 1840–1924*, Oxford Kemptall Press, London, n.d., p. 74; Dipesh Chakrabarty, 'Sasipada Banerjee: A Study in the Nature of the First Contact of the Bengal Bhadralok with Working Class in Bengal', *Indian Historical Review*, Vol. II, No. I, July 1975, pp. 343–44.

[169] The Anglo Indian Association was formed in London in 1883 by W.S. Caine and Samuel Smith, two Liberal members of the British Parliament. They took up the leadership of a number of anti-drinking movements in India. See Lucy Carnoli, 'Origin of the Kayastha Temperance Movement'.

[170] Ibid., pp. 432–47.

[171] The Indian Social Conference, during its 10th session at Calcutta in 1896, discussed the issue and passed a resolution in favour of the temperance movement. See C.Y. Chintamani, *Indian Social Reform*, Madras, 1901, 'Appendix', p. 372.

[172] The Indian National Congress took up the issue of temperance from the time of its inception. It passed several resolutions against the excise policy of the government; see the resolutions of 1888, 1889, 1890, 1900, 1901, etc. At its sixteenth session, the Congress passed a detailed resolution on this topic. See K. Iswara Dutt, *Congress Cyclopedia: The Indian National Congress, 1885–1920*, New Delhi, n.d., Vol. I, pp. 38, 48, 57, 145.

[173] In Madras Presidency, a few individuals like Venkata Ratnam Naidu, Veeresalingam and G. Subramanya Aiyer were active against intemperance. According to Venkata Ratnam Naidu, 'to an Indian temperance has no other meanings, it denotes nothing other than abstinence'; quoted in V. Ramakrishna Acharyulu, *Social Reform Movements in Andhra*, p. 299.

[174] During the period 1911–20 (1086–95 ME), the demand for arrack and toddy increased by 47 per cent and 50 per cent respectively, and the annual income of Ezhavas from the toddy business to about Rs 70 lakhs. See P.K. Madhavan, *The Life of T.K. Madhavan*, Vol. II, pp. 437–45.

[175] John D. Rogers, 'Cultural Nationalism and Social Reform: The 1904 Temperance Movement in Sri Lanka', *Indian Economic and Social History Review*, Vol. 26, No. 3, July–September 1989, p. 320.

[176] A. Ayyappan, *Social Revolution in a Kerala Village: A Study in Culture*, Asia Publishing House, Bombay, 1965, p. 154.

[177] *Private Papers of Dr Palpu*, File No. 4, p. 99, Nehru Memorial Museum and Library (NMML), New Delhi.

[178] *Madras Mail*, 5 May 1924, in *Travancore Government English Records*, Vaikom Bundle, Vol. IV, Cellar, Trivandrum Secretariat.

[179] T.K. Velu Pillai, *The Travancore State Manual*, 4 vols, Government Press, Trivandrum, 1940, Vol. III, p. 13.

[180] See the conversation between Mahatma Gandhi and T.K. Madhavan reproduced in *The Hindu*, 30 September 1921. See also *Collected Works of Mahatma Gandhi*, Vol. XX (August–December 1921), p. 187; P.K. Madhavan, *The Life of T.K. Madhavan*, Vol. II, pp. 494–95.

[181] Verse 13, chapter IV, *Bhagavad-Gita*, with commentary by Swami Gnananonda Saraswati, Trichur, 1968, p. 73.

[182] M. Srinivasa Aiyangar, *Tamil Studies or Essays on the History of the Tamil People, Language, Religion and Literature*, Guardian Press, 1914, p. 66; Elamkulam Kunjan Pillai, *Studies in Kerala History*, National Book Stall, Kottayam, 1970, pp. 371–73; Elamkulam Kunjan Pillai *Kerala Charitra Prasanangal*, National Book Stall, Kottayam, 1963, p. 119.

[183] A. Ayyappan, *Iravas and Culture Change*, p. 32.

[184] Ibid., p. 36; A. Ayyappan, *Social Revolution in a Kerala Village*, p. 154.

[185] Quoted in A. Ayyappan, *Iravas and Culture Change*, p. 37.

[186] Sasipada Banerjee started a Temperance Society among factory workers at Baranagar for making the working class 'aware of' the evils of drink and disciplining them. See Dipesh Chakrabarty, 'Sasipada Banerjeel', pp. 339–64.

[187] *Vivekodayam*, August–September 1920, as quoted in P.K. Balakrishnan, *Narayana Guru*, p. 152. This address of Sree Narayana Guru shows that he himself pointed out the evils of drink to the poor people and asked them to forsake it. Daniel Thomas writes, 'if there is one thing against which the Guru was never tired of speaking and asking his followers to speak, it was the evils of drinking'. See Daniel Thomas, *Sree Narayana Guru*, The Christian Institute for Religion and Society, Bangalore, 1965, p. 32.

[188] The most critical words used by Mahatma Gandhi to describe alcoholism were 'evil and sin'. *Young India*, 16 March 1920.

[189] Murkothu Kumaran, *Sree Narayana Guru Swamikalude Jeevacharitram*, second edition, P.K. Brothers, Calicut, 1971, p. 470; M.K. Sanoo, *Narayana Guru Swami*, p. 540.

[190] *Sahodharan*, Vol. 3, No. 5, September–October 1920 (Kanni 1096 ME), p. 162.

[191] Swami John Dharmatheerthan, *The Prophet of Peace*, Sree Narayana Publishing House, Chempazhanti, Kerala, 1931, p. 47.

[192] Ibid.

[193] V. Ramakrishna Acharyulu, *Social Reform Movements in Andhra*, p. 310.

[194] Though Travancore was predominantly an agricultural state in 1931, while agriculture accounted for 17.6 per cent of the total state revenue, the contribution of excise and customs was 34.7 per cent. See All Travancore Joint Political Congress, *Travancore: The Present Political Problems*, 1934, pp. 24–26.

[195] *Kerala Kaumudi*, 14 June 1923, p. 1.

[196] *Kerala Kaumudi*, 22 June 1922, p. 4.

[197] Ibid.

[198] *Kerala Kaumudi*, 24 May 1923, p. 3.

[199] *Kerala Kaumudi*, 12 May 1921, p. 3; *Proceedings of the Eighteenth Annual Meeting of the SNDP Yogam*, No. 17.

[200] Ibid.

[201] Ibid.

[202] P.K. Madhavan, *The Life of T.K. Madhavan*, Vol. II, pp. 438–39.

[203] Ibid., p. 339.

[204] Ibid., pp. 448–56.

[205] *Kerala Kaumudi*, 22 June 1922, p. 4.

[206] P.K. Madhavan, *The Life of T.K. Madhavan*, Vol. II, p. 446.

[207] See the conversation between Gandhi and T.K. Madhavan on prohibition in the *Collected Works of Mahatma Gandhi*, Vol. XXI (August–December, 1921), p. 187; M.K. Sanoo, *Narayana Guru Swami*, p. 408.

[208] Ibid.

[209] On 9 November 1925 (24 Thulam 1098 ME), M. Madhavan, secretary of the Liquor Abolition Samiti, and a number of others were arrested and imprisoned under Section 90 of the Travancore Criminal Code. See P.K. Madhavan, *The Life of T.K. Madhavan*, Vol. II, p. 440.

[210] Ibid., pp. 141–42.

[211] Ibid., p. 439.

[212] Ibid.

[213] Ibid., p. 436.

[214] Fuchs, *Rebellious Prophets*, p. 273.

[215] *Private Papers of Dr Palpu*, File No. 12, p. 103, Nehru Memorial Museum and Library (NMML).

[216] For details of his 'non-alcoholic madhu campaign', see ibid., File Nos. 1 and 2.

[217] According to *Vivekodayam*, in 1921, out of 1,000 workers, only 110 retained their so-called traditional occupation. See *Vivekodayam*, November–December 1912 (Vrischikam 1088 ME), p. 47.

[218] *Census of India, 1921*, Vol. XXV, Travancore, Part I, Report, p. 125.

6

Dogmatisms of the Caste System

All the social reformers of modern India, from Raja Rammohan Roy to B.R. Ambedkar, have regarded casteism as a social evil and as something to be obliterated from social life. Reform organizations like the Brahmo Samaj, the Prarthana Samaj, the Arya Samaj, the Ramakrishna Mission and the Theosophical Society have not only raised their voice against the caste system, but also held the view that it should not continue to shape social relations. However, even though these organizations and reformers were anti-caste and made constant references to the caste system as the root of India's social ills, only those among them from the lower castes – such as Jotirao Phule, founder of the Satyashodhak Samaj; Sree Narayana Guru, founder of the SNDP Yogam; and B.R. Ambedkar, organizer of the All India Depressed Classes Federation – aggressively questioned the caste structure as such.[1] Leaders like Swami Dayanand Saraswati and Mahatma Gandhi defended the Vedic notion of *chaturvarna* or the four-fold division of Hindu society. Dayanand gave it a utopian explanation and sought to maintain *chaturvarna* on the basis of virtue. According to him, no person was born into any *varna* but rather was identified as a Brahmin, Kshatriya, Vaishya or Sudra according to the kind of life he led.[2]

Like Dayanand Saraswati, Gandhi too was a defender of *chaturvarna*.[3] Although stressing the need for social equality among the four divisions, Gandhi said: 'I believe that caste has saved Hinduism from its disintegration. . . . I consider the four divisions alone to be fundamental, natural and essential. . . . I am certainly against any attempt at destroying the fundamental divisions.'[4] In an interview with T.K. Madhavan, editor of *Deshabhimani*, at Tinnevelly on 23 September 1921, in reply to a query whether he was in favour of caste, and inter-caste marriage and inter-dining, Gandhi categorically stated, 'I am for caste' and 'against both' (inter-dining and inter-marriage) 'on hygienic and spiritual grounds'.[5] He upheld the prohibition on inter-dining and inter-marriage since they foster 'self-control'; and he referred to the caste system as a beneficial 'natural institution'.[6] He even went to the extent of saying that 'Prohibition against inter-marriage and inter-dining is essential for a rapid evolution of the Soul'.[7]

However, Gandhi's views on caste, *varna*, inter-caste marriage and inter-dining underwent radical changes between 1926–47, although it cannot be stated with certainty that these changes were a direct fall-out of his involvement in the Vaikom Satyagraha, and his meeting and discussions with Narayana Guru at Sivagiri.[8] In 1925, at the time of the Vaikom Satyagraha, while conversing with Sree Narayana Guru, Gandhi asked whether it was not according to nature to have different castes in the society.[9] The allegory he used was that all the leaves of a tree are not alike.[10] The Guru responded by reinterpreting this allegory and explaining that irrespective of the apparent differences among the leaves, the juice of every leaf is essentially the same, just like men may appear to be of different kinds (castes) but are essentially the same.[11] This response of the Guru reveals his conviction about the instrumentality of caste differentiations in perpetuating a hierarchical distribution of people in society.

Later, while addressing an audience in Calcutta, Gandhi pointed to a tree and said, 'Though the leaves of this tree may appear different in looks, the content of the juice of these different leaves is the same as they belong to the same species.' This was in sharp contrast to his Sivagiri analogy where he cited the leaves of a tree to justify the caste system; in Calcutta he cited the same analogy to establish the hollowness of casteism. This turnaround in Gandhi's view may have been due to the influence of his meeting with Sree Narayana Guru.[12]

For Narayana Guru, caste discrimination was both irrational and unacceptable.[13] Caste was abhorrent to him not only on moral and ethical grounds, but also because of its rules and regulations, which 'hampered social mobility, fostered social division and sapped individual initiative'. He waged a relentless war against the institution of caste. His call for action was two-fold. The first was of course a set of actions to challenge and resist the hegemony of *savarnas*. The second was a set of actions prompting the Ezhavas to fight their own caste-based feelings towards communities they considered as lower to them. The Guru advocated that since all men belonged to 'one race and one caste',[14] people should not observe caste distinctions. The foundation of his concept of caste was, therefore, the oneness of human nature. A man who worked zealously with the Guru on these lines was Sahodharan Ayyappan.

As discussed in the previous chapter, the first move of Narayana Guru and the SNDP Yogam against caste was their attempt to encourage homogeneity within the Ezhavas by erasing the sub-caste structure. They then worked towards promoting communal equality with members of the 'lower castes'. While the Ezhavas suffered caste discrimination at the hands of the upper castes, they themselves were guilty of treating castes considered lower to them in the social hierarchy in the same way.[15] In fact, a number of Ezhava temples were not open to such castes that were considered lower to them in the caste hierarchy.[16] In Canannore, for instance, a Pulaya and his sister were severely beaten up for not having moved away from the path in order to allow some Ezhavas to pass unpolluted.[17] This caste attitude of the Ezhavas pained the Guru very much.[18] He and Sahodharan Ayyappan vehemently opposed the caste feelings of Ezhavas towards Pulayas and the Parayas, though without much headway. They felt it was a contradiction to fight against the pollution and untouchability practised by castes above them while they themselves treated Pulayas and Parayas as polluting and untouchable. Therefore, they decided that one of the first things to be done was to eradicate the feeling of caste superiority which many Ezhavas nourished. They believed that such a shift in attitude would at the same time create the feeling of caste equality, that they were neither inferior nor superior to anyone.[19] Therefore, the Guru reminded the Ezhavas that unless they changed their attitude towards the communities inferior to them in the caste structure, they had no right to fight against upper-caste domination. He told them: 'You must look upon the Pulayas and the like with love. The Ezhavas should behave towards their inferior in such a way that those who deem themselves superior to the Ezhavas should see and learn from it. This is a matter you should pay special attention to.'[20]

The uplift of communities like the Pulayas and Parayas was considered by Narayana Guru as an important part of his life's mission. He admitted students to his ashram without any distinctions of caste. Students from different communities lived, dined, bathed, prayed and studied together there.[21] He also made them cook food for guests and others. Whenever prominent caste-conscious people came to the ashram, the Pulayas would serve food to them; and on many occasions, the Guru made it a point to introduce these servers of food to the visitors as Pulayas.[22] He taught the sacred books to low-caste people, and insisted that the temples dedicated by him should be made accessible to them. At public assemblies and feasts, he treated them as equals. When quarrels arose between caste Hindus and non-caste Hindus, the Guru was always on the side of the latter.[23]

Narayana Guru stressed the fundamental unity of mankind by projecting a casteless society as the ideal for the emancipation of humankind. A few of his followers appreciated this ideal and tried to put it into practice. As a means towards achieving the Guru's dream, Sahodharan Ayyappan and some of his friends decided to organize inter-dining with Pulayas at his native place on 27 May 1917.[24] The idea behind the event was that 'those who want to root out the caste system should first accord equal status to those considered lower to them'.[25] On the appointed day, after taking an oath that they would adopt all lawful means to end the caste system, they took food in the company of

Pulayas.[26] This public violation of the custom of separate dining, considered sacred through the centuries, raised a storm in the society at large as well as within the Ezhava community.[27] The violent reaction of local Ezhava leaders did not, however, deter Ayyappan from working towards his goal.[28]

People with vested interests even spread the rumour that Narayana Guru himself was against the inter-diners.[29] The Ezhava community in general turned against Ayyappan,[30] who had been accepted as the most promising young Ezhava leader in Cochin state.[31] When the incident stirred up such a storm, Ayyappan decided to visit the Guru at Alwaye and briefed him. The Guru smiled, blessed him and said, 'The movement will grow; behave like Christ.'[32] When Ayyappan asked the Guru for a message for the Sahodhara Sangam in order to blunt the opposition to his activities relating to inter-caste marriages and inter-dining with the low castes,[33] the Guru complied by issuing a message in which he pronounced his famous dictum: 'Whatever be the difference in faith, dress or language, all humanity belongs to the same caste; there is no harm in inter-marriage and inter-dining.'[34] Narayana Guru also has the credit of being the first *sanyasi* of the traditional order to perform an inter-racial marriage in his ashram at Sivagiri, of an Ezhava youth to a German lady,[35] at a time when even Mahatma Gandhi vehemently opposed inter-caste marriage and inter-caste dining.[36]

On his part, Ayyappan started a movement called the Sahodhara *Prasthanam*, which stood for the brotherhood of all men, and with the aim of eradicating casteism, superstition and social injustice. This is how he came to be popularly known as Sahodharan Ayyappan. In 1917, he started a journal titled *Sahodharan* as the mouthpiece of the movement. Both his Prasthanam and this journal, with the blessings and special consideration of the Guru,[37] did a lot for promoting universal brotherhood, and for discouraging the caste system and other pernicious practices prevailing in the Hindu society.

Apart from Ayyappan, others like Kumaran Asan, Palpu, C.V. Kunjuraman, T.K. Madhavan, C. Krishnan, Guru Satyavradhan were also moved to act on behalf of social unity and for the breaking down of caste discrimination. But the campaign of Narayana Guru and some of his supporters for abolishing casteism did not have too many takers in Kerala. When the Guru set up the ideal of one caste before his community, though a few progressive Ezhavas appreciated it, the majority of them and the Yogam itself failed to implement it. This failure can be attributed to the following reasons: first, since the influence of traditional beliefs and practices was so deep-rooted, the advice of the Guru did not have a serious impact initially; second, Ezhavas were naturally inclined to claim rights for themselves and at the same time reluctant to yield the same to others whom they considered inferior;[38] finally, although the Guru's idea in forming the SNDP Yogam was not merely to organize the Ezhava community, but to bring together all people without any discrimination of caste, creed or religion, the middle class Ezhavas who governed the Yogam could not reconcile to this idea.

The fact is that the Yogam tended to become an exclusively Ezhava organization. From its very inception it was parochial and caste-oriented, as revealed by the bye-laws of the Yogam.[39] Its membership was strictly restricted to Ezhavas and their various denominations.[40] When the Yogam started taking on the hues of a caste organization, ignoring Sree Narayana Guru's basic principles, the Guru himself was forced to sever his ties with it.[41]

Crusade against Untouchability and Unapproachability

The initial activities of the Yogam had to do with the fight against disabilities like the denial of admission in public schools and government offices, which was their indirect crusade against untouchability and unapproachability. The Yogam and middle-class Ezhavas launched their direct fight against untouchability and unapproachability only towards the end of the second decade of the twentieth century. It was then that they turned their attention to issues like the restriction on them using public roads. Though caste-based untouchability was the bane of social life all across India,[42] it was worse in Kerala where caste rules were implemented in the most irrational manner with the triple burdens of untouchability, unapproachability and unseeabillity.

The caste bias was such that it was believed that members of the lower castes polluted the superior castes not only by touch but also by sight. On public roads leading to areas where temples and Brahmin houses were situated, signboards were put up by the government prohibiting lower castes from entering. Therefore, at the beginning of the twentieth century, there were streets, roads and pathways that were not for public use, in the sense of being open to all communities,[43] and there were several such all over Kerala.[44] In addition to this, even the distance at which Ezhavas or other low-caste people should remain when upper-caste Hindus appeared on the road was stipulated. Those who violated these rules, either knowingly or unknowingly, were not only beaten up but also dragged to the court, and quite often the court verdict went against the lower castes.[45] Such caste repressions prompted Vivekananda to describe Malabar as 'a paradise of fools where everyone was happy in his ignorance, in his superstition and in his age-long social bondage'.[46] Gandhi was equally critical of this state of affairs in Travancore.[47]

When caste restrictions became a hindrance to their socio-economic and educational progress, the emerging middle class among Ezhavas, who desired status and power, started resisting these social evils.[48] The most important factor that induced Ezhavas to fight against untouchability and unapproachability was their interest in joining government services, for securing social status and economic mobility.[49] Chapter four discusses how 'untouchability' and 'unapproachability' had an important place in the explanations given by the government for not admitting Ezhavas into the public services. The lopsided advancement of education in the Ezhava community only served to produce a large number of educated unemployed youths who were disillusioned as they were denied government jobs on the basis of caste.[50] Due to strict observance of caste rules and untouchability, departments like the army, palaces and *devaswoms* were not open to them till the year 1936.[51] In 1913, the Dewan defended the government's reluctance to employ the lower castes in certain departments in the following words: 'if too many Ezhavas are taken, the work may be obstructed as they cannot enter all places freely such as temples, Brahmin houses and the like'.[52] It was in this context that the reformers began to focus their attention on the question of unapproachability and untouchability as it dawned on them that for fulfilling their material interest and establishing social equality, removal of these caste restrictions was indispensable.[53] In short, the motive behind their movement was not only to put an end to caste discrimination, but also, by abolishing the hegemony of the *savarna*s, to secure rights of entry into government service.

Second, the humiliating treatment meted out to them challenged the Ezhavas' sense of self-respect and dignity. Rich Ezhavas and the educated Ezhava middle class especially found the notices put up in the vicinity of shrines and at public roads prohibiting backward communities from entering the locality,[54] to be insulting and humiliating. The experience of Aloommoottil Channar is a good example of the resentment of Ezhava landlords and the upper middle class of the community.

Channar was one among two individuals who owned a car in Travancore.[55] Once, when his car reached a spot beyond which Ezhavas were not allowed to proceed, Channar had to get down and take a longer route on foot to rejoin the road about a mile or so away, while his driver, who happened to be a Muslim, drove the car along the road forbidden to his 'master' and waited at the wheel for him to arrive.[56] Likewise, during temple festivals like the Thrissur Puram, Ezhavas and other untouchables who had dwellings on the roadside were required to vacate their houses in order to avoid polluting the procession of Brahmins and other upper-caste people carrying the deity.[57] Rich, well-educated and well-employed Ezhavas like C. Krishnan, Palpu, P. Velayudhan and Kumaran Asan could not travel on a large number of roads in their provinces although they held respectable positions not only among the Ezhavas but also among the *savarna*s. Palpu wrote to Gandhi in 1925 that 'the right to walk through the public road is one that even dogs and pigs enjoy everywhere without having to resort to any Satyagraha at all'.[58] Naturally, therefore, the Ezhavas viewed these disabilities as humiliating, and as seriously affecting their self-esteem and individuality.

The third reason for their dissatisfaction centered on the commercial

TABLE 20
Involvement of various communities in industry, transport and trade[59]

Community/Caste	Industry	Transport	Trade
Ezhavas	26.3	3.4	7.0
Muslims	15.5	2.3	18.9
Christians	7.8	1.8	6.7
Nairs	2.8	1.1	4.7

prosperity of the Ezhavas. We find that the Ezhavas were not just agricultural labourers, but engaged in industry and trade as well. Table 20 shows the involvement of various communities in Kerala in industry, transport and trade, and the relative position of the Ezhavas.

The contribution of the caste factor in general economic activities is evident from the table given above. The moot point is that the progress of Ezhavas in the fields of production and commerce depended on their having free access to mobility across regions and spaces, which in turn meant free use of infrastructure – especially roads. Most of the roads 'prohibited' to them led to sites of intense consumer activity. By implication, the prohibition undermined smooth functioning of their businesses. Therefore, on 13 June 1910, forty-five Ezhavas of Ramamangalam in Muvattupuzha submitted a petition requesting the government to withdraw the notification dated 23 April 1885 that prohibited entry, as it affected their economic development.[60] The petitioners pleaded that such prohibitions considerably affected the commercial prosperity of their community.[61]

The fourth reason for Ezhava discontent was non-acceptance of their civic rights. The point can be explicated with reference to concrete historical events. Till 1918, when the Ezhavas were excluded from the outer precincts of the Brahmin temples, they decided to have temples of their own and went on to establish a number of them. But this attitude of the Ezhavas began to change by the end of the second decade of the twentieth century, as they noticed the disparity in the temple income and expenditure. In 1921, government spent more than Rs 24 lakhs for the administration of temples and the maintenance of *oottupuras*, when the income from the temples was only Rs 4 lakhs.[62] While the government spent more than Rs 24 lakhs on temples and its allied institutions, the expenditure for all other departments taken together was Rs 93,52,226.[63] This shows that excess money spent on temples were derived from taxes paid by all sections of the people, while the benefits of these temples accrued only to a microscopic minority. The Ezhavas being the largest tax payers in the State felt that it was unfair on the part of the government to use their money to administer temples and construct roads while they were denied the use of either. This was a clear violation of civic rights and this awareness

TABLE 21 *Economic and educational position of Nairs and Christians in Travancore during the early 1930s*[65]

		Nairs	Syrian Christians
		(in thousands)	
(i)	Literacy		
	(a) Vernacular	453	482
	(b) English	234	322
(ii)	Average size of landholding (in acres)	3.12	4.46
(iii)	Average income per year (in Rs)	147	275

prompted them to fight for their rights.[64] The upcoming commercial and mercantile class within the Ezhava community wanted the money collected from them as tax to be spent in ways conducive to their further development.

The fifth reason was related to the economic competition between Nairs and Christians which brought the former close to the Ezhavas. The economic interest of the *savarna* community, especially the Nair middle class, suffered a setback during this time. Table 21 shows the positions of Nairs and Christians vis-à-vis education, size of landholdings and average income per year.

This inequitable distribution of economic and cultural capital between the two communities is evident from the table above. When we consider the total population of these communities, it can be found that the inequality is even more skewed than that decipherable from the table. Nairs became sensitive to this relative disadvantage during competition between the Nair and Christian middle class for the control of land, jobs, education, positions in the legislature and the government service. This rivalry for economic supremacy naturally impelled the *savarna*s to strike an intimacy with *avarna*s, especially the Ezhavas. By that time the earlier superior position of the Nairs in the field of ownership of land, education and *sarkar* jobs was reversed in favour of the Syrian Christians.[66] The Nairs of Travancore found Ezhavas to be potential junior allies in the competition with the Christians.[67] Only a consolidated Hindu community, it was felt, could stand against the growing importance of Christian middle-class businessmen, cash crop farmers and professionals.[68] The Ezhava elites also had their own reason for joining hands with the *savarna*s, especially the Nairs. As seen in the previous chapter, the experience of the Ezhavas with the Christians and Muslims while working together in the Civic Rights League had been disappointing since 'the Civic Rights League had been quick to forget the anti-untouchability aspects of its original programme, when the major grievance of educated Syrian Christians was met'.[69] Besides, leaders like Madhavan introspected about the indifferent attitude of the *savarna* Hindus towards untouchability and reached a philosophical conclusion that the feelings of those who have been experiencing untouchability is not the same as those who had not experienced it.[70] Madhavan was not ready for a confrontation with the influential *savarnas*. Instead, he wanted their cooperation and support to fight against untouchability. He realized that otherwise the Ezhavas could not make any dent in the social structure of Kerala.[71]

The last reason which accelerated the movement against untouchability was the cooperation and support of the educated middle-class sections among the *savarnas*. Though the orthodox section of *savarnas* stood for untouchability and were dead against lifting the prohibition of entry to the *avarnas*, the educated Malayalee nationalist intelligentsia, who mainly hailed from caste Hindus, began to empathize with the disabilities of the *avarnas*. We have already seen that G.P. Pillai took the grievances of the Ezhavas to the forum of the ninth session of Indian National Social Conference (a sister organization of Indian National Congress) held at Poona as early as in 1895.[72] The concept of temple entry was the brain child of Raman Thampi, an aristocratic Nair and a retired Judge of Travancore High Court, and not that of an Ezhava.[73] The cooperation and support of *savarna* community was influenced by various factors like the growth of education, nationalist sentiment, the influence of Gandhi (whose clarion call against untouchability and socio-economic inequality caught the attention of caste Hindus), impact of modern western ideas, etc. Along with the development of nationalism the caste Hindus slowly started to realize the fact that for the growth of national unity and solidarity, eradication of casteism and untouchability that had prevented the unity of people was essential.[74] The attitude of Mahatma Gandhi towards untouchability and casteism[75] to a great extent influenced the *savarna* Congress leaders in altering their approach and attitude to casteism and untouchability.[76]

While the Ezhava middle class had been waging a futile war against caste discrimination and untouchability without making any breakthrough, the two *savarna* leaders, C. Raman Thampi and Kannath Janardhana Menon, an educated aristocratic Nair from Cochin state, came out openly for opening all Hindu temples, under government and caste Hindu control, to the Ezhavas and the other deprived sections of the Hindu society.[77] This initiative of temple entry from two caste Hindu leaders themselves shook the bed rock of traditional Malayalee Hindu belief system. It was an eye opener for the Ezhavas, as it was pronounced at a time when the heterodox Ezhavas had never even dreamt of such an idea. Thus the seed of temple entry concept in Kerala was sown by these two educated *savarna* leaders.

Despite the fact that the Ezhavas started movements against untouchability and also demanded the opening of certain roads which ran past the temples closed to them, the concept of temple entry was, as a matter of fact, beyond their imagination. This is evident from the petitions the Ezhavas of Cochin submitted to their Maharaja in 1917. In this petition they humbly pleaded:

Even now we have no admission to schools. We can not go near some Anchal offices . . . We have no ambitions for high positions. We have no desire to enter the temples of cast Hindus. Our prayer is very limited. Our only request is that we have to get the rights and privileges which we would get if we were to convert to either Islam or Christianity while we remain within the fold of Hinduism.[78]

Barring a few, majority of the Ezhavas, whether educated or illiterate, could not flout tradition and therefore defended caste system and untouchability. They stringently followed caste practices and treated the different communities according to their social status in caste hierarchy.[79] The orthodox section even defied the Guru by denying entry to the Pulayas in an Ezhava temple at Trivandrum.[80] While asking the caste superior to them to recognize the equality of Ezhavas with *savarnas*, they were not ready to concede the same rights they claimed for themselves to the caste below them.[81] Notwithstanding their social status in the community, the Ezhavas were not ready to spare any one who deviated from this norm. The experience of Sahodharan Ayyappan and his friends highlight this fact. As mentioned earlier, Ayyappan and his friends organized an interdining with a few Pulayas at Pallippuram in Cochin State.[82] This infuriated the elders of the Ezhava community in Cochin, particularly in his locality in Cherayi. Its ripples spread all over Kerala.[83] The Vignana Vardhini Sabha, a local Ezhava association took various steps against Ayyappan and his friends.[84] This resulted in Ayyappan and twenty-one other families who took part in the function being subjected to severe social ostracism.[85] Ayyappan was ridiculed by many and mockingly named 'Pulayan Ayyappan'.[86] He was doused with red ants and cowdung at the instigation of prominent Ezhavas in Cherayi.[87] As the wrath of the conservatives did not subside the Ezhavas led a delegation to the Maharaja of Cochin with a request that Ayyappan be exiled from the state.[88] On the contrary, the comparatively liberal Maharaja advised the delegation that 'they must strengthen the hands of Ayyappan so that government may eventually take the measures demanded by Ayyappan'.[89] It was during the uproar of interdining, Kumaran Asan the General Secretary of the SNDP Yogam, wrote an editorial in *Vivekodayam* which criticized both the orthodox and the heterodox alike, and described the act of Ayyappan and his friends as a 'foolhardy' or suicidal step.[90] The editorial of Kumaran Asan overlooked the moral and ethical aspects of Ayyappan's interdining. The ideology behind the movement was the uplift of neither the Ezhavas nor the Pulayas[91] but an endeavour of self-purification in the sense that the Ezhavas were justified in their demand for equal rights with the *savarnas* only if they treated the communities considered below on par with them. The message Kumaran Asan conveyed to the young reformers through his editorial was that they should first learn to stand on their own feet before attempting to help others.[92] Otherwise it would be a 'suicide by leaping straight from the peaks of idealism to practical application'.[93] This reveals that the Ezhavas, in general, were only theoretically opposed to the caste system. In practice, however, a majority of them were not strictly against its existence or its continuation as long as it concerned the castes lower to them.

The situation in Travancore was not very different. When Raman Thampi for the first time mooted the idea of temple entry for Ezhavas and other despised sections of society, it was, indeed, a bold move which found very few takers even among the Ezhavas. While presiding over a meeting of Ezhava Samajam at Quilon in 1917, in connection with the sixty-third birth anniversary of Narayana Guru,[94] Raman Thampi opined that the Ezhavas no longer needed parallel temples of their own and suggested that the temples of the government and the caste Hindus should be opened to them for worship. Though this speech of Raman Thampi shocked the *savarnas* and *avarnas* alike in Travancore, and the entire Hindu Community in general, it was a shot in the arm for T.K. Madhavan and C.V. Kunjuraman. After getting inspiration from Raman Thampi, C.V. Kunjuraman wrote an article on temple entry and sent it to *Deshabhimani,* for publication. Though Madhavan was the editor of the paper, K.P. Padmanabha Channar, popularly known as K.P. Kayyalakkal, the owner of the paper, refused its publication due to the fear of a backlash from the government and the *savarnas*.[95] Only after getting an assurance from N. Kumaran, a legal expert from the Ezhava community that it would not cause any infringement of the existing law, that it was published in December 1917, a few months after it was written.[96] Thus, this article, appearing in the form of an 'editorial' in the *Deshabhimani* (in December 1917), entitiled 'Njangalkum Sarkar Kshetrangalil Onnu' (A Government Temple for Us Too), was the first expression of demand the Ezhavas made for temple entry. The article opened up the issue for discussion. In 1919 and 1920, when Madhavan wanted to raise the issue of temple entry in the legislative assembly, the then Dewan of Travancore, M. Krishnan Nair, empathized with Madhavan. He allowed him to present resolutions on temple entry for *avarnas* in the Popular Assembly,[97] despite the fact that the Assembly rule 19(D) did not permit any member to take religious matters for discussion in the Assembly.[98] Krishnan Nair, a man of liberal ideas from Malabar, who held the view that 'a government or an individual could not do much without creating general awareness among the people against untouchability',[99] permitted Madhavan to present his resolution. Besides, he was not against the freedom of expression of an Assembly member on the pretext of a mere technical excuse of an Assembly rule, which was strictly enforced by his successors.[100] When Madhavan was presenting his representation on temple entry at Sree Mulam Popular Assembly in 1919, his counterparts from the Ezhava community in the Assembly – Moolur Padmanabha Panicker and A.K. Govindan Chanar – left the seats which they occupied, adjacent to the speaker, and moved to the visitors gallery, as they considered it a matter of shame to listen to something so ludicrous and implausible.[101] This shows that even the attitude of the educated Ezhavas, the mainstream Ezhava social reformers, was influenced by their inherent inability to question traditional practices. They felt that it was a futile exercise. Though they began their demand with permission for temple entry, all of them, including Kumaran Asan and T.K. Madhavan, eventually confined their request to Ezhavas being accorded the same facilities enjoyed by the low-caste Hindu converts to Christianity, while they remained within the fold of Hinduism.[102]

The educated *savarna* community in general and Nair community in particular followed a favourable attitude towards temple entry for *avarnas*.[103] In a joint protest meeting of the *savarnas* and *avarnas*, held at Trivandrum on the 7 March 1921 (24 Kumbam 1096 ME), all prominent Nair leaders spoke in favour of temple entry for all the Hindus and criticized the attitude of the government.[104] In 1922, forty-six Hindu members of the Sree Mulam Popular Assembly – a majority of them being caste Hindus – submitted a memorandum to the government to open all Hindu temples, whether government administered or aided, to the entire Hindu community for worship for the general welfare and development of Hindus without considering their caste.[105] At Ambalapuzha Conference of Nair Samajam, P.K. Narayana Pillai even went to the extent of emphasizing that the Ezhavas should not be satisfied with just temple entry but strive to procure the right to perform rituals including *poojas*.[106] Without their support and cooperation the Vaikom Satyagraha would have mere remained as a desideratum. The *savarna* communities played a seminal role in the fight against untouchability and temple entry movement in Travancore. In other words, the moral and physical support of *savarnas* acted as a leverage to boost the courage of Ezhavas.[107]

By the end of the second decade of the twentieth century, an open and organized movement against untouchability gained extra momentum after the intervention of Sahodharan Ayyappan and T.K. Madhavan. As rationalism and universal brotherhood were his precepts, Sahodharan adopted a scientific and humanist approach to tradition. This enabled him to look at tradition critically, and the contemporary socio-religious practices from the stand point of social utility, replacing faith with rationalism and humanism.[108] The *Sahodara* movement of Ayyappan contributed considerably in spreading the message of freedom, equality, friendship and fraternity all over Kerala and thus inspired and enlightened the people. The *Sahodara* movement helped, to a large extent, to develop an independent intellectual thinking.[109] While Sahodharan was a rationalist, Madhavan was a nationalist par excellence. Being a nationalist, casteism and untouchability were abhorrent to Madhavan, as they fostered social division and discouraged patriotic feelings. He, there-fore, called for an ideological struggle representing civil liberty movement as an integral part of an evolving national consciousness.[110] The temple entry movement for Madhavan was not just a means of establishing the religious rights of Ezhavas (as Hindus) but for achieving moral rights of a citizen.[111] In other words, it was a movement for achieving citizens civil liberty rights and social equality.[112]

Both Ayyapan and Madhavan were prolific writers and eloquent speakers who used their organizational skills and employed their fiery speeches and powerful writings to develop an independent intellectual thinking for the benefit and service of the despised sections of society. Through their respective journals *Deshabhimani* and *Sahodharan*, started in 1915 and 1917, T.K. Madhavan and Sahodharan Ayyappan contributed considerably in spreading the message of freedom, equality and fraternity all over Kerala.[113] This to certain extent helped to lift the depressed classes from their moral stupor. For materializing their desire Madhavan, like his contemporary nationalists, tried to incorporate Gandhian ideologies and strategies in his movement. In other words, he began to apply the techniques of non-violent satyagraha and the mobilization of public opinion to issues which affect the internal structure of Malayalee society. As a result of their endeavour, socio-religious practices based on orthodoxy, obscurantism and fatalism were sought to be replaced by freedom, faith, reason and a sense of human dignity. Though there were differences in ideology and approach, the ultimate end of both these leaders was the liberation of the deprived section from all kinds of bondage. With the intervention of these two leaders, a revolutionary change, both in policy and strategies, took place. Till then Palpu, Kumaran Asan and others had confined themselves to submitting memorials and representations. The movement of these constitutionalists had remained confined to the urban lower and middle classes, while it failed to reach the masses of the State: the peasants, and the unlettered agricultural labourers. The emerging new leadership differed from their predecessors, as they were not satisfied with the existing method. Realizing that the method of constitutionalism – submitting petitions and memorials to the authorities – were absolutely ineffective in changing the attitude of the government and a group of *savarna* Hindus, this new leadership decided to change the tactics of mobilization from the old method of mendicancy to direct action. Taking a leaf out of the experiences of their predecessors, Madhavan and Sahodharan acknowledged that social freedom could not be achieved unless and until they converted the style of protest of the moderates into a mass movement through mobilzation of Ezhavas for non-cooperation and civil disobedience – boycotting *savarna* temples, refusing to pay taxes and defying government sign boards prohibiting entry.[114] They believed that the awareness of one in need was more potent than the awareness of the authorities. Therefore, they were determined to carry their message to the villages and secure a mass support for their agitation. Within a few months, the whole Ezhava movement underwent a sea change. What Gandhi did to the Indian National Congress, both Madhavan and Ayyappan together did to the Ezhava community. As we have already seen, while Sahodharan Ayyappan concentrated his attention on eradicating the evils of caste and popularizing the idea of interdining, T.K. Madhavan devoted his entire time and energy to put an end to casteism, untouchability and temperance. According to Madhavan, 'If Gods cease to observe untouchability man will have no justification'.[115]

During this period the Ezhavas and the Yogam launched an intense campaign against untouchability, though temple entry was not a major item on their agenda. As a result, an unprecedented awakening was witnessed among the Ezhavas. The Ezhava youths organized a large number of meetings all over Travancore and Cochin. In 1918, about five hundred Ezhava youths held a meeting at Eravavoor and took a vow to use public roads which were prohibited to them. They also raised funds to support the movement against untouchability.[116] In the same year, the Ezhava leaders asked their community to boycott Guruvayur Ekadasi.[117] In the fifteenth session of the Yogam held at Kottarakkara in 1918, the Yogam, for the first time, introduced and passed a resolution pertaining to temple entry for the untouchables.[118] This demand was reiterated in 1919 annual session at Kayamkulam and in 1920 at Alleppey.[119] It was during this period that Madhavan and his friends launched an intense campaign in the Sree Mulam Popular Assembly for establishing the right to enter the temples either run or aided by the government. Thus it became a regular feature thereafter.[120] In 1919 they advised the Ezhavas to refuse to pay taxes till the ban on using temple roads was removed.[121] In the interpellations in the Legislative Council on 27 July 1920 (12 Karkkadakam 1095 ME), N. Kumaran Asan enquired whether the government could make a public declaration providing facilities such as entrance to government schools, guest houses and other public places to all without any distinction of caste or at least provide those facilities which were being enjoyed by the low-caste Hindu converts to Christianity while they remained with in the fold of Hinduism. The reply was not positive at all.[122] As there was no response from the government to their representation on temple entry, another resolution was passed unanimously, in the annual meeting at Alleppey in 1920, to boycott all *savarna* temples till they were opened to the Ezhavas.[123] For achieving their dream concept of temple entry, participants of the seventeenth annual meeting of the Yogam were ready to face any hardship. They were even prepared to offer satyagraha till their prayers were granted.[124] At this meeting the question of en masse conversion of Ezhavas from Hinduism to Christianity also came up for the first time.[125] It is rather surprising to note that T.K. Madhavan an ardent follower of Narayana Guru and a staunch Sanatana Hindu,[126] who had always been holding the opinion that the Ezhavas should obtain all their rights without relinquishing Hinduism,[127] was the person who introduced this controversial resolution.[128] This shows the desperation and helplessness of the leaders like Madhavan. However, the audiences were not ready to accept these resolutions.[129] As Kumaran Asan, Erath Krishnan Asan and many other important leaders vehemently opposed the resolution, it was finally withdrawn.[130] Another development, in 1920, was the decision of the non-caste Hindus to defiantly enter the banned roads, close to the temple.[131] Therefore Madhavan along with Ayyappan and Swami Satyavratan crossed by the restricted area of Vaikom temple ignoring the sign board banning their entry.[132] On later occasions too Madhavan defied sign boards prohibiting entry to untouchables and even dared to inform the District Magistrate of Kottayam about the infringement of law,[133] so as to 'to demonstrate the stupidity of law'.[134]

As the reception to this agenda of conversion was not accepted positively,[135] on 31 December 1920 (17 Dhanu 1096 ME) a meeting of the untouchables was held at Sivagiri, under the Chairmanship of N. Kumaran, General Secretary of the SNDP Yogam.[136] This meeting repeated the decision of boycott of *savarna* temples more vigorously and a committee consisting of N. Kumaran, T.K. Madhavan, C.V. Kunjuraman and K.P. Kayyalakkal was constituted to prepare a charter of 'ten commandments' on temple boycott.[137] Hundreds of copies of the charter were circulated all over Travancore. Under the auspices of this committee many seminars and discussions were organized to explain and educate people about the irrationality and ignorance behind the practice of untouchability and how to implement temple boycott. As a result, a number of Ezhavas boycotted caste Hindu as well as government temples.[138] It was a big blow to *savarna* temples as this boycott caused considerable financial crisis and a few temples even found it difficult to meet the means for sweeping and sprinkling temples and buying oil to light the lamp.[139] This only strengthened their resolve to fight for temple entry. This was evident from the slogan 'Temple Entry is our birth right' on placards, used to receive the delegates of the annual meeting at Karunagappally in 1921.[140] At this meeting they decided to form a Service Fund (Seva Nidhi) for helping the temple entry movement.[141] It was during this period that a group of young Ezhava radicals entered into a temple at Kadakkavur in Cherayinkizhil forcefully[142] questioning the denial of temple entry. They were prosecuted and convicted[143] on the ground that their entry made the temple impure.[144] As this hurt the self-respect of the community, Ezhavas intensified their movement against untouchability in Travancore in various ways. The movement slowly started to spread over to the neighboring state of Cochin. In a meeting of Sree Narayana Dharma Poshini Sabha held at Trippunithura on 6 January 1923 (22 Dhanu 1098) under the chairmanship of Madhavan, a resolution was passed on the right to temple entry. Thus temple entry became an issue in Cochin as well.[145]

The orthodox section of the *savarna* Hindus did not like this organized movement of defiance by the Ezhavas. The vigour and enthusiasm of the Ezhavas to do away with the humiliating casteism on the one hand and the interest of the *savarnas* to retain their caste hegemony over untouchables on the other, caused a number of skirmishes between the *savarnas* and the Ezhavas in various parts of Travancore like Kotta, Kadakkavur, Tirunakkara, etc.[146]

Apart from opposition from the *savarna* orthodoxy, the uncompromising attitude of the government disturbed the Ezhavas. We have already seen the relentless attempts of Madhavan and his counterparts in Sree Mulam Popular assembly from 1918 onwards, for establishing the rights of Ezhavas to enter the temples either run or aided by the government. Though in 1919 and in 1920 Ezhava representatives were allowed to submit a petition on temple entry for all Hindus irrespective of caste, in 1921 they were denied even that privilege by the new Dewan Raghavaiya, on the pretext that temple entry being a religious subject, it could not be discussed in the House.[147] When T.K. Madhavan and Chavarkattu Marthadan Vaidhyan, gave a notice to submit petitions for equal rights of citizens with special emphasis on entry of all Hindus into public temples, the Chief Secretary asked them to amend the subject of the petition as equality of citizen's rights in the hope that they would not refer to the subject of temple entry.[148] This ban on presenting their representation in the Assembly was considered as an intervention by the government in the civil liberty movement of the Ezhavas.[149] Against this stand of the government, the Ezhavas organized protest meetings all over Travancore. On 7 March 1921 (24 Kumbam 1096 ME), while the session of Sree Mulam Assembly was on, a joint meeting of the *savarnas* and *avarnas* was held at LMS Hall Trivandrum to protest against the draconian law of the government.[150] At this meeting it was also decided that a deputation of the Ezhava representatives in the Assembly would meet the Dewan and if necessary, threaten to walk out in case they were not permitted to submit their representation.[151] Instead of accepting their demand the Dewan assured them that the rule 19(D) of the Assembly would be amended before the next session and that the Ezhavas would be then allowed to make their representation.[152] On the basis of this assurance the deputation dropped their old plan of boycotting the Assembly and left the place after submitting a collective memorandum to the Dewan.[153] But in the next Assembly instead of keeping his promise, Raghavaiyya reiterated his old stand and said that so far as Ezhavas remained within the fold of Hinduism, they would not be given the same right and privileges which a convert to Christianity and Islam would get.[154] Madhavan met Raghavaiyya at Bhaktivilasam, the official residence of Dewan, and sought his help for an interview with the Maharaja, in order to bring to the notice of His Highness, the request of the Ezhavas. The Dewan also declined that request. When the Dewan was not ready to budge from his stubborn position, Madhavan bemoaned, 'in such a situation what can we do; we will be forced to leave Travancore'. The Dewan promptly replied, 'for redressing your grievances you may leave Travancore'. As he had never expected such an irresponsible response from a responsible Dewan, Madhavan enquired, 'Are you seriously suggesting it'? When the Dewan maintained a stoic silence, Madhavan left the place in search of other alternatives.[155] There were three alternatives not complimentary to each other, despite their uniformity in scope: a) conversion of the Ezhavas to other religions, b) transformation of the Yogam from sectarianism to secularism by opening its membership to all without any consideration of caste, creed or religion and c) seeking political support from outside Travancore for resolving their social problems.

Options Available

Conversion

As the Ezhavas began to strongly believe that Hinduism and its caste hierarchy were solely responsible for their social, economic and political grievances,[156] many Ezhavas thought about conversion as a panacea for redressing their grievances. There was, however, no unanimity of opinion on the question of conversion and the religion to which conversion was to be sought. While C.V. Kunjuraman supported Christianity, C. Krishnan was in favour of Buddhism and Rarichhan Mooppan from Malabar opted for Brahmo religion. Conversion to Christianity was used by Ezhavas as a threat against orthodox *savarnas*, and the conservative government of Travancore.[157] C.V. Kunjuraman preferred Christianity in the light of the favours the Christians received in Travancore. The factor which induced Krishnan to opt for Buddhism was the possibility of social and moral uplift through the means of conversion.[158] The reason which persuaded Rarichchan Muppan to embrace Brahmo religion was its anti-idolatry, anti-casteism and its opposition to priesthood. He strongly criticized the Guru's consecration of temples and other religious activities. According to him, the Guru's activities were nothing but unscrupulous imitation of Brahminical practices and this would only lead to stratification of society and mutual antagonism among the Ezhavas.[159] He asked the Guru to induce the Ezhavas to adopt the Brahmo forms of worship.[160] Sahodharan Ayyappan, who propagated the philosophy of 'no caste, no religion, no God for man' was neither against Christianity, nor Buddhism. Though he embraced Buddhism[161] in the later period, in the beginning he neither supported conversion nor opposed it. However, he was to comment later that 'Past experiences taught one that so long as Hindus remained Hindus, it is impossible to wipe out caste feeling from their mind'. In support of Christianity he said, 'It is better to convert to Christianity in which there is no untouchability and unapproachability'.[162] Though T.K. Madhavan once stood for Christianity,[163] and later changed his allegiance to Aryasamaj,[164] in his heart of heart he remained always a Sanatana Hindu.[165]

Another section advocated the founding of a new religion. For this purpose some of the Guru's disciples approached him. In his letter addressed to the Guru, Sivaprasad, one of the disciples of the Guru, said that his (Guru's) teachings of Brahminical practices to the Ezhavas would not remove mutual antagonism within the community.[166] As a solution he appealed to the Guru to preach a new religion which was casteless like Buddhism, 'Otherwise let us give an open permission to convert to Buddhism or Christianity or Brahmo religion, whatever we like to provide at least our offsprings to have freedom and worldly life'.[167] The idea of conversion for social mobility did not gain much support since majority of Ezhavas and most of the prominent leaders like Kumaran Asan, Murkoth Kumaran, Erath Krishnan Asan and many other influential Ezhavas were dead against conversion. The temper of Ezhava majority revealed the fact that they passionately clung to the religion in which they were born and brought up.[168] They all believed that any attempt of en masse conversion of Ezhavas from Hinduism to any other religion was nothing but an insult to Narayana Guru, who was without doubt a *sanatana* Hindu under whose spiritual and religious guidance the Ezhavas had achieved enviable success in every walk of life. Kumaran Asan wrote a very scholarly and academic article in 1923, rejecting outright the conversion theory, and this was later published in 1933 as a booklet entitled *Mathaparivarthana Rasavadam* that meant the alchemy of religious conversion.[169]

The Guru, however, held the view that each person had the freedom to follow the religion of his choice, while advocating that the essence of all religions was the same. Regarding the claim of superiority over the other by the followers of each religion, the Guru compared this with that of the claim of seven blind men about the elephant. To the Guru, the edveavour to prove this claim of superiority was nothing but ignorance and hence he wrote;

> Religions are in essence one;
> As blind men dispute about the elephant
> The ignorant with varying arguments stray
> Behold and stray not, be at peace.[170]

In his conversation with Gandhi in 1925 at Sivagiri, the Guru stated Hinduism was as good as any other religion for spiritual salvation.[171] In fact, in the universalistic outlook of the Guru, conversion had no place. In a message to the All Religious Conference at Alwaye Advaitashram in 1924 he stated: 'This great parliament of religion makes it abundantly clear that the ultimate goal of all religion is the same and so there is no need for followers of different religions to indulge in mutual conflict.'[172] The religious conference and ripples of Vaikom satyagraha pacified the enthusiasm for conversion of a section of the Ezhavas for the time being.

Secularism as Opposed to Sectarianism

Though the Yogam claimed that it stood for the protection of 'Narayana Dharma' that was 'one caste one religion and one God for men' it always remained as an organization of the Ezhavas, for the Ezhavas and by the Ezhavas. This sectarian character of the Yogam pained the Guru, who expressed his unwillingness (in 1912–13) to be associated with such an organization, despite the fact that he was the permanent President of the Yogam.[173] This sectarian character of the Yogam kept away many influential sections of society despite their affinity to the Guru and his ideology, as they were not Ezhavas. Leaders like Madhavan realized that without the blessing of the Guru,[174] and the help and sympathy of the influential *savarna* section, Ezhavas alone would not be able to make any substantial change in social matters and if at all possible that it would be a time consuming process.[175] Therefore, for implementing the broad and liberal conception of the Guru[176] and also for attracting all sections of Malayalee population, the Yogam in its seventeenth annual meeting held at Alleppey in 1920[177] and nineteenth annual session at Quilon in 1923,[178] passed resolutions to throw open its membership to all, irrespective of caste and religion.[179] They thus made an attempt to extend this sphere of Yogam's activities for the benefit of all sections of the population, thus forming a broader and fraternal organization working for the national advancement.[180] Instead of strengthening the feeling for Ezhava identity, they decided to take a broad and liberal concept of the Guru based on universal brotherhood. As per the request of Madhavan the Guru issued a message on 30 January 1927 for the information of public in general and the Ezhavas in particular. This message was as follows, '. . . The name Ezhava does not stand for any particular caste or religion. Hence without considering caste or religion, members can be enrolled in the Yogam. I wish large number of people join the Yogam'.[181] Madhavan tried to justify the lukewarm approach and attitude of the *savarnas* towards untouchability. He observed that the feelings of *savarnas* would be different from *avarnas* for which one cannot blame them as they never experienced its (caste) bitterness.[182] As a result of this approach a large number of people from different communities, castes and religions joined the Yogam.[183] The secular character of the Yogam considerably helped get the support of *savarnas* for fighting against untouchability.

Outside Political Support

When Dewan Raghavaiyya indifferently stated that the Ezhavas may, if they so wish, leave Travancore for the redressal of their grievances, Madhavan, decided to garner political support from outside. This led him to Gandhi and the Indian National Congress. His views on politics and social reform differed sharply from that of other Ezhava leaders.[184] He minutely observed Indian National Movement of the Congress under Gandhian leadership which had attracted millions of people of different classes and ideologies into political action. This popular struggle on moral, political and ideological basis for establishing *swaraj* by which Gandhi meant 'freedom for the meanest of our countrymen . . .'[185] gave Madhavan not only a hope but also inspired him to be a part of Gandhian movement for freedom or *swaraj*. Gandhi further explained his concept of Swaraj as follows: 'I am not interested in freeing India merely from the English yoke. I am bent up on freeing India from any yoke whatsoever. I have no desire to exchange 'king log for king stork'.[186] This left no doubt in the minds of many non-Hindus and non-caste Hindus that Gandhi's concept of freedom meant freedom for all and sundry. Unlike other Ezhava leaders, who professed unswerving loyalty to the British,[187] Madhavan while admitting that the British rule had provided many facilities to the untouchables, also believed that the alien rule was not a substitute for *swaraj*.[188] The early Congress leaders did not dare take up social issues for fear of disrupting the political unity of the people, as in a country like India all communities were divided into so many sections under the influence of caste and creed.[189] However, in 1917 there was a perceptible change in the Congress policies and we find nationalist and democratic feelings, confined to the political arena, begining to invade the socio-religious space.[190] In its thirty-second session at Calcutta it passed a resolution urging upon the people 'the necessity, justice and righteousness of removing all disabilities imposed by custom upon the depressed classes'.[191] When Gandhi became the undisputed leader of the Congress party in 1920, he declared that the removal of untouchability was as important as the political struggle for freedom. According to Gandhi, 'We shall be unfit to gain Swaraj so long as we would keep in bondage a fifth of the population of Hindustan.'[192] It is no wonder, therefore, that T.K. Madhavan was attracted to the Congress and Gandhi who held the view that India would not deserve complete independence so long as untouchability existed in society.[193]

In approach and attitude of the Congress under Gandhian leadership, Madhavan found a new strategy and an alternative ideology based on broad socio-economic and political vision of self-reliance, egalitarian social order with an aptitude for democratic, libertarian and secular concept. Madhavan decided to use the newly discovered Gandhian technique of satyagraha to mobilize public opinion on issues which affected the internal structure of the Malayalee society. Madhavan had the credit of becoming the first leader of the untouchable community in India who advised the deprived section of society to use satyagraha as means for social transformation. Madhavan was the representative of the Yogam in the All Kerala Thiyya Conference, which was held at Calicut on 14 October 1918, under the auspices of the Cochin Ezhava Samajam[194] to discuss the high-handed and dastardly treatment which shook the community to its very depth that was accorded to the Ezhavas in Cochin state[195] in the guise of social and religious sanctions.[196] This conference was presided over by the noted Ezhava leader from Malabar Kottiyath Ramunni.[197] In this conference, Madhavan delivered a long and inspiring speech in which he stressed the following points:[198] a) Thiyyas should give up without reservation the practice of untouchability in respect of those they considered lower to them; b) they should oppose untouchability practiced by those they considered above them and c) the Thiyyas should observe satyagraha to put an end to untouchability. In the same conference, under the initiative and guidance of T.K. Madhavan, the Thiyya Passive Resistance League was formed to fight untouchability and for permission to enter all temples.[199] As an acceptance, Rarichan Moopan, another Thiyya leader from Malabar donated on the occasion, one hundred and one rupees, for the functioning of the League.[200] This donation of a prominent Ezhava leader could be considered as a gesture accepting political strategy of Congress for socio-religious reforms in Kerala. In the seventeenth session of the annual meeting of the Yogam at Alleppey in 1920, Ezhavas were even prepared to offer satyagraha till their prayer for temple entry was granted.[201] In a message sent to the Ezhavas, Madhavan wrote, 'Brothers, no great achievement is possible without sacrifices . . . Satyagraha is the best means to freedom for us who try to live upto the standards set up by the Guru'.[202] Here Madhavan's endeavour was to link-up the ideologies and programmes of Gandhi and Narayana Guru in order to attract Ezhavas to the satyagraha. Though Madhavan had to face stiff opposition from other Ezhavas for asserting the principles of satyagraha in the meetings and conferences of the Yogam,[203] he succeeded to a great extent in galvanizing the support of a section of the Ezhavas.

Apart from accepting the removal of untouchability as an agenda of Gandhian movement, there were various other factors responsible for inspiring Madhavan and a few Ezhavas to develop proximity to Gandhi and Indian National Congress. Though there were differences in approach and ideology between Mahatma Gandhi and Narayana Guru,[204] Madhavan noticed that many of the items listed in the constructive programme of Mahatma Gandhi such as communal harmony, removal of untouchability, khadi, village industries, economic equality, temperance, and basic education were very similar to the ideas and programmes envisaged by Narayana Guru for uplifting the untouchables.[205] Constructive works of Gandhi at the village level was envisaged as a means to bring about social and economic regeneration of villages and for reaching out to the rural masses. In actual terms, his programmes, like Narayana Guru's, were for social reform and economic equality. Gandhi's basic education, charka, khadi and village industries were meant for self-reliance and also for an effort to set up *swadeshi* or indigenous enterprises which were very similar to Narayana Guru's 'Sivagiri Free Industrial And Agricultural Gurukulam'.[206] In spite of their differences in religious matters,[207] their social and economic ideas were quite similar as both were for liberating the poor and downtrodden from the clutches of tradition and economic exploitation of the well-to-do. One may presume that the similarity in the ideas approaches and programmes of the Guru and Gandhi might be one of the reasons for attracting them to Gandhi and the Congress party.

Gandhi's endeavour in popularizing khadi and spinning as a part of *swadeshi* and as a 'vital aspect of our national movement',[208] made weaving, one of the traditional occupation of the Ezhavas, a respectable profession.[209] Till then, the Ezhavas were mockingly called *chilanthy* meaning spider[210] as weaving was one of their traditional occupations. Besides, spinning wheel and khadi made it possibile to revive handloom industry which was on the verge of dying due to the impact of machine-woven-cloths introduced by the British. In other words, Gandhian leadership had championed the revival of village industries, especially handspinning and handweaving which provided not only a new life to handloom industry from its decline but also provided the industry a new social status as a symbol of nationlism and *swadeshi*. Thus social respectability and possibility of reviving the traditional profession also encouraged them to move closer to Gandhi.

Another factor which led to their closeness to Gandhi and Congress was their doubt about the integrity and sincerity of the non-Hindus like the Christians and Muslims to fight against untouchability. The experience they had had with them during the time of Civic Rights League disappointed the Ezhavas. They had joined with the Muslims and the Christians in the League to fight for their proportionate share in the government service, legislature and also to put an end to untouchability. As a result of their combined fight, Devaswom was separated from Revenue Department which helped the non-Hindus and Ezhavas to get better share in Government service and legislature. However, as far as untouchability was concerned, Ezhavas continued to be prevented an entry into public roads, public buildings and the caste Hindu temples. After getting better share in government jobs, the non-Hindu commnuties became indifferent to the untouchability aspect of its original programme.[211] This disappointed the Ezhavas which drove them to seek help from outside.

The non-cooperation of the Ezhavas in general[212] and those in government service in particular[213] was another factor which left Madhavan with no option but to approach Gandhi and the Indian National Congress. Since the majority of Ezhavas were afraid of reprisals from their caste Hindu landlords, they kept away from the movement.[214] Those who were in the government service also did not lend any active support to Madhavan's belligerent talk of forceful temple entry,[215] as they feared that it would be interpreted as an anti-government activity. Madhavan, therefore, appealed to the Congress for support in order to activate the movement.

Transformation of a Political Technique into a Weapon for Social Emancipation

Here, I would like to examine in detail the background of how a political technique 'satyagraha' appeared as a means of social transformation. As we have already mentioned, T.K. Madhavan's views on socio-political issues differed from the other Ezhava leaders. While the latter held the view that to get their grievance redressed, it was better to cooperate with the government, Madhavan was in favour of seeking the support of the Indian National Congress.[216] Having closely watched the activities of the Congress and Gandhi, who accorded top priority to the removal of untouchability, he was inspired to seek their support.[217] First, he approached the District Congress Committee (DCC) of Quilon, when it held a meeting at Anandavalleswaram in the third week of September 1921 for including untouchability as an agenda of its programme[218] on the basis of the decision of the All India Congress Committee (AICC).[219] Gandhi had already declared that the removal of untouchabilty was no less important than the political struggle for freedom.[220] However, C. Sankara Menon, the then President of Quilon DCC, in his presidential speech, expressed his doubt whether 'the Congress Committee could take up the question without consulting the Congress authorities. . . .'[221] This doubt may perhaps have risen because of the attitude of AICC to refrain from actively interfering with the political affairs of the princely states, as Gandhi felt the time for Congress intervention in the affairs of the state was not ripe enough.[222]

It was during this time that Madhavan learned from the newspapers about Gandhi's visit to Tinnevelly. He decided as the representative of the untouchables, to use this opportunity[223] to meet Gandhi to seek his advice.[224] On 23 September 1921, he met Gandhi at his Ashram.[225] Describing his meeting with Gandhi as a unique experience, Madhavan said,

> Though I disagree with many of his views regarding caste, inter-caste-dinning and intermarriages, I cannot but respect him. I have been closely observing his way of life and activities for the last fifteen years. . . . The love and respect I felt for him when I went to meet him increased a hundredfold as I left his presence . . . .. My meeting with him and the time I spent at his feet were the most joyous moments of my life. As I returned from my meeting with him it made me feel like having been on a pilgrimage.[226]

Acknowledging the impact of Gandhi's constructive programmes, especially Khadi on Ezhavas to regain their self respect as weavers,[227] he sought Gandhi's advice on temple entry for which Ezhavas were striving hard. To Madhavan, the removal of untouchability, as a matter of reforming Hinduism, was an abstract idea and temple entry was a concrete articulation of that idea.[228] Gandhi said, 'On strategical grounds, I would ask you to drop temple entry now and begin with public wells then you may go to public schools.'[229] Gandhi drew parallel between the socio-economic and religious conditions of the Ezhavas and that of *Panchamas* in North India. After briefing Gandhi about the remarkable achievements of Ezhavas in religious matters, education, employment in government service and judiciary and also mentioning that his community produced distinguished literateurs and journalists, Madhavan very politely corrected Gandhi's erroneous notion by saying, 'You seem to mistake our position in society for something analogous to that of *Punchamas* in British India. Except half a dozen schools . . . all public schools in this state are open to us.'[230] The spontaneous response of Gandhi with his characteristic smile was, 'You are ripe for temple entry then'.[231] When Madhavan further added, 'that a good number of temples in Travancore are maintained out of public funds',[232] Gandhi's immediate response was 'Well it is a matter of civil rights even here', and added, 'I would certainly advise you to offer civil disobedience and court imprisonment, if law interferes'.[233] Gandhi might have thought of using this opportunity for trying out the political weapon satyagraha against socio-religious issues connected with untouchability. When Madhavan brought the presidential address of C. Sankara Menon at Anandavalleswaram to the notice of Gandhi he categorically stated that the stand of Sankara Menon was wrong and assured Madhavan that Travancore Congress Committee should take up this issue.[234] As per the request of Madhavan, Gandhi gave an Autoscript on Temple Entry Question to Madhavan which emphatically stated that the local Congress Committee should help Ezhavas in this matter.[235] It is rather surprising to note that Gandhi took a position which was contrary to his own position regarding the interference of Congress Party in the internal laws of the state.[236] When somebody questioned the justification of Gandhi for launching a satyagraha under Congress against an Indian state, his clarification was as follows: 'Satyagraha in an Indian State by the Congress for the attainment of its object is, I, think, clearly forbidden. But Satyagraha in an Indian State in connection with local abuses may be legitimately taken up at any time provided the other necessary conditions are fulfilled. . . . Unapproachability and untouchability have to be tackled whenever they exist'.[237] This, perhaps, might have been because of his interest to arrest the plan of enmasse conversion of the untouchables to non-Hinduism or for creating an environment for Hindu solidarity.

The publication of this interview in *The Hindu* and *Deshabhimani* played a seminal role in changing the attitude of the *savarna* community. Those who were the earlier opponents of temple entry had now become its supporters.[238] Nair Service Society, Hindu Mahajanasabha (Kerala), Namboodiri Yogakshema Sabha, and many other caste Hindu organizations extended their support. Caste Hindu leaders like Changanessery Parameswaran Pillai, Pattam Thanu Pillai, T.K. Velu Pillai, Kuroor Neelakantan Namboodiripad,[239] Harippad S. Krishna Ayer[240] and almost all *savarna* newspapers like *Mathrubhumi, Samadarshi, Swarajya, Malayalee, Janaranjini*, and *Sree Vazhumkode* published articles favouring temple entry.

Though Madhavan wanted to use this favourable attitude of *savarnas* for launching satyagraha movement, he could not do it due to the following reasons:[241] a) Kerala Provincial Congress committee (KPCC) being involved in Moppilla rebellion did not have sufficient time for the movement; b) the protest and boycott of schools by students in Travancore against hike in school fees and subsequent oppression of students created a tense atmosphere in the state and this political turbulence was not at all conducive to launch a satyagraha in Travancore for which the essential requirement was a peaceful atmosphere and c) pre-occupation of Madhavan with the socio-political issues, especially the temperance movement.

Towards Vaikom Satyagraha

After Malabar rebellion, which was squarely blamed by the *savarna* landlords and land holders 'for the activities of the Congress in arousing the passions of illiterate Muslim peasants',[242] 'there was, a lull in the national movement in Malabar following the rebellion'.[243] To regain their lost ground in Malabar after the Mopillah rebellion, Congress Party turned its attention from politics to socio-economic issues pertaining to anti-untouchability, Harijan uplift, temperance, Khadi and *swadeshi*.[244] Madhavan decided to make use of this opportunity. Though not a member of the Congress Party, he along with K.P. Kesava Menon and K.M. Panikkar attended the thirty eighth session of Indian National Congress held at Kakinada from 28 December 1923 to 1 January 1924.[245] On the basis of Madhavan's representation, 'The Request to the All India Congress Committee on behalf of untouchables of India', Indian National Congress adopted a resolution to establish a committee on untouchability.[246] For adopting this resolution, Maulana Mohamed Ali, the then President of the Indian National Congress, used his discretionary power to allow Madhavan, who was not a member of the AICC to present his demands in the subject committee, even though it was mandatory that only a member of the Congress party could do it,[247] and succeeded in getting a resolution for the removal of untouchability adopted by the committee. Madhavan was always grateful to Mohamed Ali for his help and as a gesture of gratitude the former named his only son after Mohamed Ali.[248]

As a result of relentless work of Madhavan and solid support of K.P. Kesava Menon and K.M. Panikkar, Kakinada Congress decided to take active steps against untouchability. As per the decision of the Kakinada Congress, KPCC took up the eradication of untouchability as an urgent issue and decided to intensify this programme. The Malayalee nationalist intelligentsia began to associate itself with the disabilities of the *savarnas*. Nationalist newspapers gave solid support to satyagraha; *Deshabhimani, Mathrubhumi* and *The Hindu* along with *Kerala Kaumudi, Sahodharan* and *Madras Mail* reported extensively about the development. The KPCC met at Ernakulam on 24 January 1924 and formed Kerala State Congress Anti-Untouchability Committee, consisting of T.K. Madhavan, Kurur Neelakantan Namboodiripad, T.R. Krishnaswami Ayer and K. Velayudha Menon with K. Kelappan as convenor.[249] Besides, a Propaganda Committee was also constituted with K.P. Kesava Menon, A.K. Pillai, T.K. Madhavan, Hassan Koya Mullah and Kurur Neelakantan Namboodiripad as members for adopting a basic strategy to educate and mobilize opinion among caste Hindus on untouchability.[250]

Thus due to the intervention of Gandhi, and the cooperation of AICC and KPCC 'the rising tide of nationalism and democracy began to overflow from the political to socio-religious fields effecting the downtrodden castes and class'.[251] The Anti-Untouchability Committee met at Quilon on 15 February 1924 to discuss the evils of untouchability and passed various resolutions regarding the need of establishing human rights and creating self-respect among the untouchables.[252] On Gandhi's advise of offering 'Civil Disobedience', KPCC decided to apply the newly introduced political weapon, satyagraha to fight against unapproachability at Vaikom in North Travancore where the roads around the temple were closed to the *avarna* Hindus. This satyagraha was simply for the right of the *avarnas* to use temple roads and not for temple entry. Thus the decision of Congress Party to take active steps towards eradication of untouchability appeared in the form of Vaikom Satyagraha. In other words, the nationalist challenge came to be symbolized by Vaikom Satyagraha. The selection of Vaikom temple was mainly because of its accessibility by road and boat, the popularity of Vaikom as Dakshina Kashi or Benares of South India and it was also the place which was so familiar to T.K. Madhavan, the architect of this movement.[253]

Gandhian Concept of Satyagraha[254]

When Madhavan met Gandhi, at Tinnevelly on 23 September 1921, the latter advised the former to offer civil disobedience with the condition that it should be strictly non-violent and with perfect self-restraint. As 'even the nearest followers of the Mahatma were liable to be more mistaken in their interpretation of this method which Gandhi's mind had conceived and perfected through various stages of trial and error of his life',[255] I would like to mention a few words about the philosophy of satyagraha.

While fighting for Indians in South Africa against racial discrimination and colour prejudices, Gandhi evolved a political method of direct action based upon the principles of truth, love and non-violence, which he called satyagraha;[256] meaning good will towards all, especially towards opponents.[257] In other words it was an ideology to conquer hatred by love.[258] To him this new technique of protest through action and self-reliance meant non-submission to what was considered wrong and insistence to remain peaceful under all provocation.[259] It is to be underlined that there is no place in it for fear and hatred and at the same time a willing acceptance of the pain and suffering involved in this powerful force of truth and non-violence.[260] To Nataraja Guru, the watchword of satyagraha was 'Soul Force', a special weapon of 'self-purification' of the masses.[261] The terms 'civil disobedience' and 'non-cooperation' are the other two components of satyagraha.

Many people, even his followers had a misconception that the 'passive resistance' was a synonym of 'satyagraha'. Though satyagraha implies a kind of passive resistance with ethical principle and philosophy they are poles apart. While recalling the events of 1906–1907 in South Africa Gandhi wrote,

> None of us knew what name to give to our movement. I then used the term 'passive resistance' in describing it. I did not understand the implications of 'passive resistance' as I called . . . As the struggle advanced, the phrase 'passive resistance' gave rise to confusion . . . I thus began to call the Indian movement 'Satyagraha'.[262]

Gandhi drew a sharp distinction between the two.[263] While 'passive resistance' allowed for 'internal violence',[264] satyagraha is gentle, 'it never wounds and it must not be the result of anger and malice. It is never fussy, never impatient and never vociferous.'[265] If passive resistance is a weapon of the weak which unleashes forces of prejudice and exclusiveness then satyagraha, as an ideology is a truth force, which stands for compassion and inclusiveness.[266]

After returning to India in 1915, during the first two years Gandhi kept away from political affairs, and spent the time traveling around the country and seeing things for himself. During these travels he realized the fact that none of the existing methods of political struggle were viable and non-violent satyagraha was the only panacea for facing the problem of the people. He, therefore, introduced his unique technique of struggle at Champaran in Bihar and Kaira and Ahmedabad in Gujarat, during 1917–18, to fight for the economic rights and demands of the peasants and the proletariats.[267] It achieved enviable success, which inspired millions. The power of non-violent action, identified with satyagraha, was considered by Gandhi as the most suitable instrument for achieving freedom of *swaraj*. *Swaraj* of his dream was the poor man's *swaraj* or 'real progress of the masses'.[268] The economic aspect of *swaraj* was 'welfare of all' which asserted that 'economic equality is the master-key to non-violent independence'.[269] While analysing and understanding the problem of the masses Gandhi wrote of the India of his dream:

> I shall work for an India in which the poorest shall feel that it is their country, in whose making they have an effective voice, an India in which there shall be no high class and low class of people and an India in which all communities shall live in perfect harmony . . . There can be no room in such an India for the curse of untouchability . . . Women will enjoy the rights as men . . . This is India of my dream.[270]

As Jawaharlal Nehru stated, 'The ambition of the greatest man of this century has been to wipe out every tear from every eye'.[271] While emphasizing economic equality,[272] he gave equal importance to communal harmony, uplift of women and the annihilation of caste[273] as they were the social evils acting as impediments in the way of India's march towards *swaraj*.[274] He, therefore, believed that the postponement of 'social reform till after attainment of Swaraj is not to know the meaning of swaraj'.[275] There is no wonder that when Gandhi got an opportunity for trying out the political weapon of satyagraha against socio-religious issues connected with untouchability, he used it for the first time at Vaikom. It was used not to enter temple, but to assert the right of untouchables to walk in the streets adjoining the temples,[276] which were traditionally closed to the low castes. In other words Vaikom Satyagraha was the first event which began to apply satyagraha and mobilization of public opinion to issues which affected the internal structure of Hindu society. This was the initial political blow to the notion of unapproachibility since it was basically religious in character and the avarnas' exclusion from using temple roads was symbolic of their degradation and oppression.[277]

Vaikom Satyagraha in Action

While carrying on their propaganda, the members of the committee informed the people about the decision of the KPCC to launch satyagraha movement at Vaikom on 30 March 1924. Gandhi in his letter of 19 March 1924 addressed to K.P. Kesava Menon, Secretary of the committee approved the satyagraha. However, Gandhi asserted that 'In your satyagraha you must not use force even though you are opposed . . .'[278] As a result, the satyagraha committee outlined the norms to be followed by the volunteers.[279] Though the terms and conditions were quite harsh, a large number of people from all over Kerala joined as volunteers. The satyagraha was, indeed, not for temple entry but for the right of *avarnas* to use the roads near the temple.[280] 'It is in fact a movement to purify caste by ridding it of its most pernicious result'.[281] On the pretext of preventing clashes between the satyagrahis and orthodox Hindus, the Travancore Government put up barricades on the roads leading to the temple and the District Magistrate served prohibitory orders on the leaders of the satyagraha.[282] On the appointed day of 30 March 1924 the area was crowded by supporters, general public and policemen. All were waiting to know what was going to happen. The satyagrahis led by K.P. Kesava Menon clad in khadar uniform and garland marched in rows of two towards the temple by singing devotional and national songs with great enthusiasm.[283] On the first day, three men belonging to Pulaya, Ezhava and Nair communities offered satyagraha[284] and courted arrest. They were sentenced to six months imprisonment. The succeeding batches of satyagrahis consisting of *avarnas* and *savarnas* were arrested and sentenced to imprisonment. However, rumours of possible rioting caused consternation among the caste Hindus forcing satyagrahis to stop their movement for two days.[285] As the leaders failed to arouse the conscience of *savarnas* and mobilize their active support, they had no other option but to continue the satyagraha. On the ninth day, which was on the 7 April, K.P. Kesava Menon decided that he himself along with T.K. Madhavan would offer satyagraha and court arrest. So he gave the charge to George Joseph and informed about this to Mahatma Gandhi in his letter dated 6 April 1924.[286] They were accused of fermenting trouble and arrested and sentenced to six months in prison as they refused to pay a fine of rupees five hundred.[287]

This was followed by the arrest of A.K. Pillai, K. Kelappan and K. Velayudha Menon, all except A.K. Pillai were non-Travancoreans on 9 April 1924 and sentenced to four months simple imprisonment.[288] On 11 April, George Joseph, K.G. Nair and Sebastin were also arrested and sentenced for the same period.[289] This shows that the government viewed the Vaikom Satyagraha 'not as a mere religious or social agitation, but as a political upheaval'.[290] Of the nine leaders thus arrested only five were from Travancore.[291] Except T.K. Madhavan not a single Ezhava leader came forward to court arrest.

By then Vaikom Satyagraha had gained all India fame and volunteers began to arrive from different parts of India. The most prominent among them were C. Rajagopalachari, Sreenisvasa Iyyengar, C.R. Das, Vijaya Raghavachariar, E.V. Ramaswami Naicker and C.F. Andrews.[292] E.V. Ramaswami, popularly known as Periyar, came from Madurai on 14 April 1924 to offer satyagraha and underwent imprisonment.[293] As per the instruction of the Punjab Prabhandak Shiromani Committee, a team of fifteen members under Lala Lal Singh and Kripal Singh came to Vaikom to organize a free kitchen for the satyagrahis.[294] Many Muslims representing various organizations in Kerala and Madras Presidency had already joined the satyagraha as volunteers.[295]

As Gandhi strongly believed that to be sincere and lasting all reforms must come from within,[296] he insisted that the satyagraha should be carried on without external help.[297]He was, therefore not in favour of the participation of non-Hindus, non- Malayalees except at the most from the neighbouring Madras Presidency.[298] He was against the acceptance of any material support other than sympathy[299] from non-Hindus and non-Malayalees. Gandhi considered the participation of non-Hindus and outsiders in satyagraha, and taking financial help from them as harmful to the self-respect of the local Hindus of Kerala.[300]

After the arrest of K.P. Kesava Menon and A.K. Pillai, George Joseph was nominated as the leader and the organizer of the Vaikom Satyagraha. Gandhi wrote in his letter dated 6 April 1924 to George Joseph,

> ... I think that you shall let the Hindus do the work. It is they who have to purify themselves ... Untouchability is the sin of the Hindus. They must pay the debt they owe their suppressed brothers and sisters ... You can help by your sympathy ... but not by organizing the movement and certainly not by offering satyagraha ...[301]

Though he gave his own reasons to justify his view point, one could not accept it without reservation. As a result of Gandhi's ban on their participation, Akalis left the place; Christians, Muslims and non-Malayalees, except for a few from Madras Presidency, withdrew reluctantly. Thus satyagraha was more or less restricted to the affair, of Nairs and Ezhavas, which became a cause for their unity.[302]

As prominent leaders were in jail, a satyagraha deputation consisting of Congress leaders from Kerala and Madras Presidency was constituted on the advice of Gandhi to propagate the idea and message of satyagraha among the people. As a result of their work, a stream of volunteers prepared to go to jail and join the satyagraha. Government feared that the jails would be filled in no time, therefore, the police, stopped arresting the satyagrahis and began to stand in front of the them (barring their way) in rotation.[303] Subsequently satyagrahis also changed their tactics. Accordingly, one group would go in the morning and return at 12 noon and another group would offer satyagraha from noon till 6 pm. Chathukutty Nair, who along with two other satyagrahis[304] – Krishnan Pachan and Narayanan – fasted on the road before the barricade for two days – a day and a night-became unconscious and were removed to the hospital.[305] This created a stir in the minds of the people. After getting the information of fasting from George Joseph, Gandhi immediately instructed to omit fasting saying: 'You cannot fast against a tyrant. . . . Fasting can only be resorted against a lover, not to exhort rights but to reform him,'[306] and advised satyagrahis to stand or squat in relays with quiet submission till arrested.[307] The satyagrahis behaved with dignity and upheld the values of non-violence, despite the fact that they were constantly provoked by the police and orthodox Hindus to retaliate.

On the death of Maharaja Sree Mulam Thirunal, on 7 August 1924, under the age old marumakkathayam system of inheritance, Rani Sethu Lakshmi took over the charge of administration as Regent, as his nephew and immediate successor Sri Chitra Tirunal was a minor. The new Maharani immediately released all the nineteen satyagrahis imprisoned in March–April 1924.[308] As a positive response to this gesture, Gandhi advised them to suspend satyagraha temporarily and in its place he introduced a technique of political mobilizaton called *Jatha* or procession for the first time into Kerala's political repertoire.[309] This peaceful non-violent procession was a demonstration of the feelings of caste-Hindus against untouchability and it was also to meet the Maharani to submit a representation for the removal of the disabilities of the non-caste Hindus.[310]

As a result, *savarna* Hindus organized two *Jathas;* one from Vaikom and another from Suchindram, to demonstrate their support and solidarity with the satyagrahis. While Mannath Padmanabhan and A.K. Pillai were the leaders of Vaikom *Jatha,* the Suchindram *Jatha* was headed by Dr M.E. Naidu and Sivathanu Pillai.[311] Vaikom *Jatha* which started on 2 November 1924 with hardly one hundred people, had increased to a thousand in a week's time by the time it reached Trivandrum, after covering about 150 km on foot through villages and towns.[312] Both the *Jathas* converged at Shangumukam Beach and held a mammoth rally, with more than twenty thousand people, in which many prominent *savarnas* spoke in favour of ending untouchability and opening temple roads to all Hindus irrespective of caste and creed.[313] As suggested by Gandhi, a deputation consisting of twelve members under Changanechery K. Parameswaram Pillai met Maharani Regent on 27 Thulam 1100 ME (13 November 1924) and submitted a memorial signed by 22,000 people requesting the opening of the roads around Vaikom temple to all subjects without any distinction of caste and creed.[314] In reply Her Highness said, 'As it is an important matter, there is difficulty to give a prompt reply. A resolution pertaining to this matter had already been taken up in the Council for its next meeting.[315] While taking a final decision on this resolution we will give due importance to the matters mentioned in the representation'.[316] Though the reply was disappointing, the *savarna Jatha* helped spread the aims and objectives of satyagraha among the people including caste and non-caste Hindus and non-Hindus and in terms of class its impact was significant among the peasants, workers, artisans, shopkeepers, traders, professionals and the intelligentsia.

As the reply of the Regent was not satisfactory, the satyagraha was resumed. This infuriated the orthodox *savarnas* who became restless and vindictive. They unleashed violence against satyagrahis, who were beaten up, had lime thrown into their eyes and their khaddar shirts torn from them and burnt.[317] Chettedathu Shanku Pillai was the sole martyr of the Vaikom Satyagraha, who fell prey to *savarna* goons on 28 Vrischikam 1100 ME (14 December 1925) at the age of thirty eight.[318] The satyagrahis never allowed themselves to be provoked. They behaved with dignity and upheld the values of *Ahimsa*.

As they suffered all brutality inflicted up on them without any retaliation, a peaceful situation prevailed. The dignified behaviour of satyagrahis attracted the attention of C.F. Andrews, who happened to visit Vaikom. He wrote, 'I was struck by the orderliness of volunteers and everything was very peaceful.'[319] The courage and sacrifices of the satyagrahis dispelled the notion that the desire of socio-religious freedom was the preserve of *savarnas*, and showed that it was an elemental urge common to all of society.

On 7 Feburary 1925 the resolution of N. Kumaran, was moved in the Legislative Council on 2 October 1924 calling for opening of roads around the temples in Travancore to all without distinction of caste and creed.[320] It was defeated by a single vote that too cast by an Ezhava when it came to vote.[321] The lone Ezhava vote against the resolution was Parameswaran's who was an active member of the Yogam and elder brother of Dr Palpu, the originator of the Yogam.

As per the desire of Congress leaders and the satyagrahis, Gandhi began his Kerala tour on 8 March 1925, nearly one year after the commencement of the satyagraha and met Maharani Regent, senior government officials and the trustees of Vaikom temple.[322] He visited Varkala to see Narayana Guru on 27 March 1925. He had detailed discussions with the Guru and other Ezhava leaders. Though he could not make any substantial change in the attitude of the government and the *savarnas,* a compromise was arrived at by which government agreed to withdraw police and barricades subject to the condition that the satyagrahis would not enter the roads forbidden to the *avarnas*.[323] Gandhi, therefore, sent a telegram to K. Kelappan Nair, the Secretary of the Vaikom Satyagraha Committee, on 24 March 1925, instructing that the satyagrahis should on no account cross the boundary line.[324] In November 1925, only after completing the diversionary roads that could be used by the low caste without polluting the temple, the Government of Travancore announced that all the roads used by the non-Hindus could be used by all Hindus irrespective of their caste.[325] However, certain parts of the roads on the eastern side were closed to non-Hindus and non-caste Hindus.[326] Subsequently as per the advice of Gandhi on 23 November 1925, the last satyagrahi was withdrawn.[327] Thus Vaikom Satyagraha, 'a truly glorious fight to establish the dignity of man and his right of free movement'[328] had come to an end, after twenty months with limited achievements but unlimited awareness.

A large section of educated Ezhava elites were ardent supporters of colonial rule, as Britain was viewed as a saviour rather than an enemy[329] and they were severe critics of Indian National Congress which they considered as a party of caste-Hindus or *savarnas*.[330] C. Kesavan, who later became a follower of Congress Party, very categorically stated that most of the Ezhava leaders of the time preferred British paramountcy to Indian National Congress.[331] When T.K. Madhavan was trying strenuously to get the support of Gandhi and the

Indian National Congress to launch a movement against untouchability and unapproachability, a majority of Ezhava leaders were not in favour of joining the Congress movement as they felt that it would be an act of ingratitude to the British from whom they received very many privileges and concessions. In his presidential address, at the 6th Annual meeting of the Yogam on 16 May, 1909, O. Krishnan said: 'Let me tell you here that one of the most sacred duties we have to set before ourselves is to be unswerving in our loyalty to the British. We ought never to forget that it was under the government that we first tasted the sweets of liberty and that it was its protecting arm that enabled us to elevate ourselves to our present position.'[332] They also feared that it would antagonize the British and Travancore governments.[333] Dr Palpu wrote to Gandhi saying, 'The Congressmen came here without our knowledge or permission and we have nevertheless kept aloof from them so as not to displease the authorities'.[334] Their policy was to make as much as possible friendship with the rulers.[335] They preferred to bear the humiliation of untouchability than join the Indian National Congress. Apart from the fear of evoking the resentment of the British, other significant factors which kept the Ezhavas away from the satyagraha were their awareness of civic rights and their feelings of self-respect. That was why Dr Palpu, in his letter to Mahatma Gandhi, wrote ironically that even dogs and pigs had free access to public roads without having to resort to any satyagraha.[336]

A section of the Ezhavas, who wanted to keep themselves away from the movement of the Indian National Congress and Gandhi, propagated that Narayana Guru was not in favour of Vaikom Satyagraha. Apart from anti-Congress feeling, there were various other factors also responsible for this. It was a known fact that Narayana Guru himself held considerable regard and respect for the British whom he credited with bestowing up on the untouchables the right to sanyasa or asceticism which had been so far considered the sole right of the caste-Hindus. The British made this possible as they administered the country without referring to the Hindu scriptures like the *Smritis*. He, therefore, even went to the extent of describing them as *Gurukkammar* or great teachers.[337] This soft attitude of the Guru to the British might have given an impression that he would not join the Congress movement, a known anti-British organization. According to P. Parameswaran, 'The Guru had feared that the employment of a political weapon like satyagraha for solving socio-religious problems might produce opposite effect'.[338] The Ezhavas could not have liked their spiritual leader becoming a part of a political movement to resolve socio-religious issues. Many did not want their spiritual leader to involve himself and support a movement of the Congress party, an anti-establishment organization because it could in all probability antagonize the British from whom Ezhavas received considerable help. Finally they feared that the political popularity of Mahatma Gandhi could overshadow the spiritual halo of Narayana Guru. Some of the Ezhavas and the police department of Travancore Government made some attempts to show that Narayana Guru was not in favour of Vaikom Satyagraha as he did not believe in non-violent satyagraha to put an end to untouchability. In early June 1924, K.M. Kesavan, an Ezhava journalist published an interview with Narayana Guru in the *Deshabhimani* which created a furore, as it reported that Narayana Guru did not approve of the present methods of satyagraha at Vaikom and according to the Guru volunteers 'should scale over the barricades and not only walk along the prohibited roads but enter all temples . . ..'[339] After hearing about the violent advice of the Guru for scaling barricades, Mahatma Gandhi even thought of asking the local Congress Committee to call off the satyagraha.[340] Subsequent to the appearance of this note, Narayana Guru sent a letter from Muttakkadu to Gandhi on 27 June 1924, in which Guru asserted that this interview which took place in a railway train

> seems to have been prepared without correctly understanding my meaning. That report was not shown to me before publication, nor did I see it soon after it was published . . .. I have no objection whatsoever to the satyagraha movement started by Mahatma Gandhi to fight this evil nor to the cooperation of people in the movement. Any method of work that may be adopted for eradicating the evil of untouchability must be strictly non-violent.[341]

While reporting the tour of Mahatma Gandhi in Travancore, W.H. Pitt, the Police Commissioner wrote on 24 March 1925 that Narayana Guru had told Gandhi that, 'he was not a believer in non-violence in agitations for removing social disabilities and that . . . he was anxious to secure for *his community* by any method, social equality . . . with caste-Hindus including temple entry and admission to caste-Hindu houses'.[342] This report is in contradiction to Narayana Guru's letter to Mahatma Gandhi. Besides the language and tone used by Mr Pitts, in the name of Narayana Guru, is not his style and manner of expression due to following reasons. a) The Guru never used aggressive language to provoke others; b) he never argued for social equality of his community and always stood for equality for all. This report by the Police Chief was intentionally done with malafide intention to create some sort of drift between Ezhavas and *savarnas* in the name of Narayana Guru. Though the meeting between Mahatma Gandhi and Narayana Guru were reported extensively in contemporary newspapers, nowhere was such a comment of Narayan Guru mentioned except in the report of Mr Pitts.

The Guru and Satyagraha

It is a fact that there were some ideological differences between Naryana Guru and Gandhi regarding caste, conversion, inter-caste marriages and interdining and Gandhi openly expressed his disagreement on the Guru's famous dictum, 'one caste, one religion and one God for mankind'. In his speech at Varkala on 13 March 1925, Gandhi said,

> Swamiji told me yesterday, religion was one. I combated that view and I combat it here this morning. So long as there are different human heads, so long there will be different religions, but the secret of a true religious life is to tolerate one another's religion . . . I cannot, I dare not, blind myself to existing differences. I can not rub them off the slate, if I would, but knowing those differences, I must love even those who differ from me. You will find an exemplification of this law throughout the world. No two leaves of this very tree, under whose shadow we are sitting, are alike, though they spring from the same root, but, even as the leaves live together in perfect harmony and present to us a beautiful whole, so must we, divided humanity present to the outsider looking up on us a beautiful whole. That can be done when we begin to love each other and tolerate each other in spite of differences.[343]

We have already noted Narayana Guru's arguments against Gandhi's comparison of caste and *varna* with the leaves of a tree.[344] It is no wonder that there would be some differences between 'the Silent Sage of Varkala' and political and 'historical figure of Sabarmati',[345] as their philosophical approach was different.[346] While Narayana Guru was an *advaitin*, Gandhi being a follower of *Anekantavada*[347] believed that everything has infinite number of qualities and, therefore, one cannot assert anything unconditionally. He, therefore, described himself as *Syadvatin*[348] by which every judgment ought to be qualified by 'somehow'. Though they differed in approach and attitude the ultimate aim of both the Mahatma and the Guru was same, i.e., the liberation of people from all sorts of bondages and their peaceful and harmonious co-existence.

There may be differences between them in using satyagraha as a means to solve the problems of pollution and untouchability. This probable difference had been described by Nataraja Guru as follows: 'One tried, as it were, to reach the heart of the masses from the circumstances, with variety as the starting point, while, to the other, the starting point was the recognition of the one without a second. It was natural that the leader of all India politics should differ from the solitary Guru in the point of view that he accepted as the basis of activity. One represented the peripheral and the other the central compromise of the same abstract principle. The Mahatma emphasized and voiced the master sentiment of the nation, while the Guru stood for neutral principle'.[349]

Whether Narayana Guru had any differences with Gandhi or not, he extended all cooperation and help to Vaikom Satyagraha. It is a fact that T.K. Madhavan was instrumental in bringing Narayana Guru and Mahatma Gandhi together, as he found close similarity between the Guru and Gandhi. He advocated the satyagraha as the best means to freedom for those who wanted to live up to the standards set by the Guru.[350] The Guru, as a person who stood through out his life for the emancipation of mankind from social and religious obscurantism, might have heard from T.K. Madhavan about the activities of Mahatma Gandhi in South Africa and India and his endeavour for the liberation of deprived section of society. Besides, many items listed in the constructive programme of Mahatma Gandhi were very similar to that of Narayana Guru's movements against untouchability, and for temperance, spinning and weaving, *swadeshi*, education activities, etc.[351] So the Guru did not have any objection in supporting Vaikom Satyagraha. Certainly Madhavan was the person who played a significant role in involving the Guru in Vaikom Satyagraha. The Guru gave his Vellur Madam at Vaikom for use as Satyagraha Ashram.[352] He also started a fund for providing financial help to the satyagraha and he himself contributed Rs 1000 as donation.[353] The Guru even permitted the staff of Alwaye Advaitashram to take part in the satyagraha.[354] On 27 September 1924 (12 Kanni 1100 ME) the Guru himself came to Vaikom clad in Khadi,[355] and reviewed the satyagraha.[356] He took a round of the Satyagraha Ashram and was pleased with the arrangements and was very happy to see a small Pulaya child in the kitchen.[357] Madhavan wrote, 'The visit of the Guru was more as a mentor rather than a visitor'.[358] As he was very impressed with charka and spinning of yarn at Ashram, he gave an order for thirty spinning wheels at the Alwaye Advaitashram and a special one for himself.[359] From the time of Vaikom Satyagraha onwards Narayana Guru only wore Khadar dhoti and shawl till the end of his life.[360] When Gandhi visited the Guru at Sivagiri in March 1925, the latter assured the former that he would not allow 'his followers to approach him without wearing khaddar'.[361] The dedication and discipline of the voluneteers in khadi uniform so impressed him that even though he did not like to wear it, he too was prepared to don the uniform of a volunteer at that time and offer satyagraha.[362] This shows the determination of the Guru to fight against untouchability. He ate food with the Ashram inmates. Next day a prayer meeting presided over by the Guru was held at Ashram for the health and long life of Mahatma Gandhi. He had never done such things earlier in his life before the public.[363] Narayana Guru's cooperation was indeed, a boost to the morale of the satyagrahis.

Impact of Satyagraha

Though the immediate result of the satyagraha movement was negligible in matters concerned with the eradication of untouchability and unapproach-ability, it did create an impact both in the social and political life of India. In fact, it was the Vaikom Satyagraha which for the first time revealed the depth of the evils of untouchability in India.[364] This satyagraha brought the question of civil rights of the so-called depressed classes into the forefront of Indian politics and emphasized the integral connection between Hindu temples and the disabilities of the *avarna communities*. It gained attention and sympathy from many parts of India, and the impetus it gave to the national struggle of depressed classes for equality was remarkable. Murkoth Kunhappa writes, 'When Gandhi's satyagraha movement and the spirit of *Swaraj* permeated into Kerala, it strengthened a hundredfold the urge for upward movement by the down-trodden'.[365] While admitting the differences of opinion among the Ezhavas about the intervention of the Congress Party in socio-religious issues, pertaining to untouchability, Ezhava leaders, in spite of their indifferent attitude to satyagraha, admitted two things: a) however strongly Ezhavas protested against their socio-religious grievances it could only have a limited impact which failed to go beyond the borders of Kerala; b) with the advent of Vaikom satyagraha under Gandhi and Indian National Congress, the grievances of the despised section of the Malabar region crossed the borders of Kerala as well as India and reached the British Parliament for the first time.[366] Thus Vaikom Satyagraha succeeded to a great extend in transforming a regional issue of untouchables in Kerala into a national and international issue. In short, this satyagraha created a public opinion against the system of untouchability and unapproachability in India in general and in Kerala in particular. The satyagraha movement shifted the emphasis from pure socio-religious issues to the involvement of the *avarnas* with the wider political issues of the day. The *avarnas*, the working-class section of society responded favourably to this political atmosphere. One of the significant contributions of this satyagraha was that it 'revealed the changing concept of caste and emergence of class as an important motivating force in Travancore politics'.[367] The satyagraha put an end to the idea of mass conversion into other religions for gaining social mobility. In the Pallathurithy meeting of the Yogam in 1927, it was decided to forsake the idea of conversion and ask the Ezhavas to follow the much favoured idea of the Guru, that is, 'one caste, one religion and one God for man'.[368]

Colonialism, Nationalism and SNDP Yogam

It is interesting to examine the role of the Yogam and the Ezhavas in the genesis and development of the Vaikom Satyagraha. Though Madhavan was a prominent member of the Yogam, neither the Ezhava community nor the Yogam were responsible for Vaikom Satyagraha.[369] Though the satyagraha included participants from all castes and different religions, leadership was mostly in the hands of the *savarnas*. The Ezhava community was on the whole indifferent.[370] When the satyagraha was inaugurated, the Yogam did not come out with a clear-cut policy regarding temple entry. This indecision is best reflected in C.V. Kunjuraman's words who stated that it is time for the Ezhavas to rethink seriously whether to extend support to a movement which can either turn out to be conducive for their development or detrimental to it.[371] The secretary of the Yogam issued a notice in November calling for a meeting to consider the attitude of its members towards the satyagraha till the resolution on freedom of movement was under consideration in the Assembly.[372] This shows the indecisiveness and apathy of the Yogam towards it. Though not at all a supporter of the Indian National Congress, C.V. Kunjuraman, a prominent leader of Ezhavas, was unhappy with the indifferent attitude of his community. He therefore wrote an editorial in Kerala Kaumudi requesting each member of the Ezhava community to do a soul searching in order to know whether their community had sincerely worked towards the success of the satyagraha.[373] Various factors were responsible for this lack of cooperation from the Yogam and the Ezhavas.

By this time the Yogam was divided into two different groups following entirely different and mutually incompatible ideologies. One section was influenced by the upper strata of the Ezhava community under C. Krishnan who was vehemently opposed to the Indian National Congress. The other group was led by T.K. Madhavan who represented the nationalist element in the Ezhavas taking active part in the satyagraha. C.V. Kunhiraman and Sahodharan Ayyappan did not support satyagraha whole heartedly as they believed that untouchability and unapproachability were illegal and wanted to have the sign boards indicating unapproachability removed by force.[374] But both of them actively participated in the movement. The Guru himself came out with warm expression of sympathy and support for the satyagraha movement.[375] According to the advice of Mahatma Gandhi, when the outsiders and the non-Hindus were withdrawn from the movement, C.V. Kunjuraman started a pidiyari prasthanam (a handful of rice contribution from each family every day) which helped to feed the satyagrahis.[376]

That the co-operation and support of the Ezhava community was limited was clear from the fact that of the nineteen satyagrahis, who were convicted in the first phase of the satyagraha, only one was an avarna Hindu.[377] C. Rajagopalachari was dissatisfied with the lack of co-operation from the Ezhavas.[378] Ayyamuthu Gaundar, a Congress leader and an active participant from Coimbatore in a message to the Ezhavas said, 'The number of people from amongst you who have joined the satyagraha campaign at Vaikom can be counted on fingers. Is it not your bounden duty to remedy this sad omission? If you have self-respect and a sense of duty in you, you must come forward in larger number to join the satyagraha and to make it a success'.[379]

The most important reason for this indifference of the Ezhavas towards this satyagraha stemmed from the differing attitude of a section of the Ezhava middle class towards the Indian National Congress and British imperialism.

In the twenty-first session of the Yogam held at Vaikom between 7 and 9 May 1925, the president of the session, Dr K. Kunji Kannan, and secretary, N. Kumaran, candidly admitted their differences and disagreement with the Congress. The anti-British stance of the Congress was the main reason for this. Kumaran Asan, C. Krishnan, Palpu and others believed that whatever little privileges they enjoyed were due to the foreign rule.[380] During the time of the coronation of British King as the Emperor of India, the Yogam celebrated it all over Kerala and sent a message which said:

> The SNDP Yogam, an association representing the Thiyyas, the most numerous and industrious community in Malabar, Travancore and Cochin beg respectfully to acknowledge their gratitude for the numerous benefit the community have received both directly and indirectly from the British rule to offer their most loyal and heartfelt congratulations to your Majesty's on this auspicious occasion.[381]

Some of them were made to believe without doubt that the Britishers were sent to India by God to protect the *avarnas* from their social grievances.[382] Therefore, a section of the Ezhavas considered that the improvement of untouchables in the social and economic field was due to the intervention of the British administration. Besides, they also thought that the Indian National Congress was an all India organization of the *savarnas* to retain and continue their social, political and economic hegemony over the untouchables.[383] They had little faith in the Congress and their movement for *swaraj*. As for Krishnan and other Ezhava leaders, so long as casteism exist in India, Indians did not deserve self-government. 'Reflection of a Thiyya Boy' written by Kumaran Asan in 1908, brings out his deep concern about the miserable plight of the downtrodden untouchables.

He wrote:

Why shouldst thou wail, then, O Bharat:
Thy slavery is thy destiny, O Mother;
Thy sons, blinded by caste, clash, among themselves
And get killed; what for is freedom then?[384]

This was the general feeling of a good section of the educated Ezhavas towards Indian freedom. They argued that till the time the untouchables gained necessary self-confidence to demand their rights from government, the British administration should continue in India; otherwise, they feared that the conditions of the untouchables would again be 'hewers of wood and drawers of water'.[385] According to Krishnan, the success of the Home Rule group could not be the success of the untouchables and he feared that the miserable plight of the untouchables in the princely state would spread to areas which were directly under the British control, after the success of the Home Rulers. Therefore, he asked his people to organize against the mighty *savarna* community and their organization, that is, the Indian National Congress, which wanted *swaraj*.[386] Like Ambedkar, Krishnan also considered the movement of Gandhi as, 'irresponsible' and 'insane'.

In his letters addressed to George Landbury and Mrs Lord Athol of the Labour Party, Krishnan described the activities of Mahatma Gandhi as 'destructive' and a 'Himalayan Blunder'.[387] Just like Krishnan, another prominent Ezhava leader from Malabar, Murkkoth Kumaran, also opposed Gandhi and his satyagraha movement and civil disobedience movement. This was mainly because of his belief that so long as the caste grievances existed, even if opportunity for self-government is obtained it would only be a mere transfer of power from the white man to the upper castes.[388] As this satyagraha was controlled by Mahatma Gandhi and the Indian National Congress, this influential section among the Ezhavas did not cooperate with this movement. Though this movement was started for opening the roads to the Vaikom temple, the Ezhava middle class feared that their cooperation with the Indian National Congress – the ardent enemy of the British Imperialism in India – would effect their relation with the latter. Besides as stated earlier they preferred British paramountacy to *swaraj* and nationalism or self govern-ment of the Congress[389] because they feared that the *swaraj* of the Congress meant government of the *savarnas*. Movement towards national freedom and movement towards freedom from *savarnas* had different social contexts and they were incommensurable. Therefore, those whose interest fell more on the uplift of the local communities welcomed British supremacy rather than the nationalism of the Congress.[390] T.K. Ravindran in his *Vaikom Satyagraha and Gandhi*, implicitly suggests that the satyagraha would have succeeded had it not been started by the Congress with its anti-British stance.[391]

From this, it is clear that the Ezhava elites had no grasp of the nature of British colonial rule in India and the fact that the freedom they visualized or wanted was of a limited character. As K.N. Panikkar has described about the nineteenth-century intellectuals,[392] the Ezhava elites of twentieth century were also suffering from 'false consciousness' and hence they failed to grasp the contradiction between British imperialism and the interests of the Indian people, which led them to believe that freedom from British rule would rein-force the traditional form of *savarna* hegemony both in the social and political fields. Having imbibed the colonial ideology in place of the traditional forms of authority, it was difficult for them to perceive the spirit of nationalism. They tended to identify the rise of nationalism with the reinforcement of traditional forms of authority, sanctioned by the Brahminical Hinduism.

A section of the Ezhavas who followed *misradaya* system of inheritance for achieving their narrow ends even supported the government's move to oppose the resolution to remove the ban on untouchables to use public roads and highways on being promised a few concessions in favour of their laws of inheritance, thereby sabotaging the hope and dream of Untouchables in general and Ezhavas in particular. On the 2 October 1924, when N. Kumaran introduced a resolution in the Legislative Council for removing the ban on untouchables to use public road and high ways, that resolution as stated earlier was lost by a lone vote. This solitary vote to defeat this resolution, was cast not by the *savarnas* but by Parameswaran, one of the founding leaders of the Yogam, and the younger brother of the veteran leader, Palpu.[393] In a letter to Gandhi a satyagrahi wrote, 'I am ashamed to say one member of the depressed and prohibited classes himself voted against the entry and sided with the government'.[394] The reason which persuaded Parameswaran to cast his vote against the primary civic right of his community is worth mentioning. Parameswaran and his supporters wanted to retain the *misradaya* law of inheritance.[395] Government assured him that his wants will be favoured provided he voted against the resolution which was introduced in the council for getting freedom for using public roads and highways.[396] Similarly, due to vested interests several Ezhava officials also supported the government and opposed satyagraha.[397]

Another reason was that a group of youths, who were more radical than the satyagrahis, did not have belief in the non-violent satyagraha to remove the notice board which prevented the untouchables from entering those roads. As these boards were illegal and illegitimate, they considered that it was their right to remove them by force. A big controversy ensued between the print media such as *Deshabhimani* and *Kerala Kaumudi* on this subject, As these sign boards indicating unapproachability was illegitimate, *Kerala Kaumudi* under C.V. Kunjuraman argued that these sign boards should be removed by force.[398] At the same time Madhavan argued for non-violence and asked to implement Gandhian means of satyagraha to achieve their ends.[399] This argument between these two veteran leaders also created an ideological confusion among the youth.

The other two important reasons were: (i) the vast majority of the Ezhavas were too fearful of their caste-Hindu landlords. Since the poor Ezhavas were dependent on the caste-Hindu landlords, it was impossible for them to give open support to the satyagraha. (ii) the poor illiterate and ignorant Ezhava masses were actually the slaves of tradition and found it hard to break away from the age long beliefs all at once. The poor Ezhavas, who were taken by the spiritual qualities of the Guru, had little enthusiasm for Gandhian method of satyagraha and this kept them away from the movement.[400]

Towards Temple Entry

Due to the pressure exerted by a few orthodox Hindus,[401] the government did not keep the promises which they assured during the time of Vaikom settlement. Therefore, a number of satyagrahas of this kind were organized in various parts of Travancore, like Suchindram in 1926 and Tiruvarp in 1927 and once again at Suchindram in 1930 in order to get the temple road opened. The government and the orthodox Hindus continued their efforts to suppress these satyagrahas.[402]

The untimely death of T.K. Madhavan in 1930 at the age of forty-five[403] considerably affected the unity of *savarnas*, especially the Nairs and the Ezhavas.[404] Though the Nair Service Society and the Yogam joined together to fight against the Hindu orthodoxy and obscurantism, the political turmoil of early 1930s was not conducive to their cordial relationship. The uncompromising mentality of the Nairs to retain their hegemony in the *sirkar* service and legislature on the one hand and the inequity of social disabilities of the Ezhavas and the growing class consciousness of the radical sections among the Ezhava middle class on the other were responsible for this soured relation between these two communities. A prominent Ezhava newspaper looked upon the attempt at Hindu unity as 'the exploitation of the Ezhava community for the maintenance of caste Hindu supremacy'.[405] The failure of the struggle to achieve the objective of social equality by getting the temples opened, for which thousands had suffered, especially due to the opposition of the orthodox Hindus, had irritated the radical youths of the Ezhava community. The other reason was the long awaited constitutional reform of 1932, which retained the supremacy of caste Hindus especially the Nairs in the legislature. This tended to confirm the idea that the Government of Travancore was for caste Hindus and the Ezhavas and other untouchables would not receive any benefit from this regime. Therefore, the Ezhavas naturally got attracted to the Christian and the Muslim camp once again to form a Joint Political Congress, to eliminate the influence of the Nairs who had been enjoying the political and bureaucratic monopoly of State for centuries. Noted Congress leader George Joseph later described this development as follows: 'The center of gravity has moved from the caste Hindu to Christians, Ezhavas and Muslims.'[406] This led the Nairs to leave the camp of agitation for social equality.[407] This cooperation of the Ezhavas with non-Hindus obviously rattled the government. Therefore, on 8 November 1932 with the aim of getting the Ezhavas out of the Joint Political Congress, the government appointed a Temple Entry Enquiry Committee.[408] In their report, the Committee did not advocate temple entry to the *avarnas*. According to them: 'There is a strong feeling among the *avarnas* in favour of temple entry. At the same time it has to be recognized that there is considerable opposition from a large body of the *savarnas* on the other side'.[409] But they pleaded to redeem the *avarnas* from the social economic and political grievances and to put an end to distant pollution and recommended the opening of most of the roads, wells and tanks to all castes.[410]

This reluctance of the expert committee to open the government temples to the *avarnas*, infuriated the Ezhava middle class. The question of conversion came up once again. The Ezhava youths formed various organizations in Travancore such as Samyuktha Ezhava Sangam, Ezhava Yovjana Sangam, All Travancore Ezhava Youth League, etc. On 31 July 1933 at its first meeting the Ezhava Sangam passed a resolution urging the Yogam to declare that the Ezhavas no longer wished to remain Hindus.[411] These Ezhava youths were eager to demolish the outdated practices of Hinduism and to put an end to the hegemony of caste Hindus for ever and finally to wrest civic rights for themselves from the caste Hindu Government. As for the Ezhavas, both political and religious freedom was inevitable.[412] The All Travancore Ezhava Youth League propagated the idea of the Ezhavas as an 'independent community'.[413] In 1934, All Travancore Ezhava Youth League was converted to All Kerala Thiyya Yuvajana Sangam.[414] This required considerable propaganda work to maintain the view that the Ezhavas constituted an independent community.[415] By this time, E. Madhavan published a book titled, *Swathanthra Samudayam* (an independent community) calling the Ezhavas to abandon all religion and asking them to be an independent community.[416] Such aggressive attack against Hinduism was never witnessed before or after. While presiding over the second meeting of the All Travancore Youth League at Karunagappally on 16 September 1933, Sahodharan Ayyappan urged the Ezhavas to renounce Hinduism as it was impossible to overcome all kinds of deprivation and humiliation at the hands of the upper castes.[417] From 1934 to 1936, the calls for conversion became an almost daily occurrence in the Travancore native press.[418] Though C.V. Kunjuraman was against the Abstention movement, as far as conversion was concerned he was in favour of radical youths. He supported Christianity and thousands of Ezhavas were ready to renounce Hinduism.[419] But C. Krishnan and K.P. Thayyal supported the conversion to Buddhism and Islam, respectively. A few Ezhavas embraced Sikhism.[420] Missionaries of Christianity, Buddhism and Islam came to Kerala to convert Ezhavas to their respective religions.[421] The Ezhava leaders undertook this conversion as a panacea to fight against the conservative government and orthodox caste Hindus.[422] The thirty third annual meeting of the Yogam unanimously passed a resolution to renounce Hinduism en masse by the Ezhavas to get rid of grievances under Hindu obscurantism.[423] While the choice of a particular religion varied, the determination for renouncing Hinduism was both uniform and strong.

In addition to the aggressive policy of the Ezhavas against Hinduism, the activities of the Indian National Congress also accelerated the movement for temple entry and Guruvayur Satyagraha during 1931–32[424] and Gandhi's epic fast in 1932,[425] created an unprecedented impact in favour of temple entry movement in Kerala. The activities of Harijan Seva Sangh and the historic 'Harijan tour' of Mahatma Gandhi had created an acute demand for temple entry. The Harijan Seva Sangh organized various meetings all over Travancore.

In January 1936, Sangh passed a resolution that effective steps should be taken for securing temple entry for the Harijans.[426] On 10 March 1936, another meeting of the All Kerala Harijan Seva Sangh was held at Trivandrum for preparing an elaborate agenda for future action.[427] This meeting decided to launch a temple entry movement on 5 April 1936, and also to organize public meetings in seventy other centers in Kerala.[428]

Another decision was to celebrate 19 April 1936 as an All Kerala Temple Entry day.[429] They organized processions in thirteen districts in favour of temple entry. Mrs Rameshwari Nehru presided over the All Kerala Temple Entry Conference held at Trivandrum on 9 and 10 May 1936, under the auspices of Kerala Provincial Board of the Harijan Seva Sangh.[430] This Conference appealed to the Travancore Government to open all state temples to the Harijans immediately. On 3 November 1936, the All Kerala Temple Entry Conference submitted a memorial signed by 50,522 *savarna* Hindus of Travancore demanding temple entry for the Harijans.[431] Thus the Harijan tour of Mahatma Gandhi, the continuous work of local Congress supporters and the activities of national leaders like C. Rajagopalachari, Mrs Rameshwari Nehru, etc. helped to provide a climate in favour of temple entry. In sum, on the one side the radical sections of the Ezhavas were getting restive and they even threatened to leave the Hindu fold; on the other the consistent work of the Congress and the change of the *savarnas* in their attitude towards temple entry of untouchables actually prepared the background for the temple entry proclamation in Travancore.

Besides the above mentioned reasons, the granting of temple entry can be viewed as a clever tactical move on the part of the then Dewan, Sir C.P. Ramaswamy Aiyer. Ramaswamy Aiyer had found political advantage in opening up of the temples. He perceived that the opening of temples might lead to the withdrawal of the Ezhavas, the strongest section of the Joint Political Congress, from the Abstention movement. In addition to this political acumen, he – being a staunch supporter of Hinduism and an ardent enemy of the activities of Christian missionaries[432] – did not like the idea of the Ezhavas converting to Christianity.[433] Therefore, the motive behind this proclamation of temple entry was, indeed, to put an end to the problem of conversion forever. Thus on 12 November 1936, on the occasion of the young Maharaja's birthday, a proclamation was issued, which threw open all the government temples, in the state, to all Hindus without any discrimination of caste and creed. Rajagopalachari, hailed this as 'the most non-violent and bloodless revolution in the history of man in the recent years'.[434]

What turns out from the foregone discussion about the fight against casteism and dogmatic facets of caste system that distributed communities in a hierarchical and debilitating manner is the increasing complexity involved in the fights and oppositions to them. This complexity is due to ideological incompatibilities among those fighting groups, pragmatic preferences among reformers (between those who favour the Indian National Congress and the British in India etc.), ideological presuppositions about the strategies of confrontation with the opponents, imbalance between self-interest and common-interest, etc. Besides, the feelings such as anguish due to humiliation, fear, uncertainty about the possible reprisals, reticence, conformism to traditional or customary systems, attitude towards change (be it gradual or radical), etc. had compounded the complexity. The transpositioning of satyagraha from the domain of political struggle to socio-religious space has altered the idea of satyagraha itself. Practice of this mode of resistance and opposition has also made the existing differentiation between those domains and spaces all the more complex. Whether the fights described in this chapter might or might not have produced the fruits expected out of them remains a matter of debate, the fact is that those fights, oppositions to them and strategic/tactical negotiations between them accrued certain results which can be said to be something unique and unprecedented in the history of struggles and contestations; whether these belong to the local or national topographies.

Notes and References

1 H. Charles Heimsath, *Indian Nationalism and Hindu Social Reform*, Oxford University Press, Bombay, 1964, p. 6.

2 Dayanand Saraswati, *Satyartha Prakash*, translated by Durga Prasad, New Delhi, 1972, p. 83; Heimsath, *Indian Nationalism and Hindu Social Reform*, pp. 120, 300–01; A.R. Desai, *Social Background of Indian Nationalism*, Popular Prakashan, Bombay, 1976, p. 255.

3 M.K. Gandhi, *Hindu Dharma*, Navajivan Publishing House, Ahmedabad, 1958, pp. 6, 321.

4 M.K. Gandhi, 'The Caste System', *Young India*, 8 December 1920. See also *Collected Works of Mahatma Gandhi* (henceforth *CWMG*), Vol. XIX: November 1920–April 1921, Publications Division, Government of India, New Delhi, 1994 (first published in 1966), pp. 83–84.

5 'Interview to Deshabhimani', *The Hindu*, 30 September 1921. Also see *CWMG*, Vol. XXI: August–December 1921, p. 187. However, Gandhi added: 'If one man says he will not inter-dine with another owing to repugnance, I oppose that. You must get rid of that repugnance.'

6 M.K. Gandhi, 'The Hindu Caste System', *CWMG*, Vol. XIII: January 1915–October 1917, pp. 301–03.

7 M.K. Gandhi, 'Hinduism', *Young India*, 6 October 1921. Also see *CWMG*, Vol. XXI, p. 247.

8 Sahodharan Ayyappan, 'Gandhiyude Sivagiri Sandarshanam', reproduced in *Aruvippuram Pratishta Shatabdi Smaranika*, Trivandrum, 1988, pp. 75–76. See also S. Omana, *The Philosophy of Sree Narayana Guru*, Gurukula, Varkala, 1984, p. 36.

9 Kotookoikal Velayudhan, *Sree Narayana Guru: Jeevithacharitram*, Trivandrum, 1983 (first published in 1975), p. 157.

10 M.K. Sanoo, *Narayana Guru Swami* (biography), Vivekodayam Printing and Publishing Co., Irinjalakuda, 1976, p. 441.

11 Ibid.

12 Sahodharan Ayyappan, 'Gandhiyude Sivagiri Sandarshanam'. Despite great effort to locate that speech in Calcutta, I could not succeed as Ayyappan does not mention the year of the speech.

[13] Narayana Guru, 'Jatinirnayam', in *Sree Narayana Krithikal*, Quilon, 1978, p. 154.

[14] Narayana Guru, 'Atmopadesha Shatakam', ibid., p. 115.

[15] The Ezhavas were not able to treat as their equals those who were considered traditionally lower to them, such as Parayas and Pulayas. See *Vivekodayam*, Vol. 5, No. 9, December 1908 – January 1909 (Dhanu 1084 ME), p. 5. Also see P.K. Balakrishnan, 'Kerala Navodhanathinu Charithraparamaya Oru Mukavura', *Yoganadam*, Vol. 3, No. 7, October 1977, p. 32.

[16] All over Kerala it was common for Ezhavas to practise untouchability towards Parayas and Pulayas, and many of their temples were closed to these lower castes. See Murkothu Kunhappa, *Murkothu Kumaran*, National Book Stall, Kottayam, 1975, p. 104.

[17] *Kerala Kaumudi*, 14 June 1923, p. 4.

[18] M.K. Sanoo, *Narayana Guru Swami*, pp. 240–41.

[19] P.K. Balakrishnan, (ed.), *Narayana Guru Samahara Grandham*, National Book Stall, Kottayam, 1969 (first published in 1954), p. 236.

[20] Quoted in P. Parameswaran, *Sree Narayana Guru Swamikal: Navothanathinte Pravachakan*, Jayabharath Publishers, Calicut, 1979 (first published in 1971), p. 108.

[21] Pazhamballi Achyuthan, *Sree Narayana Guru (Smaranakal)*, Sarada Book Depot, Thonnakal, 1960, p. 11.

[22] P. Parameswaran, *Sree Narayana Guru Swamikal*, pp. 107–08.

[23] Generally, in clashes between Nairs and Pulayas, Ezhavas took the side of the Nairs. This attitude of the Ezhavas deeply pained Narayana Guru. See M.K. Sanoo, *Narayana Guru Swami*, pp. 365–68.

[24] While M.K. Sanoo says that this inter-dining was organized on 27 May 1917, according to M. Prabha it was held on 29 May 1917. See M. Prabha, 'Sahodharan Ayyappan', in M. Govindan, ed., *Poetry and Renaissance: Kumaran Asan Birth Centenary Volume*, Sameeksha, Madras, 1974, p. 230.

[25] Quoted in M.K. Sanoo, *Narayana Guru Swami*, p. 257.

[26] The oath was: 'Caste differences are unprincipled, harmful and unnecessary, and I whole-heartedly pledge to employ all legal means to remove it.' See ibid., p. 258; M.K. Sanoo, *Sahodharan K. Ayyappan*, D.C. Books, Kottayam, 1980, p. 78.

[27] M. Prabha, 'Sahodharan Ayyappan', in *Poetry and Renaissance*, pp. 230–31; M.K. Sanoo, *Narayana Guru Swami*, p. 258.

[28] Sahodharan Ayyappan and twenty-one other families who took part in the inter-dining were ex-communicated from the community. The orthodox section of Ezhavas began to refer to Ayyappan as 'Pulayan Ayyappan'.

[29] M.K. Sanoo, *Narayana Guru Swami*, p. 259

[30] The impact of this was felt not only in Cherayi and Cochin, but all over Kerala. See P.K. Balakrishnan, ed., *Narayana Guru Samhara Grandham*, p. 235; M.K. Sanoo, *Narayana Guru Swami*, p. 259.

[31] See the editorial by N. Kumaran Asan, *Vivekodayam*, Vol. XIV, Nos. 2–1, April–June 1917 (Medam–Edavam 1092 ME) p. 47; P.K. Balakrishnan, ed., *Narayana Guru Samhara Grandham*, pp. 235–39.

[32] M.K. Sanoo, *Narayana Guru Swami*, p. 260; M.K. Sanoo, *Sahodharan K. Ayyappan*, p. 84.

[33] M.K. Sanoo, *Narayana Guru Swami*, p. 261.

[34] *Kerala Kaumudi*, 2 June 1921, p. 2; M.K. Sanoo, *Sahodharan K. Ayyappan*, p. 85.

[35] A. Ayyappan, 'Iravas and Cultural Change', *Bulletin: Madras Government Museum*, 1945, p. 156. See also R. Gangadharan, 'Misra Vivahathinte Arambham', *Vivekodayam Antharashtra Sree Narayana Guru Varsham Smaraka Pathippu*, March 1978, pp. 153–56; 'Adhyathe Misravivaham', *Kerala Kaumudi*, issue no. 433, 1 Jan 1984, p. 17.

[36] T.K. Madhavan's interview with Mahatma Gandhi in *CWMG*, Vol. XXI, p. 187.

[37] Pazhamballi Achyuthan, *Sree Narayana Guru (Smaranakal)*, pp. 34–38.

[38] V.T. Samuel, *One Caste, One Religion, One God: A Study of Sree Narayana Guru*, Sterling Publishers, New Delhi, 1977, p. 62.

[39] N. Kumaran, 'SNDP Yogacharitram', *SNDP Yogam Golden Jubilee Souvenir*, Quilon, 1953, p. 47. Also see Chapter 4 of this book.

40 Ibid.

41 Narayana Guru's letter to Dr Palpu dated 12 May 1916, reproduced in *Gurukulam*, Vol. 15, Nos. 6–7, September–October 1978, p. 283.

42 For details, see J.H. Hutton, *Caste in India: Its Nature, Function and Origin*, Oxford University Press, London, 1951; Bhupendranath Dutta, *Studies in Indian Polity*, Puri Publishers, Calcutta, 1944; Emile Senart, *Caste in India: The Facts and the System*, translated by Sir Edward Denison Ross, Methuen and Co., London, 1930; J.N. Bhattacharya, *Hindu Castes and Sects*, second edition, Editions India, Calcutta, 1968; L.S.S. O'Malley, *Indian Caste Customs*, second edition, Vikas Publishing House, New Delhi, 1974.

43 T.K. Ravindran, 'Consequences of Unapproachability in Travancore', *The Bulletin of the Institute of Traditional Culture*, July–December 1975, p. 57.

44 The Vaikom Temple Road in Travancore, Trippunithura Road in Cochin and Tali Road in Calicut were a few among the hundreds of highways in Kerala on which the movement of low-caste people was prohibited.

45 *Vivekodayam*, Vol. 3, No. 5, 16 September 1907 (31 Chingam 1082 ME), p. 5. See also *Mitavadi*, Vol. 5, No. 2, February 1917, p. 4.

46 *Complete Works of Swami Vivekananda*, Vol. III, Mayawati Memorial Edition, ninth edition, Calcutta, 1964, pp. 294–95.

47 Gandhi said, 'Unfortunately for Hinduism, unfortunately for the state and unfortunately even for the whole of India, there is not much credit to the state in the matter of untouchability.' Quoted in Mahadev Desai, *The Epic of Travancore*, Navajivan Karyalaya, Allahabad, 1937, p. 4.

48 P.K. Gopalakrishnan, 'Samuhya Parishkarana Prasthanangal', *Kerala Charitram*, Vol. I, pp. 1216–17.

49 *Vivekodayam*, Vol. 2, No. 3, 15 July 1905 (32 Midhunam 1080 ME), p. 3.

50 *Proceedings of the seventeenth session of Sree Mulam Popular Assembly*, 1921, p. 11.

51 *Vivekodayam*, Vol. 21, Nos. 8–12, March–August 1931 (Meenam–Karkkadakam 1106 ME), p. 22.

52 *Proceedings of Sree Mulam Popular Assembly*, 1913, p. 163.

53 *Vivekodayam*, Vol. 21, Nos. 5–12, March–August 1931, p. 23.

54 *Report of the Temple Entry Enquiry Committee*, published on 24 April 1934, Trivandrum, p. 47. See also File No. 66/1911, Judicial Department, Travancore, Kerala State Archives (KSA); *Proceedings of the seventeenth session of the Sree Mulam Popular Assembly*, 1921, p. 108.

55 C. Kesavan, *Jeevithasamaram*, Vol. I, National Book Stall, Kottayam, 1968, p. 302.

56 Ibid. See also Murkothu Kunhappa, 'The Thiyyas of Kerala', *Souvenir, Indian History Congress*, XXXVII, Calicut, 1976, p. 43.

57 *Mitavadi*, Vol. 6, No. 11, November 1918, p. 26.

58 Letter to Mahatma Gandhi dated 21 April 1925, *Dr Palpu Papers*, File No. 1, Nehru Memorial Museum and Library (NMML), New Delhi, p. 4.

59 All Travancore Joint Political Congress, *Travancore, The Present Political Problem*, Trivandrum, 1934, pp. 25–26.

60 File No. 40/4 of 1907, Judicial Department, Travancore, KSA, p. 1.

61 Ibid.

62 K. Ayyappan pointed out the discrimination between income from temples and the expenditure on temples. In 1921, the income from temples was Rs 4 lakhs, and the expenditure on temple administration and *uttupura* was Rs 24,44,249. See *Sahodharan*, Vol. 3, No. 12, May–June 1921 (Edavam 1096 ME); 'Editorial', *Kerala Kaumudi*, 2 June 1921, p. 2.

63 *Sahodharan*, Vol. 3, No. 12, May–June 1921.

64 *Mitavadi*, Vol. 7, No. 1, January 1919, pp. 9–11.

65 All Travancore Joint Political Congress, *Travancore, The Present Political Problem*, pp. 15–20.

66 Out of 503 posts with a monthly salary of Rs 150, Nair and Christian candidates were respectively 130 and 149 in number. *Kerala Kaumudi*, 16 October 1929, p. 5.

[67] Robin Jeffrey, ed., *People, Princes and Paramount Power: Society and Politics in the Indian Princely States*, Oxford University Press, London, 1978, p. 154.

[68] Robin Jeffrey, *The Decline of Nayar Dominance: Society and Politics in Travancore 1847–1908*, Vikas Publishing House, Delhi, 1976, pp. 243–51.

[69] Robin Jeffrey, *People, Princes and Paramount Power*, p. 148.

[70] P.K. Madhavan, *T.K Madhavante Jeevacharitram*, DC Books, Kottayam, 1986, p. 134.

[71] Ibid., p. 128.

[72] See G.P. Sekhar, ed., *G.P. Centenary Souvenir: Select Writings and Speeches of G.P. Pillai*, Trivandrum, 1964, p. 111.

[73] N. Kumaran, former secretary of the SNDP Yogam, wrote: 'The idea of temple entry was derived not from the brain of Ezhavas but of Raman Thampi.' See 'SNDP Yogam: Chila Smaranakal', in *SNDP Yogam Golden Jubilee Souvenir*, 1953, p. 57.

[74] In the editorial of the inaugural issue of *Mathrubhumi* (17 March 1923), the first nationalist newspaper from Kerala, it was written: 'The condition of the deprived sections in India, especially in Kerala, is a hindrance to the welfare and unity of the nation, and affects the self-respect of the untouchables. We are therefore always conscious of the need for their uplift and welfare.'

[75] In the Belgaum session of the Congress in 1924, Gandhi said: 'Untouchability is another hindrance to Swaraj. Its removal is just as essential for Swaraj as the attainment of Hindu–Muslim unity. This is an essentially Hindu question and Hindus cannot claim or take Swaraj till they have resorted to liberty of the suppressed classes.' See 'Congress Presidential Addresses', in *Silver to the Golden Jubilees*, second series, Madras, 1934, pp. 741–42. Gandhi's concept of Swaraj considered social reforms as an essential pre-requisite for India's freedom. According to Gandhi, caste and untouchability were the two social impediments in our march towards Swaraj; and to postpone social reform till after the attainment of Swaraj is not to know the meaning of Swaraj. See *CWMG*, Vol. XXXVI, p. 470.

[76] Reports of Madhavan's interview with Mahatma Gandhi – published in The *Hindu* on 30 September 1921, and later in *Deshabhimani* – worked wonders in influencing the caste Hindu opinion in favour of temple entry. Even the Brahmins and Hindu Mahajana Sabha changed their views. See P.K. Madhavan, *T.K Madhavante Jeevacharitram*, DC Books, Kottayam, 1986, p. 119-23.; M.K. Sanoo, *Narayana Guru Swami*, p. 414. See also *CWMG*, Vol. XXI: August–December 1921, pp. 185–88.

[77] M. Muralidharan, 'Nammude Avakashasamarangal', *SNDP Yogam Golden Jubilee Souvenir*, 1953, p. 57.

[78] *Mitavadi*, Vol. 5, No. 8, August 1917, pp. 31–32.

[79] On 13 September 1916, Narayana Guru consecrated a temple at Koorkenchery in Trichur. This temple was open to communities such as carpenters, goldsmiths, ironsmiths, etc., but Pulayas and Parayas were allowed only up to sacrificial altar. See *Vivekodayam*, Vol. XIII, Nos. 4–5, July–September 1916 (Karkkadakam 1091 and Chingam 1092 ME), p.106; *Kerala Kaumudi*, 14 June 1923, p. 4.

[80] P.K. Balakrishnan, 'A Mediator', in P.K. Balakrishnan, ed., *Narayana Guru Samhara Grandham*, pp. 150–51.

[81] *Vivekodayam*, Vol. 5, No. 9, June–August 1906, p. 5, and December–January 1908–09, p. 5. See also P.K. Balakrishnan, 'Kerala Navothanathinu Charitraparamaya Oru Mukhavura', *Yoganadam*, Vol. 3, No. 7, October 1977, p. 32.

[82] See editorial by N. Kumaran Asan, *Vivekodayam*, Vol. XIV, Nos. 1–2, April–June 1917 (Medam–Edavam 1092 ME), p. 46.

[83] P.K. Balakrishnan, ed., *Narayana Guru Samhara Grandham*, p. 235; M.K. Sanoo, *Narayana Guru Swami*, p. 259.

[84] M.K. Sanoo, *Sahodharan K. Ayyappan*, p. 79.

[85] Ibid.

[86] M.K. Sanoo, *Narayana Guru Swami*, p. 258; M. Prabha, 'Sahodharan Ayyappan', in *Poetry and Renaissance*, p. 230.

87 P.K. Balakrishnan, 'K. Ayyappan', in *Narayana Guru Samhara Grandham*, p. 235; M. Prabha, 'Sahodharan Ayyappan', in *Poetry and Renaissance*, p. 230.

88 Ibid.

89 Ibid., p. 231. Also see the note by T.C. Gopalan titled 'The Exile of Sahodharan', in M.K. Sanoo, *Sahodharan K. Ayyapan*, pp. 97, 125–27.

90 N. Kumaran Asan wrote an editorial under two sub-headings, 'Inter-dining Uproar' and 'For the Attention of Young Social Reformers', in *Vivekodayam*. While the first opposed the orthodox section of Ezhavas by stating that inter-dining with Pulayas was not a sin as in the eyes of God all human beings are equal, the second one described inter-dining with Pulayas as a foolish action as it could uplift neither Pulayas or Ezhavas. See *Vivekodayam*, Vol. XIV, Nos. 1–2, April–June 1917 (Medam–Edavam 1092 ME), pp. 46–47. M.K. Sanoo wrote that the editorial 'clearly implied that the holding of the inter caste dinner was really "foolhardy"'; see *Narayana Guru Swami*, p. 259.

91 According to Kumaran Asan, Ezhavas inter-dining with Pulayas and Parayas would not uplift any of them. *Vivekodayam*, Vol. XIV, Nos. 1–2, April–June 1917 (Medam–Edavam 1092 ME), p. 47.

92 Ibid.

93 Ibid.

94 P.K. Madhavan, *T.K. Madhavante Jeevacharitram*, D.C. Books, Kottayam, 1986, p. 81.

95 N. Kumaran, 'SNDP Yogam: Chila Smaranakal', in *SNDP Yogam Golden Jubilee Souvenir*, 1953, p. 57.

96 Ibid.

97 P.K. Madhavan, *T.K. Madhavante Jeevacharitram*, p. 89.

98 See the letter by N. Raja Rama Rao, Chief Secretary, dated 10 February 1921, to T.K. Madhavan, reproduced in M.K. Sanoo, *Narayana Guru Swami*, p. 405; P.S. Velayudhan, *SNDP Yoga Charitram*, pp. 214–15.

99 In a discussion in the Assembly regarding the forceful entry of a group of Ezhavas into a temple at Kadakkavur near Cherayinkizhil, and their subsequent prosecution and conviction, the Dewan expressed his view as follows: 'I am not telling that untouchability should remain forever. In due course with the spread of education it will disappear. There is a lot of difference in social fabric between now and fifty years back.' He asked Madhavan, 'Do you believe that the change you demand can be introduced successfully by an individual or a government?' Madhavan said yes, and cited the example of the Japanese government to prove that it is possible if the government so willed. See P.K. Madhavan, *T.K. Madhavante Jeevacharitram*, pp. 87–89.

100 The successors of M. Krishnan Nair were Raghavaiyya and W.E. Watts. Both of them opposed the temple entry resolution in the Assembly on the ground that it dealt with a religious subject. See T.K. Madhavan, 'Kshetrapraveshnavathathinte Charitram', in *Vaikom Satyagraha Commemoration Volume*, Vaikom, 1977, pp. 41–44.

101 P.K. Madhavan, *T.K. Madhavante Jeevacharitram*, p. 87.

102 See interpellations of Kumaran Asan in the Travancore Legislature Council, dated 12 Karkkadakam 1095 ME (27 July 1920). See also T.K. Ravindran, *Asan and Social Revolution in Kerala: A Study of His Assembly Speeches*, Kerala Historical Society, Trivandrum, 1972, pp. 86–88; P.S. Velayudhan, *SNDP Yoga Charitram*, pp. 217–18.

103 C.V. Kunjuraman, 'Nangalkum Sarkar Kshetrangalil Onnu' (A Government Temple for Us Too), in P.K. Balakrishnan, ed., *Narayana Guru Samhara Grandham*, pp. 77–79.

104 P.S. Velayudhan, *SNDP Yoga Charitram*, pp. 215–16.

105 Ibid., p. 219.

106 P.K. Madhavan, *T.K. Madhavante Jeevacharitram*, p. 79.

107 Ibid., p. 135.

108 Sahodharan Ayyappan changed his mentor Narayana Guru's dictum, 'One caste one religion and one God for mankind', to 'No caste no religion and no God for mankind'. See M.K. Sanoo, *Sahodharan K. Ayyappan*, pp. 143–51; M.K. Sanoo, *Narayana Guru Swami*, p. 262.

[109] Sukumaran Pottekkadu, 'Sahodara Prasthanam', *Vivekodayam Antharashtra Sree Narayana Guru Varsha Smaraka Pathippu*, March 1978, p. 160.

[110] P.K. Madhavan, *T.K. Madhavante Jeevacharitram*, p. 14. In his paper *Deshabhimani*, for over one-and-a-half decades, Madhavan highlighted the need for civil liberties and social equality. See the back volumes of *Deshabhimani*, which are available with Priyadarshan, a schoolteacher whose hobby was to collect and preserve old documents and make them available to scholars for consultation. He settled near Quilon in Kerala.

[111] See T.K. Madhavan's speech, 'Kshetrapraveshanavathathinte Charitram: Oravalokanam', delivered at Ochra in a mammoth meeting organized on 21 November 1929 (6 Vrichikam 1105 ME) around the demand for temple entry for all, irrespective of caste; reproduced in *Vaikom Satyagraha Commemoration Volume*, pp. 41–45.

[112] P.K. Madhavan, *The Life of T.K. Madhavan*, Vol. II, pp. 414–17.

[113] Sukumaran Pottekkadu, 'Sahodara Prasthanam', *Vivekodayam Antharashtra Sree Narayana Guru Varsha Smaraka Pathippu*, pp. 60–68; M.K. Sanoo, *Sahodharan K. Ayyappan*, pp. 76–127; M.K. Sanoo, *Narayana Guru Swami*, pp. 401–16.

[114] *Mitavadi*, Vol. 6, No. 12, 9 August 1918, pp. 24–26 and Vol. 7, No. 1, January 1919, pp. 9–11; *Madras Mail*, 18 May 1920, p. 5 and 24 May 1921; File No. 554/1920 (Confidential), *Travancore Government English Records*, KSA.

[115] K.M. Panikkar, 'Introduction', in P.K. Madhavan, *The Life of T.K. Madhavan*, Vol. II, pp. IV and V.

[116] *Mitavadi*, August 1918, p. 6.

[117] *Mitavadi*, Vol. 6, No. 12, December 1918, pp. 24–26.

[118] M.K. Narayanan, 'SNDP Yogavum T.K. Madhavanum', in *SNDP Yogam Platinum Jubilee Souvenir*, 1978, p. 150.

[119] Ibid.

[120] See proceeding nos. 16 and 19 of the seventeenth session, proceeding no. 15 of the eighteenth session and proceeding no. 16 of the twentieth session. Also see P.S. Velayudhan, *SNDP Yoga Charitram*, p. 203.

[121] *Mitavadi*, Vol. 7, No. 1, January 1919, pp. 9–11

[122] P.K. Madhavan, *T.K. Madhavante Jeevacharitram*, pp. 130–131. See also T.K. Ravindran, *Asan and Social Revolution in Kerala*, pp. 86–88; P.S. Velayudhan, *SNDP Yoga Charitram*, pp. 217–18.

[123] Proceeding no. 16 of the seventeenth session of the SNDP Yogam; P.S. Velayudhan, *SNDP Yoga Charitram*, p. 203.

[124] Editorial, *Kerala Kaumudi*, 27 May 1920, p. 2.

[125] M.K. Narayanan, 'SNDP Yogavum T.K. Madhavanum', in *SNDP Yogam Platinum Jubilee Souvenir*, 1978, p. 150.

[126] M.K. Sanoo, *Narayana Guru Swami*, p. 420.

[127] P.K. Madhavan, *T.K. Madhavante Jeevacharitram*, p. 126.

[128] See proceedings of the seventeenth session of the SNDP Yogam, item no. 27. See also P.K. Madhavan, *The Life of T.K. Madhavan*, Vol. II, p. 416; P.S. Velayudhan, *SNDP Yoga Charitram*, p. 201.

[129] The question of conversion was as emphatically repudiated as the resolution on temple admission was enthusiastically supported. The temper of the audience showed how passionately they clung to the religion in which they were born and brought up. See Editorial, *Kerala Kaumudi*, 27 May 1920, p. 2.

[130] While this resolution was supported by Aanasthanathu Kunju Panicker, Kunnakottu Kunju Sankaran Chanar and P.K. Panicker, it was vehemently opposed by Kumaran Asan, Erathu Krishnan Asan, K.C. Kunjuraman and Krishnan Ayyappa. See also P.S. Velayudhan, *SNDP Yoga Charitram*, p. 201.

[131] M.K. Sanoo, *Narayana Guru Swami*, p. 418.

[132] *Madras Mail*, 18 May 1920, p. 5.

[133] Letter from T.K. Madhavan to the District Magistrate dated 13 Vrichikam 1096 ME (30

November 1920), File No. 554/1920 (Confidential), *Travancore Government English Records*, KSA.

[134] Robin Jeffrey, 'Travancore: Status, Class and the Growth of Radical Politics', in Jeffrey, ed., *People, Princes and Paramount Power*, p. 150.

[135] Many Ezhavas all over Kerala opposed this idea of conversion. See 'Mathaparivarthanam' (Religious Conversion) by Mathamauly in *Kerala Kaumudi*, 19 August 1920 (4 Chingam 1098 ME), p. 3. Also see Editorial, *Kerala Kaumudi*, 27 May 1920, p. 2.

[136] Ibid.

[137] P.S. Velayudhan, *SNDP Yoga Charitram*, p. 214.

[138] C. Kesavan, *Jeevitasamaram*,Vol. I, p. 354.

[139] The Vellarvattom Koil authorities faced severe financial difficulties in managing the day-to-day affairs of the temple due to the boycott of *avarnas*. See P.K. Madhavan, *T.K. Madhavante Jeevacharitram*, p. 92; P.S. Velyaudhan, *SNDP Yoga Charitram*, p. 214.

[140] M.K. Narayanan, 'SNDP Yogavum T.K. Madhavanum', in *SNDP Yogam Platinum Jubilee Souvenir*, 1978, p. 150.

[141] P.K. Madhavan, *T.K. Madhavante Jeevacharitram*, p. 97.

[142] Ibid., pp. 87–88; P.S. Velayudhan, *SNDP Yoga Charitram*, p. 212.

[143] Though Madhavan protested in the Assembly, the Dewan clearly stated that untouchability being a religious matter, it was not right on the part of the government to interfere in it. See P.K. Madhavan, *T.K. Madhavante Jeevacharitram*, pp. 88–89.

[144] P.S. Velayudhan, *SNDP Yoga Charitram*, p. 212.

[145] P.K. Madhavan, *T.K. Madhavante Jeevacharitram*, p. 126.

[146] *Mitavadi*, April 1918, pp. 25–26; *Mitavadi*, May 1918; *Mitavadi*, March 1920, p. 80.

[147] P.K.K. Menon, *The History of Freedom Movement in Kerala*, Vol. II, Regional Records Survey Committee, Trivandrum, 1972, p. 297.

[148] See the letter from N. Rajarama Rao, Chief Secretary to Government, dated 10 February 1921, to T.K. Madhavan, quoted in P.K. Madhavan, *T.K. Madhavante Jeevacharitram*, p. 92.

[149] See the proceedings of the eighteenth session of the SNDP Yogam, item no. 15; P.S. Velayudhan, *SNDP Yoga Charitram*, p. 202.

[150] P.K. Madhavan, *T.K. Madhavante Jeevacharitram*, p. 92; P.S. Velayudhan, *SNDP Yoga Charitram*, pp. 215–16.

[151] Ibid.

[152] Ibid.

[153] Komalizhathu Madhavan, 'Samudhayodharakan T.K. Madhavan', in *Yoganatham International Narayana Guru Varsha Visheshal Prathi*, 1977, p. 50.

[154] P.K. Madhavan, *T.K. Madhavante Jeevacharitram*, pp. 130–31.

[155] Komalizhathu Madhavan, 'Samudhayodharakam T.K. Madhavan', p. 5; *Vaikom Satyagraha Commemoration Volume*, p. 43.

[156] *Mitavadi*, April 1918; *Mitavadi*, March 1920, p. 80; P.K. Madhavan, *T.K. Madhavante Jeevacharitram*, pp. 126–27.

[157] Robin Jeffrey, 'The Social Origin of a Caste Association', *South Asia*, No. 4, 1974, p. 53.

[158] C. Krishnan, 'Ee Mathamaanu Nammude Abhimanathe Keduthiyathu', in P.K. Balakrishnan, ed., *Narayana Guru Samhara Grandham*, pp. 86–87.

[159] *Mitavadi*, Vol. 5, No. 4, April 1917, pp. 38–40.

[160] Ibid.

[161] M.K. Sanoo, *Narayana Guru Swami*, p. 351.

[162] *Sahodharan*, Vol. 2, Nos. 11–12, March–May 1920 (Meenam–Medam 1095 ME), p. 290.

[163] We have already seen that T.K. Madhavan had introduced a resolution in the seventeenth session of the SNDP Yogam at Alleppey in 1920 for *en masse* conversion to Christianity. See proceeding no. 27 of the seventeenth session; also see *Kerala Kaumudi*, 19 August 1920, p. 3.

[164] P.K. Madhavan, *T.K. Madhavante Jeevacharitram*, pp. 126–27.

[165] P.K. Madhavan, *The Life of T.K. Madhavan,* Vol. II, pp. 622–26; M.K. Sanoo, *Narayana Guru Swami,* p. 416.

[166] Letter dated 12 February 1917 (1st Kumbam 1092 ME), quoted in *Mitavadi,* Vol. 5, No. 3, March 1917, pp. 252–53.

[167] Ibid.

[168] *Kerala Kaumudi,* 27 May 1920, p. 2.

[169] In his presidential address to the SNDP Yogam in 1923 at Quilon, while opposing the conversion theory, N. Kumaran Asan was equally critical about the limitations of Buddhism, which irritated C. Krishnan, a staunch supporter of Buddhism. In reply to Asan he wrote two editorial articles, one in English and another in Malayalam, in *Mitavadi* on 28 May 1923. In response to these articles, Asan, a distinguished scholar of Buddhism, wrote an elaborate academic article and sent it to *Mitavadi* on 15 June 1923 for publication. However, it was returned without being published. This unpublished article was brought out ten years later, in 1933, as a booklet entitled *Mathaparivarthana Rasavadam* (Alchemy of Religious Conversion) by his wife Bhanumathi Amma, with an introduction by Murkoth Kumaran.

[170] Narayana Guru, 'Atmopadesha Shathakam', stanza no. 44, reproduced in T. Bhaskaran, ed., *Sree Narayana Guruvinte Sampoorna Krithikal,* p. 366.

[171] In a discussion between Mahatma Gandhi and Narayana Guru at Sivagiri on 28 Kumbam 1100 ME (11 March 1925), the former asked whether Hinduism would be sufficient to achieve spiritual salvation apropos the hue and cry among Ezhavas for conversion to other religions. Narayana Guru replied that though the Hindu religion is sufficient for spiritual salvation, there are equal means of salvation in other religions also. However, he added, people are more concerned with worldly freedom than spiritual salvation. This implied that the untouchables and unapproachables, so long as they remained within Hinduism, would be deprived of worldly freedom. For details of this conversation, see Kotookoikal Velayudhan, *Sree Narayana Guru Jeevithacharitram,* pp. 157 and 207–09. Also see P.K. Balakrishnan, ed., *Narayana Guru Samhara Grandham,* pp. 164–67; M.K. Sanoo, *Narayana Guru Swami,* pp. 438–43.

[172] This message was issued by the Guru at the end of the two-0day conference. See P. Parameswaran, *Sree Narayana Guru Swamikal,* p. 140.

[173] *Kerala Kaumudi,* 27 May 1920, p. 2.

[174] When T.K. Madhavan was elected as organizational secretary of the SNDP Yogam, he decided to commence his work from Sivagiri after taking the blessing of the Guru. On that occasion, as per Madhavan's request, the Guru issued the following message on 17 Makaram 1102 ME (30 January 1927): 'No community can be improved and strengthened without the backing of an organization. It was based on this principle, I established the Yogam twenty-five years back. The name Ezhava does not stand for any particular caste or religion. Hence without considering caste or religion members can be enrolled in the Yogam. I wish large number of people join the Yogam.' The message has been reproduced in P.K. Madhavan, *The Life of T.K. Madhavan,* Vol. II, p. 498. Also see P.S. Velayudhan, *SNDP Yoga Charitram,* p. 238.

[175] P.K. Madhavan, *T.K. Madhavante Jeevacharitram,* p. 28.

[176] *Kerala Kaumudi,* 27 May 1920, p. 2; P.S. Velayudhan, *SNDP Yoga Charitram,* p. 181.

[177] Ibid.

[178] M.K. Narayanan, 'SNDP Yogavum T.K. Madhavanum', in *SNDP Yogam Platinum Jubilee Souvenir,* 1978, p. 152.

[179] *Kerala Kaumudi,* 27 May 1920, p. 2.

[180] Ibid.

[181] *Vivekodayam,* March 1978, p. VIII; P.K. Madhavan, *The Life of T.K. Madhavan,* Vol. II, p. 498.

[182] P.K. Madhavan, *T.K. Madhavante Jeevacharitram,* p. 134.

[183] P.S. Velayudhan, *SNDP Yoga Charitram,* p. 181.

[184] M.K. Sanoo, *Narayana Guru Swami,* p. 420.

[185] *CWMG,* Vol. XXIV, p. 227.

[186] Ibid.

[187] See the presidential address of O. Krishnan at the sixth annual meeting of the SNDP Yogam

held at Ernakulam on 16 May 1909, reproduced in *Vivekodayam*, Vol. 6, Nos. 1–2, April–June 1909, p. 7.

[188] P.K. Madhavan, *T.K. Madhavante Jeevacharitram*, pp. 128–29.

[189] See the presidential addresses of early Congress leaders such as Dadabhai Naoroji, Badruddin Tyabji and W.C. Bonerjee, in *Congress Presidential Addresses*, First Series, 1885 to 1910, G. A. Natesan & Co., Madras, 1935.

[190] File No. I/1885–1920, All India Congress Committee (AICC) Papers: Resolutions, p. 190, Nehru Memorial Museum and Library, New Delhi.

[191] Resolution No. XV, 'The Grievances of the Depressed Classes', passed in the thirty–second session of Indian National Congress held at Calcutta in 1917. This resolution was proposed by G.A. Natesan who said: 'This Congress urges up on the people of India the necessity, justice and righteousness of removing all disabilities imposed by customs upon the depressed classes, the disabilities of a most vexatious and oppressive character subjecting those classes to considerable hardship and inconveniences.' It was seconded by Desai and supported by Rama Iyer and Asaf Ali. See File No. I/1885–1920, All India Congress Committee (AICC) Papers: Resolutions, p. 190, Nehru Memorial Museum and Library, New Delhi.

[192] See *CWMG*, Vol. XIX, p. 20.

[193] K.P. Kesava Menon, *Kazhinja Kalam*, p. 157.

[194] *Mitavadi*, November 1918, pp. 30–32.

[195] M.K. Narayanan, 'SNDP Yogavum T.K. Madhavanum', in *SNDP Yogam Platinum Jubilee Souvenir*, p. 149.

[196] *Kerala Kaumudi* (editorial), 27 May 1920, p. 2.

[197] *Mitavadi*, November 1918, pp. 30–32.

[198] M.K. Narayanan, 'SNDP Yogavum T.K. Madhavanum', in *SNDP Yogam Platinum Jubilee Souvenir*, p.149; M.K. Sanoo, *Narayana Guru Swami*, pp. 403–04.

[199] *Mitavadi*, November 1918, pp. 8 and 27.

[200] M.K. Narayanan, 'SNDP Yogavum T.K. Madhavanum', in *SNDP Yogam Platinum Jubilee Souvenir*, p. 149.

[201] *Kerala Kaumudi*, 27 May 1920, p. 2.

[202] Quoted in M.K. Sanoo, *Narayana Guru Swami*, p. 421.

[203] A controversy arose between *Deshabhimani* of T.K. Madhavan and *Kerala Kaumudi* of C.V. Kunjuraman in this regard. See back volumes of these papers, i.e. 1920–21 and 1924–25. Also see M.K. Sanoo, *Narayana Guru Swami*, p. 419.

[204] See the discussion between Mahatma Gandhi and Sree Narayana Guru at Sivagiri on 12/13 March 1925. See P.K. Balakrishnan, ed., *Narayana Guru Samhara Grandham*, pp. 164–65; M.K. Sanoo, *Narayana Guru Swami*, pp. 438–41.

[205] See T.K. Madhavan's interview with Gandhi in *The Hindu*, 30 September 1921, in *CWMG*, Vol. XXI: August–December 1921, p. 187. See also T.K. Madhavan's report regarding his meeting with Mahatma Gandhi in *Deshabhimani*, 1 October 1921 (15 Kanni 1097 ME).

[206] This centre for technical and vocational training was designed with the help of Earnest Kirk, the first European disciple of Narayana Guru, to impart job-oriented education and training in small-scale industries, which included handicrafts, weaving, carpentry, dairy farming, metal works, farming and pottery, for making them economically self-reliant. See *Kala Kaumudi*, 1 January 1984, p. 40; 'Sree Narayana Guru Special – Sivagiri Pilgrimage', *Kerala Kaumudi*, 1994, p. 54.

[207] See the discussion between Mahatma Gandhi and Sree Narayana Guru at Sivagiri on 12/13 March 1925. See P.K. Balakrishnan, ed., *Narayana Guru Samhara Grandham*, pp. 164–65, and M.K. Sanoo, *Narayana Guru Swami*, pp. 438–41.

[208] See the presidential address by S. Srinivasa Aiyangar at the forty-first session of the Indian National Congress in 1926, in *Congress Presidential Addresses*, 1911–1934, Second Series, pp. 800–01.

[209] See the interview of Mahatma Gandhi by T.K. Madhavan published in *Deshabhimani* on 15 Kanni 1097 ME (1 October 1921). Also see *CWMG*, Vol. XXI: August–December 1921, p. 185; P.K. Madhavan, *T.K. Madhavante Jeevacharitram*, p. 115.

[210] Ibid.

[211] Robin Jeffrey, 'Temple Entry Movement in Travancore 1860–1940', *Social Scientist*, Vol. IV, No. 8, 1976b, p. 12.

[212] M.P. Sreekumaran Nair (1976), 'Review' of *Vaikom Satyagraha and Gandhi* by T.K. Ravindran, *Journal of Indian History*, Vol. XIV, Part III, December 1976, p. 763.

[213] *Madras Mail*, 18 May 1920, p. 5.

[214] Robin Jeffrey, *People, Princes and Paramount Power*, p. 153.

[215] *Madras Mail*, 18 May 1920, p. 5.

[216] In one of his messages he requested the Ezhavas to join the Congress and work for the freedom of their country and themselves. See M.K. Sanoo, *Narayana Guru Swami*, p. 420.

[217] See the excerpts of his speech in the Travancore Congress Committee held at Ananda-valleswaram in November 1921, in P.K. Madhavan, *T.K. Madhavante Jeevacharitram*, pp. 103–04.

[218] Ibid., pp. 103–05.

[219] The Calcutta session of the Indian National Congress in 1917 passed a resolution urging the people to seriously consider 'the necessity, justice and righteousness of removing all disabilities imposed by custom upon the depressed classes'; Resolution No. XV in File No. I/1885–1920, *AICC Papers*, p. 190, Nehru Memorial Museum and Library, New Delhi.

[220] See the interview of Mahatma Gandhi by T.K. Madhavan, editor, *Deshabhimani* on 23 September 1921 in *The Hindu*, 30 September 1921; CWMG, Vol. XXI: August–December 1921, p. 186.

[221] P.K. Madhavan, *T.K. Madhavante Jeevacharitram*, pp. 103–04; interview of Gandhi by T.K. Madhavan in *CWMG*, Vol. XXI, p. 87.

[222] Vishnu Dayal Mathur, 'Congress Attitude Towards States' People's Conference', in *State's People's Conference: Origin and Role in Rajasthan*, Publication Scheme, Jaipur, 1984, p. 53. Also see the booklet *Congress Policy Towards States* by All India State's People's Conference, Bombay, 1938.

[223] P.K. Madhavan, *T.K. Madhavante Jeevacharitram*, p. 107; T.K. Madhavan at Ochra on 6 Vrichikam 1105 (21 November 1929), reproduced under the title 'History of Temple Entry Movement – A Review', in *Vaikom Satyagraha Commemoration Volume*, pp. 41–45.

[224] M.K. Sanoo, *Narayana Guru Swami*, p. 406.

[225] T.K. Madhavan in his article mentions 8 Kanni 1097, i.e. 24 September 1921, as the date of his meeting with Gandhi, *Deshabhimani*, 15 Kanni 1097 ME (1 October 1921), while *The Hindu* dated 30 September 1921 reported the date of the meeting as 23 September 1921. See also P.K.Madhavan, *T.K. Madhavante Jeevacharitram*, p. 107.

[226] Ibid., p. 114.

[227] Madhavan told Gandhi, 'My community has been much benefited – morally much more than materially – by your *charkha* movement . . . weaving and toddy drawing are the two heredi-tary professions of my community. Before you took up *Swadeshi* and the boycott of foreign clothes other communities used to mock at us by addressing as *chilanthy* meaning spider . . . and *kotty*, in connection with our traditional occupation of weaving and toddy making respectively. The enthusiasm you have created for Indian made clothes is partly responsible for the removal of social stigma attached to weaving.' See the conversation between Mahatma Gandhi and Madhavan in *The Hindu*, 30 September 1921, and *CWMG*, Vol. XXI, p. 185.

[228] *CWMG*, Vol. XXI, p. 186.

[229] Ibid.

[230] Ibid.

[231] Ibid.

[232] Ibid.

[233] Ibid.

[234] Ibid., p. 187.

[235] Mahatma Gandhi's writing on the Temple Entry Question, reproduced in *Vaikom Satyagraha Commemoration Volume*, p. 154.

[236] Gandhi always advised the Congress to refrain from actively interfering with the political

affairs of the state. See Vishnu Dayal Mathur, 'Congress Attitude Towards States' People's Conference', in *States' People's Conference: Origin and Role in Rajasthan*, p. 53; also M.K. Gandhi, *The Indian States' Problem*, Navajivan Press, Ahmedabad, 1941 (1948), p. 64.

237 *Young India*, 1 May 1924; CWMG, Vol. XXIII: March 1922–May 1924, p. 518. The other 'necessary conditions' are waiting in deputations on the Dewan and Maharaja, and submitting monster petitions to the authorities.

238 P.K. Madhavan, *T.K. Madhavante Jeevacharitram*, pp. 122–23; speech of T.K. Madhavan at Ochra on 21 November 1929 (6 Vrichikam 1105 ME), reproduced in *Vaikom Satyagraha Commemoration Volume*, p. 42.

239 M.K. Sanoo, *Narayana Guru Swami*, p. 415.

240 Speech of T.K. Madhavan at Ochra on 21 November 1929 (6 Vrichikam 1105 ME), reproduced in *Vaikom Satyagraha Commemoration Volume*, p. 42.

241 P.K. Madhavan, *T.K. Madhavante Jeevacharitram*, p. 125.

242 Robin Jeffrey, 'Temple Entry Movement in Travancore', p. 14.

243 K.P. Kesava Menon, *Kazhinja Kalam*, p. 157; K. Gopalan Kutty, 'The Guruvayur Satyagraha' *Journal of Kerala Studies*, Vol. VIII, 1981, p. 42.

244 Ibid.

245 P.K. Madhavan, *T.K. Madhavante Jeevacharitram*, p. 127; K.P. Kesava Menon, *Kazhinja Kalam*, p. 158.

246 P.K. Madhavan, *T.K. Madhavante Jeevacharitram*, p. 133; K.P. Kesava Menon, *Kazhinja Kalam*, 1969, p. 158.

247 See P.K. Madhavan, *T.K. Madhavante Jeevacharitram*, pp. 131–33.

248 However, as per the request of Mrs Narayani Madhavan, Mahatma Gandhi, without knowing that the child was already named after Mohamed Ali, called him Babu Vijayanath; this became his permanent name and he became one of the early economic management experts in the country. See Vechuchira Madhu, 'A great son of a great father', *Mathrubhumi*, 20 November 2011, p. 8; *Malayala Manorama*, 20 November 2011, p. 1.

249 *Vaikom Satyagraha Commemoration Volume*, p. 62.

250 Ibid.; A.K. Pillai, *Congressum Keralavum*, DC Books, Kottayam, 1986, pp. 312–15 (first published in 1935).

251 Bipan Chandra *et al.*, *India's Struggle for Independence, 1857–1947*, Viking, New Delhi, 1988, p. 224.

252 See 'The Kerala State Congress Untouchability Eradication Committee Resolutions', in *Vaikom Satyagraha Commemoration Volume*, p. 62.

253 Robin Jeffrey, 'Temple Entry Movement in Travancore', p. 14; M.K. Sanoo, *Narayana Guru Swami*, p. 417.

254 On 26 November 1923, when he was in the Yervada Central Jail, Gandhi started writing *The History of Satyagraha in South Africa* in Gujarati. It is reproduced in English translation in CWMG, Vol. 29: November 1925–February 1926, pp. 1–269.

255 Nataraja Guru, *The Word of the Guru*, pp. 38–39.

256 According to Gandhi, *satyagraha* was the power 'born of Truth and Love or non-violence'. See CWMG, Vol. 29: November 1925–February 1926, p. 92.

257 Jawaharlal Nehru, *Discovery of India*, Asia Publishing House, Bombay, 1977, p. 434 (first published in 1946).

258 CWMG, Vol. 7: June–December 1907, p. 108.

259 Nehru, *Discovery of India*, p. 360.

260 Ibid.

261 Nataraja Guru, *The Word of the Guru*, p. 38.

262 CWMG, Vol. 29: November 1925–February 1926, p. 92.

263 Gandhi distinguished them at length in CWMG, Vol. 10: November 1909–March 1911, pp. 10–11, 13, 15–16, 20, 35–36.

264 Internal violence in the sense that the resisters intentionally or unintentionally harbour enmity, anger and prejudice towards their opponents. See CWMG, Vol. 54: 6 March–22 April 1933, p. 416; CWMG, Vol. 19, p. 466.

[265] *CWMG*, Vol. 54, 6 March–22 April 1933, p. 416.

[266] Ibid., pp. 10–13 and 20.

[267] The *satyagraha* of Champaran and Kaira (Kheda) involved peasants, and the one in Ahmedabad involved industrial workers. For details, see B.R. Nanda, *Mahatma Gandhi: A Biography*, Allied Publishers, New Delhi, 1968, pp. 156–71.

[268] *CWMG*, Vol. 31: June–November 1926, p. 46.

[269] *CWMG*, Vol. 75: 11 October 1941–31 March 1942, p. 158.

[270] *Young India*, 10 September 1931, reproduced in M.K. Gandhi (1962), *India of My Dream*, compiled and edited by R.K. Prabhu, Navajivan Publishing House, Ahmedabad, 1962, p. 6 (first published in 1947).

[271] Jawaharlal Nehru, 'A Tyrst with Destiny', speech in the Constituent Assembly, 14 August 1947. See S. Gopal and Uma Iyengar, eds, *The Essential Writings of Jawaharlal Nehru*, Oxford University Press, New Delhi, 2003, pp. 346–47.

[272] *CWMG*, Vol. 75: 11 October 1941–31 March 1942, p. 158.

[273] Ibid.

[274] Ibid.

[275] Ibid., Vol. 36: February–June 1928, p. 470.

[276] *CWMG*, Vol. 26: January–April 1925, pp. 420–21.

[277] Bipan Chandra *et al.*, *India's Struggle for Independence, 1857–1947*, p. 230.

[278] *The Hindu*, 3 April 1924; *CWMG*, Vol. XXIII: March 1922–May 1924, pp. 272–73.

[279] Each individual had to take an oath before enrolling as a volunteer. See *Vaikom Satyagraha Commemoration Volume*, p. 63.

[280] *Kerala Kaumudi*, 1 May 1924, p. 1.

[281] *Young India*, 1 May 1924; 'Vaikom Satyagraha', in *CWMG*, Vol. XXIII: March 1922–May 1924, pp. 515–19.

[282] Official notes on Vaikom Satyagraha, dated 17 April 1924, Vaikom Bundle, No. I, *Travancore Government Records*, Kerala Secretariat.

[283] K.P. Kesava Menon, *Kazhinja Kalam*, pp. 164–65; Kotookoikal Velayudhan, *Sree Narayana Guru Jeevithacharitram*, pp. 151–55; Robin Jeffrey, 'Temple Entry Movement in Travancore', p. 15; P.K. Madhavan, *T.K. Madhavante Jeevacharitram*, pp. 148–73.

[284] Three *satyagrahi*s were Kunhappi (a Pulaya), Bahuleyan (an Ezhava) and Govinda Panikkar (a Nair). See K.P. Kesava Menon, *Kazhinja Kalam*, p. 164.

[285] Ibid., p. 168.

[286] Ibid., pp. 169–70.

[287] Ibid., pp. 169–70; K.P. Kesava Menon, *Bandhanathil Ninnu*, third edition, Mathrubhumi Printing and Publishing Co. Ltd., Kozhikode, 1963, pp. 19–20; *The Hindu*, 11 April 1924; 'Magistratente Vidhi', in *Vaikom Satyagraha Commemoration Volume*, p. 80; *Souvenir: Indian History Congress*, Calicut, 1976, p. 59.

[288] *Vaikom Satyagraha Commemoration Volume*, pp. 83–85.

[289] T.K. Ravindran, *Vaikom Satyagraha and Gandhi*, Sree Narayana Institute of Social and Cultural Development, Trichur, 1975, p. 63.

[290] Ibid.

[291] C.W.E. Cotton, Resident of Travancore, to Chief Secretary to the Government of Madras, 21 April 1924, GO No. 151, Political Department, Ordinary Series, Kerala Secretariat.

[292] See *Vaikom Satyagraha Commemoration Volume*, pp. 99, 105, 120, 123, etc.

[293] Ibid., p. 125; T.K. Ravindran, *Vaikom Satyagraha and Gandhi*, p. 88.

[294] *Kerala Kaumudi*, 19 June 1924, p. 1; *Vaikom Satyagraha Commemoration Volume*, p. 127.

[295] News Bulletin, 6 Medam 1099 ME (21 April 1924), *Vaikom Satyagraha Commemoration Volume*, p. 103.

[296] *Young India*, 1 May 1924; *CWMG*, Vol. XXIII: March 1922–May 1924, p. 516.

[297] Ibid., p. 478.

[298] Interview in *The Hindu*, 17 May 1924, reproduced in *CWMG*, Vol. XXIV: May–August 1924, p. 67.

[299] Gandhi's letter to George Joseph, dated 6 April 1924, in CWMG, Vol. XXII: March 1922–May 1924, p. 515.

[300] For Gandhi's view, see 'Notes' and 'Vaikom Satyagraha' in *Young India*, 1 May 1924, reproduced in CWMG, Vol. XXIII: March 1922–May 1924, pp. 477–519.

[301] *Young India*, 1 May 1924; see also CWMG, Vol XXIII, March 1922 – May 1924, p. 515.

[302] Robin Jeffrey, 'Temple Entry Movement in Travancore', pp. 16–17.

[303] K.P. Kesava Menon, *Kazhinja Kalam*, p. 176.

[304] The other two persons who fasted along with the Nair were Krishnanpachan and Narayanan.

[305] Ibid.; 'Satyagraha News Bulletins', dated 10 April 1924 (28 Menam 1099 ME), in *Vaikom Satyagraha Commemoration Volume*, p. 86.

[306] Gandhi's letter to George Joseph dated 12 April 1924 in *Young India*, 1 May 1924, CWMG, Vol. XXIII: March 1922–May 1924, p. 517.

[307] Ibid.

[308] Jeffrey, ed., *People, Princes and Paramount Power*, p. 152; T.K. Ravindran, *Vaikom Satyagraha and Gandhi*, p. 96.

[309] 'Interview to Vaikom Deputation' on 20 May 1924, *The Hindu*, 26 May 1924, reproduced in CWMG, Vol. XXIV: May–August 1924, p. 94; A.K. Pillai, *Keralavum Congressum*, p. 319.

[310] 'Interview to Vaikom Deputation' on 20 May 1924.

[311] For details of *Savarna Jatha*, see Sadhu M.P. Nair, *The Vaikom Satyagraha*, 1100 ME, pp. 204–26; 'Savarna Jathayum Memorialum', in *Vaikom Satyagraha Commemoration Volume*, pp. 170–79.

[312] A.K. Pillai, *Keralavum Congressum*, p. 320; *Malayala Manorama*, 31 October and 12 November 1924, p. 4.

[313] 'Savarna Jathayum Memorialum', in *Vaikom Satyagraha Commemoration Volume*, p. 175.

[314] Ibid., p. 176; T.K. Ravindran, *Vaikom Satyagraha and Gandhi*, p. 97.

[315] N. Kumaran, general secretary of the SNDP Yogam and a nominated member of the Legislative Council, moved a resolution in the Council on 2 October 1924 demanding that all roads around the temples be opened. The Maharani referred to this resolution in her reply. See *Travancore Legislative Council Proceedings*, Vol. VI, February 1925, pp. 767–73. Also see *Vaikom Satyagraha Commemoration Volume*, p. 177.

[316] 'Savarna Jathayum Memorialum', in *Vaikom Satyagraha Commemoration Volume*, p. 177; T.K. Ravindran, *Vaikom Satyagraha and Gandhi*, p. 99.

[317] 'Gandhi's interview to Associate Press of India', *The Hindu*, 2 July 1924, reproduced in CWMG, Vol. XXIV: May–August 1924, p. 333; *Vaikom Satyagraha Commemoration Volume*, pp. 122–24.

[318] Ibid., p. 108.

[319] Quoted in K.P. Kesava Menon, 'Memories of the Satyagraha', in *SNDP Yogam Golden Jubilee Souvenir*, 1953, pp. 91–92.

[320] *Proceedings of the Travancore Legislative Council*, 2 October 1924, Vol. VI, Part I, p. 318.

[321] N. Kumaran, 'Sanchara Swatanthra Prameyam Niyamasabhayil', in *Vaikom Satyagraha Commemoration Volume*, pp. 184–196; *Travancore Legislative Council Proceedings*, Vol. VI, Part I, p. 317 onwards; *Young India*, 19 May 1925; CWMG, Vol. XXVI: January–April 1925, pp. 158–59.

[322] For detailed accounts of Gandhi's Kerala tour, see CWMG, Vol. XXVI: January–April 1925. Gandhi wrote a series of article in *Young India* in 1925 about his Travancore tour. Also see *Vaikom Satyagraha Commemoration Volume*, pp. 262–64; *The Hindu*, 14 March 1925.

[323] 'A Statement' by N. Kumaran, C.V. Kunjuraman and K.P. Kayyalakkal, in *Vaikom Satyagraha Commemoration Volume*, p. 261.

[324] Gandhi's telegram to K. Kelappan Nair dated 24 March 1925, reproduced in CWMG, Vol. XXVI: January–April 1925, p. 386.

[325] See 'Editorial', *Mathrubhumi*, 21 November 1925; *Vaikom Satyagraha Commemoration Volume*, pp. 269–73.

[326] Ibid., p. 270.

[327] Ibid., p. 272; *Madras Mail,* 9 February 1925, p. 4.

[328] An observation of *The Hindu* correspondent on 31 March 1924.

[329] In almost all early presidential addresses of the SNDP Yogam, Ezhava leaders expressed their loyalty to the Biritish government. See the presidential address of Mr O. Krishnan at the sixth annual general meeting of the SNDP Yogam held at Ernakulam on 16 May 1909, *Vivekodayam,* 10 May 1909 (28 Medam 1084 ME), p. 7.

[330] C. Kesavan, *Jeevithasamaram*, pp. 356–57.

[331] Ibid., p. 357.

[332] See *Vivekodayam,* 10 May 1909 (28 Medam 1084 ME), p. 7.

[333] Jeffrey, 'Temple Entry Movement in Travancore, 1860–1940', p. 14.

[334] *Dr Palpu Papers,* File No. 7, p. 4, Nehru Memorial Museum and Library, New Delhi.

[335] M.K. Sanoo, *Narayana Guru Swami,* p. 420.

[336] Letter from Dr Palpu to Gandhi on 21 April 1925, *Dr Palpu Papers,* File No. 1, p. 4, Nehru Memorial Museum and Library, New Delhi.

[337] On many occasions Narayana Guru showed great regard to the British as they used to take administrative decisions without any caste or communal considerations. See 'Nammude Gurukkammar', in P.K. Balakrishana, *Narayana Guru,* p. 163; N. Kumaran, 'Sree Narayana Prasthanavum Britishkarum', in *Vivekodayam Antharashtra Sree Narayana Guruvarsham Smaraka Pattippu,* March 1978, pp. 28–35.

[338] P. Parameswaran, *Narayana Guru Swamikal,* p. 145.

[339] *The Hindu,* 6 June 1924; *CWMG,* Vol. XXIV: May–August 1924, pp. 259–60.

[340] 'Notes on Vaikom Satyagraha', *Young India,* 19 June 1924, reproduced in *CWMG,* Vol. XXIV: May–August 1924, pp. 259–60.

[341] *Young India,* 10 July 1924, reproduced in *CWMG,* Vol. XXIV: May–August 1924, pp. 364–65.

[342] W.H. Pitt, 'Report on the Tour of M.K. Gandhi in Travancore', 24 March 1925, Vaikom Bundle, No. 7, Kerala Secretariat.

[343] 'Gandhi's Speech in Reply to Ezhavas' at Varkala on 13 March 1925, reproduced in *CWMG,* Vol. XXVI: January–April 1925, p. 296.

[344] See paras 2 to 4 of this chapter.

[345] Nataraja Guru, *The Word of the Guru,* p. 39.

[346] While Narayana Guru was an *Advaitin,* Gandhi followed *Anekantavada.* An *Advaitin* is a follower of Advaita Vedanta, a school of Hindu philosophy which stands for 'non-duality'or 'absolutism'. This philosophy teaches the oneness of God, soul and universe. Its chief exponent was Sankaracharya. *Anekantavada* is one of the three fundamental doctrines of Jainism, the other two being *Syadvada* and *Nyayavada. Anekantavada* is the theory of the multi-faceted nature of reality or principle of pluralism. In other words, it represents the 'doctrine of non-exclusiveness' or 'multiple viewpoints' or 'non-absolutism'. As per this notion truth and reality are perceived differently by each person according to their understanding, and no single point of view is the complete truth. *Syadvada* is derived from Sanskrit word '*syad*' meaning 'perhaps', or 'somehow' or 'possible'. *Syadvada* is the theory of conditional predication. The Jain view is that perspectival knowledge can be expressed through *syad.* As reality is complex, no single proposition can fully express the nature of reality. Thus the *syad* should be prefixed before each proposition giving it a sense of a conditional point of view, and thus removing any dogmatism in statements. For details, see *CWMG,* Vol. XXIX, pp. 411–12; Vol. LIV, p. 170; Vol. LXIV, p. 380; and Vol. LXXII, p. 209. Also see Satish Chandra Chatterjee and Dhirendra Mohan Datta, *An Introduction to Indian Philosophy,* University of Calcutta, 1984; and Bina Gupta, *An Introduction to Indian Philosophy: Perspectives on Reality, Knowledge and Freedom,* Routledge, New York, 2012. *Nyayavada* is a theory of the limited perspectival nature of much of human knowledge.

[347] See *CWMG,* Vol. XXIX, p. 411; Vol. LIV, p. 170; and Vol. LXIV, p. 380.

[348] *CWMG,* Vol. XXIX, p. 411 and Vol. LXXII, p. 209.

349 Nataraja Guru, *The Word of the Guru*, pp. 40–41.

350 Quoted in M.K. Sanoo, *Narayana Guru Swami*, p. 421.

351 'Interview to *Deshabhimani*' by T.K. Madhavan on 23 September 1921, *The Hindu*, 30 September 1921; *CWMG*, Vol. XXI: August–December 1921, pp. 185–86.

352 'Sree Narayanaguruvum Vaikom Satyagrahavum', *Deshabhimani*, 11 Ocotber 1924. The editorial was on the Guru's visit to the Satyagraha Ashram on 27 September 1924, reproduced in *Vaikom Satyagraha Commemoration Volume*, p. 168. Also see Kotookoikal Velayudhan, *Sree Narayana Guru Jeevithacharitram*, p. 152.

353 The report of the *Mathrubhumi* regarding the Guru's visit to the Satyagraha Ashram, reproduced in M.K. Sanoo, *Narayana Guru Swami*, p. 426 .

354 Kotookoikal Velayudhan, *Sree Narayana Guru Jeevithacharitram*, p. 153.

355 M.K. Sanoo, *Narayana Guru Swami*, p. 423.

356 Ibid., pp. 423–24; 'Sree Narayana Guruvum Vaikom Satyagrahavum', in *Vaikom Satyagaha Commemoration Volume*, p. 168.

357 Kotookoikal Velayudhan, *Sree Narayana Guru Jeevithacharitram*, p. 153; M.K. Sanoo, *Narayana Guru Swami*, pp. 423–24.

358 See *Deshabhimani* editorial by T.K. Madhavan titled 'Sree Narayana Guruvum Vaikom Satyagrahavum', 11 October 1924. Also M.K. Sanoo, *Narayana Guru Swami*, pp. 424–26.

359 M.K. Sanoo, *Narayana Guru Swami*, p. 423; Kotookoikal Velayudhan, *Sree Narayana Guru Jeevithacharitram*, p. 153.

360 P.K. Gopalakrishnan, 'Samuhya Parishkarana Prasthanagal', in *Kerala Charitram*, Vol. I, p. 1242; K. Damodaran, *Sree Narayana Guru Swami*, p. 99.

361 *The Bombay Chronicle*, 27 March 1925, reproduced in *CWMG*, Vol. XXVI: January–April 1925, p. 421.

362 Kotookoikal Velayudhan, *Sree Narayana Guru Jeevithacharitram*, p. 154; M.K. Sanoo, *Narayana Guru Swami*, pp. 424–25.

363 'Sree Narayana Guruvum Vaikom Satyagrahavum', in *Vaikom Satyagraha Commemoration Volume*, p. 168; Kotookoikal Velayudhan, *Sree Narayana Guru Jeevithacharitram*, p. 154; M.K. Sanoo, *Narayana Guru Swami*, p. 425.

364 Anima Bose, 'Gandhi's Stand on Human Rights in the Vaikom Satyagraha', *Gandhi Marg*, Vol. II, No 1, April 1980, p. 24.

365 Murkothu Kunhappa, 'Thiyyas of Kerala', *Souvenir: Indian History Congress*, p. 50.

366 In 'An Appeal to the Ezhava Community' issued on 1 Mithunam 1099 ME (15 June 1924) by N. Kumaran, C.V. Kunjuraman, K.P. Kayyalakkal and P.R. Narayanan. See *Kerala Kaumudi*, Vol. 6, No. 14, 19 June 1924; *Vaikom Satyagraha Commemoration Volume*, pp. 148–50 (esp. p. 149).

367 Jeffrey, 'Temple Entry Movement in Kerala', p. 23.

368 P.K. Gopalakrishnan, 'Samuhya Parishkarana Prasthanangal', *Kerala Charitram*, Vol. I, pp. 1245–46.

369 *Kerala Kaumudi*, 10 April 1924, p. 1.

370 M.P. Sreekumaran Nair, 'Review' of *Vaikom Satyagraha and Gandhi*, p. 763.

371 *Kerala Kaumudi*, 10 April 1924, p. 1.

372 *Kerala Kaumudi*, 27 November 1924, p. 1.

373 See the editorial of *Kerala Kaumudi*, Vol. 7, No. 1, 6 March 1925.

374 M.K. Sanoo, *Narayana Guru Swami*, pp. 418–19.

375 G. Priyadarsanan, 'Narayana Guruvum Vaikom Satyagrahavum', *SNDP Yogam Platinum Jubilee Souvenir*, pp. 143–45. However, P. Parameswaran says that there are ample reasons to believe that the Guru was not in complete agreement with the Satyagraha movement. He says it cannot be assumed that the Guru held the same views as Gandhi regarding *satyagraha* as a means of solving the problem of pollution and untouchability. See P. Parameswaran, *Sree Narayana Guru Swamikal*, p. 145.

376 C. Kesavan, *Jeevitasamaram*, p. 145.

377 Jeffrey, ed., *People, Princes and Paramount Power*, p. 153.

[378] *The Hindu*, 27 May 1924.

[379] Quoted in Sadhu M.P. Nair, *The Vaikom Satyagraha*, Vol. I, 1925, pp. 137–38. Also see T.K. Ravindran, *Vaikom Satyagraha and Gandhi*, p. 73.

[380] K.R. Achutan, *C. Krishnan*, pp. 141–42.

[381] *Vivekodayam*, Vol. VIII, Nos. 8–9, November 1911 to January 1912 (Vrischikam–Dhanu 1087 ME), p. 184. N. Kumaran Asan wrote a poem titled 'Delhi Kireedadharanam', in which he extolled British imperialism and its benevolent rule. Ibid., pp. 179–98.

[382] *Vivekodayam*, Vol. XIII, No. 10, January–February 1916 (Makaram 1091 ME), p. 351.

[383] *Mitavadi*, Vol. 5, No. 12, December 1917, pp. 31–32.

[384] Poem reproduced after translation in M. Govindan, *Poetry and Renaissance*, p. 238. The translation was done by K. Ayyappa Paniker.

[385] K.R. Achutan, *C. Krishnan*, p. 141; *Mitavadi*, Vol. 5, No. 12, December 1917, p. 31.

[386] *Mitavadi*, Vol. 5, No. 10, October 1917, pp. 2–3.

[387] Letter dated 28 March 1938, quoted in K.R. Achutan, *C. Krishnan*, p. 196.

[388] Murkothu Kunhappa, *Murkoth Kumaran*, pp. 167–68.

[389] *Vivekodayam*, Vol. 4, No. 7, 1907 (1083 ME), p. 5.

[390] C. Kesavan, *Jeevitasamaram*, Vol. I, p. 357.

[391] T.K. Ravindran, *Vaikom Satyagraha and Gandhi*, pp. 144–49.

[392] See K.N. Panikkar, *Presidential Address*, Section III, Indian History Congress, 36th session, Aligarh, 1975, pp. 17–18.

[393] *Travancore Legislative Council Proceedings*, 6 February 1925, pp. 767–73.

[394] *Young India*, 19 February 1925.

[395] By that time the Ezhavas were divided into two groups on the question of law of inheritance: modern, educated Ezhavas who opposed both matriliny and *misradayam* (mixture of matriliny and patriliny), and others led by P. Parameswaran who wanted to retain *misradayam* law of inheritance.

[396] *Vivekodayam*, Vol. 18, No. 19, January–February 1925 (Makaram 1100 ME), p. 302; C. Kesavan, *Jeevitasamaram*, Vol. I, p. 367.

[397] C.O. Madhavan, a high ranking officer in Travancore government service, wrote to the Chief Secretary on 31 October 1933 that the SNDP Yogam had fallen into the hands of 'a few misguided Ezhava young men'. See Confidential Section (CS), 1338/1933, Kerala Secretariat.

[398] C. Kesavan, *Jeevitasamaram*, Vol. I, p. 356.

[399] Ibid.; M.K. Sanoo, *Narayana Guru Swami*, p. 419.

[400] Jeffrey, ed., *People, Princes and Paramount Power*, p. 153.

[401] The Vaikom settlement was 'flimsy in one respect' as Gandhi described it, for the government had taken shelter under the term 'open to non-Hindus'. See Mahadev Desai, *The Epic of Travancore*, pp. 21–22.

[402] *Kerala Kaumudi*, 21 September 1927, p. 1; Mahadev Desai, *The Epic of Travancore*, p. 22.

[403] P.K. Balakrishnan, 'T.K. Madhavan', in *Narayana Guru*, p. 226; P.K. Madhavan, *T.K. Madhavante Jeevacharithram*, p. 368.

[404] P.K. Madhavan stated that the death of T.K. Madhavan considerably affected the attitude of Ezhavas to the concept of religion, nation and social relations with other communities. See P.K. Madhavan, *The Life of T.K. Madhavan*, Vol. II, p. 623.

[405] *Fortnightly Reports of Madras States*, Home Political, 18/1/1933, National Archives of India; *The Hindu*, 27 January 1933, p. 14; *Kerala Kaumudi*, 23 April 1936.

[406] *Kerala Kaumudi*, 29 November 1935; File No. 776/1940, Travancore Government English Records, Confidential Section (CS).

[407] R. Velayudhan, *Kerala: The Red Rain Land*, Indian Institute of Social Affairs, New Delhi, 1958, p. 17.

[408] A committee of eight members under V.S. Subramanya Iyyer, a retired Dewan of Travancore, was constituted to report on the question of temple entry. See B. Dis No. 648/Dev., dated 25 November 1932, English Records, Trivandrum; P.K.K. Menon, *The History of the Freedom Movement in Kerala*, Vol. II, p. 303.

[409] *The Report of the Temple Entry Enquiry Committee*, 1934, p. 80.

[410] Ibid., p. 82.

[411] P.S. Velayudhan, *SNDP Yoga Charitram*, p. 321; *The Report of the Thirtieth Annual Meeting of the SNDP Yogam by Secretary, K.M. Kesavan,* 1933, p. 7.

[412] Ibid.

[413] P.S. Velayudhan, *SNDP Yoga Charitram,* p. 331.

[414] Ibid.

[415] *The Report of the Thirty-first Annual Meeting of the SNDP Yogam by C. Kesavan,* 1934, p. 11.

[416] E. Madhavan, *Swathanthra Samudayam,* Prabhat Book House, Trivandrum, 1979, pp. 111–16 (first edition 1939).

[417] C. Kesavan, *Jeevitasamaram,* Vol. II, p. 112.

[418] See back volumes of *Kerala Kaumudi, Deepika, Malayala Manorama,* etc., for the year 1935–36.

[419] *Kerala Kaumudi,* 15 March 1936, p. 7.

[420] The Rawalpindi Report says that five Ezhavas converted to Sikhism in order to get rid of the stigma faced by them for being born as low-caste Hindus. Ibid., 30 April 1936, p. 3.

[421] C.V. Kunjuraman, *Ezhavarude Matha Parivarthana Samrambham.*

[422] *Kerala Kaumudi,* 26 March 1936, p. 1.

[423] *Kerala Kaumudi,* 7 May 1936, p. 10.

[424] The Guruvayur Satyagraha under K. Kelappan started on 1 November 1931, which was observed as 'All Kerala Temple Entry Day', and continued till 2 October 1932, on the issue of granting the right of temple entry to lower castes. For details, see K. Gopalan Kutty, 'The Guruvayur Satyagraha', pp. 44–55.

[425] When the British Prime Minister, MacDonald, announced the Communal Award in July 1932 for creating separate electorates for the depressed classes and other minorities, Gandhi, who was opposed to any separate electorate, went on 'a fast unto death'. This resulted in the Poona Pact which, while maintaining the joint Hindu electorate, reserved more seats for the depressed classes than the Communal Award. See *CWMG,* Vols. 51, 52, 54, 56, 57, 61, 63, 64, 71, 82 and 85. Also see Ravinder Kumar, 'Gandhi, Ambedkar and the Poona Pact', *Occasional Papers on History and Society,* No. XX, Centre for Contemporary Studies, Nehru Memorial Museum and Library, New Delhi.

[426] Mahadev Desai, *The Epic of Travancore,* p. 34.

[427] *Kerala Kaumudi,* 26 March 1936, p. 6.

[428] Ibid.

[429] Ibid.

[430] Mahadev Desai, *The Epic of Travancore,* p. 34.

[431] P.K.K. Menon, *The History of the Freedom Movement in Kerala,* Vol. II, p. 309.

[432] K. Sukumaran, 'V.K. Velayudhan', *SNDP Yogam Golden Jubilee Souvenir,* p. 200.

[433] In a conference, the Ezhava Maha Yogam passed a resolution for wholesale conversion of Ezhavas to Christianity. See *Kerala Kaumudi,* 26 March 1936, p. 9.

[434] Quoted in Dr C.C. Karunakaran, 'The Temple Entry Proclamation', *SNDP Yogam Golden Jubilee Souvenir,* p. 109.

Politics and Protest

The history of the spread of the caste-based socio-religious movement to the political sphere can be traced back to the *Malayali Memorial* of 1891. The political protest movement led by the Yogam had more than one purpose. Its aims included getting representation in the public services and the legislature in proportion to the population strength of Ezhavas; abolishing the property qualification of suffrage; introducing adult franchise and communal electorates; ensuring communal representation in the legislature; and, finally, putting an end to the dominance of caste Hindus, especially Nairs, in the legislature and in public services.

Though the role played by Ezhavas in the *Malayali Memorial*, the first political protest movement in Travancore, was very nominal, the impact of that movement was quite remarkable on the community, particularly on its middle class. The *Malayali Memorial* was organized by Nair elites against the dominance of non-Malayali Brahmins in the Travancore administration. Non-Malayali Brahmins not only occupied 35 per cent of the topmost offices of the state, but almost all the lucrative and powerful posts worth Rs 600 per month and above in the Travancore Public Service.[1] During the period between 1817 and 1914, almost all the Dewans of Travancore, except N. Nanu Pillai,[2] were non-Malayali Brahmins. This dominance of the non-Malayali Brahmins was resented by the Nairs, who had earlier enjoyed political authority as well as a major share in the administrative posts. The Nairs had begun to find it difficult to get into government service due to the influence of the non-Malayali Brahmins in the Maharaja's palace and in administration.[3] Their inability to reach the higher realms of administration led them to advocate the claim of 'Travancore for Travancoreans'. The disgruntled Nairs began to highlight the hegemony of the non-Malayali Brahmins as the dominance of 'foreigners'. Their choice of a native Travancore theme and an anti-Brahmin tone to launch their movement attracted the attention and cooperation of other castes and communities like the Christians, the Ezhavas and the Muslims. This paved the way for conceiving a collectivity consisting of homogenous national citizens, as against the heterogenous sociality of various communities. With the support of these Travancoreans, a memorial known as the '*Malayali Memorial*' signed by 10,037 citizens from various communities, was submitted to Shri Mulam Thirunal Maharaja on 11 January 1891.[4] The memorial reflected the sentiments and aspirations of the vast majority of the subjects of the kingdom. In the memorial, they protested against 'the denial to them of a fair share in the government of their country and their systematic exclusion from the higher grades of its governmental machinery'.[5]

This was the first mass attempt by Travancoreans as a whole against the Brahmin domination for securing rights and privileges. The interests of all the communities were not uniform. While the Nairs tried to recover their lost position, the effort of the Christians was to get more posts in government service, and the Muslims and the Ezhavas agitated for entry into government service.[6] The memorial worked well for the Nairs, the key organizers of this movement, and they got much of what they sought.[7] We have seen that the Ezhavas received an unfavourable reply even though the memorialists stressed the point that

> there is not a single representative of the Thiyya community holding any govern-
> ment appointment at Rs 5 or upwards a month in the state, though intelligent and
> educated men were not wanting among them, whereas several of their caste men
> in Malabar were advanced to some of the highest offices of the uncovenanted civil
> service open to the natives of India.[8]

They also pointed out that the public departments of Travancore remained closed to the Ezhavas till 1906. The Christians too were dissatisfied with the results of the *Malayali Memorial*. Therefore, the educated members of these other communities looked upon the memorial as basically a petition of over 10,000 Nairs.[9] The achievement of the Nairs and the rejection of other communities from government service indeed infuriated the Christians, Ezhavas and Muslims. These communities followed the example of the *Malayali Memorial* by submitting memorials and memorandums representing their separate caste and community to the Maharaja of Travancore. In 1895, an Ezhava memorial signed by Palpu was submitted to S. Sankara Soobiar, the then Dewan to the Maharaja of Travancore.[10] It stated that the backward position of their community was mainly due 'to the political and educational disabilities to which the Thiyyas of Travancore are subjected'.[11] As that memorial did not benefit the Ezhavas, in 1896, a community memorial, popularly known as the Ezhava Memorial, signed by 13,176 Ezhavas, was submitted to the Maharaja of Travancore. This memorial requested in humble terms the granting of ordinary civic rights, which were given to converts to Islam or Christianity, to Ezhavas who chose to remain within the fold of Hinduism. But this memorial too failed to produce any results.

Not only the memorials of the Ezhavas, but also those of the Christians and the Muslims were rejected by the government, on the ground that these memorials came into being to serve the self-interest of these communities. At the same time, the *Malayali Memorial*ists, instead of stressing the grievances of the Nairs, gave a Travancorean hue to their petition, describing the movement as an anti-Brahmin movement.[12] Therefore, the Ezhava and the Christian memorials, which represented the grievances of their respective communities, could not create the kind of impact *Malayali Memorial* achieved. Instead of stressing the grievances of separate communities, had it been a movement of non-Hindus and non-caste Hindus against the domination of caste Hindus, it would have been more successful. But this could not be achieved till 1918.

When the individual attempts of these communities failed, the educated elites among Ezhavas, Christians and Muslims realized that an alliance of non-Hindu, non-*savarna* communities was essential to fight against the caste Hindu hegemony in Travancore. Thus the Christians, Ezhavas and Muslims formed an alliance for the same cause on the Syrian Christian initiative, which they had fought in association with the Nairs. But by that time the Nairs had become their formidable foe. We have also seen how, twenty-seven years after the *Malayali Memorial*, elite Christians, Ezhavas and Muslims struggled for more than three years under the common umbrella of the League for Equal Civic Rights,[13] and eventually, in 1922, succeeded in getting employment in all government departments except the *Dewaswam* and *Kottaram*.[14] However, though all these communities received some benefits in the matter of government jobs, they did not match their numerical strength and educational qualifications. The constitution of the Public Service Bureau by the SNDP Yogam took place under such circumstances. But all these activities did not make much of a difference regarding the monopoly of the caste Hindus or non-Malayali Brahmins in government service. In 1932, the Nairs and non-Malayali Brahmins, who constituted about 18 per cent of the total population of Travancore, accounted for 74 per cent of the total appointments in the state. At the same time all other communities, who constituted about 82 per cent of the total population of the state, occupied only 26 per cent of the total jobs in the state. The military and *Dewaswam* departments were excluded from this account. Both these were staffed exclusively by caste Hindus, of whom the large majority were the Nairs.

The unemployment problem, another important reason for political protest in Travancore, reached an acute stage in this educationally advanced princely state by the beginning of the 1930s. This problem was associated with various factors, such as the rapid growth of population, increase in the number of educated people, lack of industrial development coupled with the renunciation of 'traditional' occupations by most castes, caste restrictions imposed on the untouchables and non-Hindus, the monopoly of government service by caste Hindus, the decline of the *marumakkathayam* system of inheritance and subsequent disintegration of *taravad*s (joint families), etc. In the period between 1901 and 1921, the population of Travancore increased by more than one million.[15] After the modernization and practical recognition of English as the official language of the state, almost all castes and communities started sending their children to schools and colleges with a view to qualify them for government service. As a consequence of this, the number of qualified candidates was in excess of the demand.[16] Being a predominantly agricultural country, industries had not yet developed sufficiently to accommodate the increase in educated population – which therefore remained more or less unemployed. Modern education and its associated discourses had already represented 'traditional' occupations as inferior and this received widespread acceptance, as a result of which a number of communities drifted away from the traditional occupations which they had monopolized for a long time.[17] Due to the partition of joint families, the small holdings of land became uneconomic and inadequate to meet the increased needs of the rising number of unemployed members of households.[18] Therefore, the younger generation of the educated left their traditional fields of engagement in search of wage employment.

While government service was mainly reserved for upper-caste Hindus, educated youths from non-Hindu communities as well as non-caste Hindus remained unemployed. 25.1 per cent of vernacular-educated Christians, and 9.2 per cent of English-educated and 8.9 per cent of vernacular-educated Ezhavas remained unemployed.[19] Frustrated and annoyed, they organized themselves in order to secure their due share in government service, and to demolish the hegemony of caste Hindus in government service. At the same time, the Nairs had among them about 32.8 per cent of English-educated and 51.1 per cent of vernacular-educated persons who were not employed,[20] although they could retain their control over the government service. While the educated unemployed sections among non-caste Hindus and non-Hindus tended to question the ways of the caste Hindus, especially the Nairs in the government service, the Nairs strove to retain their old position. Thus the early 1930s saw a clash of interests between both these groups.

Legislative Reforms and the Abstention Movement

Travancore enjoyed special prerogatives among the princely states: it had the distinction of being the first Indian state to set up a Legislative Council in 1888, for the purpose of wider participation of different sections of its population in the framing of laws and regulations.[21] It was a small Council of eight members, of which at least two were non-official members nominated by the government. The Dewan was the ex-officio president, and the tenure of the Council was three years. It was a purely deliberative body for the purposes of legislation and had no executive role or administrative powers. Though all the members had the right of discussion as well as voting rights, the Council had plenary powers of legislation, subject to the ruler's assent, before a measure could pass into law. No measure relating to public revenues could be introduced in the Council except with the previous sanction of the Dewan.[22] In 1898, the Legislative Council was enlarged by increasing the minimum number of members from five to eight, and the upper limit of membership from eight to fifteen.[23] This time the proportion of non-official members nominated by the government was fixed at two-fifths of the total number. The principle of electing members was not conceded. Previous sanction of the Dewan was made necessary not only for measures affecting public revenues, but also for those affecting religion or religious rites and usage of any class.[24]

Besides establishing the Legislative Council, Maharaja Sree Mulam Thirunal extended his administrative experimentation by setting a Praja Sabha called the Sree Mulam Popular Assembly in 1904. In 1905–06, the Maharaja of Travancore granted the people the right to elect members to the Assembly, but the right to franchise was mainly determined by the land revenue accruing from the members.[25] In the beginning, only those who paid more than hundred rupees per annum as land tax were eligible to cast their vote.[26] But later this tax amount was reduced to fifty rupees.[27] That was why Henry Bruce commented:

> The contribution and the working of the Assembly show that however genuinely popular it may be, it is neither legislative nor executive nor widely representative. No such body would for a moment satisfy the modern agitators in British India. In order to elect or to be elected a person has essentially to have a yearly income of 3,000 rupees.[28]

In short, this was an 'Assembly of the representatives of the land holders and merchants in the country'.[29]

In 1919, the Legislative Council was again remodelled by Regulation I. The new Council was enlarged not only by raising the minimum number of members to twenty-five, but also by granting to the people the privilege of electing the members to the Council. Eight out of the eleven non-official seats were thrown open to elected members: four by the general electorate (one for each of the four revenue divisions of the state); one by the *jenmies*; one by the European planting community; one by the merchants, traders and factory owners.[30] A limited right was granted to the Council to interpellate the government and to discuss the annual budget. According to the Legislative Council Regulation II of 1921, all persons who paid an annual land tax of not less than Rs 5 or a municipal tax of Rs 3, and in the town of Trivandrum, which returned one member, of Re 1 or professional tax to a municipality or income tax to the government, and all graduates of recognized universities were eligible to vote in the general constituencies, provided they were not under twenty-one years of age.[31] Women were placed on a footing of complete equality with men in the matter of voting and membership.[32] The Legislative Council Regulation of 1931 again expanded the voting rights to include various categories such as retired persons from 'State Forces', government services, registered land-holders, tenants or *kudiyan* who had been paying the tax of one rupee or more, etc.[33] The franchise qualification for the Council was fixed at a higher rate than that of the Sree Mulam Popular Assembly.[34] The franchise qualification shows that both these constituent bodies were dominated by landlords and the upper middle-class section of the society. According to this amended regulation of 1921, the total number of electors during 1922–23 was about 96,316, which formed only 2.5 per cent of the total population of the state.[35] Though some rules were relaxed following various constitutional reforms introduced in the Council and Assembly, land tax continued to be the main criteria of franchise; as a result, the traditional land-holding *savarna* communities, especially Nairs, monopolized the legislature and most of communities like the Ezhavas and the Muslims were completely excluded from it.

As long as the suffrage was based upon property qualification, the Nairs, being the largest body of tax payers, would get more seats than legitimate on the basis of their population. This situation was a result of the steps taken by the government to change the existing land relations. After the Pattom Proclamation Law of 1865, Nairs, the then tenants of the state, became landlords. When partition took place in the Nair *taravad*s, most of their land was mortgaged to Christians and other communities. Though the Christians and other communities purchased the partitioned land of the Nairs and practically enjoyed permanent occupancy rights, they were not legally recognized as the owners of the land as the land taxes continued to be paid by the mortgagers.[36] This naturally gave more voting rights to the Nairs than their property qualification actually warranted. In addition to this, the partition of the *taravad*s had a favourable impact on the Nairs. The new branches of Nair families had enough land to qualify them for franchise. This was demonstrated by the deeds executed during the five-year period after the proclamation of the 'Nair Regulation' in 1925. The Nairs executed 32,903 partition deeds covering an area of 334,300 acres of land which were distributed among 400,864 individuals.[37] This naturally increased the number of both landowners and small-scale landholders among Nairs. The actual changes in the landholdings, therefore, did not materially affect the dominance of the Nairs in the legislature. Table 22 shows the position of the Nairs and other communities in the legislature.

The table above shows that Nairs, who constituted about 17 per cent of the total population, captured a majority of seats in the Council – 52 per cent in 1922, 57 per cent in 1925, 61 per cent in 1928 and 65 per cent in 1931. As a consequence, the Sree Mulam Assembly got dominated by Nairs. In 1933, the

TABLE 22 *Representation of different castes and communities in the Travancore Legislative Assembly between 1922 and 1931*[38]

Community	Population	Members in the Legislative Council			
		1922	1925	1928	1931
TOTAL	50.59	23	23	23	23
Nairs	8.68	12	13	14	15
Christians	16.04	7	7	6	4
Ezhavas	8.69	0	0	0	0
Muslims	3.53	0	0	1	0
Other caste Hindus	4.29	4	3	2	3
Depressed classes	9.17	0	0	0	1

43 seats in the Assembly were distributed as follows: 24 Nairs, 8 Christians, 3 Ezhavas, 5 caste Hindus, 1 Muslim and 1 from the depressed classes.[39]

In the first four elections, the Ezhavas did not get even a single seat in the Council. The Muslims and Christians were also dissatisfied, both with their non-representation and their nominal representation. The Ezhavas and the Yogam made attempts to get their due share in the Legislative Council, the Sree Mulam Assembly and other representative bodies from 1904 onwards.

After the formation of the Sree Mulam Popular Assembly in 1904, the Ezhava middle class demanded adequate representation in various democratic bodies such as the Legislative Council, Sree Mulam Popular Assembly, etc., on the basis of their population strength. In 1905, Kumaran Asan pleaded in the Sree Mulam Popular Assembly for providing adequate representation to the Ezhavas in the Legislative Council and in the various Town Improvement Committees.[40] In 1914, the Ezhava representatives in the Assembly argued for a special electorate for their community in order to get adequate representation. According to K.M. Krishnan: 'Since the institution of Assembly only one Ezhava had been elected as a member by the Taluk voters in one year, they had little or no chance of being adequately represented in the Assembly under the ordinary rules.'[41] The Yogam, both inside and outside the Assembly, time and again complained about their grievances. On 5 August 1927, the Yogam submitted a memorial to the Maharani Regent to redress their grievances in the Legislative Council. In this memorial they stated that the electoral rules pertaining to the Legislative Council did not enable them to get elected from the general constituency.[42]

Though we are a land-owning class owing to the high franchise now fixed by the rules, we have not got a majority of voters in any one of the electorates. . . . We also beg to submit that a great majority of our men . . . are workers and the electoral rules fortunately do not make any provision for a labour constituency, although the government were careful to make adequate provision for capitalists, viz. *jenmis*, the planters and the commercial and industrial interests. Our prayer, therefore, for a proper and adequate representation in the Council is justified by the large interests that we have to safeguard. We have waited in 1924 on deputation to the Dewan and submitted a memorial on the subject for this consideration, when he promised to consider our claim for separate representation if we fail to win any seat in the second general election. Though we have contested more than one seat, we failed to secure any. The third general election is fast approaching and, we, therefore, pray that this question may be taken up for consideration and adequate provision made in the rules so that we may be enabled to return our own candidates for the Ezhavas or by the formation of plural constituencies with seats reserved for the Ezhavas.[43]

A community of which the majority of people were agricultural labourers and industrial workers had been denied franchise rights, as the suffrage was based upon land revenue. Though the Ezhavas, through excise and customs, contributed a good portion of their income to the state treasury, the government excluded these kinds of revenue in the fixation of franchise qualification. Therefore, they described the suffrage as aristocratic, semi-feudal and oligarchic in character. As far as education was concerned, the percentage of literates among Ezhavas was 42, which was greater than the state average. As far as industrial activities were concerned, their contribution was more than any other community. That was why Dewan Watt once said: 'The Ezhavas are entitled to special consideration and gratitude of all Travancore.'[44]

The franchise based on land tax was unsuited to the conditions that prevailed in Travancore because at that time only 54.3 per cent of the population were dependent on agriculture, and the income from land was only 17.6 per cent of the total income of the state.[45] At the same time, excise and customs contributed 34.7 per cent of the total income of the state.[46] The excise and customs revenue had mainly been the contribution of Christians, Ezhavas and Muslims. The exclusion of excise and customs contribution for the purpose of franchise qualification annoyed these communities, and they demanded abolition of property qualification. Another factor that induced the Ezhavas, Christians and Muslims to oppose property qualification was that persons who were in possession of land and who actually paid land tax were not entitled for franchise since the taxes were still paid in the name of the mortgagers. Therefore, they demanded that if property qualification was regarded as a criterion of eligibility to vote, the actual payer of the land tax, though in another man's name, should be entitled to vote rather than the nominal registry-holder.[47] Had the franchise not been confined to land tax alone, the position of the Ezhavas, the Christians and the Muslims, who were mainly engaged in industry, transport and trade, would have come into prominence. That was why the meeting of the Ezhava Mahajana Sabha, which was held at Alleppey on 27 November 1932, under the auspices of the Yogam with K. Ayyapan as president, and under the presidentship of K. Ayyappan, opposed the land revenue qualification.[48] On 26 May 1928, during the time of the Simon Commission's visit to India, C.V. Kunjuraman, general secretary of the Yogam, submitted a representation to the Commission enumerating the existing disabilities, pointed out the need to retain the communal electorate to provide separate electorate for the Ezhavas, and requested the introduction of adult franchise.[49] In addition to this, several representations were sent to the Dewan and the Resident demanding adult franchise and reservation of seats. On 18 March 1932, the Ezhava members of the Sree Mulam Popular Assembly submitted a representation to Dewan Watts, pointing out that Ezhavas would not be able to elect a single candidate if the franchise was on the basis of land revenue, and requesting him to introduce either adult franchise or special electorate for the Ezhavas.[50] But there was no change in the attitude of the authorities.

Meanwhile, in June 1932, an announcement regarding constitutional reform was made by the government.[51] Immediately, on 29 June, the Yogam summoned a meeting at Quilon under the presidentship of K.P. Asan, and demanded adult franchise – and if this was not possible, that all tax payers, irrespective of the quantum of tax paid, be made eligible to vote.[52] The meeting proposed to the government to reserve 17 per cent of the seats in the Assembly and the Council for Ezhavas on the basis of population strength. The Yogam decided to form a new political organization by the name of Ezhava Rashtriya Sabha, which came into existence in 1932.[53] When this new organization met at Quilon on 31 July 1932, the need for adult franchise and reservation for communal representation of the Ezhavas was stressed.[54] But the government rejected these demands on the ground that 'the formation of communal electorate is altogether unsuited to Travancore', and it would only help 'to create a communal cleavage in the country'.[55] On the question of adult franchise, the government's answer was: 'The decision in Travancore is at present based on communal or sectional interests and unless popular parties formed on political lines come into existence the introduction of adult franchise would endanger the larger interest of the state.'[56] The Legislative Council Reform was passed on 28 October 1932 and it came into force with effect from 1 January 1933. The main feature of this regulation was that the Sree Mulam Popular Assembly and the Legislative Council were abolished, and a bicameral legislature was created: namely, the Travancore Sree Mulam Assembly and the Travancore Sri Chitra State Council.[57] This new reform neither changed the franchise nor made it in any way responsible to the legislature. The principle of autocracy remained unchanged. The new regulation once again stressed the property qualification. In the Sree Mulam Assembly, eligibility required annual land tax of Rs 5 or more, and in the Council it was fixed on a higher standard of annual land tax of Rs 25 or municipal tax of Rs 5.[58]

Thus this long-awaited administrative reform, instead of providing new opportunities to the untouchables and minority communities, once again retained the supremacy of caste Hindus by giving undue importance to land tax for anyone to have franchise. This naturally increased the frustration of the Ezhavas, the Christians and the Muslims. They understood that as long as the franchise was based on property qualification, the Nairs would continue to have a majority in the legislature for they constituted the largest number of payers of land tax in the state.

According to the reformers, 'the autocracy of one individual is infinitely better than the predominance of a single community in an Indian state when there are conflicting communal interests'.[59] They also thought that 'so long as the Nair community maintains predominance in the public service and in the legislature, no truly democratic aim is realizable'.[60]

As soon as the announcement of constitutional reforms was made, a meeting of the Ezhava Mahajana Sabha was held at Quilon on 27 November 1932, under the auspices of the Yogam, to protest against the new reform; the Sabha demanded adult franchise, and reservation of four seats in the Council and ten seats in the Assembly for Ezhavas.[61] The Yogam appointed a committee to formulate a programme of action in association with like-minded organizations.[62] According to R. Velayudhan, 'the sociological process of the crisis among the Ezhavas brought them shoulder to shoulder with the Christians and the Muslims'.[63] The Ezhavas, led by C. Kesavan, began to turn towards the aggrieved and disappointed Christians and Muslims to launch a crusade for political and bureaucratic representation on the basis of community.

Thus the middle class among Ezhavas, Christians and Muslims stood as a united body and resolved to work along strictly constitutional lines to get their grievances redressed.[64] On 17 December 1932, they held a combined meeting at Trivandrum under the presidentship of A.J. John. This meeting gave birth to the Travancore Joint Political Conference.[65] The conference submitted a memorandum to the Dewan on 9 January 1933 which demanded the introduction of communal representation and reserved seats for particular communities in the legislature.[66]

But the press note issued by the government on 27 January 1933 revealed the reluctance of the government to reserve seats in joint electorates.[67] This led to a strong and tempestuous political agitation in Travancore. Once again, on 25 January 1933, a meeting of the Joint Political Conference was held at L.M.S. Hall, Trivandrum, under the presidentship of A.J. John, when the famous *Nivarthanam* or Abstention resolution was passed. The famous Malayalam scholar I.C. Chacko coined the word '*nivarthanam*' which means abstention. The Joint Political Conference did not want to identify their movement with the Non-Cooperation Movement under Mahatma Gandhi in British India. This was mainly because the Abstentionists wanted the sympathy of the

British rulers. To avoid being misunderstood that their movement was a part of the Non-Cooperation Movement, they intentionally chose *nivarthanam* or abstention, instead of *nissahakaranam* or non-cooperation.[68]

According to the resolution, the Joint Political Conference planned to launch an agitation aimed at boycotting elections to the new legislative bodies,[69] and requested persons who had filed their nominations to withdraw their candidature as a protest against the discrimination of the government towards non-Hindus and the untouchables.[70] On behalf of the Ezhavas and the Yogam, C. Kesavan, C.V. Kunjuraman and M. Govindan supported the *Nivarthanam* resolution.

Meanwhile, the government had admitted the demands of the Ezhavas and the Muslims. On 7 February 1933, C.V. Kunjuraman and M. Govindan of the Yogam, along with Komalizethu Sankaran and M. Madhavan Vaidhyar, met the Maharaja at Kanyakumari.[71] At this meeting the Maharaja assured the Ezhava representatives that provision would be made to secure seven seats in the Assembly and two seats in the Council for the Ezhavas, through representation, election and nomination.[72] As this assurance was felt to be a genuine one, both C.V. Kunjuraman and M. Govindan changed their prior stance towards the Abstention movement. With the aim of creating an atmosphere to retreat from the movement the leaders of the community met at Kaithamukku SNDP office in Trivandrum, at a meeting summoned by the Yogam president, Madhavan Viadyar.[73] But C. Kesavan and other radical sections among the Ezhavas abstained from the meeting in protest against the change of attitude of C.V. Kunjuraman and M. Govindan.[74] A special meeting of the Yogam was summoned at Changanachery on 14 March 1933 under the presidentship of K. Ayyappan. At this meeting both C.V. Kunjuraman and M. Govindan tried to convince the audience about the positive implications of their stand. But the Yogam in general was against this new turn, and the Abstention resolution was ratified with 1,491 votes in favour and 9 votes against.[75] Various Ezhava organizations arranged meetings to support the Abstention movement.[76]

Due to the combined efforts of the Ezhavas, Christians and Muslims, under the leadership of C. Kesavan, N.V. Joseph, T.M. Varghese, M.M. Varkey, P.K. Kunju, etc., the *Nivarthanam* agitation spread all over Travancore. Even though the activities of the Joint Political Conference had succeeded in marshalling the support of the bulk of these three communities, the government managed to conduct elections in June 1933 and some members belonging to these communities contested in the election; in this election and through nomination, Ezhavas got seven seats in the Assembly and two seats in the Council.[77] That is, more than 60 per cent in the Assembly and about 59 per cent of the seats in the Council were elected without contest.[78] This reveals the success of the Abstention movement.

After the elections, the Abstentionists continued their agitation for dissolution of the legislature. On 21 August 1933, the Travancore Joint Political Conference met at Trivandrum and changed its name to All Travancore Joint Political Congress. At this meeting it was declared that the aim of the Congress was to achieve sufficient representation in the legislature, the public service and the Nair Brigade – in proportion to the numerical strength of each community, the introduction of adult franchise, and, finally, to usher in a responsible government.[79] On 31 July 1933, the Ezhava Mahajana Sabha under the presidentship of C. Kesavan passed a resolution demanding that the Yogam move a motion of no-confidence against those who had submitted nominations for the elections against the decisions of the Yogam.[80] Subsequently, the Yogam passed a no-confidence resolution against K.M. Krishnan Vakil and K.C. Karunakaran, for submitting nomination and accepting nomination of the government, respectively.[81] A similar resolution was also passed at the meeting of the Ezhava Mahajana Sabha held at Quilon against K. Sankaran and C.V. Kunjuraman.[82] The Yogam, at its thirtieth annual meeting held at Alleppey on 27 August 1933, passed a resolution demanding the dissolution of the legislature. On the day of the first meeting of the newly constituted Council, the members of these three communities organized a mass fast to protest against the new Council.[83] At that time there was a strong movement against Sir C.P. Ramaswamy Aiyer, who was considered to be the root cause of all the problems in the state. At a historical meeting of the Joint Political Congress held at Kozhencheri on 13 May 1935, C. Kesavan, who presided over the meeting, openly demanded the dismissal of Sir C.P. Ramaswamy Aiyer.[84] Kesavan was arrested on 7 June 1935 for his inciting speech at Kozhancheri,[85] and sentenced to two years imprisonment and fined Rs 500.[86] In addition, the government prohibited Joint Political Congress from holding meetings. The arrest of Kesavan came as a shock to the Ezhavas and the Yogam. They sent telegrams and memorandums to the Viceroy, the Maharaja and other officials protesting against oppression by the government and the arrest of their leaders.[87]

The political unrest in the state persuaded Sir C.P. Ramaswamy Aiyer to advise the Maharaja to introduce various reforms to redress the grievances of the non-Hindus and the untouchables. A Public Service Commission was constituted to ensure fair representation for the backward communities in the public services and 40 per cent of the jobs in the intermediate division were reserved for backward communities.[88] All lower-level posts were to be filled in proportion to the population of each caste or community.[89] The second victory of the Abstentionists was the government decision to reorganize the Nair Brigade and the Travancore military force, and to bring them under the Indian state forces.[90]

From then onwards recruitment was open to all, in contrast to the earlier practice of recruitment of Nairs alone into the Brigade. The franchise qualification was also widened by reducing the property qualification and communal representation in the legislature. According to the new reform, eight seats for Ezhavas and three seats for Muslims and Latin Catholics were reserved in the Assembly; and in the Council, two seats for Ezhavas and one each for Muslims and Latin Catholics were reserved.[91] The first general election on the basis of this communal representation was held in April 1937 and there was no contest for any of the eight seats reserved in the Assembly and two seats reserved in the Council for Ezhavas.[92] In the election, the Travancore Joint Political Congress obtained an absolute majority, and T.M. Varghese was elected as the deputy president, which was the highest elected office of the Legislative Assembly. He defeated Puthuppally S. Krishna Pillai, S. Subramanya Iyyer, Pattam Thanu Pillai and Vaikom Rama Krishna Pillai.[93]

Due to the consistent work of the Yogam along with members of the Christian and Muslim communities, the dominance of the Nairs in the legislature, public service and the military was reduced considerably. The achievement of the Yogam in its fight against discrimination in various fields like education, employment, politics and religion was supplemented by this new gain.

The Abstention movement was indeed the first mass political movement in Travancore and a precursor of the Travancore State Congress, but the nature of this movement was communal and therefore against the unity of the entire people. The movement became reactionary and undemocratic when it became organized on caste basis for securing communal electorates, and for demanding the reservation of seats on communal basis in the legislature as well as in the public service. It is indeed an irony that the SNDP Yogam, which was named after Sree Narayana Guru who lived and worked for the unity of all, contributed to the growth of communal division.

Notes and References

[1] *Malayali Memorial*, p. 6, reproduced in *Kerala Archives News Letters*, Vol. II, Nos. II and III, Directorate of Archives, March 1976.

[2] In 1877, N. Nanu Pillai was appointed Dewan of Travancore by Ayilyam Thirunal and he continued in that post till 1880. When Vishakham Tirunal became the Maharaja in 1880, he asked him to resign and appointed V. Ramiengar, a non-Malayali Brahmin, as the Dewan. See Robin Jeffrey, *The Decline of Nayar Dominance: Society and Politics in Travancore 1847–1908*, Vikas Publishing House, Delhi, 1976, pp. 340 and 344; K.R. Elenkath, *Dewan Nanu Pillai, with His Selected Writings and Letters*, Dewan Nanu Pillai Memorial Reading Room, Trivandrum, 1975. Chapters IV–VI, pp. 30–85.

[3] *Malayali Memorial*, pp. 110–12.

[4] Ibid., p. 1.

[5] Ibid., p. 2, para 2.

[6] Ibid., p. 5.

[7] *Vivekodayam*, June–July 1905 (Mithunam 1080 ME), p. 32.

[8] *Malayali Memorial*, p. 5.

[9] *Madras Mail*, 16 November 1896, p. 3.

[10] The *Ezhava Memorial*, Bangalore, 12 May 1895, was signed by Dr P. Palpu and submitted to S. Sankara Soobiar, Dewan of Travancore. See T.K. Ravindran, *Vaikom Satyagraha and Gandhi*, Sri Narayana Institute of Social and Cultural Development, Trichur, 1975, p. 27.

[11] Quoted in ibid.

[12] 'Save us from the Foreign Brahmins is the burden of the cry . . .', *Madras Times*, 20 January 1891, as quoted in Robin Jeffrey, 'A Note on the Malayali Origins of Anti Brahmanism in South India', *Indian Economic and Social History Review*, Vol. XIV, No. 2, 1977, p. 263.

[13] *Caste and Citizenship in Travancore*, Travancore Civic Rights League, Kottayam, 1919, p. 3.

[14] The activities and demands of the Civic Rights League have already been discussed in detail in chapter 4.

[15] According to the 1901 Census, the total population of Travancore was 29,52,151 (see *Census of India, 1901*, Vol. XXVI, Travancore, Part I, Report, p. 88). In 1921, it increased to 40,06,062 (see *Census of India*, Vol. XXV, Travancore, Part I, Report, p. 34).

[16] According to the estimate of the Unemployment Enquiry Committee, the total number of educated people seeking employment every year in Travancore was 3,500. At the same time, the number of people absorbed both in government and private service was 1,360. This shows that 2,140 out of 3,500 persons remained unemployed. See *Census of India, 1931*, Vol. XXVIII, Travancore, Part I, Report, p. 258.

[17] Among the Ezhavas, only 8 in every 100 followed toddy-drawing, and among the Brahmins, only 17 in every 100 continued their 'traditional' occupation of priesthood. *Census of India, 1921*, Vol. XXV, Travancore, Part I, Report, p. 125. But Velu Pillai says that only 38 in a 1,000 among Ezhavas and 161 in a 1,000 among Brahmins followed their traditional occupations; see *The Travancore State Manual*, Vol. III, p. 12.

[18] According to the 1931 Census, about 38 per cent of the holdings were below the size of 1 acre. Of the total number of holdings, more than 87 per cent were less than 5 acres. See *Census of India, 1931*, Vol. XXVIII, Travancore, Part I, Report, p. 490.

[19] Ibid., pp. 258–59.

[20] Ibid.

[21] *The Travancore Government Gazette*, 10 April 1888, Part II, Chapter I, No. I.

[22] *Administration Report of Travancore*, 1937–38, p. 12.

[23] Ibid.

[24] Ibid.

[25] See *Proceedings of the Second Meeting of the Sree Mulam Popular Assembly*, Travancore, 1905, p. 1; P.K.K. Menon, *The History of the Freedom Movement in Kerala*, Vol. II, The Regional Records Survey Committee, Trivandrum, 1970–72, p. 62.

[26] *Proceedings of Sree Mulam Popular Assembly*, 1905, p. 1.

[27] Ibid., Appendix 'A', tenth session, 1911, p. V.

[28] Letters from Malabar, p. xxvi, quoted in P.K.K. Menon, *The History of the Freedom Movement in Kerala*, Vol. II, p. 59.

[29] *The Travancore Government Gazette*, 4 October 1904, Part II, Chapter I, No. 3.

[30] R. Ramakrishnan Nair, *Constitutional Experiments in Kerala*, Trivandrum, 1964, p. 9.

[31] See *Travancore Administration Report*, 1937–38, pp. 13–14; see also P.K.K. Menon, *The History of the Freedom Movement in Kerala*, Vol. II, p. 64.

[32] *Travancore Administration Report*, 1937–38, p. 14.

[33] *Travancore Administration Report*, 1936–37, p. 23.

[34] Ibid.

[35] Ibid.

[36] All Travancore Joint Political Congress, *Travancore, The Present Political Problem*, Trivandrum, 1934, pp. 24–25.

[37] Ibid., p. 7.

[38] Ibid., p. 24.

[39] Ibid., p. 21.

[40] *Proceedings of Sree Mulam Popular Assembly*, 1905, p. 73.

[41] *Proceedings of Sree Mulam Popular Assembly*, 1914, p. 113.

[42] All Travancore Joint Political Congress, *Travancore, The Present Political Problem*, p. 22.

[43] Quoted in ibid.

[44] Quoted in ibid.

[45] Ibid., p. 26.

[46] Ibid.

[47] Ibid., p. 24.

[48] P.S. Velayudhan, *SNDP Yoga Charitram*, p. 284.

[49] Ibid., Appendix 22, p. CL-CLVI; N. Muralidharan, 'Nammude Avakasa Samarangal', *SNDP Yogam Plantinum Jubilee Souvenir*, p. 309.

[50] Thazhava Kesavan, 'Nivarthana Prakshobhanam', *SNDP Yogam Golden Jubilee Souvenir*, p. 226; P.K.K. Menon, *The History of Freedom Movement in Kerala*, Vol. II, p. 335.

[51] The Press Communique, 2 June 1931, Ibid., p. 325.

[52] C. Kesavan, *Jeevitasamaram*, Vol. II, p. 39.

[53] P.S. Velayudhan, *SNDP Yoga Charitram*, SNDP Yogam, Quilon, 1978, p. 282.

[54] C. Kesavan, *Jeevitasamaram*, Vol. II, NBS, Kottayam, 1971, pp. 40–41.

[55] P.S. Velayudhan, *SNDP Yoga Charitram*, p. 279.

[56] *Dasan*, Vol. 6, No. 11, 31 October 1932.

[57] *Administration Report of Travancore*, 1936–37, p. 22.

[58] Ibid.

[59] *Travancore, The Present Political Problem*, p. 22.

[60] Ibid.

[61] Thazhava Kesavan, 'Nivarthana Prakshobhanam', in *SNDP Yogam Golden Jubilee Souvenir*, SNDP Yogam, Quilon, 1953, p. 227.

[62] Ibid.

[63] R. Velayudhan, *SNDP Yoga Charitram*, p. 17.

[64] All Travancore Joint Political Congress, *Travancore, the Present Political Problem*, p. 1.

[65] Thazhava Kesavan, 'Nivarthana Prakshobhanam', in *SNDP Yogam Golden Jubilee Souvenir*, p. 227.

[66] The Memorandum reproduced in *Dasan*, Vol. 6, No. 21, 14 January 1936.

[67] K.K. Kusuman, *The Abstention Movement*, Kerala Historical Society, Trivandrum, 1976, p. 33.

[68] M.M. Varkey, *Ormakalilude*, NBS, Kottayam, 1971, p. 96.

[69] All Travancore Joint Political Congress, *Travancore, the Present Political Problem*, p. 221.

[70] Ibid.

[71] *30th Annual Report of the General Secretary of the SNDP Yogam*, 1933 (1109–1–11), p. 4.

[72] *Kerala Kaumudi*, 7 May 1936, p. 1.

[73] C. Kesavan, *Jeevitasamaram*, Vol. II, p. 68.

[74] Ibid.

[75] Thazhava Kesavan, 'Nivarthana Prakshobhanam', in *SNDP Yogam Golden Jubilee Souvenir*, p. 228.

[76] C. Kesavan, *Jeevitasamaram*, Vol. II, p. 71.

[77] In the Assembly, out of seven members, three were elected and four were nominated, while in the Council, two were nominated. See P.S. Velayudhan, *SNDP Yoga Charitram*, p. 319.

[78] On the whole, twenty-nine seats out of forty-eight seats in the Assembly, and in the Council, thirteen seats out of twenty-two seats, were filled unopposed. See A. Balakrishna Pillai, *Kesariyude Mukaprasangangal*, NBS, Kottayam, 1961, pp. 84–87.

[79] *Yuvabharathy*, Vol. II, No. 2, 26 August 1933.

[80] P.S. Velayudhan, *SNDP Yoga Charitram*, p. 332.

[81] C. Kesavan, *Jeevitasamaram*, Vol. II, p. 86.

[82] Apart from no-confidence, the resolution also decided to impose ostracism on C.V. Kunjuraman and K. Sankaran. See ibid.

[83] Ibid., p. 87.

[84] Thazhava Kesavan, 'Nivarthana Prakshobhanam', in *SNDP Yogam Golden Jubilee Souvenir,* p. 228. See also P.K.K. Menon, *The History of Freedom Movement in Kerala*, Vol. II, p. 369; *Malayala Manorama, 14 May 1935.*

[85] *Malayala Manorama,* 8 June 1935.

[86] Though the Sessions Judge at Quilon sentenced him to one year's simple imprisonment and a fine of Rs 500, in the High Court his sentence was increased to two years and a fine of Rs 500. See *Thirty-third Annual Report of the General Secretary of SNDP Yogam*, 1936, p. 6.

[87] In the telegram to the Viceroy it was stated: 'The SNDP Yogam Council protest Travancore Government's highly repressive measures against oppressive communities. Their leaders and general secretary of the Yogam arrested and prosecuted public meetings banned and individuals gagged. Discontent aggravated. Prayer your Excellency intervene, alleviate suffering, redress grievances.' See *Malayala Manorama*, 18 June 1935, p. 3.

[88] Thazhava Kesavan, 'Nivarthana Prakshobhanam', in *SNDP Yogam Golden Jubilee Souvenir*, p. 230.

[89] Ibid.

[90] P.K.K. Menon, *The History of the Freedom Movement in Kerala*, Vol. II, p. 368.

[91] *The Administration Report of Travancore*, 1936–37, pp. 22 and 98–99; Thazhava Kesavan, 'Nivarthana Prakshobhanam', in *SNDP Yogam Golden Jubilee Souvenir*, p. 230.

[92] Ibid.; *The Administration Report of Travancore*, 1936–37, p. 99.

[93] E.M. Kovoor, *T.M. Verghese*, NBS, Kottayam, 1965, p. 83.

Conclusion

From the second half of the nineteenth century, the princely state of Travancore witnessed an unprecedented transition in which continuities and discontinuities in social relations coexisted. Many social relations were altered and redefined; others were perpetuated and reinstated. Travancore witnessed a social transformation in which new agents of change were formed, new forms of organizations and institutions became visible. These agents influenced the nature and course of the transformation which in turn refashioned the nature of those agents as well.

The factors that influenced the changes in the social and economic spheres were the introduction of laws patterned on the western concept of private property in land; growth of a cash economy due to the development of plantation industries; development of infrastructure such as transport, communications and hydroelectric projects; growth of small-scale industries and increased overseas trade; and the spread of English education. The emergence of a middle class in Travancore was a result of the social transformations brought about by these factors. Its impact was not limited to the upper castes; it percolated to marginal groups such as untouchables like the Ezhavas as well. The middle class in Travancore, therefore, included almost every religion and caste.

But members of the middle class belonging to lower castes like the Ezhava faced discrimination from the upper castes. This caste replicated the existing hierarchical distribution of people within it as well. Most public facilities and opportunities were denied to them, affecting their social and economic mobility. Therefore, their immediate material interest necessitated a change in the existing caste and social practices, which kept them segregated from the mainstream of social and political life. The Travancore Ezhava Sabha founded by Palpu in 1896 to bring the various denominations of Ezhavas within a common organization was an expression of the new need. But this endeavour failed to get the support of the masses, since its arguments appealed only to a small group of educated, upper sections of Ezhavas.

It was spiritual leadership and the ideas of Sree Narayana Guru that attracted the masses. By that time the Guru had become popular after his famous consecration of 'Ezhava Shiva' at Aruvippuram. The consecration was a revolt against the existing tradition and customs of the society. In other words, it was a symbolic protest and challenge against Brahmin domination in religious matters, which spilled over to the political and economic spheres as well. From that day onwards, the lower castes enjoyed the freedom to worship gods belonging to the upper-caste Hindu pantheon. Apart from the religious significance, the Guru's ideas on caste, customs and rituals, on western education, and on the importance of industry and commerce were also in conformity with the aspirations of the middle class. The new class immediately adopted these ideas into their reform activities to achieve progress and upward social mobility.

It is generally held that the SNDP Yogam was organized for the propagation of the philosophy of Sree Narayana Guru.[1] Kumaran Asan traced the genesis of the Yogam to the consecration of Shiva by the Guru. Though it is true that the Yogam was an extension of the Aruvippuram Kshetrayogam, which was formed to protect the temple and *math* adjacent to it, the ideas behind the consecration at Aruvippuram temple and the motives behind the formation of the Yogam were entirely different. It has been enumerated in detail that the consecration was conducted with the sacred objective of creating a world of brotherhood devoid of any discrimination based on caste and creed. The words of the Guru inscribed in front of the temple wall eloquently declare his vision of the oneness of man. At the same time, the Yogam was formed not with the objective of organizing all communities for their spiritual and material advancement but with the single aim of attaining the social and economic progress of the Ezhava community. The objective of the Yogam, as mentioned by P. Parameswaran to the Dewan of Travancore, was to promote and encourage religious and secular education and industrial habits among the Ezhava community.[3] Its by-laws specified that it was an organization formed with the objective of social and economic progress of Ezhavas.

In short, all the activities of the Yogam were confined to the Ezhava community. This shows that the Yogam was totally a caste-based association formed with the aim of redressing the grievances of the Ezhava community, rather than introducing and propagating the idea of the oneness of man as preached by the Guru. It is therefore not correct to view the Yogam as a vehicle for the propagation of the philosophy of Sanatana Dharma. Sree Narayana Guru's support and cooperation were available to the Yogam in its early years. When he supported the Yogam, his aim was not to organize the Ezhava community as a new religious community, but to bring about a religious and social reformulation in the society as a whole. He said: 'This organization must bring all men together. Religions must lead people to the ultimate aim.' The Sanatana principle of 'one caste, one religion and one God' will be acceptable to such a religion.[4] The Yogam could not come anywhere near such a religious environment; hence the union of all castes and creeds which the Guru had in mind was hardly realized.[5] When the Yogam openly renounced the ideals of the Guru and became totally caste-oriented, he broke away from it. In 1916, he wrote to Dr Palpu: 'Since it is seen that the Yogam takes all its decisions without my knowledge, that it is not showing any favour in matters of my interest and that it is becoming increasingly caste-oriented, I am severing my connections with the Yogam.'[6]

Soon, even Palpu was alienated from the Yogam. A thoroughly dejected and disappointed Palpu wrote a letter on 6 May 1923, to the special secretary of the Yogam in which he said: 'It has come to my notice that for a long time the SNDP Yogam, though showed respect to the Guru in public, has been doing things which were acting against the interest of the public... Though I tried to set right things in consultation with the Guru, these people were opposing me. They are continuing to do things according to their own free will. Since I would not like to work and spend money on such an organization where a group of "bandicoots" are operating for their benefit...'[7] Though the Guru was above caste feelings, the organization that was named after him became exclusively a communal organization.[8] The Guru felt that his name was being misused. He therefore made a public declaration:

> It is a few years since I eschewed all caste and religious considerations. I no longer consider myself as belonging to any caste or religion. Though this is my real and true position, today, a certain caste seems to still consider me one of them. This, it appears, has created some misunderstanding in the minds of some people regarding my true position. . . . I do not belong to any particular caste or religion. . . . I publish this for the information of the public.[9]

He also bemoaned, 'How I wish to establish a society without caste! I have told several men about it. Unfortunately there is none to work for it.'[10] In fact the Guru established an alternative association, the Sree Narayana Dharma Sangam, in 1927.[11] That he considered this association to be the one wedded to his ideas is testified by the fact that he bequeathed all his property to it.[12]

This does not mean that the Yogam and the Ezhava community did nothing against casteism. Though its activities were confined to the benefit of its own caste, during the first four decades of the twentieth century the Yogam consistently fought against caste discrimination. Two important persons in the forefront of this movement were Sahodharan Ayyappan and T.K. Madhavan. The Sahodhara Sangham of K. Ayyappan worked towards eradicating untouchability and other caste evils, and popularizing the idea of inter-dining among Ezhavas and other untouchable castes such as the Pulayas and the Parayas.

In 1920 the Yogam formed a Passive Resistance League to put an end to untouchability. T.K. Madhavan, who was one of its important leaders, was the real organizer of the Vaikom Satyagraha. The Vaikom Satyagraha and consequent *satyagraha*s in Travancore were launched for securing the right to use public roads around Hindu temples for the untouchables. A number of educated Ezhavas took part in these *satyagraha*s either directly or indirectly. Though various factors were responsible for getting all temples thrown open to all Hindus by the Travancore government in 1936, one of the most important was the social and political protest of Ezhavas led by the Yogam. No other caste organization of untouchables anywhere in India has succeeded in removing the stigma of untouchability and unapproachability as compared to what the Yogam achieved in Travancore. By their consistent struggle for more than three decades, finally, the Ezhavas, with the cooperation and support of caste-Hindu intelligentsia and Indian National Congress under Gandhi, could effectively challenge untouchability and unapproachability, and thus make a definite dent in caste consciousness.

Moreover, the Yogam was very keen on introducing social reform activities connected with life-cycle rituals such as puberty, marriage, pregnancy, birth, death, etc. This again suited the ideological and economic prospects of the middle classes who were well entrenched in the opposition between tradition and modernity. Sree Narayana Guru's call against ignorance, laziness, extravagance and expensive social customs helped the development of modern virtues like thrift, frugality and hard work which were conducive to the Ezhava middle class. Therefore they took to these reforms with great enthusiasm, which helped the development of bourgeois ideas within the Ezhava community.

The social reform movement in Kerala under Sree Narayana Guru and the Yogam was not an isolated phenomenon; though hardly influenced by reform movements in other parts of India, especially Bengal and Maharashtra, it was certainly a part of an all-India reform movement. This movement awakened the Ezhava community and brought about many changes in the life and thoughts of Hindu society in Kerala. No doubt, it helped to bring Kerala into the mainstream of national awakening in India. It is true that this reform movement focused its attention on local and regional problems to which the lower-caste communities were subjected to for generations. The contribution of the Yogam in the awakening of the Ezhavas through the campaign for literacy, abolition of expensive ceremonies and obscurantist social rituals and customs, their call for temperance and demand for a new law of inheritance was quite significant. Yet the movement failed to bring the lower sections of the community within its fold.

Though the SNDP Yogam was formed initially for a non-political purpose, it gradually got entangled in politics. The important reasons which induced the Yogam to enter politics were related to the disappointment of the Ezhavas with their marginal representation in public service and in the legislature.

They demanded a share in public service and in the legislature on the basis of their population strength. The constitutional reform of 1932, instead of providing better opportunities to the Christians, the Ezhavas and the Muslims, preserved the supremacy of the caste Hindus. Therefore, the disgruntled middle-class sections of these communities came together and formed the Joint Political Congress to fight against the hegemony of the caste Hindus. In its first meeting, on 31 August 1933, it was declared that the aim of the Joint Political Congress was to achieve representation in the legislature, public service and the Nair Brigade in proportion to the numerical strength of each community; abolition of property qualification for franchise; introduction of adult franchise; communal electorate; reservation of seats for particular communities in the legislature; and finally, to press for responsible government.[13] Though it was the first mass political movement in Travancore, its communal character severely restricted its contribution. Nevertheless, it emphasized the political rights of the Ezhavas and other non-caste Hindus and non-Hindus. As a consequence of this movement, the Government of Travancore took steps to redress some of the grievances of non-caste Hindus and non-Hindus.

Thus job reservation was granted; franchise rights were extended by reducing property qualifications and introducing communal representation in the legislature; the Nair Brigade was reorganized and brought under the Indian state; and government temples in the state were thrown open to all Hindus without any caste discrimination.

Though the Yogam was born under the inspiration of Sree Narayana Guru, ideologically it deviated from his teachings. This caste-based reform movement found extensions in the social, political and economic domains, including the independence movement. But then, the practice of the Yogam turned out to be quite contrary to the egalitarian and universal ideals of the Guru. Caste organizations have now become a way of public life in Kerala. One of the early efforts in this direction was provided by the SNDP Yogam. It is a good example of how a caste reform movement developed to become a caste solidarity movement.

Notes and References

[1] M.S.A. Rao, *Social Movements and Social Transformation: A Study of Two Backward Classes Movements in India*, Macmillan, New Delhi, 1979, p. VII; P.S. Velayudhan, 'Sree Narayana Guru: A Peep into His Life and Work', in *SNDP Yogam Platinum Jubilee Souvenir*, Quilon, 1978, p. 16.

[2] See chapter 2.

[3] P. Parameswaran to the Dewan of Travancore, 8 January 1903, *Travancore Government, English Records, Cover No. 8338*, Kerala Secretariat, Trivandrum.

[4] *Sree Narayana Guru Centenary Souvenir*, Sree Rama Vilasom Press, 1954, p. 182.

[5] Stephen Fuchs, *Rebellious Prophets: A Study of Messianic Movements in Indian Religion*, Asia Publishing House, Bombay, 1965, p. 274–5.

[6] Letter dated 22 May 1916, reproduced in *Gurukulam*, Vol. 15, No. 67, September–October 1978, p. 283.

[7] *Dr Palpu Papers*, File No. 19, Nehru Memorial Museum and Library, New Delhi.

[8] V.K. Sukumaran Nair, 'Communal Interest Groups in Kerala', in Donald E. Smith, ed., *South Asian Politics and Religion*, Princeton University Press, Princeton, 1966, pp. 182–83. The Yogam was named after the Guru to attract those whose imagination had been stirred by his personality and activities. See George Woodcock, *Kerala: A Portrait of Malabar Coast*, Faber and Faber, London, 1967, p. 230.

[9] *Vivekodayam Antharashtra Sree Narayana Guru Varsha Smaraka Pathippu*, March 1978, p. 1.

[10] M.K. Sanoo, *Narayana Guru Swami*, Vivekodayam Printing and Publishing, Irinjalakuda, 1976, pp. 345–46.

[11] Sree Nijananda Swami, 'Sree Narayana Dharma Sangam Trust', *Vivekodayam Viseshal Prathi*, Vol. II, No. 9, 1968, p. 169.

[12] Murkothu Kumaran, *Sree Narayana Guru Swamikalude Jeevacharitram*, second edition, P.K. Brothers, Calicut, 1971, p. 300. For the property of Sree Narayana Guru, there was long court litigation between the Dharma Sangam and the SNDP Yogam. For details, see Sree Nijananda Swami, 'Sree Narayana Dharma Sangam Trust', p. 169. Also see *Dr Palpu Papers*, File No. 19, pp. 100–01, and A.R. Bhaskaran, *Sree Narayana Trust Casente Highkkodathi Vithi*, Quilon, 1978.

[13] *Yuvabharathy*, Vol. II, No. 2, 26 August 1933.

Glossary

abkari	manufacture/sale of intoxicating liquors or drugs; excise on the manufacture/sale of intoxicating liquors or drugs
acharam	established custom
adiyan	form of reference to oneself adopted by a low-caste person before a high-caste person; *adiyan* means 'dependant'
Advaita	philosophy of non-dualism, in which the *paramatma* (supreme being) and *jeevatma* (the soul) are considered one and the same
advaitin	a non-dualist
agni/Agni	fire; fire deity
ahimsa	non-violence in thought and action
anantharavan	junior male member of a *taravad*
anekantavada	doctrine which states that a thing has infinite aspects
antarala jati	intermediate caste, such as that of *ambalavasi*s
arrack	country liquor or spirit
amsam	an administrative unit in Malabar; a sub-division of *taluk*
asan	village schoolmaster
ashram	the abode of *rishi*s or ascetics
ashtamangalyam	eight holy/auspicious objects: *val kannadi* (mirror of polished brass), flowers, rice/paddy, *grantham* (holy book), *kindi* (bell-metal vessel with spout), *pav mundu* (unused, unbleached loin cloth), *kumkumam* (powder prepared from the flower of *Crocus sativus*, used for marking the forehead), betel leaf with areca nut
avadhuta	free from worldly ties
avadhutan	one who has abandoned all worldly ties and relations
avarna	not belonging to the four-fold division of the Hindu caste structure

ayurveda	a system of traditional medical practice in India
bhakti	devotion
bhikshu	one who wanders begging alms
brahmaswam	relating to brahmins
charkha	instrument for spinning – made almost a symbol of the nationalist spirit by Gandhiji
cheruman	the slave caste *pulaya* is known as *cheruman* in Malabar region
cherumappad	the distance at which a *pulaya* has to stand before an upper-caste person
chilanti	spider; Ezhavas were called *chilanti* mockingly by the upper caste as weaving was their traditional occupation
chogan/chovan	name by which Ezhavas were known in north Travancore and Cochin
dewan	prime minister of a native state
devaswom	religious endowments and property belonging to temples
dharma	ordained mode of action or procedure
dwipa	island
Ekadasi	the eleventh day from new moon or full moon, observed as a day of fasting by devout Hindus
Ezhavas	a backward Hindu community mainly involved in the trade of liquor, weaving and farming
guru	preceptor
gurukulam	abode of the guru
illam	the house of Namboodiri brahmins; exogenous group of Ezhavas
Jacobites	a sect of Syrian Christians who recognize, in theory, the authority of West Asian patriarchs
jati	caste
jenmi	one who possesses free-hold rights over landed property
jenmikkaram	*jenmi*'s dues: commuted value of rent fixed by the state for the lands covered by the Travancore *Jenmi–Kudiyan* Act of 1896
jenmom	absolute ownership: tenure in which no tax or rent is paid
kachcha	a piece of cloth used as waist-belt
kalyanam	marriage ceremony
kanam	land leased from a *jenmi* or the state on which tax or rent is paid

kanamdar/ *kanakkar*	holders of *kanam* land; tenants
kara	sub-division of a revenue village in Travancore
karanavan	male head of the matrilineal joint family of Kerala
kindi	a bell-metal vessel with a spout
kotty	literally, beater; used to mockingly refer to Ezhavas who beat or press the inflorescence of the palm during toddy-making
kozhivettu	fowl sacrifice
kshatriya	warrior community in the Hindu caste system who were traditional rulers of the land
kshetram	temple
kshetrayogam	temple association
kudiveppu	the process of installing the bride as a member of her husband's family after the marriage
kudiyan	usually the holder of *jenmikkaram* land, but sometimes used to refer to a *kanam* tenant
madam/mutt	monastery, *gurukula*, university or temple
madambi	a baron or titled member of the Nair aristocracy
makkathayam	system of patrilineal descent
mangalasutram	a nuptial string with *tali* or pendant in the shape of a pipal leaf
mangalavadyam	the music played for weddings or other auspicious ceremonies
Marthomite	Syrian Christians who remained with Mar Thomas Athanasius after his defeat in the civil suit Jacobite property in 1889 (close connection with Church Missionary Society)
marumakkathayam	system of matrilineal descent
misradayam	system according to which both the children and the nephews get equal shares of one's self-acquired property
*mlechcha*s	literally, 'impure people'
mukkuvatti	fisherwoman
muri	a division of land, a parish in Travancore
Namboodiri	Malayali brahmin caste in Travancore, Cochin and Malabar
Namboodiripad	an exalted section of Namboodiris
Nair/Nayar	*savarna* Hindu caste constituting warriors, landed gentry and influential sections in government service

nikrishta	despised or condemned
nilavilakku	five-wick oil lamp made of gun metal or brass on a pedestal
nirapara	a measuring container that holds 10 *edankazhi*s (roughly 12 litres) of paddy/rice filled to the brim
nivarthanam	abstention or non-cooperation
Nyaya	philosophical system of logical thinking and the means of determining the right thing
Nyayavada	theory of the limited perspectival nature of much of human knowledge
otti	type of tenure in which land is mortgaged to the holder
panchamas	caste outside the four-fold division of the Hindu caste system
pandaravaka	belonging to the state
pandaravaka otti	favourable tenure of government lands having the characteristic of mortgage
pandaravaka pattom	non-favourable tenure of government lands on which full rate of land revenue is charged
pandal	temporary loggia in which the *tali* rite of a marriage ceremony is held
para	a solid measure of 10 *edankazhi*s (roughly 12 litres) used for measuring grains, especially paddy/rice
paripalanam	protection, propagation, fostering care
pattakkaran	lease holder
pattom	rent or tenancy
pooja	adoration; sacrifice made to the deity with accompaniments of ceremonial offerings and other rites
pradhanikal	literally, important persons or chiefs
prasthanam	movement
rajabogam	light revenue assessment on land under the control of certain *jenmie*s
sahayikal	literally, helping hands
sahodaran	brother
samajikanmar	persons pertaining to an assembly or *samajam*
sambandham	literally, 'connection'; the simple marriage ceremony of Nairs involving the presentation of a cloth by the man to the woman

satyagraha	a political method of direct action, evolved by Gandhiji, based upon the principles of truth, love and non-violence
savarna	caste Hindus; one belonging to any of the four high castes
shanar	Tamil-speaking toddy tappers in south Travancore
Shivalinga	phallic emblem of Lord Shiva
sirkar	government
Sree Pandaravaka	belonging to the temple of Shree Padmanabha Swamy at Tiruvananthapuram
swadeshi	produced in one's own country
swaraj	freedom
syad	possibly, perhaps, somehow
Syadavada	doctrine of conditional predication
tali	small gold pendant (in the shape of a pipal leaf) tied by the bridegroom round the neck of the bride at the time of marriage
taluk	revenue sub-division of a district
taravad	matrilineal joint family of Nairs
tavazhi	branch of matrilineal joint family
thampuran	master; form of address for males of upper-caste communities by the lower castes. The males in royal families as at Calicut were similarly addressed by other castes, including upper castes.
thampuratti	feminine gender of *thampuran*
thiyyapad	distance at which a Thiyya or Ezhava had to stand before a high caste
toddy	country liquor extracted from the palmyra or coconut tree
uralimar	brahmin managers of temples
uriyam/uliyam	forced labour demanded by the *sirkar*
uttupura	free feeding house for brahmins
val kannadi	mirror of polished brass
verumpattakkaran	tenant at will
verumpattam	ordinary lease for a year; tenancy at will
viruthi/virutti	land granted at concessionary rent/tax in return for performance of services
yogam	organization

Select Bibliography

Manuscript Sources

National Archives of India, New Delhi

Crown Representative Records Madras States (Travancore and Cochin)
Madras Political Proceedings (MPP)
Madras Residency Records (Travancore State)
Madras Native Newspaper Records / Fortnightly Reports, 1870–1911
Foreign Department, 1870–1930
Foreign Political Department, 1914–1936

Nehru Memorial Museum and Library (NMML), New Delhi

Institutional Collections
All India Congress Committee (AICC) Papers
All India State People's Conference

Individual Collections
G.P. Pillai
Dr P. Palpu
Diaries of Kumaran Asan
A.K. Pillai
K.P. Kesava Menon
Pattom Thanu Pillai
Sir C.P. Ramaswami Aiyer

Kerala Secretariat, Trivandrum

Travancore Government English Records
Confidential Section Files
Cover System Files
Education Department Files
Development Department Files
General Department Files
Judicial Department Files
Political Department Files
Uplift Department Files
Vaikom Satyagraha Files

Official Publications and Printed Materials

Madras Government

Madras Native Newspaper Reports, 1908–1933
Report of the Malabar Marriage Commission, 1891
Report of the Malabar Tenancy Committee, Vol. II, 1940

Government of Kerala

Kerala Archives Newsletters, Directorate of Archives, Trivandrum, 1975–78

Travancore Government

Administration Reports, 1860–1938
Census of India, Travancore (1875–1941)
Lists of Public Servants of the Travancore Government, 1870–71, 1893–94
Regulations and Proclamations of Travancore, 5 volumes, 1800–1929
Report of the Marumakkatayam Committee, Travancore, 1908
Travancore Government Gazette, 1863–1905
Travancore Land Revenue Manual, 5 volumes, 1915
Report of the Industrial Survey of Travancore, 1921
Proceedings of the Third Conference of Head Masters of English High Schools, 1921
Report of Unemployment Enquiry Committee of Travancore, 1928
Report of the Temple Entry Enquiry Committee, 1934
Travancore Legislative Council Proceedings
Travancore Sree Mulam Popular Assembly Proceedings, 1905–1938
Travancore Jenmi–Kudiyan Regulation of 1071 ME *(1895–96)*
Travancore Jenmi–Kudiyan Report , 1915
Abstract of Travancore Legislative Council Proceedings, Vols I to III
Report of University Committee, Travancore, 1923–24
Sree Chitra State Council Proceedings, 1933–38
Report on the Scheme for the Introduction of Basic Land Tax and Revision of Agricultural Income Tax, 1946

Cochin Government

Census Reports, 1891–1921

Non–Governmental Documents

Annual Report of the Secretary, SNDP Yogam, 1905–36.
Proceedings of the Annual Meetings of SNDP Yogam, 1905–36.
Caste and Citizenships in Travancore, Travancore Civic Rights League, Kottayam, 1919.
All Travancore Joint Political Congress, *Travancore: The Present Political Problem* Trivandrum, 1934.
Congress Presidential Addresses, First Series, 1885 to 1910, G.A. Natesan & Co., Madras, 1935.
Congress Presidential Addresses, Second Series, 1911 to 1934, G.A. Natesan & Co., Madras, 1937.

Congress Policy Towards States, All India State's People's Conference, Bombay, 1938.

Newspapers and Periodicals

Common Weal, 1914–20
Dasan, 1932
Deepika, 1888–1940
Deshabhimani, 1921–30
Gurukulam, 1938
Gurunathan, 1105 ME, 1110 ME (1929–35)
The Hindu, 1924–26
Indian Social Reformer, 1898–1940
Kerala Kaumudi, 1919–31
Kerala Society Papers, 1932
Madras Mail, 1896–1925
Madras Times, 1890–92
Malabar Quarterly Review, 1904
Malayala Manorama, 1890–1904, 2011
Mathrubhumi, 1923–40, 2011
Mitavadi, 1913–20
Prabudha Keralam, 1929–35
Sahodaran, 1920–22
Service, 1924–26
Unni Namboodiri, 1931–33
Vivekodayam, 1903–36
Yoganadham, 1977–78
Yogakshemam, 1920–37
Young India, 1924–26
Yuva Bharati, 1933

Books

Achutan, K.R., *C. Krishnan* (biography, Malayalam), National Book Stall, Kottayam, 1971.
Agur, C.M., *Church History of Travancore*, S.P.S. Press, Madras, 1903.
Aiya, Nagam, *The Travancore State Manual*, 3 vols, Government Press, Trivandrum, 1906.
Aiyangar, M. Srinivasa, *Tamil Studies or Essays on the History of the Tamil People, Language, Religion and Literature*, Guardian Press, 1914.
Aiyer, L.A. Krishna, *The Travancore Tribes and Castes*, 2 vols, Government Press, Trivandrum, 1937–39.
Aiyer, L.A. Krishna, *Kerala and Her People*, Education Supplies Depot, Palghat, 1961.
Aiyer, L.A. Krishna, *Social History of Kerala*, 2 vols: Vol. I, Book Centre Publications, Madras, 1963; Vol. II, The Dravidian Vol. II, 1970.
Aiyar, S. Ramanathan, *Brief Sketch of Travancore, The Model State of India: Its People and Its Progress under the Maharaja*, Western Star Press, Trivandrum, 1903.

Aiyar, S. Ramanathan, *Progressive Travancore*, Anantha Rama Press, Trivandrum, 1923.

Alexander, K.C., *Social Mobility in Kerala*, Deccan College Post Graduate and Research Institute, Poona, 1968.

Alexander, P.C., *Buddhism in Kerala*, Annamalai University, Annamalai Nagar, 1949.

All Travancore Joint Political Congress, *Travancore: The Present Political Problem*, Trivandrum, 1934.

Ambedkar, B.R., *Annihilation of Caste with a Reply to Mahatma Gandhi*, B.R. Kadnekar, 1937.

Ambedkar, B.R., *What Congress and Gandhi Have Done to the Untouchables*, Thacker and Co., Bombay, 1945.

Ambedkar, B.R., *The Untouchables*, Amrit Book Co., New Delhi, 1948.

Asan, N. Kumaran, *Mathaparivarthana Rasavadam* (Malayalam), Sarada Book Depot, Thonnakkal, 1971; first published 1933.

Asan, N. Kumaran, *Brahmasri Sri Narayana Guruvinte Jeevacharithra Samgraham* (Malayalam), Kumaran Asan Memorial Committee, Thonnakkal, 1984; first published 1979.

Ayyappan, A., 'Iravas and Culture Change', *Madras Government Museum Bulletin*, Madras, 1945; first published in *Madras Government Museum Bulletin*, Vol. V, No. 1, 1943.

Ayyappan, A., *Social Revolution in a Kerala Village: A Study in Culture*, Asia Publishing House, Bombay, 1965.

Ayyar, K.V. Krishna, *A Short History of Kerala*, Pai and Company, Ernakulam, 1966.

Balakrishnan, P.K., *Narayana Guru Samahara Grandham* (an anthology, Malayalam), National Book Stall, Kottayam, 1969; first published 1954.

Balakrishnan, P.K., *Kavyakala Kumaranasanilude* (Malayalam), Sreeni Printers and Publishers, Trivandrum, 1970.

Balu, M. Peter and W. Richard Scott, *Formal Organizations: A Comparative Approach*, Chandler, San Francisco, 1962.

Banerjee, Albion Raja Kumar, *An Indian Path Finder, Being the Memoirs of Sevabrata Sasipada Banerjee 1840–1924*, Oxford Kemptall Press, London, n.d.

Barbosa, Durate, *A Description of the Coast of Africa and Malabar in the Beginning of the Sixteenth Century*, translated and edited by E.J. Stanler Henry, London, 1866.

Barbosa, Durate, *The Book of Durate Barbosa*, Vol II, translated by M.L. Dames, The Hakluyt Society, London, 1921.

Basu, Prem Sundar, comp., *Life and Works of Brahmanand Keshav*, Navavidhan Publishing Company, Calcutta, second edition, 1940.

Bhaskaran, A.R., *Sree Narayana Trust Casente High Kodathi Vidhi* (Malayalam), Quilon, 1978.

Bhaskaran, T., ed., *Sree Narayana Guruvinte Sampoorna Krithikal* (Malayalam), Mathrubhumi Press, Calicut, 1985.

Bhaskaranunni, P., *Pathonpatham Noottantile Keralam* (Malayalam), Kerala Sahitya Akademi, Trichur, 1988.

Bhaskaranunni, P., *Keralam Irupathamnootantinte Arambathil* (Malayalam), Kerala Sahitya Akademi, Trichur, 2005.

Bhattacharya, J.N., *Hindu Castes and Sects*, second edition, Editions India, Calcutta, 1968.

Bhattathiripad, V.T., *Adukkaleyilninnu Arengethekku* (drama, Malayalam), Mathrubhumi Printing and Publishing Company, Kozhikode, 1957.

Bhattathiripad, V.T., *Kanneerum Kinavum* (autobiography, Malayalam), National Book Stall, Kottayam, 1970.

Bourdieu, Pierre, *Outline of a Theory of Practice*, Cambridge University Press, London, 1977.

Bourdieu, Pierre, *Distinction: A Social Critique of the Judgement of Taste*, Harvard University Press, 1979.

Bourdieu, Pierre, *The Logic of Practice*, Stanford University Press, 1990.

Buchanan, Francis, *A Journey from Madras through the Countries of Mysore, Canara and Malabar*, 2 vols, Higginbotham, Madras, 1870.

Chaitanya, Krishna, *Kerala*, National Book Trust, New Delhi, 1972.

Chandra, Bipan, et al., *India's Struggle for Independence, 1857–1947*, Viking, New Delhi, 1988.

Chatterjee, Satish Chandra and Dhirendra Mohan Datta, *An Introduction to Indian Philosophy*, University of Calcutta, Calcutta, 1984.

Chintamani, C.Y., *Indian Social Reform*, Madras, 1901.

Chopra, P.N. and N. Subramanian, N., *History of South India*, 3 vols, S. Chand and Co., New Delhi, 1979.

Damodaran, K., *Shri Narayana Guru Swami Tripadangalude Jeevacharitram* (Malayalam), Quilon, 1929.

Damodaran, K., *Ezhava Charitram* (Malayalam), Trivandrum, 1935–36 (1110 ME), Vol. I.

Damodaran, K., *Kerala Charitram* (Malayalam), Trichur, 1962.

Day, Francis, *The Lands of the Perumals or Cochin, its Past and its Present*, Asian Education Services, New Delhi, 1990; first published by Gantz Brothers, Madras, 1863.

De, Barun, ed., *Perspectives in Social Sciences: Historical Dimensions*, Oxford University Press, Calcutta, 1977.

Desai, A.R., *Social Background of Indian Nationalism*, fifth edition, Popular Prakashan, Bombay, 1976.

Desai, Mahadev, *The Epic of Travancore*, Navajivan Karyalaya, Allahabad, 1937.

Dharmanandaji, Swami, *Sree Narayana Gurudevan*, National Book Stall, Kottayam, 1965.

Dharma Theertha, Swami, *The Menace of Hindu Imperialism*, Har Bhagwan, Lahore, 1946.

Dharmatheerthan, Swami John, *The Prophet of Peace*, Sree Narayana Publishing House, Chempazhanti, Kerala, 1931.

Directorate of Archives, *Kerala Archives Newsletters*, Trivandrum, 1975–78.

Dutt, K. Iswara, *Congress Cyclopedia, the Indian National Congress, 1885–1920*, Vol. I, New Delhi, n.d.

Dutta, Bupendranath, *Studies in Indian Polity*, Puri Publishers, Calcutta, 1944.

Elenkath, K.R., *Dewan Nanoo Pillai With His Selected Writings and Letters*, Dewan Nanoo Pillai Memorial Reading Room, Neyyoor, West Trivandrum, 1975.

Erikson, Erik, *Childhood and Society*, Grafton Books, London, 1987.

Fuchs, Stephen, *Rebellious Prophets: A Study in Messianic Movements in Indian Religion*, Asia Publishing House, Bombay, 1965.

Fuller, C.J., *The Nayars Today*, Cambridge University Press, London, 1976.

Fuller, C.J., *The Renewal of the Priesthood: Modernity and Traditionalism in a South Indian Temple*, Princeton University Press, Princeton, 2003.

Gandhi, M.K., *Collected Works of Mahatma Gandhi (CWMG]*: Vols VII (7), X (10), XIII (13), XIX (19), XXI (21), XXII (22), XXIII (23), XXIV (24), XXVI (26), XXIX (29), XXXI (31), XXXVI (36), LIV (54), LXIV (64), LXXII (72), LXXV (75), Publications Division, Ministry of Information and Broadcasting, Government of India, New Delhi.

Gandhi, M.K., *The Indian States' Problem*, Navajivan Press, Ahmedabad, 1941.

Gandhi, M.K., *Hindu Dharma*, Navajivan Publishing House, Ahmedabad, 1958.

Gandhi, M.K., *India of My Dream*, compiled and edited by R.K. Prabhu, Navajivan Publishing House, Ahmedabad, 1962; first published 1947.

Ghose J.C., ed., *The English Works of Raja Ram Mohan Roy*, 3 vols, Panini Office, Allahabad, 1906.

Gidden, Antony, *New Rules of Sociological Method: A Positive Critique of Interpretative Sociology*, Hutchinson, London, 1976.

Gidden, Antony, *The Constitution of Society: Outline of the Theory of Structuration*, Polity Press, Cambridge, 1984.

Gidden, Antony, *The Consequences of Modernity*, Polity Press, Cambridge, 1990.

Gidden, Antony, *Modernity and Self: Identity, Self and Society in the Late Modern Age*, Polity Press, Cambridge, 1991.

Goody, Jack, ed., *Literacy in Traditional Societies*, Cambridge University Press, 1981; first published in 1968.

Gopal, S. and Uma Iyengar, eds., *The Essential Writings of Jawaharlal Nehru*, Oxford University Press, Delhi, 2003.

Gopalakrishnan, P.K., *Keralathinte Samskarika Charitram (A Cultural History of Kerala)* (Malayalam), Kerala Basha Institute, Trivandrum, 1974.

Gopalan, A.K., *In the Cause of the People*, Orient Longman, Madras, 1983.

Govindan, M. (ed.), *Poetry and Renaissance: Kumaran Asan Birth Centenary Volume*, Sameeksha, Madras, 1974.

Gregor, Mary J., ed. and trans., *Immanuel Kant: Practical Philosophy*, Cambridge University Press, 1996.

Griffiths, Sir Percival, *The History of the Indian Tea Industry*, Wiedenfield and Nicolson, London, 1967.

Gupta, Bina, *An Introduction to Indian Philosophy: Perspectives on Reality, Knowledge and Freedom, Routledge,* New York, 2012

Hawksworth, *A Day Dawns in Travancore*, C.M.S. Press, Kottayam, 1860.

Heimsath, H. Charles, *Indian Nationalism and Hindu Social Reform*, Oxford University Press, Bombay, 1964.

Hutton, J.H., *Caste in India: Its Nature, Functions and Origins*, fourth edition, Oxford University Press, Bombay, 1963.

Innes, C.A., *Madras District Gazetteer*, Vol. I, Malabar, Madras, 1908; first published 1904.

Iyer, L.K. Ananthakrishna, *Anthropology of Syrian Christians*, Government Press, Ernakulam–Cochin, 1926.

Iyer, L.K. Ananthakrishna, *The Cochin Tribes and Castes*, 2 vols, Higginbotham, Madras, 1909 and 1912; reprint, Johnson Reprint Corporation, New York, 1969.

Jamal, *Kunju Sahab* (biography), National Book Stall, Kottayam, 1975.

Jayakumar, Vijayalayam, *Sree Narayana Guru: A Critical Study*, New Delhi, 1999.

Jeffrey, Robin, *The Decline of Nayar Dominance: Society and Politics in Travancore 1847–1908*, Vikas Publishing House, 1976.

Jeffrey, Robin, *Politics, Women and Well–Being: How Kerala Became 'a Model'* Macmillan, London, 1992.

Jeffrey, Robin, *Media and Modernity: Communications, Women and the State in India*, Permanent Black, New Delhi, 2010.

Jeffrey, Robin, ed., *People, Princes and Paramount Power: Society and Politics in the Indian Princely States*, Oxford University Press, London, 1978.

John, K.J., ed., *Christian Heritage of Kerala*, published by Fr. George Veliparampil, Cochin, 1981.

Jones, Kenneth W., *The New Cambridge History of India, III.I: Socio–Religious Movements in British India*, Cambridge University Press, 1989.

Joshi, V.C., ed., *Rammohun Roy and the Process of Modernization*, Vikas Publishing House, New Delhi, 1975.

Kant, Immanuel, 'An Answer to the Question, What is Enlightenment?' [1784], in *Immanuel Kant: Practical Philosophy*, translated and edited by Mary J. Gregor, Cambridge University Press, 1996.

Kerala History Association, *Kerala Charitram* (Malayalam), 2 vols., Government Press, Ernakulam; Vol. I: 1973, Vol. II: 1974.

Kesavan, C., *Jeevitasamaram* (autobiography, Malayalam), 2 vols, National Book Stall, Kottayam; Vol. I: 1968, Vol. II: 1971.

Kesavan, C.O., *Mahakavi Kumaran Asan*, Chandra Mohan Press, Trivandrum, 1958.

Kooiman, Dick, *Conversion and Social Equality in Kerala: The London Missionary Society in South Travancore in the Ninteenth Century*, Manohar, Delhi, 1989.

Kopf, David, *British Orientalism and Bengal Renaissance: The Dynamics of Indian Modernization, 1773–1835*, University of California Press, Berkeley, 1969.

Koshy, M.J., *Genesis of Political Consciousness in Kerala*, Kerala Historical Society, Trivandrum, 1972.

Kovoor, E.M., *T.M. Verghese* (biography, Malayalam), National Book Stall, Kottayam, 1965.

Krishnan, N.R., *Ezhavar Annum Innum* (Malayalam), Seena Publications, Engadiyar, Trichur, 1967.

Kumar, Ravinder, 'Gandhi, Ambedkar and the Poona Pact', Occasional Papers on History and Society, No. XX, Nehru Memorial Museum and Library (NMML), New Delhi.

Kumaran, Murkothu, *Sree Narayana Guru Swamikalude Jeevacharitram* (Malayalam), P.K. Brothers, Calicut, 1971.

Kunhappa, Murkothu, *Murkothu Kumaran* (biography), National Book Stall, Kottayam, 1975.

Kunjuraman, C.V., *Ezhavarude Matha Parivartana Samrambham* (Malayalam), C.M.S., Kottayam, 1935.

Kusuman, K.K., *The Abstention Movement*, Kerala Historical Society, Trivandrum, 1975.

Kusuman, K.K., *Slavery in Travancore*, Kerala Historical Society, Trivandrum, n.d.

Lemercinier, Genevieve, *Religion and Ideology in Kerala*, New Delhi, 1984.

Logan, William, *Malabar*, 2 vols, Government Press, Madras, 1951.

Lopez, Lawrence, *A Social History of Modern Kerala*, Trivandrum, 1988.

Madhavan, E., *Swathantra Samudayam* (Malayalam), Prabhat Book House, Trivandrum, 1979; first published 1934.

Madhavan, P.K., *The Life of T.K. Madhavan (T.K. Madhavante Jeevacharitram)*, Vol. II, Sarada Book Depot, Trivandrum, 1936.

Madhavan, P.K., *T.K. Madhavante Jeevacharitram*, edited and abridged by N.K. Damodaran, D.C. Books, Kottayam, 1986.

Madhavan, T.K., *Dr. Palpu* (biography), Vol. I, fully revised by Pallipattu Kunju Krishnan, Cheppad, Alleppey, 1969.

Mankekar, D.R., *The Red Riddle of Kerala*, Manaktalas, Bombay, 1965.

Mateer, Rev. Samuel, *Native Life of Travancore*, W.H. Allen, London, 1883.

Mateer, Rev. Samuel, *The Land of Charity*, John Snow, London, 1871.

Mateer, Rev. Samuel, *Travancore and Its People*, John Snow, London, 1871.

Mathur, Vishnu Dayal, *States' Peoples' Conference: Origin and Role in Rajasthan*, Publication Scheme, Jaipur, 1984.

Menon, A. Sreedhara, *A Survey of Kerala History*, National Book Stall, Kottayam, 1973.

Menon, A. Sreedhara, *Social and Cultural History of Kerala*, Sterling Publishers, New Delhi, 1979.

Menon, C. Achuta, *Cochin State Manual*, Ernakulam, 1911.

Menon, K.P. Kesava, *Bandhanathil Ninnu* (Malayalam), third edition, Mathrubhumi Printing and Publishing Co., Kozhikode, 1963.

Menon, K.P. Kesava, *Kazhinja Kalam* (Malayalam), third edition, Mathrubhumi Printing and Publishing Co., Kozhikode, 1969.

Menon, K.P. Padmanabha, *History of Kerala*, 4 vols, Government Press, Ernakulam, Vol. I: 1924, Vol. II: 1929, Vol. III: 1933 and Vol. IV: 1937.

Menon, O. Chandu, *Indulekha* (novel), National Book Stall, Kottayam, 1971; first published 1889.

Menon, P.K.K., *The History of the Freedom Movement in Kerala*, Vol. II: 1885–1938, Regional Record Survey Committee, Government of Kerala, Trivandrum, 1972.

Meyer, C. Adrian, *Land and Society in Malabar*, Oxford University Press, London, 1952.

Misra, B.B., *The Indian Middle Class: Their Growth in Modern Times*, Oxford University Press, New Delhi, 1978; first published 1961.

Mohandas, S., ed., *Vishwaguru: a book on Sree Narayana Guru*, S.N. Club, Thiruvananthapuram, 1998.

Muni, Narayana Prasad, *Narayana Guru's Complete Works*, National Book Trust, New Delhi, 2006.

Nag, Kalidas and Deb Jyoti Burman, eds, *The English Works of Raja Rammohun Roy*, Part II, Sadharan Brahmo Samaj, Calcutta, 1946.

Nair, M.P., *The Vaikom Satyagraha*, Vol. I, 1925.

Nair, R. Ramakrishnan, *Constitutional Experiments in Kerala*, Kerala Academy of Political Science, Trivandrum, 1964.

Nair, R. Ramakrishnan, *Social Structure and Political Development in Kerala*, Kerala Academy of Political Science, Trivandrum, 1976.

Namboodiripad, E.M.S., *The National Question in Kerala*, People's Publishing House, Bombay, 1952.

Namboodiripad, E.M.S., *Kerala Yesterday, Today and Tomorrow*, National Book Agency, Calcutta, 1967.

Nanda, B.R., *Mahatma Gandhi: A Biography*, Allied Publishers, New Delhi, 1968.

Narayana Guru, *Darshana Mala* (Malayalam), Lalitha Printing Works, Varkala, 1962.

Narayana Guru, *Sree Narayana Guru Deva Krithikal* (Malayalam), Sree Narayana Dharma Sangam, Varkala, 1967.

Narayanan, K.G., *Ezhava–Thiyya Charitra Padanam*, Anaswara Publishers, Kayamkulam, 1984.

Nataraja Guru, *The Word of the Guru: The Life and Teachings of the Guru Narayana*, Paico Publishing House, Ernakulam, Cochin, 1968; first published in 1952.

Nehru, Jawaharlal, *Discovery of India*, Asia Publishing House, Bombay, 1977; first published 1946.

O'Hanlon, Rosalind, *Caste, Conflict and Ideology: Mahatma Jotirao Phule and Low Caste Protest in Nineteenth Century Western India*, Orient Longman, Hyderabad, 1985.

O'Malley, L.S.S., *Indian Caste Customs*, Vikas Publishing House, New Delhi, 1974.

Omana, S., *The Philosophy of Sree Narayana Guru*, Narayana Gurukulam, Varkala, 1984.

Ouwerkerk, Louise, *The Untouchables of India*, Oxford University Press, Bombay 1945.

Padmanabhan, Mannath, *Ente Jeevitha Smaranakal* (Malayalam), Vol. I, Nair Service Society Press, Trivandrum, 1964.

Panicker, K.K., *Sree Narayana Paramahamsan* (biography), Vidyarambham Press, Alleppey, 1968.

Panikkar, K.M., *A History of Kerala*, Annamalai University, Annamalainagar, 1959.

Panikkar, K.M., *Asia and Western Dominance: A Survey of Vasco da Gama Epoch of Asian History, 1498–1945*, George Allen and Unwin, London, 1953.

Panikkar, K.M., *Hindu Society at Cross Roads*, Asia Publishing House, New York, 1961.

Panikkar, K.N., 'Presidential Address', Section III, Indian History Congress, 36th Session, Aligarh, 1975.

Panikkar, K.N., *Culture, Ideology, Hegemony: Intellectuals and Social Consciousness in Colonial India*, Tulika Books, New Delhi, 1995.

Panikkar, K.N., *An Agenda for Cultural Action and Other Essays*, Three Essays, New Delhi, 2002.

Parameswaran, P., *Sree Narayana Guru Swamikal: Navothanathinte Pravachakan* Malayalam), Jayabharath Publishers, Calicut, 1979; first published 1971.

Pazhamballi, Achyuthan, *Sree Narayana Guru (Smaranakal)* (Malayalam), Sarada Book Depot, Thonnakal, 1960.

Pillai, A. Balakrishna, *Kesariyude Mukhaprasangangal*, National Book Stall, Kottayam, 1961

Pillai, A.K., *Keralavum Congressum*, D.C. Books, Kottayam, 1986; first published 1935.

Pillai, Elamkulam P.N.N Kunjan, *Kerala Charithrathinte Iruladanja Edukal* (Malayalam), National Book Stall, Kottayam, 1963.

Pillai, Elamkulam P.N.N Kunjan, *Kerala Charitra Prasnangal* (Malayalam), National Book Stall, Kottayam, 1963.

Pillai, Elamkulam P.N.N Kunjan, *Keralam Anchum Arum Noottandukalil* (Malayalam), National Book Stall, Kottayam, 1967.

Pillai, Elamkulam P.N.N Kunjan, *Studies in Kerala History*, National Book Stall, Kottayam, 1970.

Pillai, Elamkulam P.N.N Kunjan, *Annathe Keralam* (Malayalam), National Book Stall, Kottayam, 1973.

Pillai, Parameswaran P., *Report on the Scheme for the Introduction of Basic Land Tax and Revision of Agricultural Income Tax*, Government Press, Trivandrum, 1946.

Pillai, T.K. Velu, *The Travancore State Manual*, 4 vols, Trivandrum Government Press, 1940.

Powell, B.R. Baden, *The Land Systems of British India*, Oriental Publishers, 1974.

Raghavan, Puthupally, ed., *C.V. Kunjuramante Thiranjedutha Krithikal* (Malayalam), Prathibha Publications, Quilon, 1971.

Rajendran, G., *The Ezhava Community and Kerala Politics*, Kerala Academy of Political Science, Trivandrum, 1974.

Ranade, Mahadev Govind, *The Miscellaneous Writings of the Late Hon'ble Mr. Justice M.G. Ranade with an Introduction by D.E. Wacha*, published by Mrs Ramabai Ranade, Manoranjan Press, Bombay, 1915.

Rangaswami, Vanaja, 'The Democratic Movement in the British Indian States of Mysore, Travancore and Cochin 1900–1948', unpublished Ph.D. thesis, Delhi University, Delhi, 1977.

Rao, M.S.A., *Social Movements and Social Transformation: A Study of Two Backward Classes Movements in India*, Macmillan India, New Delhi, 1979.

Ravindran, T.K., *Asan and Social Revolution in Kerala: A Study of His Assembly Speeches*, Kerala Historical Society, Trivandrum, 1972.

Ravindran, T.K., *Vaikom Satyagraha and Gandhi*, Sri Narayana Institute of Social and Cultural Development, Trichur, 1975.

Ravindran, T.K., *Historical Views and Reviews*, College Book House, Trivandrum, 1980.

Regional Records Survey Committee, *The History of the Freedom Movement in Kerala*, Vol. I: 1600–1885, Government of Kerala, Trivandrum, 1970.

Said, Edward, *Orientalism*, Random House, New York, 1979.

Said, Edward, *Culture and Imperialism*, Vintage Books, 1994.

Samuel, V.T., *One Caste, One Religion, One God: A Study of Sree Narayana Guru*, Sterling Publishers, New Delhi, 1977.

Sanoo, M.K., *Narayana Guru Swami* (biography), Vivekodayam Printing and Publishing Co., Irinjalakuda, 1976.

Sanoo, M.K., *Sahodharan K. Ayyappan*, D.C. Books, Kottayam, 1980.

Shekar, G.P., ed., *G.P. Centenary Souvenir: Selected Writings and Speeches of G.P. Pillai*, Trivandrum, 1964.

Saraswati, Dayananda, *Satyartha Prakash*, translated by Durga Prasad, New Delhi, 1972.

Saraswati, Swami Gnanananda, *Bhagavad-Gita* (commentary), Trichur, 1968.

Schneider, D.M. and Kathleen E. Gough, eds, *Matrilineal Kinship*, University of California Press, Berkeley, 1961.

Senart, Emile, *Caste in India: The Facts and the System*, translated by Sir E. Denison Ross, Methuen and Co., London, 1930.

Shan, Mohammad, ed., *Writings and Speeches of Sir Syed Ahmed Khan*, Nachiketa Publications, Bombay, 1972.

Smith, Donald E., ed., *South Asian Politics and Religion*, Princeton University Press, Princeton, 1966.

Sreedharan, K.P., ed., *Travancore Reborn*, Good Shepherd Press, Kottayam, 1933.

Srinivasan, M.N., *Social Change in Modern India*, University of California Press, Berkeley, 1966.

Surendran, K., *Kumaran Asan* (literary biography), National Book Stall, Kottayam, 1971.

Thomas, Daniel, *Sree Narayana Guru*, Christian Institute for Religion and Society, Bangalore, 1965.

Thurston, Edgar, *Castes and Tribes of Southern India*, 7 vols, Government Press, Madras, 1909; second edition, Johnson Reprint Corporation, New York, 1965.

Varkey, M.M., *Ormakalilude* (autobiography, Malayalam), National Book Stall, Kottayam, 1971.

Vaidyar, C.R. Kesavan, *Vichara Darpanam* (Malayalam), Vivekodayam Printing and Publishing Co., Irinjalakuda, 1976.

Vaidyar, C.R. Kesavan, *Sree Narayana Chintakal* (Malayalam), Vivekodayam Printing and Publishing Co., Irinjalakuda, 1977; first published 1972.

Varma, Rama, *Our Industrial Status*, Trivandrum Debating Society, C.M.S Press, Kottayam, 1874.

Velayudhan, Kotookoikal, *Sree Narayana Guru: Jeevithacharitram*, Trivandrum, 1983; first published 1975.

Velayudhan, Panikkassery, *Doctor Palpu* (biography), Seena Publishers, Engadiyar, Trichur, 1970.

Velayudhan, P.S., *S.N.D.P. Yoga Charitram*, S.N.D.P. Yogam, Quilon, 1978.

Velayudhan, R., *Kerala: The Red Rain Land*, Indian Institute of Social Affairs, New Delhi, 1958.

Verghese, T.C., *Agrarian Change and Economic Consequences: Land Tenures in Kerala 1850–1960*, Calcutta, 1970.

Visscher, Jacob Canter, *Letters from Malabar*, Gantz Brothers, Madras, 1882.

Vivekananda, Swami, *Complete Works of Swami Vivekananda*, Vol. III, ninth edition, Mayavati Memorial Edition, Advaita Ashram, Calcutta, 1963.

Ward and Conner (Lieutenants), *Memoirs of the Survey of the Travancore and Cochin States*, Sirkar Press, Trivandrum, 1863; reprinted 1898 and in 1994 by Kerala Gazetteers Department, Trivandrum.

Weber, Max, *Theory of Social and Economic Organisation*, Oxford University Press, 1947.

Weber, Max, *The Sociology of Religion*, Methuen, London, 1965.

Weber, Max, *Max Weber on Law in Economy and Society*, edited with introduction and annotation by Max Rheinstein, A Clarion Book, New York, 1967.

Wood, Ananda E., *Knowledge Before Printing and After: The Indian Tradition in Changing Kerala*, Oxford University Press, New Delhi, 1985.

Woodcock, George, *Kerala: A Portrait of Malabar Coast*, Faber and Faber, London, 1967.

Yesudas, R.N., *A People's Revolt in Travancore: A Backward Class Movement for Social Freedom*, Kerala Historical Society, Trivandrum, 1975.
Yesudas, R.N., *British Policy in Travancore*, Kerala Historical Society, Trivandrum, 1977.

Souvenirs

SNDP Yogam Golden Jubilee Souvenir, SNDP Yogam, Quilon, 1953.
Sree Narayana Guru Centenary Souvenir, Sree Rama Vilasom Press, 1954.
G.P. Sekhar, ed., *G.P. Centenary Souvenir: Select Writings and Speeches of G.P. Pillai*, Trivandrum, 1964.
Souvenir, Indian History Congress, Calicut, 1976.
Vaikom Satyagraha Commemoration Volume, Vaikom, 1977.
S.N.D.P. Yogam Platinum Jubilee Souvenir, Quilon, 1978.
Kala Kaumudi Weekly Special Issue in connection with completion of fifty years Shivagiri Pilgrimage, 1 January 1984.
Aruvippuram Prathishta Shatabdi Smaranika, Tiruvananthapuram, 1988.
Souvenir, South Indian History Congress, XI Session, 1–3 February 1991, Department of History, University of Calicut.
Kerala Kaumudi Sree Narayana Guru Special, Shivagiri Theerthadanam, 1994.

Special Issues

Shri Chattampi Swami Shatabda Smaraka Grantham, Quilon, 1953.
Vivekodayam Viseshal Prathi, Vol. II, No. 9, Vivekodayam Press, 1968.
Yoganadham Antharashtra Sree Narayana Guru Varsha Visheshal Prathi, SNDP Yogam, Quilon, 1977.
Vivekodayam Antharashtra Sree Narayana Guru Varsham Smaraka Pathippu, Vivekodayam Press, 1978.
Asan Samskarika Pradarshana Souvenir, Kaikkara, 1978.

Articles

Aboo, C., 'Shriman Churayyi Kanaran', *SNDP Yogam Golden Jubilee Souvenir*, Quilon, 1953.
Aiyer, L.A. Krishna, 'Matriliny in Kerala', *Man in India*, Vol. 24, March 1944.
Ayyappan, A., 'The Meaning of Tali Rite', *Bulletin of Rama Varma Research Institute*, Vol. IX, Trichur, July 1941.
Ayyappan, Sahodharan K., 'Gandhijiyude Sivagiri Sandarshanam', reproduced in *Aruvippuram Pratishta Shatabdi Smaranika*, Trivandrum, 1988.
Balakrishnan, P.K., 'The Caste System in Kerala', *Quest*, March–April 1976.
Balakrishnan, P.K., 'Keralathinte Navothanthinnu Charitraparamaya Oru Mukhavura', *Yoganadham*, Vol. 3, No. 7, October 1977.
Bhatia, B.M., 'Growth and Composition of Middle Class in South India in Nineteenth Century', *Indian Economic and Social History Review*, Vol. II, No. 4, October 1965.

Bhattathiripad, Bhavadasan, 'Antharjanagaludeyum Kuttikaludeyum Anathasthithi', *Mitavadi*, 16 June 1916.

Bose, Anima, 'Gandhi's Stand on Human Rights in the Vaikom Satyagraha', *Gandhi Marg*, Vol. II, No. 1, April 1980.

Carnoli, Lucy, 'Origin of the Kayastha Temperance Movement', *Indian Economic and Social History Review*, Vol. III, No. 4, December 1974.

Chakrabarty, Dipesh, 'Sasipada Banerjee: A Study in the Nature of the First Contact of the Bengal Bhadralok with Working Class in Bengal', *Indian Historical Review*, Vol. II, No. 1, July 1975.

Champadan, Vijayan, 'Sree Narayana Sahityam Malayalathil', *Mathrubhumi Varanthappathippu*, 16 September 1900, p. III.

Chandramohan, P., 'Struggle against Untouchability: Ezhava Community of Kerala', *State and Society*, Vol. 4, No. 3, July–September 1983.

Chandramohan, P., 'Popular Culture and Socio–Religious Reform: Narayana Guru and Ezhavas of Travancore', *Studies in History*, Vol. 3, No. 1, New Delhi, 1987.

Chandramohan, P., 'Growth of Social Reform Movement in Kerala', *Perspective on Kerala History: The Second Mellenium, Kerala State Gazeteer*, Vol. II, Part 2, Trivandrum, 1999.

Chandramohan, P., 'Colonial Connections of Protestant Missionaries in Travancore', *Indian Historical Review*, Vol. XXVI, July 1999.

Chandramohan, P., 'Ideas and Idols: Narayana Guru and the SNDP Yogam', *Journal of South Indian History*, Vol. I, No. 2, Calicut University March–August 2004.

Chandramohan, P., 'Casteism, Nationalism and Imperialism: The Ezhavas of Kerala, 1885–1925', in Charles Dias, ed., *Kerala Spectrum: Aspects of Cultural Inheritance*, Dr K.J. John Felicitation Volume, Cochin, 2006.

Chandramohan, P., 'Education and Social Consciousness in the Making of Modern Kerala', in Suresh Jnaneswaran, ed., *Historiography: Structure and Practice*, Festschrift in Honour of Dr T.K. Ravindran, Thiruvananthapuram, 2010.

Dumont, Louis, 'Nair Marriage as Indian Fact', *Affinity as a Value in South India with Comparative Essays on Australia*, University of Chicago Press, Chicago, 1983.

Edwin, P.G., 'British Impact in Kerala', *Journal of Kerala Studies*, Vol. V, Part II, June 1978.

Fuller, C.J., 'The Renewal of the Priesthood: Modernity and Traditionalism in a South Indian Temple', *Princeton University Press*, Oxford, 2003.

Gangadharan, R., 'Misra Vivahathinte Arambam', *Vivekodayam, Antharashtra Sree Narayana Guru Varsham Smaraka Pathippu*, March 1978.

Gopalakrishnan, P.K., 'Ezhavar', *Kerala Charitram*, Vol. I, 1973.

Gopalakrishnan, P.K., 'Samudaya Parishkarna Prasthanangal', *Kerala Charitram*, Vol. I, 1973.

Gopalan Kutty, 'The Guruvayur Satyagraha', *Journal of Kerala Studies*, Vol. VIII, March–June, September, December, 1981.

Gopi, 'Cochin SNDP Yogam', *SNDP Yogam Golden Jubilee Souvenir*, Quilon, 1953.

Gough, Kathleen E., 'Literacy in Kerala', in Jack Goody, ed., *Literacy in Traditional Societies*, Cambridge University Press, 1981, reprint.

Gough, Kathleen E., 'Female Initiation Rites in Malabar Coast', *Journal of Royal Anthropological Institute*, Vol. LXXXV, Part II, 1955.

Gough, Kathleen E., 'Nayars and the Definition of Marriage', *Journal of Royal Anthropological Institute*, Vol. LXXXIX, 1959.

Govindan, M., 'Rao Bahadur P. Velayudhan', *SNDP Yogam Golden Jubilee Souvenir,* Quilon, 1953.

Hardgrave, L. Robert, 'The Breast Cloth Controversy: Caste Consciousness and Social Change in Southern Travancore', *Indian Economic and Social History Review,* Vol. 5, No. 2, June 1968.

Heimsath, H. Charles, 'The Function of Hindu Social Reformers – With Special Reference to Kerala', *Indian Economic and Social History Review,* Vol. XV, No. 1, January–March 1978.

Heimsath, H. Charles, 'From Social Reform to Social Struggle', *Man and Development,* Vol. IV, No. 3, September 1982.

Houtart, Francis and Genevieve Lemercinier, 'Socio–Religious Movements in Kerala: A Reaction to the Capitalist Mode of Production', *Social Scientist,* Vol. VI, No. 11, June 1978.

Jeffrey, Robin, 'Social Origins of a Caste Association, 1875–1906: The Founding of the S.N.D.P. Yogam', *South Asia,* No. 4, 1974.

Jeffrey, Robin, 'Temple Entry Movement in Travancore 1860–1940', *Social Scientist,* Vol. IV, No. 8, 1976.

Jeffrey, Robin, 'A Note on the Malayali Origin of Anti–Brahminism in South India', *Indian Economic and Social History Review,* Vol. XIV, No. 2, 1977.

Jeffrey, Robin, 'Travancore: Status, Class and the Growth of Radical Politics, 1860–1940, Temple Entry Movement', in Robin Jeffrey, ed., *People, Princes and Paramount Power: Society and Politics in the Indian States,* Oxford University Press, Delhi, 1978.

Jeffrey, Robin, 'Matriliny, Marxism and the Birth of the Communist Party in Kerala 1930–1940', *Journal of Asian Studies,* Vol. XXXVIII, No. 1, November 1978.

Jeffrey, Robin, David Arnold and James Manor, 'Caste Associations in South India: A Comparative Analysis', *Indian Economic and Social History Review,* Vol. XIII, No. 3, 1976.

Karunakaran, C.C., 'Temple Entry Proclamation', *SNDP Yogam Golden Jubilee Souvenir,* Quilon, 1953.

Kesavan, Thazhava, 'Nivarthana Prakshobanam', *SNDP Yogam Golden Jubilee Souvenir,* Quilon, 1953.

Kooiman, Dick, 'The Gospel of Coffee: Mission, Education and Employment in 19th Century Travancore', *Economic and Political Weekly,* Vol. XIX, No. 35, 1 September 1984

Krishnan, C., 'Ee Mathamanu Nammude Abhimanate Keduthiyathu', in P. K. Balakrishnan, ed., *Narayana Guru Samahara Grandham* (an anthology), National Book Stall, Kottayam, 1969; first published 1954.

Krishnan, E.K., 'A Brief Account of the Life of the Late Mr Churai Kanaran: Deputy Collector of Malabar', *Malabar Quarterly Review,* Vol. III, No. 3, September 1904.

Kumaran, N., 'SNDP Yogam Chila Smaranakal', *SNDP Yogam Golden Jubilee Souvenir,* Quilon, 1953.

Kumaran, N., 'Sanchara Swatanthra Prameyam Niyamasabhayil', *Vaikom Satyagraha Commemoration Volume,* 1977.

Kumaran, N., 'Sree Narayana Prasthanavum Britishukarum', *Vivekodayam Antharashtra Sree Narayana Guruvarsham Smaraka Pathippu*, March 1978.

Kumaran, V.K., 'Malabar SNDP Yogam', *SNDP Yogam Golden Jubilee Souvenir*, Quilon, 1953.

Kunhappa, Murkothu, 'The Thiyyas of Kerala', *Souvenir*, Indian History Congress, Calicut, 1976.

Kunhappa, Murkothu, 'Thiyyarude Charitram Oru Vihaga Veekshanam', *SNDP Yogam Platinum Jubilee Celebration Committee*, Quilon, 1978.

Kunjuraman, C.V., 'Samuhya Parishkaranam', *Vivekodayam*, 15 November 1904 (30 Thulam 1080 ME), Vol. I, No. 4.

Kunjuraman, C.V., 'The Thiyyas', *Mitavadi*, March 1916.

Lanternari, Vittoria, 'Nativistic and Socio–Religious Movements: A Reconsideration', *Comparative Studies in Society and History*, Vol. 16, 1974.

Mathamauly (pen name), 'Matha Parivarthanam', *Kerala Kaumudi*, 19 August 1920.

Madhavan, C.O., 'Ezhavarum Nayar Regulationum', *Vivekodayam*, Vol. IX, Nos. 9–10, December 1912 to February 1913 (Dhanu–Makaram 1088 ME).

Madhavan, Komalizhathu, 'Samudhayodharakan T. K. Madhavan', *Yoganatham International Narayana Guruvarsha Visheshal Prathi*, 1977.

Mencher, P. Joan, 'Namboodiri Brahmins: An Analysis of Traditional Elite in Kerala', *Journal of Asian African Studies*, Vol. I, 1966.

Menon, K.P. Kesava, 'Memories of the Satyagraha', *SNDP Yogam Golden Jubilee Souvenir*, Quilon, 1953.

Miller, Eric J., 'Village Structure in North Kerala', *Economic Weekly*, Vol. IV, No. 6, 9 February 1952.

Miller, Eric J., 'Caste and Territory in Malabar', *American Anthropologist*, Vol. LVI, 1954.

Muralidharan, N., 'Nammude Avakasha Samarangal', *SNDP Yogam Platinum Jubilee Celebration Committee*, Quilon, 1978.

Nair, U. Balakrishnan, 'The Marriage System in Malabar', *Calcutta Review*, Vol. XCIX, 1894.

Nair, B.N., 'Towards a Typological Phenomenology of Society and Religion in Kerala', *Journal of Kerala Studies*, Vol. IV, Part I, March 1977.

Nair, B.N., 'The Problematic of Kerala Society', *Journal of Kerala Studies*, Vol. IV, Part II, June 1977.

Nair, P.R. Gopinathan, 'Education and Socio–Economic Change in Kerala, 1793–1947', *Social Scientist*, Vol. IV, No. 8, March 1976.

Nair, Ramakrishnan, 'Ruling Class and Its Governing Elites of Kerala', *Journal of Kerala Studies*, Vol. I, No. 1, July 1973.

Nair, M.P. Sreekumaran, 'Review of *Vaikom Satyagraha and Gandhi* by T.K. Ravindran', *Journal of Indian History*, Vol. XIV, Part III, December 1976.

Nair, V.K. Sukumaran, 'Communal Interest Group in Kerala', in D.E. Smith, ed., *South Asian Politics and Religion*, Princeton, 1966.

Narayanan, K.R., 'Shri T.K. Madhavan: Chila Anusmaranakal', *SNDP Yogam Golden Jubilee Souvenir*, Quilon, 1953.

Narayanan, M.K., 'SNDP Yogavum T.K. Madhavanum', *SNDP Yogam Platinum Jubilee Celebration Committee*, Quilon, 1978.

O'Hanlon, Rosalind, 'Maratha History as Polemic: Low Caste Ideology and Political

Debate in Late Nineteenth Century Western India', *Modern Asian Studies*, Vol. 17, No. 1, 1983.

Omvedt, Gail, 'Jotirao Phule and the Idea of Revolution in India', *Economic and Political Weekly*, Vol. 6, No. 37, 11 September 1971.

Panikkar, K.M., 'Some Aspects of Dravidian Culture', *Journal of the Royal Anthropological Institute*, London, 1919.

Panikkar, K.N., 'Rationalism in the Religious Thought of Rammohun Roy', *Indian History Congress Proceedings*, Vol. 34, Part II, 1973.

Panikkar, K.N., 'Land Control Ideology and Reform, A Study of Change in Family Organizations and Marriage Systems in Kerala', *Indian Historical Review*, Vol. IV, No. 1, July 1977.

Panikkar, K.N., 'Social and Cultural Trends in Eighteenth Century India: An Overview', in *Eighteenth Century India* (Essays in honour of Prof. A.P. Ibrahim Kunju), Trivandrum, 1979.

Panikkar, K.N., 'Breaking with the Past, Yet Looking Back to It', *The Telegraph*, 7 June 1985, p. 7.

Panikkar, K.N., 'Intellectual History of Colonial India, Some Historical and Conceptual Question', in Sabyasachi Bhattacharya and Romila Thapar, eds, *Situating Indian History: For Sarvepalli Gopal*, New Delhi, 1986.

Panikkar, K.N., 'Culture and Ideology: Contradictions in Intellectual Transformation of Colonial Society in India', *Economic and Political Weekly*, Vol. XXII, No. 49, 5 December 1987.

Panikkar, K.N., 'Culture and Consciousness in Modern India: A Historical Perspective', *Social Scientist*, Vol. 18, No. 4, April 1990.

Pottekkat, Sukumaran, 'Sahodara Prastanam', *Vivekodayam Antarashtra Sree Narayana Guruvarsha Smaraka Pattippu*, March 1978.

Prabha, M., 'Sahodaran Ayyappan', in M. Govindan, ed., *Poetry and Renaissance: Kumaran Asan Birth Centenary Volume*, Sameeksha, Madras, 1974.

Priyadarshan, G., 'Narayana Guruvum Vaikom Satyagrahavum', *SNDP Yogam Platinum Jubilee Souvenir*, 1978.

Rao, M.S.A., 'Supernatural Possessions in Kerala', *Man*, Vol. 66, No. 1, March 1986.

Ravindran, T.K., 'Consequences of Unapproachability in Travancore', *Bulletin of the Institute of Traditional Culture*, Madras University, July–December 1975.

Rogers, John D., 'Cultural Nationalism and Social Reform: The 1904 Temperance Movement in Sri Lanka', *Indian Economic and Social History Review*, Vol. 26, No. 3, July–September 1989.

Sree Nijananda, Swami, 'Sree Narayana Dharma Sangam Trust', *Vivekodayam Visheshal Prathi*, Vol. II, No. 9, 1968.

Sukumaran, K., 'V. K. Velayudhan', *SNDP Yogam Golden Jubilee Souvenir*, Quilon, 1953.

Vaidyar, C.R. Kesavan, 'Ayurvedavum Ezhava Samudhayavum', *SNDP Platinum Jubilee Souvenir*, 1978.

Varma, L.A. Ravi, 'Caste in Malabar', *Kerala Society Papers*, Vol. II, Series 9, 1932.

Velayudhan, P.S., 'SNDP Yogam Oru Charitravalokhanam', *Yoganatham Antharashtra Sree Narayana Guruvarsha Visheshal Prathi*, SNDP Yogam, Quilon, 1977.

Velayudhan, P.S., 'Sree Narayana Guru: A Peep into His Life and Work', *SNDP Yogam Platinum Jubilee Souvenir*, Quilon, 1978.

Unpublished Works

Acharyulu, Ramakrishna V., 'Social Reform Movements in Andhra (1848–1919)', Ph.D. thesis, Jawaharlal Nehru University, New Delhi, 1977.

Chandramohan, P., 'Social and Political Protest in Travancore', M.Phil. dissertation, Jawaharlal Nehru University, New Delhi, 1981.

Gopalakrishnan, P.K., 'Sree Narayana Guru: Torch Bearer of Enlightenment for Revolutionary Changes', paper presented at a seminar on *History of Political Development in Kerala*, organized by Department of Political Science under the sponsorship of the ICHR and University of Kerala at Trivandrum, 11 and 12 December 1985.

Shah, Syed Yusuf, 'Politicization of Education in British India: A Case Study of the Establishment of Aligarh Muslim University (1875–1920)', Ph.D. thesis, Jawaharlal Nehru University, New Delhi, 1981.

Index